‖‖‖‖‖‖‖ P9-DFR-661

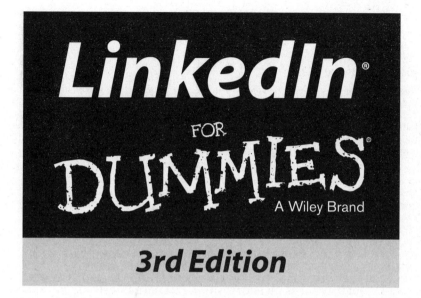

LinkedIn®

FOR DUMMIES®

A Wiley Brand

3rd Edition

by Joel Elad, MBA

FOR DUMMIES®

A Wiley Brand

JESSAMINE COUNTY PUBLIC LIBRARY
600 South Main Street
Nicholasville, KY 40356
(859)885-3523

LinkedIn® For Dummies,® 3rd Edition

Published by: **John Wiley & Sons, Inc.,** 111 River Street, Hoboken, NJ 07030-5774, www.wiley.com

Copyright © 2014 by John Wiley & Sons, Inc., Hoboken, New Jersey

Published simultaneously in Canada

No part of this publication may be reproduced, stored in a retrieval system or transmitted in any form or by any means, electronic, mechanical, photocopying, recording, scanning or otherwise, except as permitted under Sections 107 or 108 of the 1976 United States Copyright Act, without the prior written permission of the Publisher. Requests to the Publisher for permission should be addressed to the Permissions Department, John Wiley & Sons, Inc., 111 River Street, Hoboken, NJ 07030, (201) 748-6011, fax (201) 748-6008, or online at http://www.wiley.com/go/permissions.

Trademarks: Wiley, For Dummies, the Dummies Man logo, Dummies.com, Making Everything Easier, and related trade dress are trademarks or registered trademarks of John Wiley & Sons, Inc. and may not be used without written permission. LinkedIn is a registered trademark of LinkedIn, Ltd. All other trademarks are the property of their respective owners. John Wiley & Sons, Inc. is not associated with any product or vendor mentioned in this book.

LIMIT OF LIABILITY/DISCLAIMER OF WARRANTY: THE PUBLISHER AND THE AUTHOR MAKE NO REPRESENTATIONS OR WARRANTIES WITH RESPECT TO THE ACCURACY OR COMPLETENESS OF THE CONTENTS OF THIS WORK AND SPECIFICALLY DISCLAIM ALL WARRANTIES, INCLUDING WITHOUT LIMITATION WARRANTIES OF FITNESS FOR A PARTICULAR PURPOSE. NO WARRANTY MAY BE CREATED OR EXTENDED BY SALES OR PROMOTIONAL MATERIALS. THE ADVICE AND STRATEGIES CONTAINED HEREIN MAY NOT BE SUITABLE FOR EVERY SITUATION. THIS WORK IS SOLD WITH THE UNDERSTANDING THAT THE PUBLISHER IS NOT ENGAGED IN RENDERING LEGAL, ACCOUNTING, OR OTHER PROFESSIONAL SERVICES. IF PROFESSIONAL ASSISTANCE IS REQUIRED, THE SERVICES OF A COMPETENT PROFESSIONAL PERSON SHOULD BE SOUGHT. NEITHER THE PUBLISHER NOR THE AUTHOR SHALL BE LIABLE FOR DAMAGES ARISING HEREFROM. THE FACT THAT AN ORGANIZATION OR WEBSITE IS REFERRED TO IN THIS WORK AS A CITATION AND/OR A POTENTIAL SOURCE OF FURTHER INFORMATION DOES NOT MEAN THAT THE AUTHOR OR THE PUBLISHER ENDORSES THE INFORMATION THE ORGANIZATION OR WEBSITE MAY PROVIDE OR RECOMMENDATIONS IT MAY MAKE. FURTHER, READERS SHOULD BE AWARE THAT INTERNET WEBSITES LISTED IN THIS WORK MAY HAVE CHANGED OR DISAPPEARED BETWEEN WHEN THIS WORK WAS WRITTEN AND WHEN IT IS READ.

For general information on our other products and services, please contact our Customer Care Department within the U.S. at 877-762-2974, outside the U.S. at 317-572-3993, or fax 317-572-4002. For technical support, please visit www.wiley.com/techsupport.

Wiley publishes in a variety of print and electronic formats and by print-on-demand. Some material included with standard print versions of this book may not be included in e-books or in print-on-demand. If this book refers to media such as a CD or DVD that is not included in the version you purchased, you may download this material at http://booksupport.wiley.com. For more information about Wiley products, visit www.wiley.com.

Library of Congress Control Number: 2013954197

ISBN: 978-1-118-82221-0

ISBN 978-1-118-82221-0 (pbk); ISBN 978-1-118-82589-1 (ebk); ISBN 978-1-118-82578-5 (ebk)

Manufactured in the United States of America

10 9 8 7 6 5 4 3 2 1

MICHIGAN COLLEGE PUBLIC LIBRARY
305 South Main Street
Michigantown, IN 46057
(930)893-3423

Contents at a Glance

Table of Contents

Introduction

. . . .

*R*elationships matter. Ever since the dawn of time, when Fred Flintstone asked Barney Rubble whether there was any work down at the quarry, human beings have always networked. We're social creatures who like to reach out and talk to someone. As the Internet developed and grew in popularity, people rapidly took advantage of this new technology for communication, with e-mail, instant messaging, personal Web pages sharing voice, video, and data with each other, and lots of other applications to keep everybody connected. But how can the Internet help you do a better job with your professional networking? I'm glad you asked. Welcome to *LinkedIn For Dummies,* Third Edition.

LinkedIn was founded in 2003 by a guy named Reid Hoffman, who felt that he could create a better way to handle your professional networking needs. He saw lots of Web sites that let you build your own page and show it to the world, extolling your virtues and talents. But a lot of the popular Web sites that Hoffman came across focused more on the social aspects of your life and not that much on the professional side. LinkedIn changed all that with its approach of augmenting all the professional networking you do (or should do) on a daily basis. You don't have to be looking for a job to use LinkedIn, but if you're looking, LinkedIn should be a part of your search. As Hoffman put it, LinkedIn was designed to "find and contact the people you need through the people you already trust."

In short, LinkedIn allows you to coordinate your professional identity on the Internet and make you more effective in your career. The site is designed to make the aspects of networking less time consuming and more powerful, so you can open doors with your professional connections and tap the connections of people you know who make up your extended network. LinkedIn doesn't require a huge amount of time or usage to be effective, and is focused only on providing tools that help your professional career.

Perhaps you've heard of LinkedIn, but you don't understand fully what it is, how it works, and most importantly, why you should care about it. Maybe you got an invitation to join the LinkedIn Web site. Perhaps you've gotten multiple invitations, or you keep hearing about it and want to find out more. Well, you're taking the right first step by reading this book. In it, I talk about the *whys* as well as the *hows*. If you're looking to enhance your professional life, I truly believe you need to look at LinkedIn. If you want to go straight to the beach and retire, though, maybe this isn't the book for you!

This book covers LinkedIn from start to finish. In case you haven't already joined, I show you how you can sign up. If you're already a member, this book is also very useful because I show you how to build your identity and take advantage of LinkedIn's functionality. This book is useful regardless of your skill level, whether you want to join or you've been on LinkedIn for years but feel stuck.

About This Book

This book covers all aspects of using the LinkedIn site: from signing up and building your profile, to growing your network of contacts, to taking advantage of some of the sophisticated options, and everything in between. I include a lot of advice and discussion of networking concepts, but you also find a lot of step-by-step instructions to get things done. In this third edition, I revisit some of the newer facets of LinkedIn, including its Groups, Contacts, and Companies sections, and have updated all the core processes, from creating your profile to looking for a job.

This book is organized as a guide; you can read each chapter one after the other, or you can go straight to the chapter on the topic you're interested in. After you start using LinkedIn, think of this book as a reference where you can find the knowledge nugget you need to know and then be on your merry way. Lots of details are cross-referenced, so if you need to look elsewhere in the book for more information, you can easily find it.

How This Book Is Organized

I divide this book into six handy parts:

Part I: LinkedIn Basics

This part starts with the basics: I talk about the benefits of LinkedIn, how to sign up, and how to build your online profile.

Part II: Finding Others and Getting Connected

In Part II, I go a step further and discuss your network of connections. I go through how to search the LinkedIn database of tens of millions of professionals, how to introduce yourself to other people, how to grow your own personal network, and how to coordinate the way you communicate with and endorse your network.

Part III: Growing and Managing Your Network

In Part III, I heat things up by covering some of the built-in functionality of LinkedIn, such as getting and receiving recommendations, adding LinkedIn tools to your e-mail and Web browser, and importing and exporting your network to other applications, such as Microsoft Outlook.

Part IV: Finding Employees, Jobs, and Companies

Part IV takes everything I cover in the first three parts of the book and applies it to the top reasons why people use LinkedIn: namely, searching for a job, finding an employee, and finding valuable companies.

Part V: Using LinkedIn for Everyday Business

In this part, I continue on the trend of showing the real application of LinkedIn by applying the site's capabilities to different professions. I talk about how to use LinkedIn for marketing, sales, venture capital and start-up, and even some creative uses you may have never thought of doing with LinkedIn.

Part VI: The Part of Tens

Part VI is the traditional *For Dummies* Part of Tens — it contains lists that detail a number of LinkedIn functions and resources you can find on the Internet to help you with your LinkedIn experience.

And Just Who Are You?

I assume that you know how to use your computer, at least for the basic operations, like checking e-mail, typing up a document, or surfing the great big World Wide Web. If you're worried that you need a Ph.D. in Computer Operations to handle LinkedIn, relax. If you can navigate your way around a Web site, you can use LinkedIn.

You may be utterly new to the idea of social networking, or the specific ins and outs of using a site like LinkedIn. LinkedIn allows you to do some really cool stuff and enhance your professional life. There's more to it, and this book is here to show you the ropes — and help you take full advantage of what LinkedIn has to offer.

This book assumes that you have a computer that can access the Internet; any PC or Macintosh line of computer is fine, as well as Linux or any other operating system with a Web browser. All the main Web browsers can access LinkedIn just fine. In some parts of the book, I discuss specific applications such as Microsoft Outlook; if you have Outlook, I assume you know how to use it for the purposes of importing and exporting names from your address book.

Icons Used in This Book

As you go through this book, you'll see the following icons in the margins.

The Tip icon notifies you about something cool, handy, or nifty that I highly recommend. For example, "Here's a quicker way to do the described task the next time you have to do it."

Don't forget! When you see this icon, you can be sure that it points out something you should remember, possibly even something I said earlier that I'm repeating because it's very important. For example, "If you are only going to do one of my bullet point suggestions, do the last one because it's the most powerful."

Danger! Ah-*oo*-gah! Ah-*oo*-gah! When you see the Warning icon, pay careful attention to the text. This icon flags something that's bad or that could cause trouble. For example, "Although you may be tempted to go into personal details in your profile, you should never post anything that could embarrass you in a future job interview."

This icon alerts you to something technical, an aside or some trivial tidbit that I just cannot suppress the urge to share. For example, "It would be as ludicrous for me to recommend the 802.11q standard as it would be for me to insist that 1 is a prime number." Feel free to skip over this book's technical information as you please.

Beyond the Book

In addition to the material in the book you're reading right now, I provide some helpful bonus articles on the Web. Check out the free Cheat Sheet at www.dummies.com/cheatsheet/LinkedIn for tips on uploading your photo to your LinkedIn profile, staying involved with your network through status updates, using LinkedIn to search for a job, getting the most out of LinkedIn Groups, and avoiding the ten most common mistakes people make on LinkedIn.

Where to Go from Here

You can start reading this book anywhere. Open the Table of Contents and pick a spot that amuses you or concerns you or has piqued your curiosity. Everything is explained in the text, and important details are cross-referenced so that you don't waste your time reading repeated information.

Good luck with LinkedIn. Happy networking!

Part I
LinkedIn Basics

getting started with

LinkedIn

web extras

Visit www.dummies.com for great Dummies content online.

In this part...

✔ Explore all that LinkedIn has to offer.

✔ Navigate the LinkedIn Web site.

✔ Sign up with LinkedIn and create an account.

✔ Build a LinkedIn profile that details your professional and educational experience.

Chapter 1

Looking into LinkedIn

*W*hen I hear the terms "social networking" and "business networking," I always go back to one of my favorite phrases: "It's not *what* you know; it's *who* you know." Now imagine a Web site where both concepts are true, where you can demonstrate *what* you know and see the power of *who* you know. That's just one way to describe LinkedIn, one of the top Web sites today where you can do professional networking and so much more. Social networking has gotten a lot of attention over the years, and the two sites that everyone talks about are Twitter and Facebook. Let me state right now, in the first paragraph of the first chapter, that LinkedIn is *not* one of those sites. You can find some elements of similarity, but LinkedIn isn't the place to tweet about what you had for lunch or show pictures of last Friday's beach bonfire.

LinkedIn is a place where Relationships Matter (the LinkedIn slogan). It was developed primarily for professional networking. When you look at its mission statement, LinkedIn's goal "is to help you be more effective in your daily work and open doors to opportunities using the professional relationships you already have." This is not a Web site that requires a lot of constant work to be effective. It's designed to work in the background and help you reach out to whomever you need while learning and growing yourself. The key is to set up your online identity, build your network, and steadily take advantage of the opportunities that most affect you or greatly interest you.

In this chapter, I introduce you to LinkedIn and the basic services it has to offer. I answer the questions "What is LinkedIn?" and, more importantly, "Why should I be using LinkedIn?" I talk about how LinkedIn fits in with the rest of your online activities, and then I move into the tangible benefits that LinkedIn can provide you, regardless of your profession or career situation. I discuss some of the premium account capabilities that you can pay to use, but rest assured, LinkedIn has a lot of features that are free. The last part of the chapter covers basic navigation of the LinkedIn site. I show you the different menus and navigation bars, which you use throughout this book.

Discovering Your New Contact Management and Networking Toolkit

When describing how people can be connected with each other, think of a tangible network. For example, roads connect cities. The Internet connects computers. A quilt is a series of connected pieces of fabric. But what about the intangible networks? You can describe the relationship among family members using a family tree metaphor. People now use the term "social network" to describe the intangible connections between them and other people, whether they're friends, co-workers, or acquaintances.

People used to rely on address books or contact organizers (PDAs) to keep track of their social networks. You could grow your social networks by attending networking events or by being introduced in person to new contacts, and then you would continue to communicate with these new contacts, and eventually the new contacts were considered a part of your social network.

As people began to rely more and more on technology, though, new tools were created to help manage social networks. Salespeople started using contact management systems like ACT! to keep track of communications. Phone calls replaced written letters, and cellular phones replaced landline phones. E-mail has replaced phone calls and letters, and with the mass adoption of cell phones, text messaging increasingly handles short bursts of communication.

Internet tools have advanced to what people refer to as Web 2.0 systems, where online communication within your network is much more automated and accessible. Sites such as LinkedIn have started to replace the older ways of accessing your social network. For example, instead of asking your friend Michael to call his friend Eric to see whether Eric's friend has a job available, you can use LinkedIn to see whether Eric's friend works for a company you want to contact, and you can then use LinkedIn to send a message through Michael to Eric (or in some cases, directly to Eric's friend) to accomplish the same task. (Of course, this assumes you, Michael, and Eric are all members of LinkedIn.)

In the past, you had no way of viewing other people's social networks (collections of friends and other contacts). Now, though, when folks put their social networks on LinkedIn, you can see your friends' networks as well as their friends' networks, and suddenly hidden opportunities start to become available to you.

This means you can spend more time doing research on potential opportunities (like finding a job or a new employee for your business) as well as receiving information from the larger network and not just your immediate friends. This makes the network more useful because you can literally see the map that connects you with other people.

However, just because this information is more readily available, that doesn't mean there's no work involved in networking. You still have to manage your connections and use the network to gain more connections or knowledge. Remember, too, that nothing can replace the power of meeting people in person. But because LinkedIn works in the background to guide the way in finding contacts and starting the process, you spend your time more productively instead of making blind requests and relying solely on other people to make something happen.

Keeping track of your contacts

You made a connection with someone — say, your roommate from college. It's graduation day; you give him your contact information, he gives you his information, and you tell him to keep in touch. As both of you move to different places, start new jobs, and live your lives, you eventually lose track of each other, and all your contact information grows out of date. How do you find this person again?

One of the benefits of LinkedIn is that after you connect with someone you know who also has an account on LinkedIn, you always have a live link to that person. Even when that person changes e-mail addresses, you'll be updated with his new e-mail address. In this sense, LinkedIn always keeps you connected with people in your network, regardless of how their lives change. LinkedIn shows you a list of your connections, as shown in Figure 1-1.

Understanding the different degrees of network connections

In the LinkedIn universe, the word *connection* means a person who is connected to you through the site. The number of connections you have simply means the number of people who are directly connected to you in your professional network.

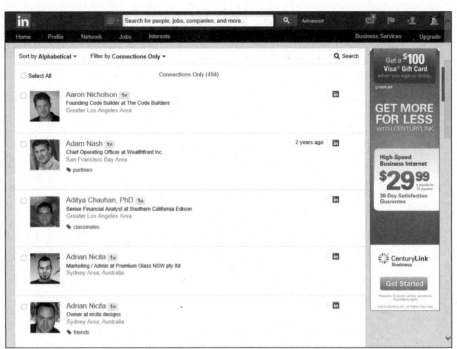

Get a $100
Visa® Gift Card
when you sign up today.

GET MORE
FOR LESS
WITH CENTURYLINK

High-Speed
Business Internet

$29.99
a month for
12 months

30-Day Satisfaction
Guarantee

CenturyLink·
Business

Get Started

Figure 1-1:
See all your
connections
in one
centralized
alphabetical
list.

Here are the different degrees of how you're connected with people on LinkedIn:

✔ **First-degree connections:** People you know personally; they have a direct relationship from their account to your account. These first-degree connections make up your immediate network and are usually your past colleagues, classmates, group members, friends, family, and close associates. Unlike Facebook, where everyone you connect to is a "friend," on LinkedIn, you can connect to friends who don't necessarily have a work, school, or group connection to you, but are people who you know personally outside those criteria. Similar to Facebook, though, you can see your first-degree connections' contact list and they can see yours.

✔ **Second-degree network members:** People who know at least one member of your first-degree connections: in other words, the friends of your friends. You can reach any second-degree network member by asking your first-degree connection to pass along an introduction from you to his friend. (I discuss introductions in Chapter 5.)

✔ **Third-degree network members:** People who know at least one of your second-degree network members: in other words, friends of your friends of your friends. You can reach any third-degree network member by asking your friend to pass along an introduction from you to her friend, who then passes it to her friend, who is the third-degree network member.

The result is a large chain of connections and network members, with a core of trusted friends who help you reach out and tap your friends' networks and extended networks. Take the concept of Six Degrees of Separation (which says that, on average, a chain of six people can connect you to anyone else on Earth), put everyone's network online, and you have LinkedIn.

So, how powerful can these connections be? Figure 1-2 shows a snapshot of how someone's network on LinkedIn used to look.

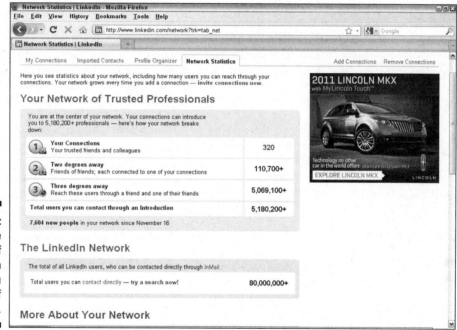

Figure 1-2:
Only three degrees of separation can give you a network of millions.

The account in Figure 1-2 had 320 first-degree connections. When you add all the network connections that each of these 320 people have, the user of this account could reach more than 110,700 different people on LinkedIn. Add in third-degree network members, and the user could have access to almost 5.1 million members, part of a vast professional network that stretches across the world into companies and industries of all sizes. Such a network can help you advance your career or professional goals — and in turn, you can help advance others' careers or goals. Of course, as of this writing, the LinkedIn community has more than 238 million members, and LinkedIn focuses on your first-degree connections instead of your second- and third-degree network members, but the concept is still valid. Your network can be vast, thanks to the power of LinkedIn.

The difference between a user and a LION

Given all this power and potential to reach people around the world, some people — LinkedIn open networkers (LIONs) — want to network with anyone and everyone who's eager to connect with them. Their goal is to network with as many people as possible, regardless of past interaction or communication with that person.

One of your most prominently displayed LinkedIn statistics is the number of first-degree connections you have. After you surpass 500 connections, LinkedIn doesn't display your current count of first-degree connections, but just the message 500+. (It's kind of like how McDonald's stopped displaying the running total of hamburgers sold on its signs. Or am I the only one who remembers that?) Part of the reason LinkedIn stops displaying updated counts past 500 is to discourage people from collecting connections. Many LIONs have thousands or even tens of thousands of first-degree connections, and the 500+ statistic is a badge of honor to them.

LIONs encourage open networking (that is, the ability to connect with someone you have never met or worked with in the past) by advertising their e-mail address as part of their professional headline (for example, John Doe; Manager >firstname@lastname.com<), so anyone can request this person be added to their network. You can find more information at sites such as www.opennetworker.com.

LinkedIn offers a formal program — OpenLink — for people interested in networking with the larger community. You can sign up for this premium service any time after you establish a premium account. When you enable the OpenLink feature, you can send and receive messages with any other OpenLink member. I discuss this in the upcoming section, "Understanding LinkedIn Costs and Benefits."

I've been asked many times whether it's okay to be a LION: if there is any meaning or benefit to having so many connections. My answer is that I don't endorse being a LION, *at all!* Although some people feel that they can find some quality hidden in the quantity, LinkedIn is designed to cultivate the real quality connections that people have. Not only does LinkedIn heavily discourage a user being a LION to the point of almost banning them, but also the random connections make it next to impossible to tap the real power and potential of LinkedIn.

Learning About What You Can Do with LinkedIn

Time to find out what kinds of things you can do on LinkedIn. The following sections introduce you to the topics you need to know to get your foot in the LinkedIn door and really make the site start working for you.

Building your brand and profile

On LinkedIn, you can build your own brand. Your name, your identity, is a brand — just like Ford or Facebook — in terms of what people think of when they think of you. It's your professional reputation. Companies spend billions to ensure that you have a certain opinion of their products, and that opinion, that perception, is their brand image. You have your own brand image in your professional life, and it's up to you to own, define, and push your brand.

Most people today have different online representations of their personal brand. Some people have their own Web sites, others create and write blogs, and others create profile pages on sites like Facebook. LinkedIn allows you to define a profile and build your own brand based on your professional and educational background. I use my profile as an example in Figure 1-3.

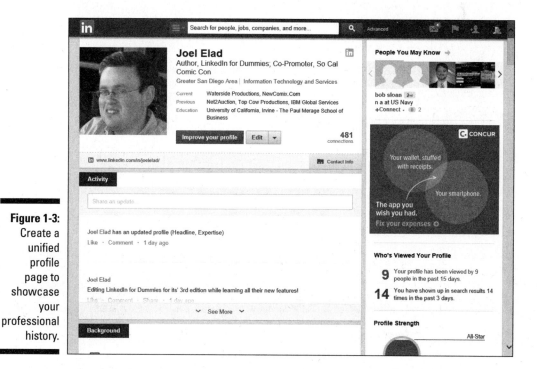

Figure 1-3:
Create a unified profile page to showcase your professional history.

Your LinkedIn profile can become a jumping-off point, where any visitor can get a rich and detailed idea of all the skills, experiences, and interests you bring to the table. Unlike a resume, where you have to worry about page length and formatting, you can provide substance and detail on your LinkedIn profile, including any part-time, contract, nonprofit, and consulting work in addition to traditional professional experience. You also have other options to consider; for example, you can

- ✔ Write your own summary.
- ✔ List any groups you belong to.
- ✔ Show any memberships or affiliations you have.
- ✔ Cite honors and awards you have received.
- ✔ Identify any patents or certifications you have earned.
- ✔ Provide links to any publications you've written or published.
- ✔ Give and receive endorsements of people's skills. (I discuss endorsements in Chapter 7.)
- ✔ Give and receive recommendations from other people. (I discuss recommendations in Chapter 8.)
- ✔ Indicate your professional interests.
- ✔ Upload presentations, graphic design projects, or portfolio examples for others to view.
- ✔ Post Web site links to other parts of your professional identity, such as a blog, a Web site, or an e-commerce store you operate.

The best part is that *you* control and shape your professional identity. You decide what the content should be. You decide what to emphasize and what to omit. You decide how much information is visible to the world and how much is visible to your first-degree connections. (I talk more about the power of your profile in Chapter 3.)

Looking for a job now or later

At some point in your life, you'll probably have to look for a job. It might be today, it might be a year from now, or it may be ten years from now. The job search is, in itself, a full-time job, and studies show that 60 to 80 percent of all jobs are found not through a job board like Monster.com or a newspaper classified ad, but rather through a formal or informal network of contacts where the job isn't even posted yet. LinkedIn makes it easy to do some of the following tedious job search tasks:

- ✔ **Finding the right person** at a target company, like a hiring manager in a certain department, to discuss immediate and future job openings

✔ **Getting a reference** from a past boss or co-worker to use for a future job application

✔ **Finding information** about a company and position before the interview

✔ **Enabling the right employers to find you** and validate your experience and job potential before an interview

✔ **Searching posted job listings** on a job board like the one on LinkedIn

The hidden power of LinkedIn is that it helps you find jobs you weren't looking for or applying to directly. This is when you're a *passive job seeker,* currently employed but interested in the right opportunity. As of this writing, hundreds of thousands of recruiters are members of LinkedIn, and they constantly use the search functions to go through the database and find skilled members who match their job search requirements. Instead of companies paying big money for resume books, they now have instant access to millions of qualified professionals, each of whom has a detailed profile with skills, experience, and recommendations already available.

This practice of finding passive job seekers is growing quickly on LinkedIn, mainly because of the following reasons:

✔ **Companies can run detailed searches** to find the perfect candidate with all the right keywords and skills in his profile, and they then contact the person to see whether he is interested.

✔ **LinkedIn users demonstrate their capabilities** by providing knowledge on the site, which gives companies insight into the passive job seeker's capabilities. Not only does LinkedIn give users the opportunity to share updates and knowledge, but it also hosts an extensive network of groups on the site. Each group runs its own "discussion board" of conversations, where LinkedIn users can pose a question or start a conversation, and other LinkedIn members can provide insight or link to relevant articles and continue the discussion.

✔ **Companies can review a person's profile** to do reference checks ahead of time and interview only people they feel would be a great match with their corporate culture.

✔ **Employed individuals can quietly run their own searches** at any time to see what's available, and they can follow up online without taking off a day for an in-person or phone interview.

LinkedIn research shows that "People with more than 20 connections are 34 times more likely to be approached with a job opportunity than people with fewer than 5 connections." Therefore, your connections definitely influence your active or passive job search.

Finding out all kinds of valuable information

Beyond getting information about your job search, you can use the immense LinkedIn database of professionals to find out what skills seem to be the most popular in a certain industry and job title. You can learn how many project managers live within 50 miles of you. You can even find current or past employees of a company and interview them about that job. LinkedIn now has hundreds of thousands of detailed Company pages that not only show company statistics but also recent hires, promotions, changes, and lists of employees closely connected with you. (Read more about Company pages in Chapter 13.)

Best of all, LinkedIn can help you find specific information on a variety of topics. You can do a search to find out the interests of your next sales prospect, the name of a former employee you can talk to about a company you like, or how you can join a start-up in your target industry by reaching out to the co-founder. You can sit back and skim the news, or you can dive in and hunt for the facts. It all depends on what method best fits your goals. (I discuss LinkedIn search techniques in depth in Chapter 6.)

Expanding your network

You have your network today, but what about the future? Whether you want to move up in your industry, look for a new job, start your own company, or achieve some other goal, one way to do it is to expand your network. LinkedIn provides a fertile ground to reach like-minded and well-connected professionals who share a common interest, experience, or group membership. The site also provides several online mechanisms to reduce the friction of communication, so you can spend more time building your network instead of searching for the right person.

First and foremost, LinkedIn helps you identify and contact members of other people's professional networks, and best of all, you don't have to contact them via a cold call, but with your friend's recommendation or introduction. (See Chapters 8 and 5, respectively, for more information.) In addition, you can find out more about your new contact before you send the first message, so you don't have to waste time figuring out whether this is someone who could be beneficial to have in your network.

You can also meet new people through various groups on LinkedIn, whether it's an alumni group from your old school, a group of past employees from the same company, or a group of people interested in improving their public speaking skills and contacts. LinkedIn Groups help you connect with other like-minded members, search for specific group members, and share information about the group with other members. (I cover LinkedIn Groups in Chapter 14.)

Understanding LinkedIn Costs and Benefits

Signing up for LinkedIn is free, and many functions are open to all account holders, so you can take advantage of most of the opportunities that LinkedIn offers. You don't have to pay a setup or registration fee, but you can pay a monthly fee for a premium account to get additional functions or communication options. Finally, tailored solutions are available for corporations that want to use LinkedIn as a source for hiring quality candidates.

Weighing free versus paid accounts

There's not much difference between a free account and paid account on LinkedIn. And the basic account is anything but basic in usage.

Your free account with LinkedIn allows you to use most of LinkedIn's most popular features, including

- ✔ Building a network of connections with no limits on size or numbers
- ✔ Reconnecting with any member of the LinkedIn network, provided that he knows you and agrees to connect to you
- ✔ Creating a professional and detailed LinkedIn profile
- ✔ Giving and receiving an unlimited number of recommendations
- ✔ Joining or creating up to 50 different LinkedIn Groups
- ✔ Requesting up to five introductions at one time (after someone accepts an introduction, you can request a new introduction in its place)
- ✔ Performing an unlimited number of searches for LinkedIn members in your extended network

If you want to step up to a paid account, some of the main features include

- ✔ Sending a message to anyone in the LinkedIn community — regardless of whether she is in your extended network — through an InMail messaging service

✔ Sending more introductions than the basic account allows

✔ Viewing more LinkedIn profile information of people not in your LinkedIn network when you conduct advanced searches

✔ Seeing more LinkedIn network profile information when you conduct advanced searches

✔ Seeing exactly who has viewed your profile and how they arrived at your profile

✔ Performing a reference check on someone (explained in Chapter 11)

✔ Obtaining membership in the OpenLink program, which gives you unlimited OpenLink messages

Comparing the paid accounts

LinkedIn offers a few levels of paid accounts, each with a specific level of benefits. For the most up-to-date packages that LinkedIn offers, check out the Compare Accounts Type page at www.linkedin.com/static?key=business_info_more, which should look like what you see in Figure 1-4. You can also click the Upgrade link at the top right of your screen, below your Account & Settings button (the thumbnail of your photo), to see a comparison of the paid accounts.

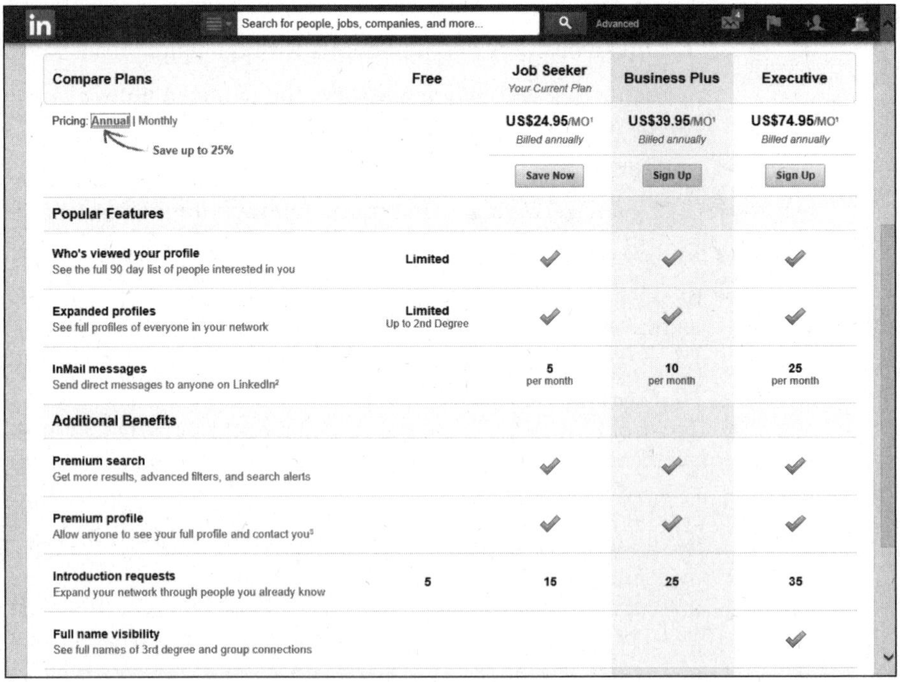

Figure 1-4: Compare different paid account features on LinkedIn.

Compare Plans	Free	Job Seeker *Your Current Plan*	Business Plus	Executive
Pricing: Annual	Monthly — Save up to 25%		US$24.95/MO¹ Billed annually	US$39.95/MO¹ Billed annually	US$74.95/MO¹ Billed annually
		Save Now	Sign Up	Sign Up
Popular Features				
Who's viewed your profile See the full 90 day list of people interested in you	Limited	✔	✔	✔
Expanded profiles See full profiles of everyone in your network	Limited Up to 2nd Degree	✔	✔	✔
InMail messages Send direct messages to anyone on LinkedIn²		5 per month	10 per month	25 per month
Additional Benefits				
Premium search Get more results, advanced filters, and search alerts		✔	✔	✔
Premium profile Allow anyone to see your full profile and contact you³		✔	✔	✔
Introduction requests Expand your network through people you already know	5	15	25	35
Full name visibility See full names of 3rd degree and group connections				✔

Every premium account comes with certain benefits regardless of the level you choose. These benefits include

- Unlimited one-click reference searches
- OpenLink network membership
- Unlimited OpenLink messages
- Ability to see who viewed your profile
- Access to premium content
- One-business-day customer service for your LinkedIn questions

As of this writing, LinkedIn offers three premium packages targeted at individual users: Job Seeker (formerly Business), Business Plus, and Executive. Each account level comes with specific benefits:

- **Job Seeker:** $29.95 per month, billed monthly, or $24.95 per month when billed annually. This account includes

  - Five InMails per month, with a seven-day response guarantee that states that if you don't receive a response to your InMail within seven days, you will receive that InMail credit back. (Unused InMail credits roll over each month, up to a maximum of nine credits. I discuss InMail in Chapter 5.)

  - Expanded profile views and a total of 250 search results outside your network when you search.

  - Fifteen introductions that you can use to have your connections introduce you to their connections.

- **Business Plus:** $49.95 per month, billed monthly, or $39.95 per month when billed annually. This account includes

  - Ten InMails per month, with a seven-day response guarantee. (Unused InMail credits roll over each month, up to a maximum of 30 credits. See Chapter 5 for more on InMail.)

  - Expanded profile views and a total of 500 search results outside your network when you search.

  - Twenty-five introductions that you can use to have your connections introduce you to their connections.

- **Executive:** $99.95 per month, billed monthly, or $74.95 per month when billed annually. This account includes

  - Twenty-five InMails per month, with a seven-day response guarantee. (Unused InMail credits roll over each month, up to a maximum of 30 credits. I discuss InMail in detail in Chapter 5.)

  - Expanded profile views and a total of 700 search results outside your network when you search.

- Thirty-five introductions that you can use to have your connections introduce you to their connections.

- Full name visibility when looking at your third-degree network members or group connections (other plans display only limited name information for these people).

Upgrading to a premium account

What's the value in getting a premium account? Besides the features listed in the previous section for each account level, premium accounts are designed to give you more attention in areas like job search. When an employer lists a job posting and collects applications through LinkedIn, premium account holders show up at the top of the applicant list (similar to the Sponsored result in a Google search) with a LinkedIn "badge" next to their name. LinkedIn provides special content in the form of e-mails, video tutorials, and articles that provide job search and professional development tips and advice from leaders in the industry. Finally, you get to see who has viewed your profile, which can be helpful when you're applying for jobs or trying to set up business deals. A premium account is not essential for everyone, so consider what you need from your LinkedIn experience and decide if upgrading is right for you.

To upgrade to a premium account, I highly recommend starting by creating your free account and using the various functions on LinkedIn. If you find that after some usage, you need to reach the larger community and take advantage of some of the premium account features, you can always upgrade your account and keep all your profile and network information that you previously defined.

If you're in charge of human resource functions at a small, medium, or large company and you are interested in using the Talent Advantage functions for your company, don't follow the steps in this section. Instead, visit http://talent.linkedin.com for more information.

To subscribe to a premium account, just follow these steps. (You must have created a LinkedIn account already; see Chapter 2 for details.)

1. **Go to the LinkedIn home page at** www.linkedin.com**. Hover your mouse over your photo or Account & Settings icon in the top-right corner of the home page, then click the Review link next to Privacy & Settings.**

2. **At the Account & Settings page (shown in Figure 1-5), click the yellow Upgrade button to bring up the premium account options, as shown in Figure 1-6.**

LinkedIn accepts Visa, MasterCard, American Express, or Discover to pay for your premium account. Make sure the billing address you provide matches the credit card billing address on file.

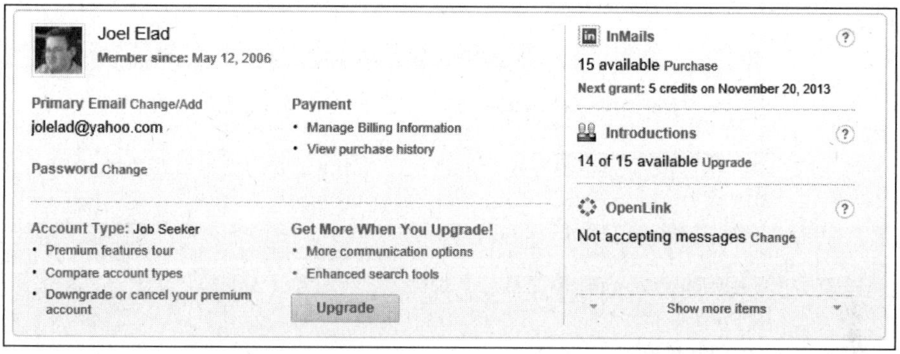

Figure 1-5:
Upgrade
your
account
from the
Account
& Settings
page.

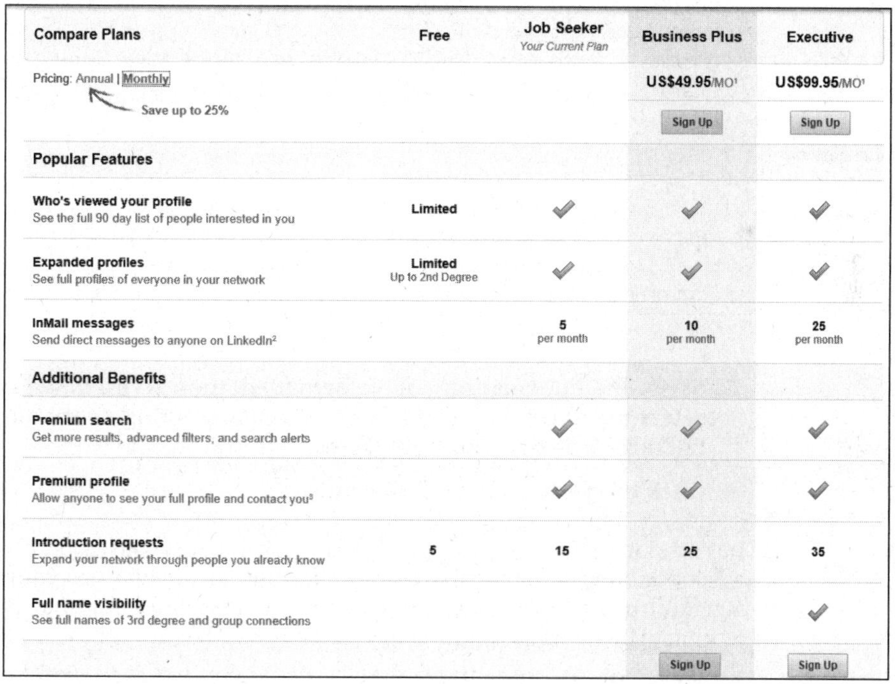

Figure 1-6:
Choose the
premium
account
that's right
for you.

3. **Click the Sign Up button for the premium level to which you want to upgrade.**

4. **Fill in the appropriate billing information, as shown in Figure 1-7, then click the Review Order button.**

Linked in. Secure Checkout 🔒

Enter your payment information

Credit or Debit Card Information:

First Name	Joel	
Last Name	Elad	
Card Number		VISA ⬤⬤⬤ ⬤⬤⬤ ⬤⬤⬤
Expires	01 ⌄	2013 ⌄
Security Code		▦ ?

Billing Information:

Country	United States ⌄
Company Name	Optional
Billing Address	123 Easy St
	Address line 2
City	Anytown
State	CA ⌄
Postal Code	12345
Phone	9495551212 ×

[Review order] [Cancel]

YOUR ORDER

Business Plus Subscription (Monthly)	US$49.95
From October 27, 2013 to November 27, 2013	
Credit from previous subscription purchase	(US$24.62)
Total purchases	US$49.95
Discounts/Credits	(US$24.62)
Estimated tax	US$0.00
Total	US$25.33

Figure 1-7:
Enter your billing information.

5. **Verify the information you've provided, then scroll down and select the check box to agree to automatic billing every month and LinkedIn's Terms and Conditions.**

6. **Click the yellow Place Order button.**

That's it! LinkedIn prorates your first month's charge based on how many days are left in the billing cycle, and it automatically charges your credit card each month afterward for the full amount, unless you bought a yearly plan, for which the charges renew every 12 months.

If you decide to stop subscribing to a LinkedIn premium account, you must go to your settings page, click Account on the left side of the screen, and then click the Downgrade or Cancel Your Premium Account link so you won't get billed anymore.

Navigating LinkedIn

When you're ready to get started, you can sign up for an account by checking out Chapter 2. Before you do, however, take a look at the following sections, which walk you through the different parts of the LinkedIn Web site so you know how to find all the cool features I discuss in this book.

After you log on to your LinkedIn account, you see your personal LinkedIn home page, as shown in Figure 1-8. There are two important areas on your LinkedIn home page that you'll use a lot, and I cover those areas in the following sections.

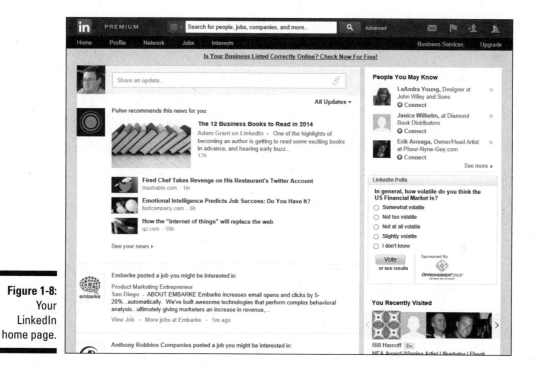

Figure 1-8: Your LinkedIn home page.

Touring the top navigation bar

Every page on LinkedIn contains certain links to the major parts of the site, and I call this top set of links the "top navigation bar" throughout this book. As of this writing, the major parts of the top navigation bar are

- ✔ **Home:** Link to your personal LinkedIn home page.
- ✔ **Profile:** Links to the profile part of LinkedIn.

✓ **Network:** Links to view your connections on LinkedIn or add/import new connections.

✓ **Jobs:** Links to the different job searches and postings you can do on LinkedIn.

✓ **Interests:** Links to search LinkedIn Company pages or keep track of companies you can follow using LinkedIn, as well as links to LinkedIn Groups, individual people known as LinkedIn Influencers, or LinkedIn Education (which includes schools and students on LinkedIn).

✓ **Business Services:** Links to post a job on LinkedIn, use the Talent Solutions section of LinkedIn, or create a LinkedIn ad to run on the site.

When you hover your mouse next to any of these words, you can see the various options in each section, like the Profile options shown in Figure 1-9.

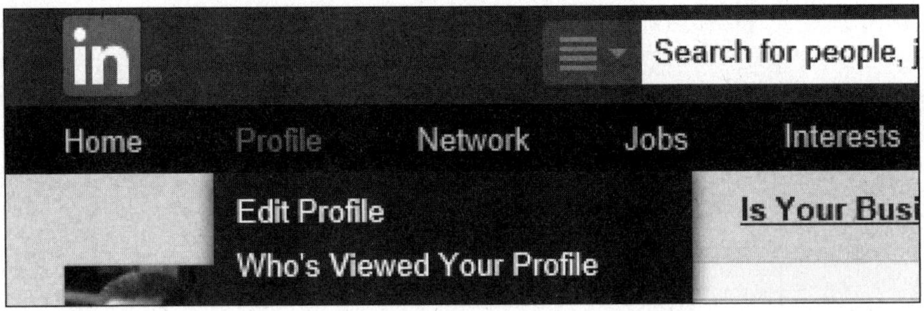

Figure 1-9: Hover your mouse over each menu element to see options for each section.

If you simply click the word, like Profile or Jobs, you're taken to the main page for that section. You can also click the Advanced link to the right of the Search box, above the top navigation bar, to bring up an Advanced People search, or you can click the drop-down list before the Search box to search for Jobs, Companies, or Groups from any page on the site. If you already changed the search criteria to another function, like Jobs, Companies, or Groups, clicking the Advanced link brings up the appropriate search page.

Finally, there are several icons along the top right of the screen:

✓ **Inbox:** The picture of an envelope opens up the LinkedIn Inbox, where you can see incoming messages and invitations.

✓ **Notifications:** The flag icon indicates new actions you should be aware of when using LinkedIn, like when you are mentioned, receive an endorsement or recommendation, or have a new connection.

✔ **Add Connections:** The picture of the + with a person is a quick link to bring up the tools to add more connections to your LinkedIn network.

✔ **Account & Settings:** After you add a profile picture, this is a thumbnail of your profile photo, and clicking this button expands a list of options that allow you to check your settings, check your job posting or Company page (if applicable), and reach the LinkedIn Help Center.

Looking at the Account & Settings page

If you need to update any aspect of your LinkedIn account, go to the Account & Settings page, shown in Figure 1-10. You can always find a link to this page at the top right of any page within LinkedIn by hovering your mouse over the Account & Settings button, and then clicking the Review link next to the Privacy & Settings header.

Figure 1-10:
See the details of your LinkedIn account.

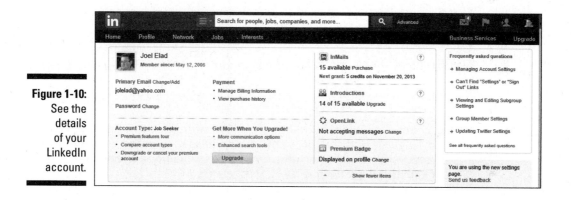

At the Account & Settings page, you first see the settings for your particular account level, especially if you have a premium account. I cover this earlier in the chapter, in the section "Upgrading to a premium account."

Scroll down to see all the different settings you can update for your LinkedIn account, as shown in Figure 1-11.

The settings you can access from this page are

✔ **Profile:** Set how much of your profile is accessible by your contacts, and also how much information you want to make available to your network in terms of profile or status updates. Update any part of your profile, add a profile photo, change your status and public profile settings, and manage your recommendations.

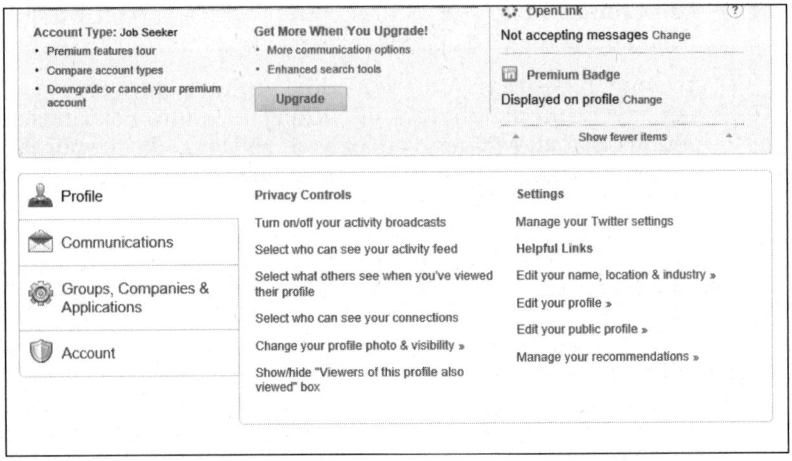

Figure 1-11:
Update your
account
settings for
LinkedIn
here.

✔ **Communications:** Set the frequency of e-mails from LinkedIn, as well as who from LinkedIn's partners can reach you. Select how other LinkedIn members can communicate with you and who can send you invitations.

✔ **Groups, Companies & Applications:** Update settings for your memberships with different LinkedIn Groups, view companies that you're following, and view or add applications that you're using with LinkedIn.

✔ **Account:** Update privacy settings, e-mail addresses and password on file, language and security settings, and links to upgrade, downgrade, or cancel your LinkedIn account. You can also enable an RSS feed of your LinkedIn account from a link in this category.

Chapter 2

Sign Me Up!

· ·

In This Chapter

▶ Joining LinkedIn with or without an invitation

▶ Registering and setting your preferences

▶ Deciding how to use LinkedIn

▶ Connecting with people you already know on LinkedIn

· ·

*W*hen LinkedIn first launched, it grew primarily through invitations — you joined only if someone who was already a member invited you and encouraged you to join. However, membership is now open to anyone 13 years or older (as long as the user hasn't previously been suspended or removed from LinkedIn, of course). You can have only one active account, but you can attach multiple e-mail addresses, past and present, to your account so that people can more easily find you.

You'll be presented with some configuration settings during the signup process that you might not know what to do with until you get more familiar with the system. Fortunately, you can customize all those settings later, but for now, I suggest some initial settings. In addition, based on your initial settings, LinkedIn recommends people to invite to your network. In Chapter 6, I discuss the ways you can grow your network more extensively, but this chapter touches on this initial recommendation process.

Joining LinkedIn

Many people join LinkedIn because a friend or colleague invited them. You can join just as easily without receiving an invitation, though. Everyone joins at the basic level, which is free. (You can opt for different levels of paid membership, as spelled out in Chapter 1.) Being able to start at the basic level makes the signup process quite straightforward. Most importantly, the basic level still gives users the ability to take advantage of the most powerful tools that LinkedIn offers.

Joining with an invitation

When a friend or colleague invites you to join, you receive an e-mail invitation. The e-mail clearly identifies the sender and usually has `Invitation to connect on LinkedIn` as its subject line. (There's a chance, though, that the sender came up with a custom header, but hopefully that message still has the word LinkedIn in the subject line.)

When you open the message, you see an invitation to join LinkedIn, like the message shown in Figure 2-1. There might be some extra text if the person inviting you personalized the message. You also see a button or link that takes you back to LinkedIn to create your account, such as the Confirm That You Know Joel button shown in Figure 2-1.

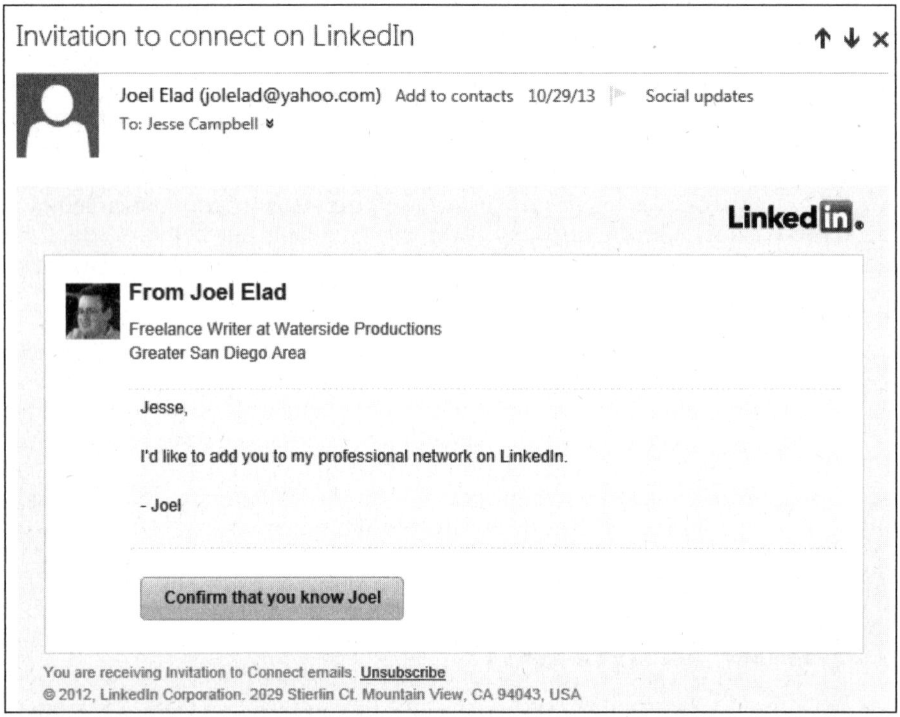

Invitation to connect on LinkedIn   ↑ ↓ ✕

Joel Elad (jolelad@yahoo.com) Add to contacts 10/29/13   Social updates
To: Jesse Campbell ⌄

Linked **in**.

From Joel Elad
Freelance Writer at Waterside Productions
Greater San Diego Area

Jesse,

I'd like to add you to my professional network on LinkedIn.

- Joel

      Confirm that you know Joel

You are receiving Invitation to Connect emails. <u>Unsubscribe</u>
© 2012, LinkedIn Corporation. 2029 Stierlin Ct. Mountain View, CA 94043, USA

Figure 2-1:
An invitation
to connect
on LinkedIn.

When you're ready to join LinkedIn with an invitation, just follow these steps:

1. **Click the button or link from your invitation e-mail.**

   You should see a new window open that goes to the LinkedIn Web site and asks to verify your name and e-mail address, as well as enter a password for your new LinkedIn account, as shown in Figure 2-2.

If you want to be known on LinkedIn by another version of your name (say a nickname, maiden name, middle initial, or proper name), or if you want to use a different e-mail address from the one used for your invitation, you can change the details in those fields — First Name, Last Name, Email.

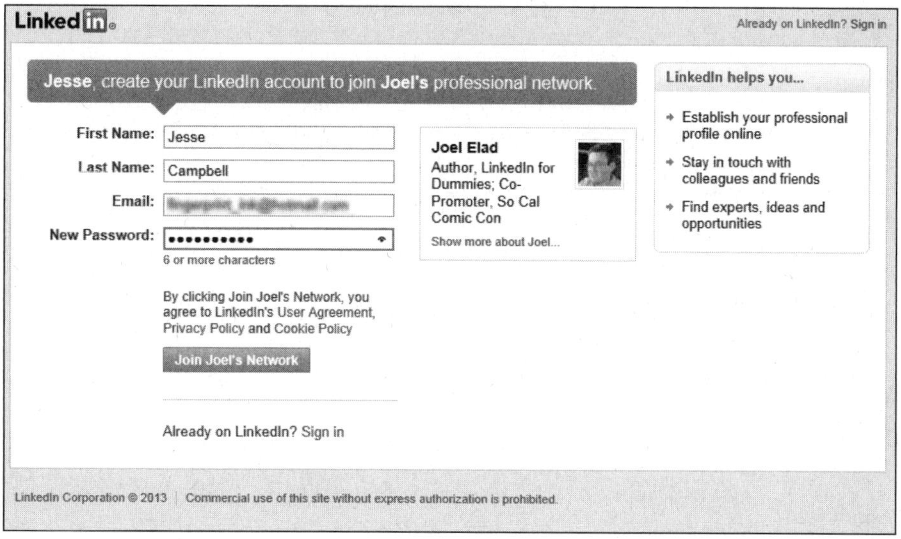

Figure 2-2:
Confirm
your name
and create a
password.

2. **Enter your correct first name and last name, and create a new password for your account. Then click the Join *Name's* Network button.**

You'll be taken to the Create a LinkedIn Profile Like (the name of your inviter), as shown in Figure 2-3. At this point, LinkedIn wants to collect some basic information it will use to create your account.

Try to pick a password that no one else can guess. You should use a combination of letters and numbers, and avoid commonly used passwords like your name, the word "password," a string of letters or numbers that are next to each other on the keyboard (for example, "qwerty"), or a password that you use on many other sites.

3. **Complete the fields presented on the Create a LinkedIn Profile page to tell LinkedIn your current employment status, company name, job title, industry, country, and ZIP code.**

In the first set of radio buttons, you can choose between three options to identify your current employment status:

- Employed
- Job Seeker
- A student

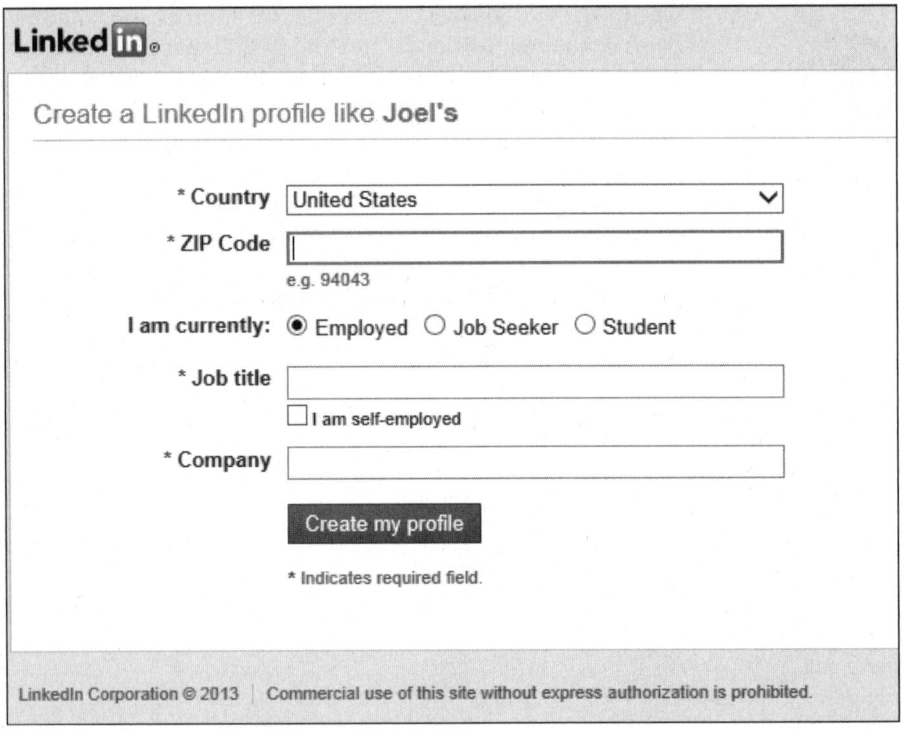

Linked in®

Create a LinkedIn profile like **Joel's**

* Country	United States ⌄
* ZIP Code	[ ]
	e.g. 94043
I am currently:	● Employed ○ Job Seeker ○ Student
* Job title	[ ]
	☐ I am self-employed
* Company	[ ]

[Create my profile]

* Indicates required field.

LinkedIn Corporation © 2013 │ Commercial use of this site without express authorization is prohibited.

Figure 2-3:
Start to give
LinkedIn
some basic
information
about
yourself.

Confirm your country of residence by selecting your country from the drop-down list provided, and then enter your ZIP or postal code in the box provided.

Enter your Job Title, and the name of the Company where you are currently employed in the boxes provided. (This includes any self-employed folks out there.) Depending on your employment status, LinkedIn may reload the page with a new field, Industry. Use the drop-down list to identify which industry you feel you belong to, as shown in Figure 2-4. If you're not employed at the moment, LinkedIn will ask you for your most recent job title and company.

4. Click the Create My Profile button to proceed.

LinkedIn offers to import your contacts from your e-mail program, as shown in Figure 2-5. LinkedIn walks you through the steps of importing your address book, offering you the chance to connect to existing members of LinkedIn. If you like, you can click the Skip This Step link and come back to this after you create your account.

It might be tempting to start inviting friends and colleagues to connect with you right away, but you might want to work on your profile or think of a strategy first before flooding people's e-mail inboxes with invitations. You can always invite people to connect with you at any time.

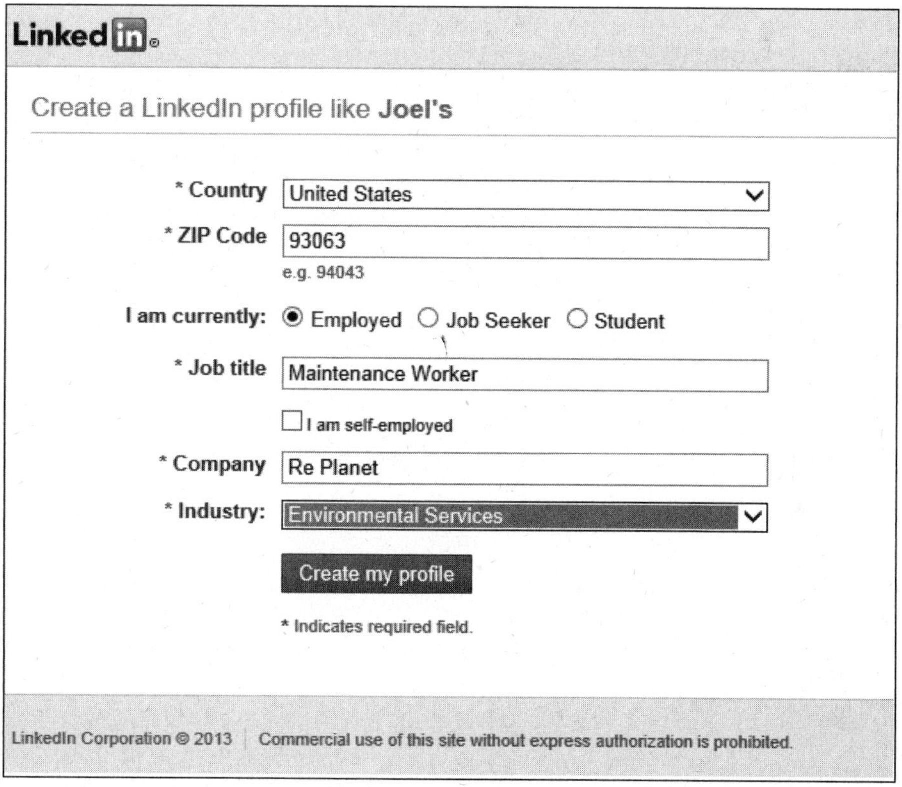

Linked in.

Create a LinkedIn profile like **Joel's**

* Country	United States ⌄
* ZIP Code	93063
	e.g. 94043

I am currently: ● Employed ○ Job Seeker ○ Student

* Job title	Maintenance Worker
	☐ I am self-employed
* Company	Re Planet
* Industry:	Environmental Services ⌄

Create my profile

* Indicates required field.

LinkedIn Corporation © 2013 | Commercial use of this site without express authorization is prohibited.

Figure 2-4:
Pick the industry that best matches your job.

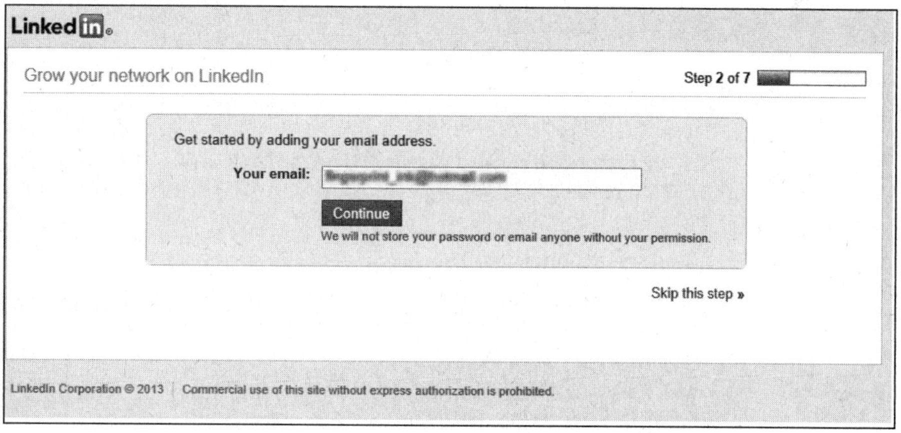

Linked in.

Grow your network on LinkedIn   Step **2** of **7**

Get started by adding your email address.

Your email: ▓▓▓▓▓▓▓▓▓▓▓

Continue

We will not store your password or email anyone without your permission.

Skip this step »

LinkedIn Corporation © 2013 | Commercial use of this site without express authorization is prohibited.

Figure 2-5:
LinkedIn can help you identify who to add to your network.

5. **Decide who you want to connect with using your new LinkedIn account.**

   After you import your e-mail contacts, LinkedIn confirms your connection to the person who invited you, and asks whether you want to invite anybody else by looking at your e-mail contacts and showing you which contacts are already on LinkedIn that you can connect with, as shown in Figure 2-6. You can select the check boxes to Add Connections now or you can click Skip This Step and invite people later. (I discuss this process in Chapter 6.)

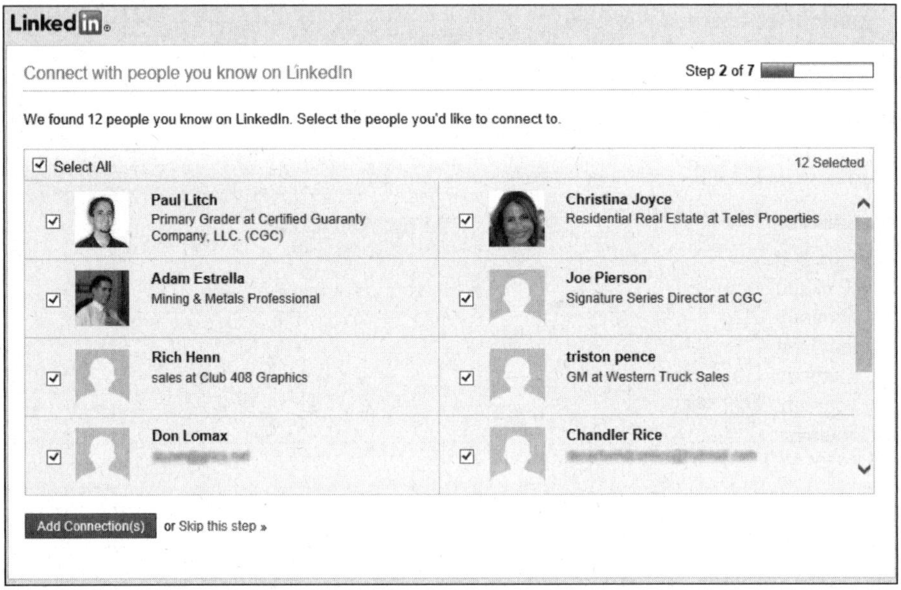

Figure 2-6: LinkedIn offers you a chance to make more connections.

6. **Click either the Add Connection(s) button or the Skip This Step link.**

   LinkedIn offers the ability to send e-mails to those contacts who are not yet on LinkedIn. It then recommends people you may know and suggests you download the mobile application. After that point, LinkedIn creates your account and takes you to your home page, as shown in Figure 2-7.

   If you want to take a break to check your e-mail, you'll find a nice Welcome to LinkedIn! message there from LinkedIn Updates, assuring you that you're now a registered LinkedIn user. The e-mail (shown in Figure 2-8) includes connection links to people you may know on LinkedIn and lets you look at other people you may know so that you can connect with them as well.

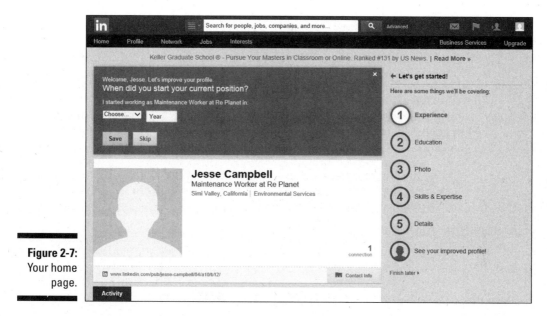

Figure 2-7:
Your home
page.

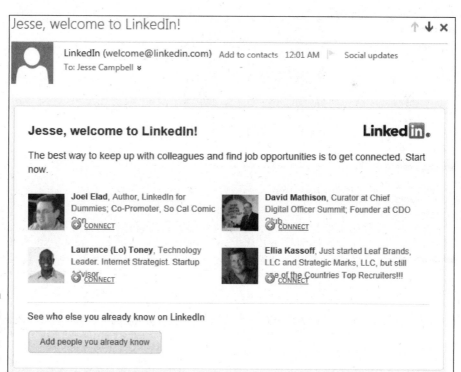

Figure 2-8:
LinkedIn
sends you
a welcome
e-mail.

Joining without an invitation

If you haven't gotten an invitation to join LinkedIn, don't let that turn you into a wallflower. You can join LinkedIn directly, without an invitation from an existing user.

Open your Web browser and go to www.linkedin.com. You see the initial LinkedIn home page, as shown in Figure 2-9. When you're ready to join LinkedIn, just follow these steps:

1. **In the Get Started section in the middle of the page, provide your first name, last name, e-mail address, and a password in the boxes provided, as shown in Figure 2-9.**

Figure 2-9: Join LinkedIn from its home page.

2. **Click the Join Now button.**

   You're taken to the next step, where LinkedIn starts to build your professional profile by asking about your current employment status and location, as shown in Figure 2-10.

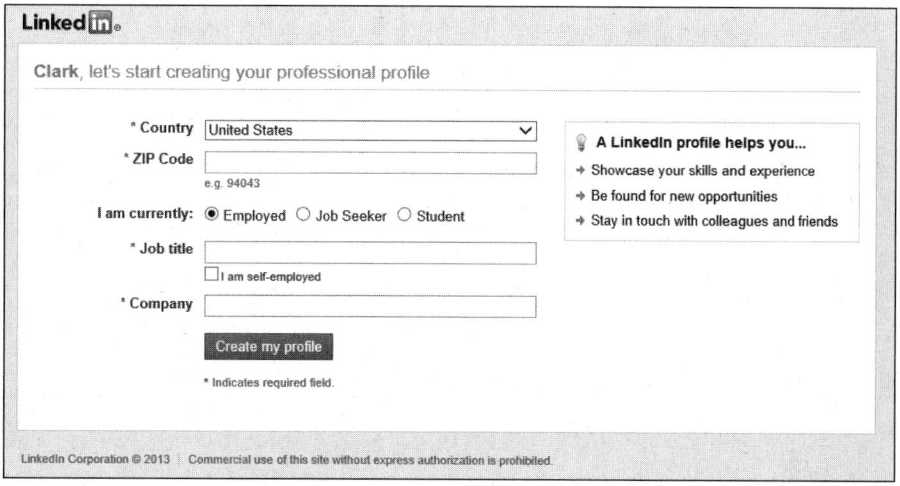
LinkedIn
Clark, let's start creating your professional profile
* Country
United States
* ZIP Code
e.g. 94043
I am currently:
Employed
Job Seeker
Student
* Job title
I am self-employed
* Company
Create my profile
* Indicates required field.
A LinkedIn profile helps you...
Showcase your skills and experience
Be found for new opportunities
Stay in touch with colleagues and friends
LinkedIn Corporation © 2013
Commercial use of this site without express authorization is prohibited.

Figure 2-10: Tell LinkedIn a little about yourself to create your account.

3. **Complete the fields regarding your current employment status and location.**

   Specifically, you need to provide the following information:

   - **Country and ZIP code:** LinkedIn won't display your ZIP code, but it does use it to assign a Region to your profile so others know the general area where you reside.
   - **I am currently:** Indicate whether you're employed, a job seeker, or a student.
   - **Details about your status:** Depending on your status, LinkedIn asks for a Company, Job Title, and Industry if you are employed, or asks for your most recent job title and company, if you're looking for work, as shown in Figure 2-11.

   If you find it difficult to choose an industry that best describes your primary expertise, just choose one that's closest. You can always change the selection later. If you're employed but looking for another job, you should still pick the industry of your current profession.

4. **Click the blue Create My Profile button to continue.**

   LinkedIn then offers to import your contacts from your e-mail program, as shown in Figure 2-12. LinkedIn walks you through the steps of importing your address book and offers you the chance to connect with existing members of LinkedIn. You can also do this after you create your account by clicking the Skip This Step link.

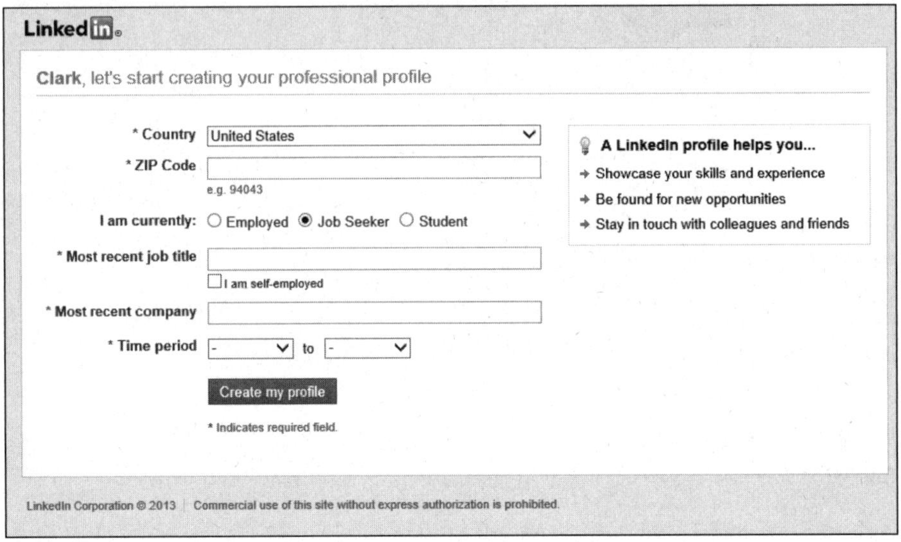

Figure 2-11: Depending on your work status, LinkedIn asks for different information.

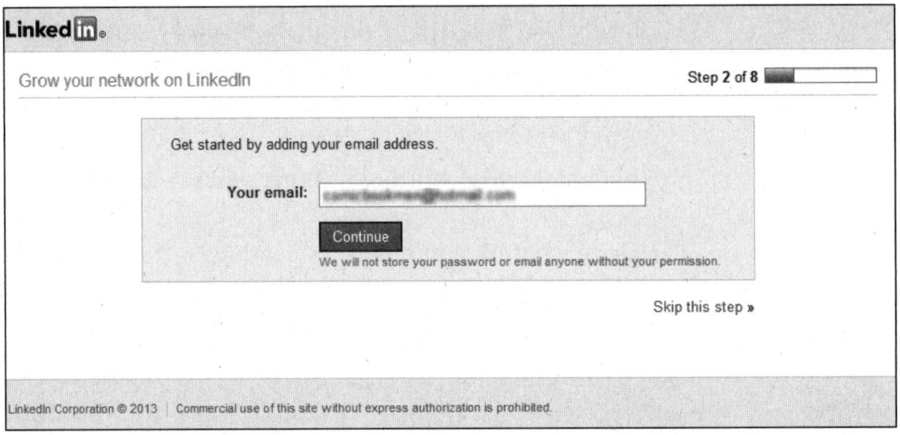

Figure 2-12: LinkedIn can help you identify who to add to your network.

5. LinkedIn asks you to confirm the e-mail address for your account.

Depending on the e-mail account you used to register the account, LinkedIn may be able to log directly into that e-mail account and confirm your e-mail address. (For example, I can click the Confirm My Hotmail Account button illustrated in Figure 2-13 to confirm the sample account I'm creating.) Otherwise, LinkedIn e-mails you a confirmation, which you can choose to receive instead of using LinkedIn to log directly into your e-mail account.

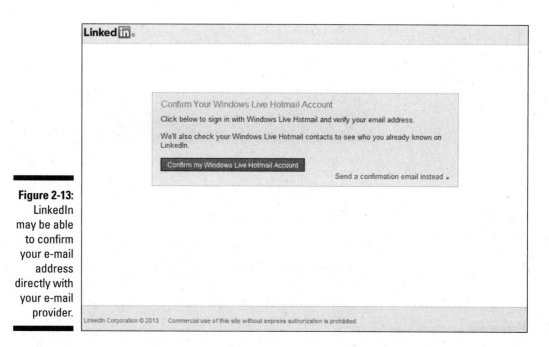

Linked in.

Confirm Your Windows Live Hotmail Account

Click below to sign in with Windows Live Hotmail and verify your email address.

We'll also check your Windows Live Hotmail contacts to see who you already known on LinkedIn.

Confirm my Windows Live Hotmail Account

Send a confirmation email instead »

LinkedIn Corporation © 2013   Commercial use of this site without express authorization is prohibited.

Figure 2-13:
LinkedIn
may be able
to confirm
your e-mail
address
directly with
your e-mail
provider.

If you choose (or have) to receive a confirmation e-mail, open
your e-mail program and look for an e-mail from LinkedIn Email
Confirmation with the subject line Please confirm your e-mail address.
When you open that e-mail, you should see a request for confirmation,
as shown in Figure 2-14. Either click the Confirm Your Email Address
button or copy and paste the URL provided in the e-mail into your Web
browser.

When you click the button, you're taken back to LinkedIn and it confirms your address, as shown in Figure 2-15. You may be asked to log in
to your account, so simply provide your e-mail address and password
when prompted.

You are asked to connect your e-mail account to look for new contacts, prompted to install the LinkedIn mobile application, and
offered the chance to upgrade your account to a paid account. (I discuss paid accounts in Chapter 1.) You can always click Skip This Step
to move along the account creation process and save those tasks for
later.

If you skip this step of confirming your e-mail with LinkedIn, you won't
be able to invite any connections, apply for jobs on the LinkedIn job
board, or take advantage of most other LinkedIn functions.

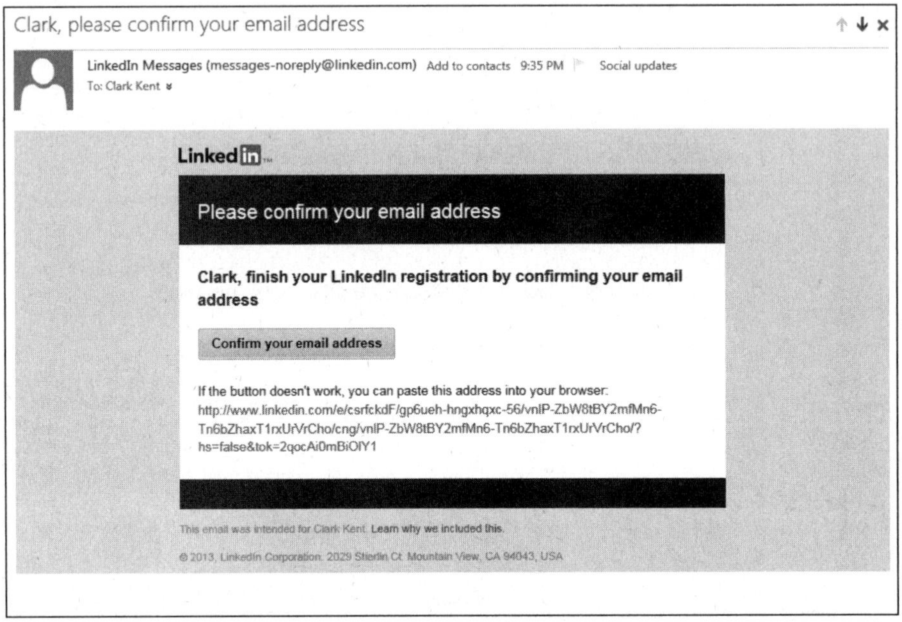

Figure 2-14:
Confirm
your e-mail
address
with
LinkedIn.

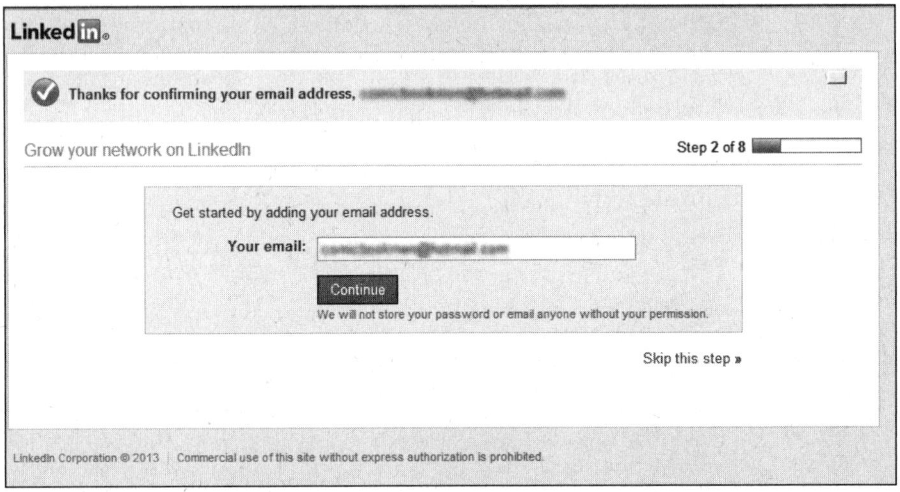

Figure 2-15:
LinkedIn
confirms
your e-mail
address.

6. **Your account is created, and you are now free to start building your network and updating your profile!**

   You are taken to your home page, as shown in Figure 2-16, where LinkedIn asks for information to help build your profile.

In the meantime, if you want to take a break to check your e-mail, you'll find a nice Welcome to LinkedIn! message there from LinkedIn Updates, assuring you that you're now a registered LinkedIn user. The e-mail encourages you to connect with people you may know and offers to take you back to the Web site to search for more people to add to your network.

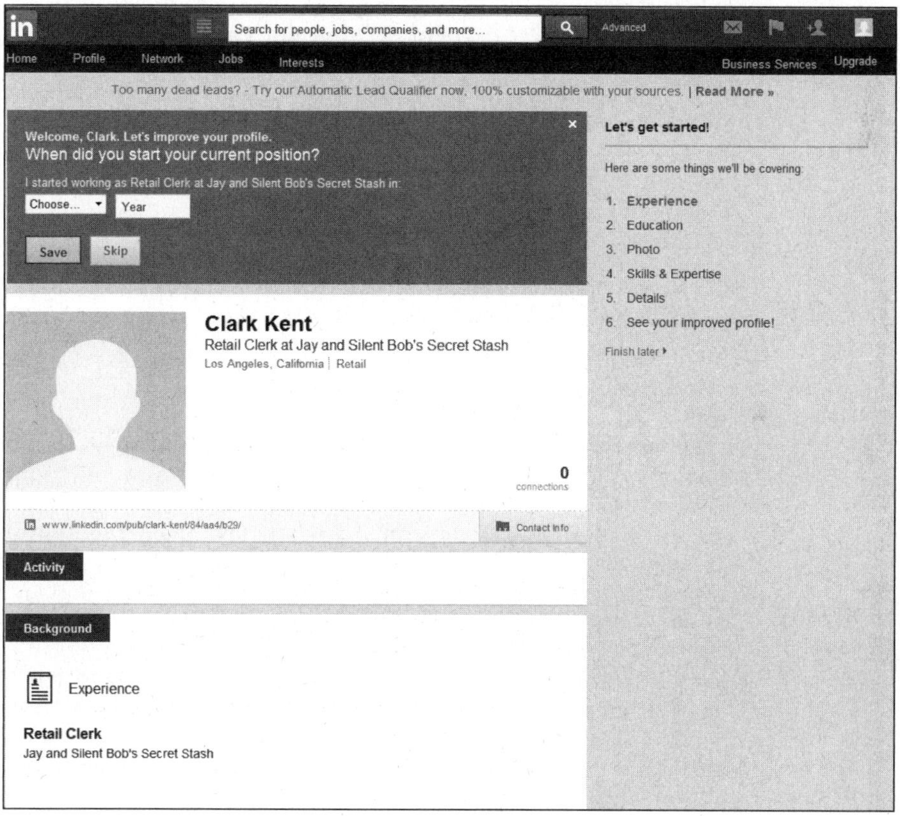

Figure 2-16:
Welcome to
LinkedIn!

Starting to Build Your Network

You're ready to look at how to build your network, with tools and forms provided by LinkedIn. Your first step is to decide who you want to invite to connect with you on LinkedIn.

Your profile is so important it gets its own chapter (Chapter 3 if you really must know). Be sure to completely fill out your profile before you start inviting people to connect. Having a complete profile makes it easier to find former colleagues and classmates. After all, if you invite someone to connect who you haven't spoken to recently, he'll probably take a quick look at your profile before responding. If he doesn't see a part of your professional history where he knows you, he will most likely ignore your invitation.

Your best bet now is to start using LinkedIn with some thought and planning. Here are some common pitfalls after signing up:

✔ You feel compelled to start inviting friends and colleagues to connect with you right away, before working on your profile or thinking of a strategy.

✔ You get nervous and decide not to invite anybody beyond one or two close friends or family members.

✔ You wonder about the value of LinkedIn and leave your account alone for a long period of time with no activity.

I've seen all three scenarios occur with various people who have joined LinkedIn, so don't feel bad if one of these is your natural reaction.

When you want to start using LinkedIn, begin by navigating to the home page and clicking Sign In. You are asked for your e-mail address and LinkedIn password, which you provided when you joined the site. After you are logged in, you can access any of the functions from the top navigation bar.

To start building your profile, hover your mouse over the Profile link in the top navigation bar and then click Edit Profile. You see your Edit Profile page, as shown in Figure 2-17. Simply click the links that look like pencils (those are Edit links) or click the Add links and follow the instructions to fill out your profile. I discuss this in greater detail in Chapter 3.

Next, start thinking about who you'd like to invite to join your network. LinkedIn provides some neat tools to help you identify, in your existing networks, people you know and trust well enough to feel confident about inviting them and expecting that they will accept.

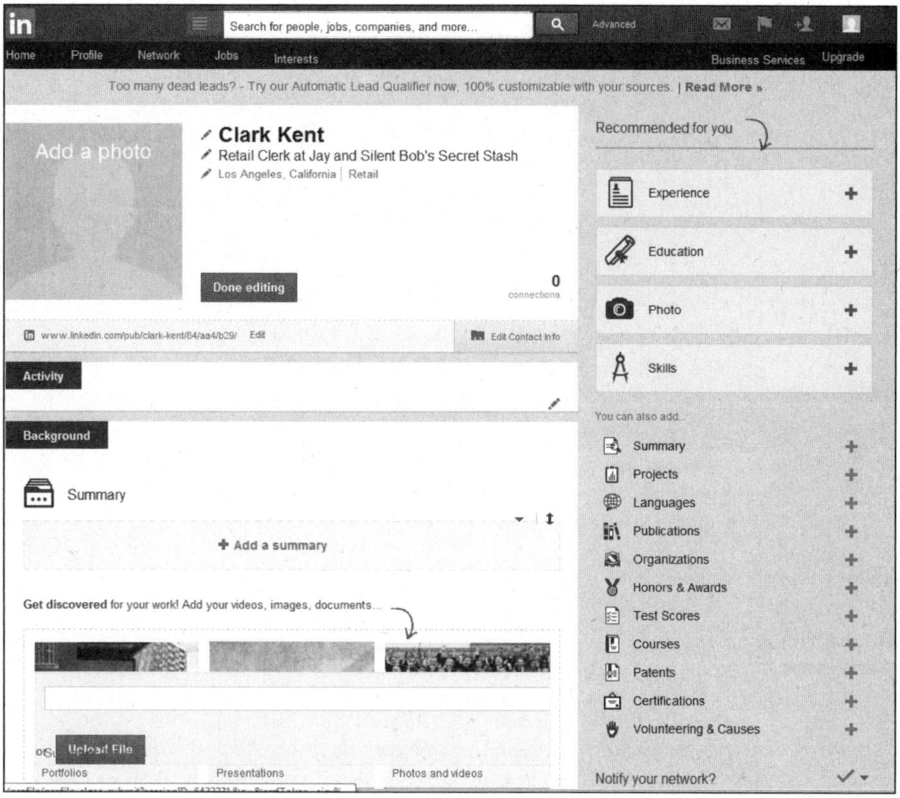

Figure 2-17: Start building your profile on LinkedIn.

The Add Connections section of LinkedIn, as shown in Figure 2-18, is always available by clicking the Network link from the top of any LinkedIn page, and then clicking the Add Connections link from the drop-down list that appears. The Add Connections section incorporates some basic options to identify and grow your network, which I cover in more depth in Chapter 6:

- ✔ Check the address book for your Web-based e-mail system, like Yahoo! Mail, Gmail, Hotmail, and AOL.

- ✔ Check your address book for contacts to invite with options for systems like Microsoft Outlook and Apple's Mail app by importing your desktop e-mail contacts with the link provided.

- ✔ Upload contact files from other applications.

- ✔ Invite people by their e-mail address. (By specifying people's individual e-mail addresses, you can decide who you want to invite without sending a blind invitation to everyone in your address book.)

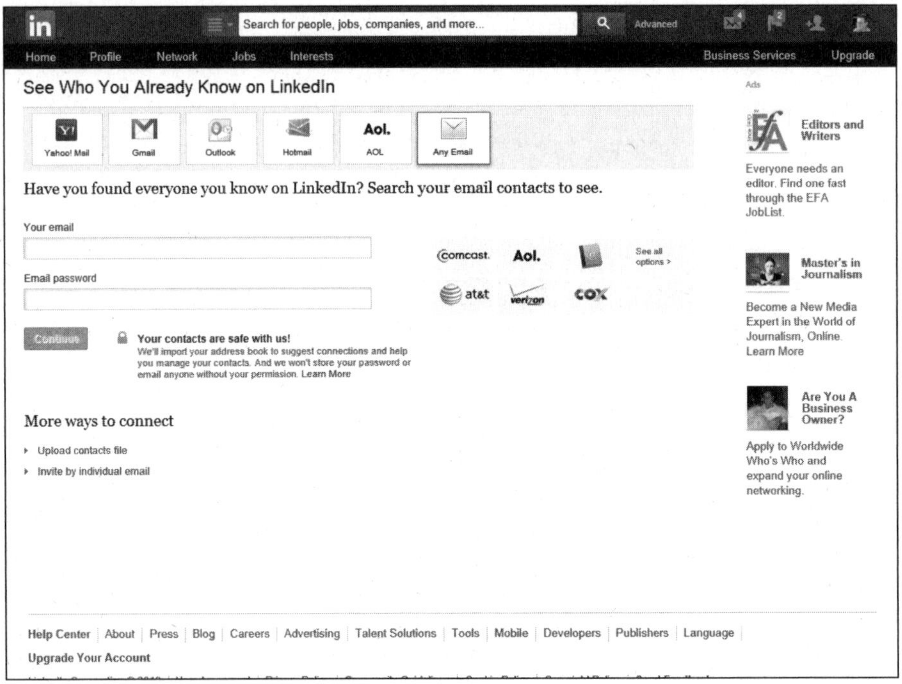

Ads

Editors and Writers

Everyone needs an editor. Find one fast through the EFA JobList.

Master's in Journalism

Become a New Media Expert in the World of Journalism, Online. Learn More

Are You A Business Owner?

Apply to Worldwide Who's Who and expand your online networking.

Figure 2-18:
Use this
handy
section
to add
connections
to your
network.

I cover these techniques in greater detail in Chapter 6. I definitely recommend that you first spend a little time thinking about who you want to invite. Then focus on getting your profile set up, and then invite people.

Privacy confidential

When you give LinkedIn access to your existing contact lists (such as on Gmail or Yahoo! Mail), rest assured that LinkedIn respects your privacy.

LinkedIn is a licensee of the TRUSTe Privacy Program. In its Privacy Policy, LinkedIn declares its adherence to the following key privacy principles:

✔ LinkedIn will never rent or sell your personally identifiable information to third parties for marketing purposes.

✔ LinkedIn will never share your contact information with another user without your consent.

✔ Any sensitive information that you provide will be secured with all industry standard protocols and technology.

Chapter 3

Building Your Profile

*A*fter you register with LinkedIn and work to build your network by looking outward, it's time to look inward by focusing on your profile. Think of your LinkedIn profile as your personal home page to the professional world: This profile exists to give anyone a complete picture of your background, qualifications, and skills as well as paint a picture of who you are beyond the numbers and bullet points.

In this chapter, I walk you through all the different sections of your profile and explain how to update them and put the right information in a concise and appealing manner. I take you through adding information at each stage so you can update your profile now or down the road (say, when you finish that amazing project or get that spiffy promotion you've been working toward).

At any time, you can go to www.linkedin.com and click the Profile link in the top navigation bar to access your LinkedIn profile to view or make changes.

Determining the Contact Settings for Your Profile

Before you dive right in and start updating your profile, stop and think about what kind of profile you want to construct and show to the world. Specifically, think about how you want to use LinkedIn. For example, some people just want to add to their network, but others are actively looking for a job. You can have many reasons for using LinkedIn, and you can identify yourself through setting up your contact settings on LinkedIn. The settings you choose mainly depend on how you plan to use LinkedIn. You can always go back and update your contact settings as your situation changes.

You can select from eight main contact settings in your LinkedIn profile. Each describes a type of opportunity that lets other people know how to approach you on the site:

- **Career opportunities:** You're looking to augment your skill set so you can advance your career, or you want to network with people who could approach you with a career opportunity now or in the future.

- **Expertise requests:** You're available to provide expertise on your main subject areas to someone with a question or opportunity.

- **Consulting offers:** You're open to receiving offers for consulting work.

- **Business deals:** You're open to doing a business deal, either for your main job or an entrepreneurial venture. Deals here could range from supplier/vendor requests, launching a new line of products, or doing a joint venture.

- **New ventures:** You're interested in participating in a new company as an employee, co-owner, financier, or anything else.

- **Personal reference requests:** You're open to providing references for your first-degree connections. (Read what defines a first-degree connection in Chapter 1.)

- **Job inquiries:** You're open to receiving job offers or interests.

- **Requests to reconnect:** You're interested in old friends, colleagues, and classmates and wouldn't mind if such folks sent a request to connect with you on LinkedIn.

After you select your settings, they appear as a bulleted list on your profile. In addition, they help determine (and potentially block) the type of communication that you receive on LinkedIn. For example, if you aren't interested in job inquiries, you shouldn't receive any direct solicitations to apply for a job.

Adding Your Summary and Basic Information to LinkedIn

Your LinkedIn profile Summary section, which appears in the top third of your profile, should give any reader a quick idea of who you are, what you've accomplished, and most importantly, what you're looking for on LinkedIn. Some people think of their summary as their "elevator pitch," or their 30-second introduction of themselves that they tell to any new contact. Other people think of their summary as simply their resume summary, which gives a high-level overview of their experience and job goals. Each summary is as individual as the person writing it, but there are right ways and wrong ways to prepare and update your summary. You should always keep in mind what your professional or career goals are, and what kind of image, or brand, you are trying to portray in support of those goals, because those goals should give you direction on how to write your summary.

LinkedIn divides the Summary section into two distinct parts:

- **Your professional experience and goals:** This is typically a one-paragraph summary of your current and past accomplishments and future goals. See the next section, "Writing your summary first," for more on how to construct the right paragraph for this part.

- **Your specialties in your industry of expertise:** This is a list of your specific skills and talents. It is separate from your professional experience in that this section allows you to list specific job skills (for example, contract negotiation or writing HTML software code) as opposed to the daily responsibilities or accomplishments from your job that you would list in the professional experience and goals paragraph.

Other core elements of your LinkedIn profile are stored in the Basic Information section. Be sure to polish these elements so they reflect well on you:

- **Your name:** Believe it or not, defining your name properly can positively or negatively affect your LinkedIn activity. Because people are searching for you to connect to you, it's important that LinkedIn knows any sort of variations, nicknames, maiden names, or former names that you may have held, so be sure you correctly fill in your First, Last, and Former/Maiden name fields. Also, LinkedIn allows you to choose a display name of your first name and last initial, in case you want to keep your name private from the larger LinkedIn community outside of your connections.

You can also include your middle name in the First Name field, which is highly recommended if you have a common name (for example, John Smith) so people can find the "right you" when searching.

✔ **Your professional headline:** Think of this as your job title. It is displayed below your name on LinkedIn, in search results, in connections lists, and on your profile. Therefore, you want a headline that grabs people's attention. Some people put their job titles; other people add some colorful adjectives and include two or three different professions. For example, I use "Author, LinkedIn for Dummies; Co-Promoter, So Cal Comic Con" indicating two of my main professions. Your headline changes only when you update the headline field, so if you add a new position to your profile, your headline doesn't update to show that addition. You have to decide what changes are worth reflecting in your headline.

Don't overload your headline with too many titles, keywords, or unrelated job skills. Although the headline does not have to be a complete sentence, it should read well and make sense. You're not scoring points with a Google search here — that's what your entire profile is for.

✔ **Your primary location and industry of experience:** As location becomes a more important element when networking online, LinkedIn wants to know your main location (in other words, where you hang your hat . . . if you wear a hat) so it can help identify connections close to you. Then, LinkedIn provides a list of industries you can choose from to indicate your main industry affiliation.

Writing your summary first

Before you update your summary on LinkedIn, I advise writing it out, using a program like Microsoft Word so that you can easily copy and paste it. This allows you to organize your thoughts, decide the right order of your statements, and pick and choose the most important statements to put in your summary.

Of course, the goals of your summary should be the same as your goals for using LinkedIn. After all, your summary is the starting point for most people when they read your profile. As you write your summary, keep these points in mind:

✔ **Be concise.** Remember, this is a summary, not a 300-page memoir of your life. Most summaries are one paragraph long, with a separate paragraph to list your skills and/or specialties. Give the highlights of what you've done and are planning to do. Save the detailed information for when you add your individual employment positions to your profile.

✔ **Pick three to five of your most important accomplishments.** Your profile can have lots of detail regarding your jobs, skill sets, education, and honors, but your summary needs to reflect the three to five items throughout your career that you most want people to know. Think of it this way: If someone were introducing you to another person, what would you want this new person to know about you right away?

Depending on your goals for LinkedIn, the accomplishments you put in your summary might not be your biggest accomplishments overall. For example, if you're trying to use LinkedIn to get a new job, your summary should include accomplishments that matter most to an employer in your desired field.

✔ **Organize your summary in a who, what, goals format.** Typically, the first sentence of your summary should be a statement of *who* you are currently, meaning your current profession or status; for example, "Software project manager with extensive experience in Fortune 500 firms." The next few sentences should focus on *what* you've done so far in your career, and the end of your summary should focus on your *goals*.

✔ **Use the right keywords in your summary.** Keywords are especially important if you're looking for a new job or hoping to pick up some consulting work. Although you should use a few keywords in your professional experience paragraph, you should really use all the appropriate keywords for skills you've acquired when you write the Specialties section of your summary. Potential employers scan that section looking for the right qualifications first, before making any contact. If you're unsure what keywords are the most important, scan the profiles of people in your industry, see what articles they are posting, or look at job opportunity postings in your field to see what employers want when they hire personnel with your title.

✔ **Be honest with your specialties, but don't be shy.** Your Specialties section is your opportunity to list any skill or trade you feel you've learned and demonstrated with some ability. Some people stuff their Summary section with the buzzworthy skills for their industry (even if the person doesn't know those skills at all) in hopes of catching a potential employer's eye. Typically, a prospective employer can detect this resume skill padding during the interview phase, which wastes everybody's time. Conversely, however, some people don't list a skill here unless they feel they're an expert at it. You should list any skill or specialty that you believe puts you above the level of a novice or pure beginner.

If you need help coming up with your various summary sections, click the See Examples link below each section header to see examples provided by LinkedIn, or you can view profiles of other people in similar industries. Reach out to your LinkedIn network or find people in your industry or field for help.

Updating your LinkedIn profile's Summary and Basic Information sections

When you have an idea of what you want to put in your profile's Summary and Basic Information sections, it's time to go into LinkedIn and plug that data into the correct fields. When you're ready, follow these steps:

1. **Go to LinkedIn and log in:**

   www.linkedin.com/secure/login?trk=hb_signin

2. **Click the Profile link in the top navigation bar.**

   You're taken to the profile page, as shown in Figure 3-1.

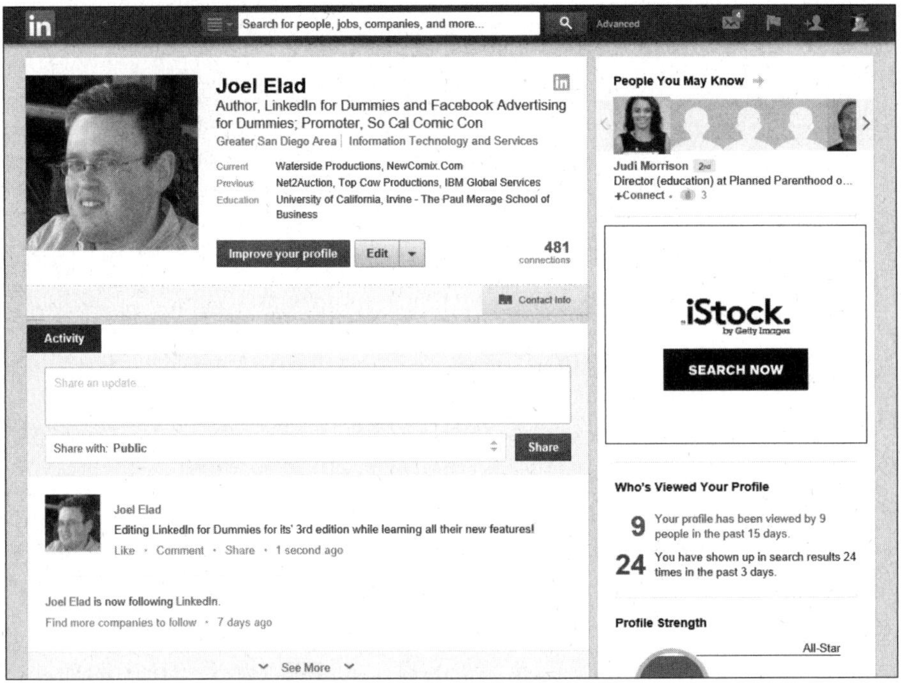

Figure 3-1:
Bring
up your
LinkedIn
profile page.

3. **Click the Edit button, then scroll down to the Summary section and click the Add Summary link below the Summary section header.**

   You see the Professional Summary page, as shown in Figure 3-2.

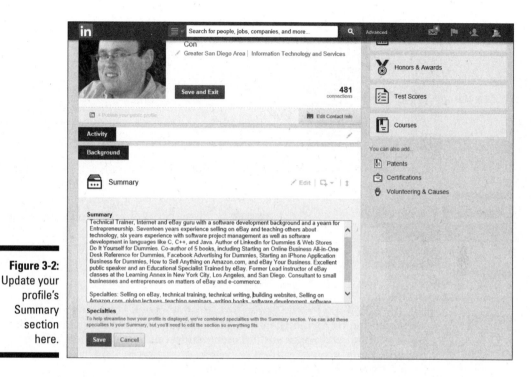

Figure 3-2: Update your profile's Summary section here.

4. **In the Summary text box, enter a paragraph or two that sums you up professionally (as discussed in the previous section).**

   You're limited to 2,000 characters, but keep your text concise and focused.

5. **In the same box, enter your skills and/or specialties as a separate list, as shown in Figure 3-2.**

   Separate each item with a comma and don't put any punctuation after the last item in your list. You don't need to press Enter/Return between skills.

6. **Click the blue Save button to save your summary.**

   You're taken back to your profile page. Next, you need to update the Basic Information section of your LinkedIn profile.

7. **Click the Edit link (it looks like a pencil) next to your name to update your name.**

   You now see the Edit Your Profile Name box, as shown in Figure 3-3.

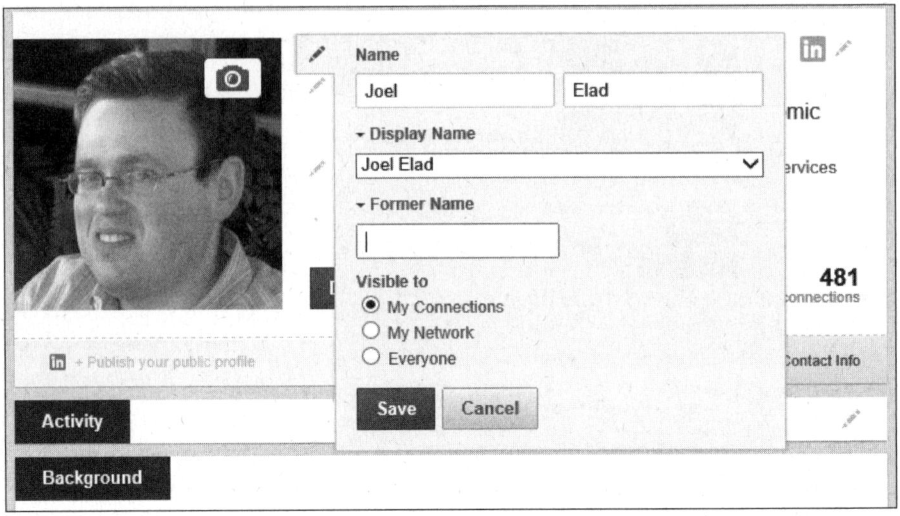

Figure 3-3:
Define your
name on
LinkedIn.

8. **In the Edit Your Profile Name box, double-check your name and add any maiden or former name in the text box provided. Decide whether you want your display and former/maiden names visible to just your connections, your extended network, or everyone on LinkedIn. When you're done, click the blue Save button.**

   If you want to maintain a higher level of privacy for your profile, you can choose the Display Name option by clicking the drop-down arrow next to the Display Name box so only your first name and last initial appear on your public profile. If you select that option, your first-degree connections see your full name, but the general public sees only your first name and last initial, such as Joel E. for me.

9. **Click the Edit link next to your headline to enter your professional headline (your main job title).**

   You can put any job title here, but make sure it conveys your main role as you want others to see it. (See the previous sections for what to include in your headline.) When you're done, click the blue Save button.

10. **Click the Edit link next to your Location and Industry line to update your location and select the industry you most associate with your career.**

   You can choose from more than 140 designations, so take a few moments to scan the list. Note that some of the industries listed are more specific than others. You want to pick the best match possible. For example, if you create custom graphics for Web sites, you could select Internet as your industry, but an even better choice would be Online Media.

The $5,000 profile update

I have a great example of why you should update your profile. Jefre Outlaw's LinkedIn profile says that he's a "portfolio entrepreneur." His profile doesn't mention, however, that he spent more than 25 years as a real estate investor and developer, nor that he obtained his own real estate license and joined his cousin Blake's agency, Outlaw Real Estate Group. He realized a golden opportunity was available to him through LinkedIn.

Outlaw was interviewed for the LinkedIntelligence blog (www.linkedintelligence.com/the-5000-profile-update). "At first I completely forgot about updating my LinkedIn profile," he said. "But I got a request to forward an introduction, and it reminded me that I should probably go update my profile to include my new gig as a Realtor."

This turned out to be a valuable update for Outlaw.

Several weeks later, someone from his extended network was using LinkedIn to search for Realtors and saw Outlaw's profile.

This person contacted Outlaw about listing a home for sale. Well, the potential client signed up with Outlaw's agency, which was able to sell the house quickly for $170,000. When you do the math, $170,000 home × 3% commission = about $5,000 to the brokerage.

As Outlaw relayed his experience to LinkedIntelligence, he wanted his story to be clear. "Let's not overstate what happened," said Outlaw. "Being on LinkedIn didn't get me the business. We [Outlaw's real estate agency] were one of several Realtors the client talked to, and I brought in my cousin, who's a great closer and more experienced than I, to meet with the client. But the fact that I was in [LinkedIn], that my profile was up-to-date, that I have over 20 really good recommendations on my profile — all that put us on the short list."

The moral of the story is simple. Keep your profile up to date on everything you're doing. If your profile isn't up to date, plan to update it right away — you may never know what opportunities you're missing by ignoring your profile.

11. Click the Save and Exit button.

You're taken back to your profile page.

You've now covered the core of your LinkedIn profile. In the next sections, you find out about the other essential elements to include in your profile, namely your current/past experience and education.

Adding a Position to Your LinkedIn Profile

One of the most important aspects of your LinkedIn profile is the list of positions you've held over the years, including your current job. This list is especially important if you're using LinkedIn to find a new or different career or to reconnect with past colleagues. Hiring managers want to see your complete history to know what skills you offer, and past colleagues can't find you as easily through LinkedIn if the job they knew you from isn't on your profile. Therefore, it's critical to make sure you have all the positions posted on your profile with the correct information, as long as that fits with the brand or image you want to portray to the professional world.

For a company in LinkedIn's directory, you need to fill in the following fields:

- ✔ Company name (and display name, if your company goes by more than one name)
- ✔ Your job title while working for the company
- ✔ The time period you worked for the company
- ✔ Description of your job duties

If your company is *not* listed in LinkedIn's directory, you need to fill in the industry and Web site for the company when you're adding your position to your LinkedIn profile.

Use your resume when completing this section, because most resumes include all or most of the information required.

To add a position to your LinkedIn profile, follow these steps:

1. **Go to LinkedIn and log in. Hover your mouse over the Profile link in the top navigation bar, then click Edit Profile from the drop-down list that appears.**

   This step takes you to your profile page. Scroll down your profile until you see the Experience header, shown in Figure 3-4.

2. **Click the Add a Position link to the right of the Experience header.**

   You see an expanded Experience section with all the necessary text boxes, as shown in Figure 3-5.

3. **In the text boxes provided, enter the information about your position, including company, title, location, time period, and job description.**

   When you type in your company name, LinkedIn checks that name against its Company pages of thousands of companies from its records,

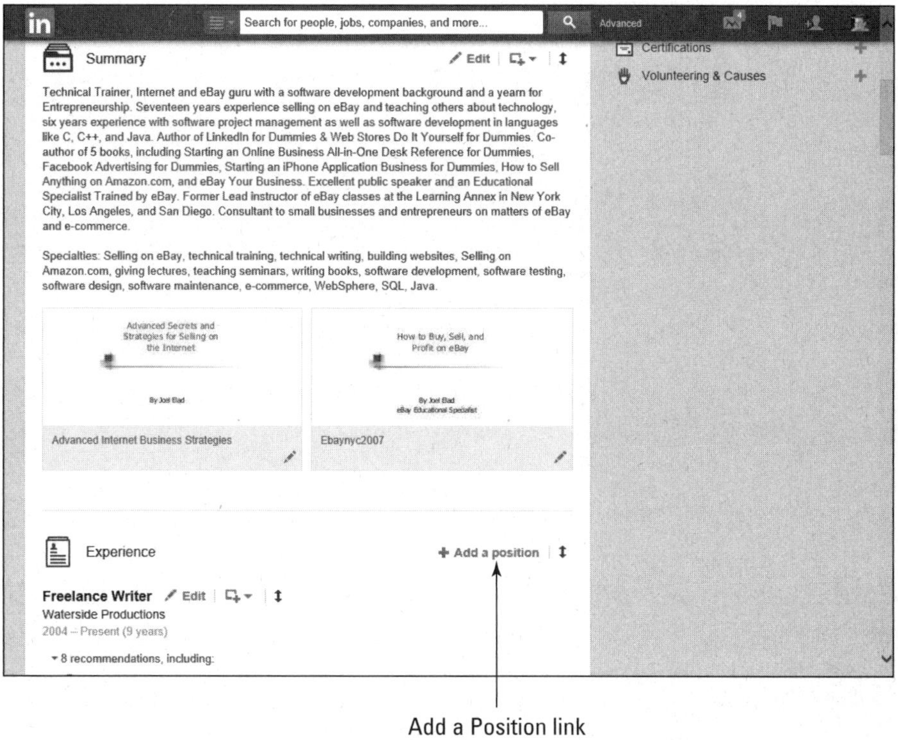

Figure 3-4:
Start at your
Experience
section
within your
profile.

Add a Position link

and you see suggested company names while you type. (An example is shown in Figure 3-6.) If you see your company name in that list, click the name, and LinkedIn automatically fills in all the company detail information for you.

After entering the company name, enter your title, job location, the time period when you worked there, and a description of your position.

4. **Click the Save button.**

   This adds the newly entered position into your profile, and you're taken back to your profile page.

5. **Repeat Steps 2–4 for any additional position you want to enter.**

To edit a position you already listed, click the Edit link next to that record in the Experience section instead of clicking the Add a Position link.

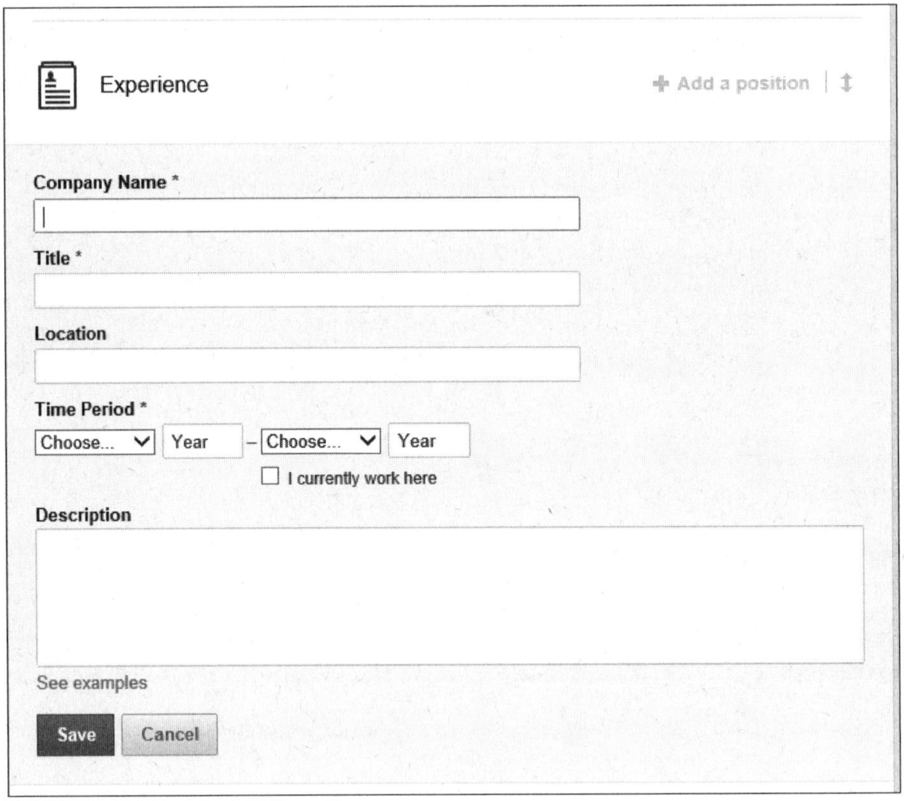

Experience   ✚ Add a position | ↕

Company Name *

Title *

Location

Time Period *

| Choose... ▾ | Year | – | Choose... ▾ | Year |

☐ I currently work here

Description

See examples

Save   Cancel

Figure 3-5:
Enter your
job informa-
tion here.

The Experience section isn't just for paid full-time employment. You can add position information for any contract work, nonprofit volunteer assignments, board of director membership, or other valid work experience that added to your skill set. If you've written a book, maintain a blog, or have a regular magazine column, you might want to list that as a separate position.

If you have most of the information that LinkedIn asks for a given position but you're missing a few details in the description, go ahead and add what you have. (You must provide a job title, company, and time period to save the position in your profile.) You can fill in any missing information later. In addition, if you make your profile public (as discussed later in the section "Setting your profile URL and public view"), make sure any position information you enter is something you don't mind the whole world — including past employers — seeing on your profile.

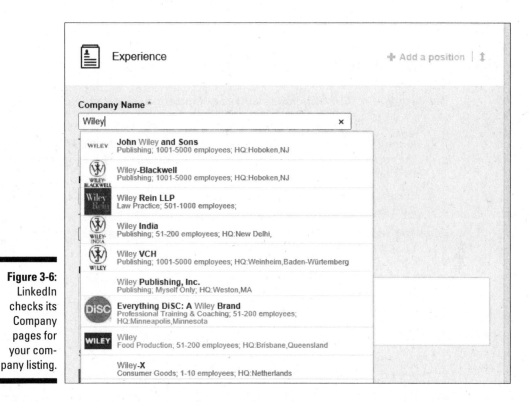

Figure 3-6:
LinkedIn
checks its
Company
pages for
your com-
pany listing.

Reporting Your Education on Your Profile

After you document your past and current jobs, it's time to move on to the next part of your profile: education. After all, besides at your jobs, where else are you going to meet and stay in touch with so many people? At school, of course! Your Education section says a lot about you, especially to potential employers and to former schoolmates who are looking to reconnect with you.

When you signed up with LinkedIn, you might have been asked to provide your basic education information. Maybe you have more than one school to list, or perhaps you didn't create a full listing for the schools you put down upon registration. In either case, you can go back to make sure that your profile is up to date and lists all your education.

Some people ask how much education to list on their profiles. Although you could theoretically go all the way back to preschool or kindergarten, most people start with high school or undergraduate college. This is up to you, but keep in mind that the more items you list, the greater the opportunity that your past schoolmates can locate and contact you.

This section isn't limited to high school, undergraduate, and post-graduate education. You should also list any vocational education, certification courses, and any other stint at an educational institution that matters to your career or personal direction.

When you're ready to update or add your education information, follow these steps:

1. **Go to LinkedIn and log in. Hover your mouse over the Profile link in the top navigation bar, then click Edit Profile from the drop-down list that appears.**

2. **Scroll down your profile until you see the Education header. Click the Add education link.**

   You see an expanded Education section with all the necessary text boxes, as shown in Figure 3-7.

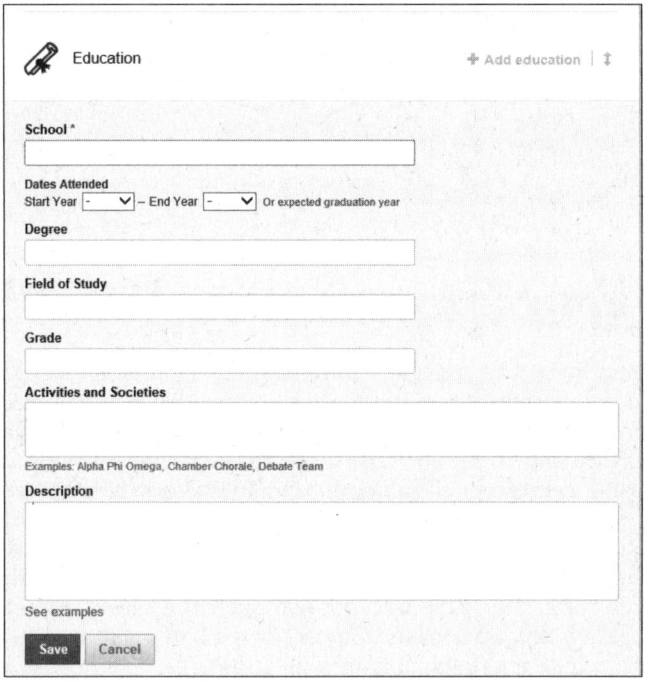

Education   + Add education | ↕

School *

Dates Attended
Start Year [- ▾] – End Year [- ▾] Or expected graduation year

Degree

Field of Study

Grade

Activities and Societies

Examples: Alpha Phi Omega, Chamber Chorale, Debate Team

Description

See examples

[Save] [Cancel]

Figure 3-7:
Enter your school information into the Education section of your profile.

---

3. **In the School text box, start entering the school name you wish to add to your profile.**

   As you're typing, LinkedIn displays a drop-down list of schools, as shown in Figure 3-8.

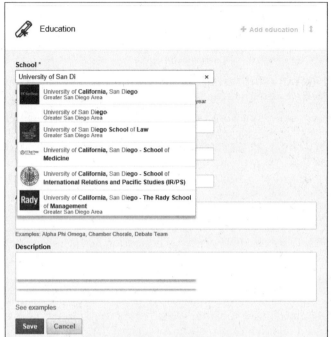

Figure 3-8:
Pick your
school from
the list
provided.

4. **Look through the alphabetized list to find your school and select it. If your school name doesn't appear, just finish typing the name of your school in the text box.**

5. **Complete the degree information about your education.**

   This includes filling in your degree type, fields of study (if applicable), grade you received (optional), and the years you attended this institution. For your degree type, you can either provide an abbreviation (BS, BA, and so on) or write the entire degree name (Masters of Science, Doctorate, and so on). The Field of Study text box is optional, but if you had a specific major or emphasis, this is where to put that information. Finally, for dates attended, if you're still attending this institution, simply fill in your expected graduation date. If you are an older worker and concerned about age discrimination, you can leave the dates of attendance blank; this is optional information.

6. **Scroll down to the Activities and Societies text box and fill it in.**

   Enter any extracurricular activities you participated in while attending this school. Also list any clubs or organizations you belonged to (including any officer positions you held in those clubs) and any societies you joined or were given membership to, such as honor societies, fraternities, or sororities.

Decide if listing these activities will support or enhance your overall professional goals and brand image. Make sure to list any activities, like current alumni organization activities, that apply to your situation today.

Separate each activity with a comma.

7. **Scroll down to the Description text box and enter any additional information about your education experience.**

   Enter any awards or honors received from this school, as well as any special events or experiences that didn't fit in the Activities and Societies box, such as studying abroad, events you organized, or committees that you served on at this school.

   You can separate each item with a period if you want.

8. **When you're done entering information, scroll down and click the Save button.**

   This step adds the newly entered education listing into your profile, and you're taken back to your profile page.

9. **Repeat Steps 2–8 for any additional education listings you want to enter.**

   To edit an existing education record, click the Edit link next to that record in the Education section, instead of the Add Education link.

Completing the Contact Info and Additional Information for Your Profile

Whenever you meet someone, the most common questions you ask are, "So, what do you do?" and "Where did you go to school?" However, there's more to you than your jobs and education, and LinkedIn has two sections, Contact Info and Additional Information, to tie your LinkedIn profile to your other Internet and real-life identities.

These sections allow you to provide lots of information in these areas:

✔ **Web sites:** LinkedIn allows you to add up to three different Web site links, which point from your LinkedIn profile to whatever Web site(s) you designate, such as your personal Web site, your company Web site, a blog, an RSS feed, or any other promotional mechanisms you use online.

Adding a link from your LinkedIn profile to your other Web sites helps boost search engine rankings for those pages. Those rankings are partially determined by the quantity and quality of Web pages that link to them, and LinkedIn is a high-quality site as far as the search engines are concerned. *Note:* You must make your profile public to receive these benefits. You can find out more about your public setting later in the chapter, in the section "Setting your profile URL and public view."

✔ **Twitter:** You can link your Twitter and LinkedIn accounts so that your Twitter updates show up on your LinkedIn profile, and your LinkedIn network activity can be tweeted to your Twitter followers automatically.

✔ **Interests:** Highlight your extracurricular activities to allow potential contacts to see what they have in common with you (favorite hobbies or sports) and give potential employers a glimpse into what else interests you outside a job.

✔ **Groups and Associations:** Illustrate what organizations you belong to and what formal activities you do in your spare time. Many people use this section to highlight charity work, networking groups they belong to, or affiliations with religious or political groups.

These items are completely optional for you to complete, but a strong, well-rounded profile usually helps you in your career or networking goals because it gives you more opportunities to connect with someone ("Hey, Joel's a big travel fan. So am I!") or allows people to identify with your situation.

When you're ready to update the rest of the information on your profile, simply follow these steps:

1. **Go to LinkedIn and log in. Click the Profile link in the top navigation bar.**

2. **On your profile page, click the Edit button. Click the Edit Contact Info link below your profile picture, name, and headline.**

   You see an Expanded contact information section, as shown in Figure 3-9, where you can update your contact information, including e-mail, phone, IM, and physical address. Click the Edit link (the pencil icon) to add the appropriate information.

   If you want to update your Twitter setting, click the Edit link next to the Twitter header to bring up the Twitter Settings page, as shown in Figure 3-10, to add or edit your Twitter account that's connected with LinkedIn.

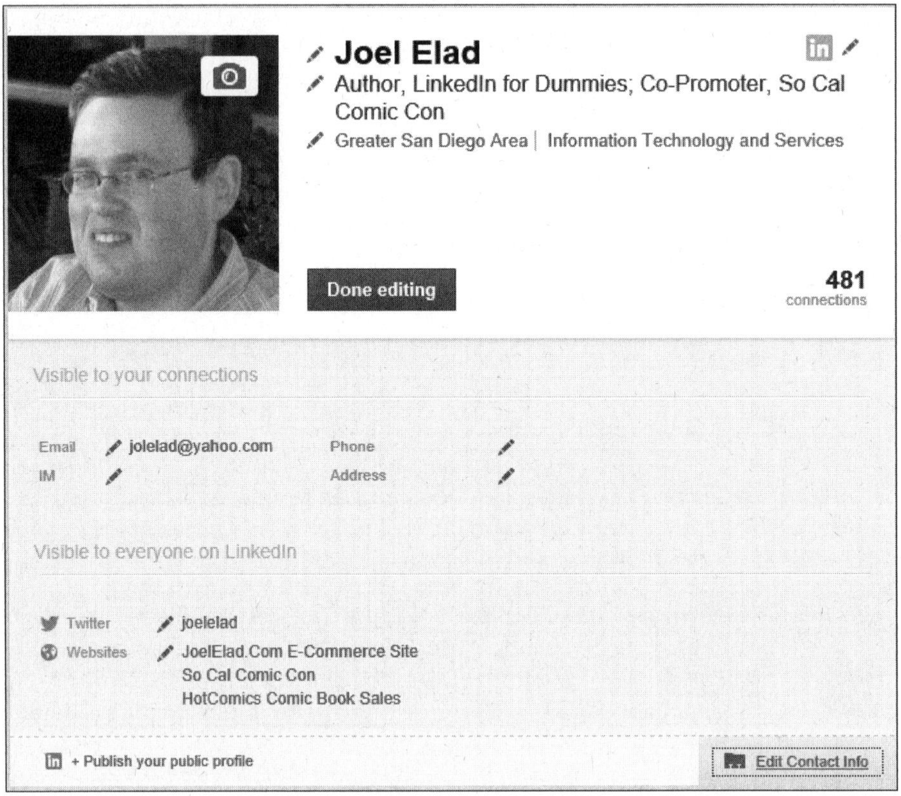

Figure 3-9: Update your contact information here.

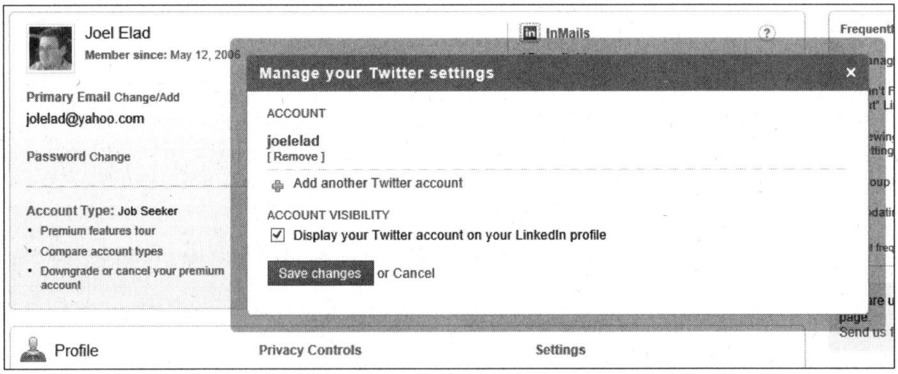

Figure 3-10: This page is where you define your Twitter account to be referenced.

3. **Under Websites, in the drop-down lists on the left, select short descriptions for the sites you intend to display.**

   You can pick from the predefined list of descriptions (My Company, My Website, and so on). Or, you can pick Other, as shown in Figure 3-11; in the blank text box that appears, type in a brief custom description for your Web site link (like My E-Commerce Site or the name of your activity).

   This description appears as a link on your profile — the reader doesn't see the site's URL.

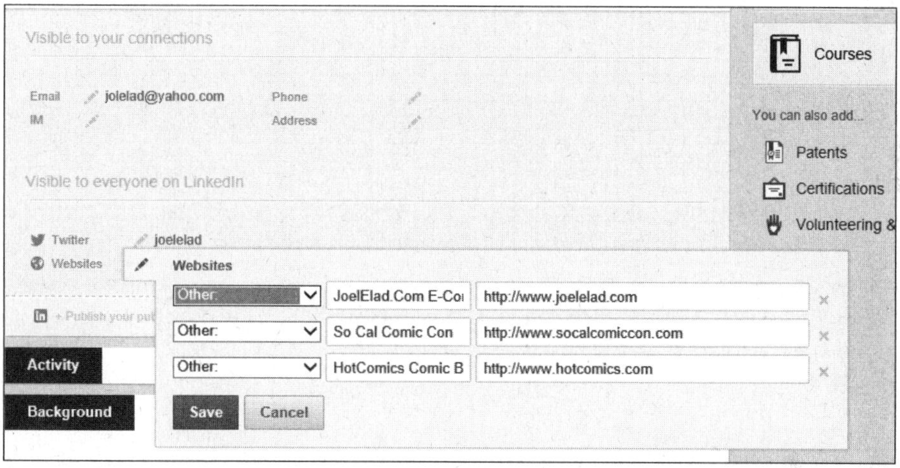

Figure 3-11: You can give custom names to your Web site links.

Visible to your connections

Email ✎ jolelad@yahoo.com   Phone ✎
IM ✎   Address ✎

Visible to everyone on LinkedIn

🐦 Twitter ✎ joelelad
🌐 Websites ✎   **Websites**

Other:▼   JoelElad.Com E-Coi   http://www.joelelad.com   ✕
Other: ▼   So Cal Comic Con   http://www.socalcomiccon.com   ✕
Other: ▼   HotComics Comic B   http://www.hotcomics.com   ✕

Save   Cancel

Courses

You can also add...

📇 Patents
📜 Certifications
✋ Volunteering &

Activity

Background

TIP

Search engines look at the text used in these links when calculating rankings. So if there are certain keywords you want to include to rank your site higher, include them in the link text. For example, you might want to say "Springfield Toastmasters" rather than "My Toastmasters Club."

4. **Still in the Websites section, in the text boxes to the right, enter the URLs of the Web sites you want to list on your profile, corresponding to the correct descriptions on the left.**

   You can add up to three URLs to your LinkedIn profile, so use them wisely.

WARNING!

This might seem obvious, but, well, people are going to be able to click those links and check out your Web sites. Sure, that's the point, but do you remember that hilarious yet embarrassing picture of yourself you added to your personal site, or that tirade you posted in your blog about a co-worker or tough project? Before you link to a site from your LinkedIn profile, scour it and make sure you won't end up scaring off or offending your contacts.

5. **Scroll down your profile until you get to the Additional Info section, as shown in Figure 3-12. Click the Edit icon to complete the Interests text box.**

   Use this section to tell the world a little more about you besides your jobs and education. Make sure to separate each interest with a comma.

   You probably want to omit any interests that a potential employer wouldn't like to see. For example, if you work in the entertainment industry, talking about how you love to download pirated movies will not make any hiring manager happy. Talk instead about how you love to watch licensed content from approved sources like iTunes or Amazon Unbox!

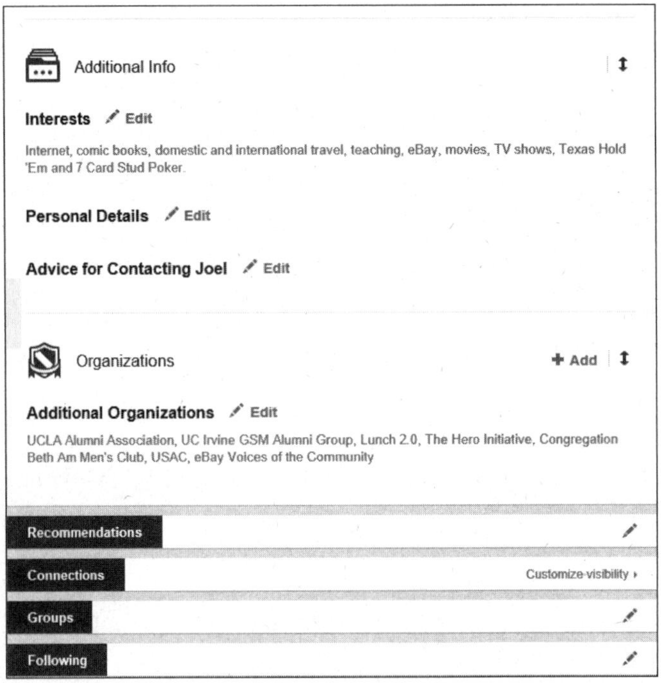

Additional Info   ↕

Interests ✎ Edit

Internet, comic books, domestic and international travel, teaching, eBay, movies, TV shows, Texas Hold 'Em and 7 Card Stud Poker.

Personal Details ✎ Edit

Advice for Contacting Joel ✎ Edit

Organizations   ➕ Add | ↕

Additional Organizations ✎ Edit

UCLA Alumni Association, UC Irvine GSM Alumni Group, Lunch 2.0, The Hero Initiative, Congregation Beth Am Men's Club, USAC, eBay Voices of the Community

Recommendations		✎
Connections	Customize visibility ▸	
Groups		✎
Following		✎

Figure 3-12: Edit your Interests and Additional Organizations here.

6. **When you're done, click the Save button. Scroll down and click the Edit link next to Additional Organizations to fill in your other groups and associations.**

   Here you can list your groups not listed under any school, such as any charity groups, religious organizations, alumni associations, and rotary clubs.

7. **Click the Save button.**

This step updates your Additional Information section in your profile, and you're taken back to your profile page.

LinkedIn is continuing to add lots of exciting sections for you to use to highlight all of your achievements and skills. If you edit your profile, you see a list of recommended sections you can add to your profile, as shown in Figure 3-13. Simply click each section and fill in the appropriate information.

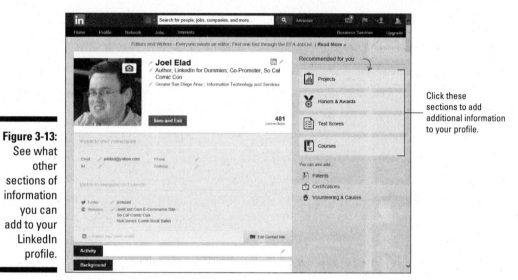

Figure 3-13: See what other sections of information you can add to your LinkedIn profile.

Click these sections to add additional information to your profile.

Reviewing Your LinkedIn Profile

After you go through the various sections of your LinkedIn profile and add the critical information, review your profile to make sure it appears exactly the way you want other people to see it, as well as decide how much information is visible to the public and what others on LinkedIn can contact you about.

Viewing your profile as others see it

While you're updating your LinkedIn profile, take a minute to view your profile to see how it is displayed on the computer screen when anyone clicks to view it. The easiest way is to click the Profile link from the top navigation bar, to see your profile, as shown in Figure 3-14.

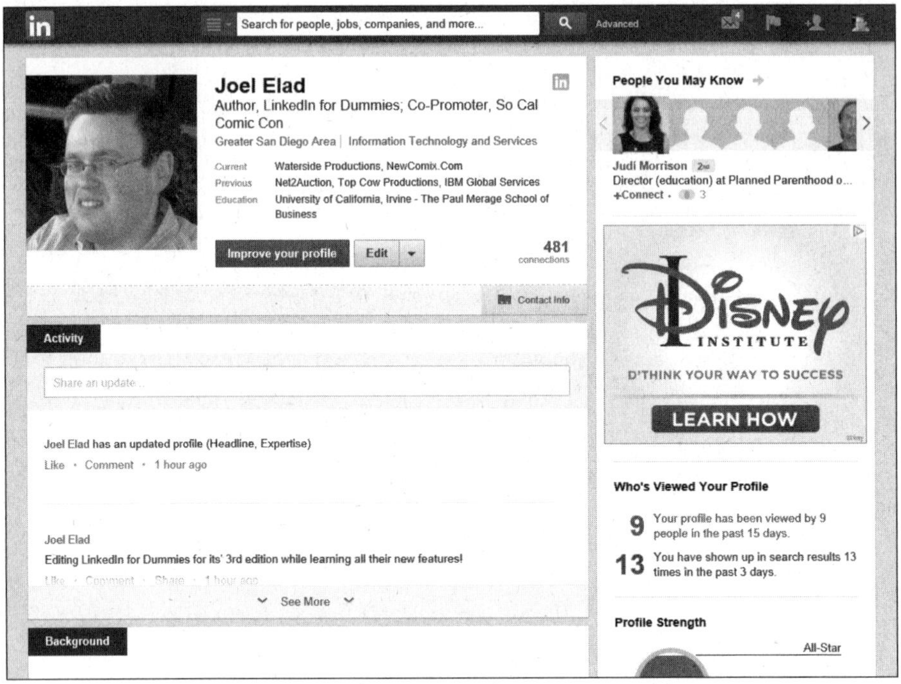

ADVERTISEMENT

DISNEY INSTITUTE

D'THINK YOUR WAY TO SUCCESS

LEARN HOW

Figure 3-14:
View your
LinkedIn
profile in
action.

Setting your profile URL and public view

After you fully update your LinkedIn profile, your next goal is probably to share it with the entire world, not just your LinkedIn network. The best way to accomplish this is to set up your profile so that your full profile is available for public viewing.

Setting your profile to full public view gives you several advantages:

✔ Anyone looking for you has a better chance of finding you because of the increased information tied to your name.

✔ When you make your profile public, it gets indexed in both the Google and Yahoo! search databases. This makes your online identity accessible and controlled by your access to LinkedIn.

✔ You give increased exposure to any companies, projects, or initiatives that you're working on by having that credit published on your LinkedIn profile.

When you're ready to set your profile to Public, just follow these steps:

1. **Go to LinkedIn and log in. Hover your mouse over the Profile link in the top navigation bar, and click Edit Profile.**

   You arrive at your profile page. Below your photo, headline, and name, look for the Publish Your Public Profile link as shown in Figure 3-15.

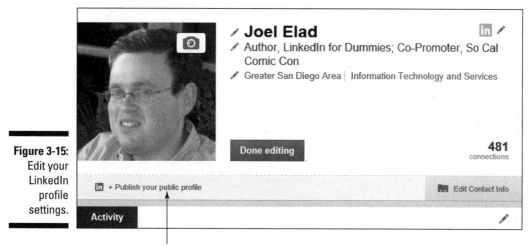

Figure 3-15: Edit your LinkedIn profile settings.

Publish Your Public
Profile link

2. **Click the Publish Your Public Profile link.**

   This step takes you to the Public Profile settings page, as shown in Figure 3-16.

3. **(Optional) To set a custom URL for your LinkedIn profile, click the Customize Your Public Profile URL link and fill in the text box that appears.**

   You can type anywhere between 5 and 30 numbers or letters, but don't include any spaces, symbols, or special characters. When you're done, click the Set Custom URL button to save your changes.

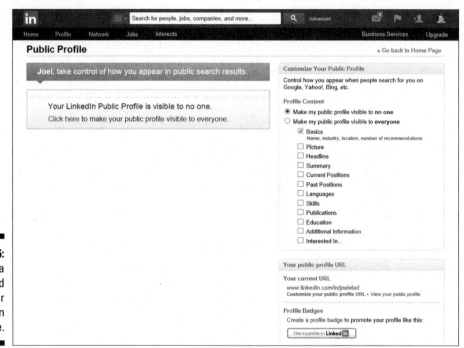

Figure 3-16:
Create a
customized
URL for your
LinkedIn
profile.

Keep in mind it's much easier to point people to www.linkedin.com/in/joelelad/ than to www.linkedin.com/5a6e4b/.

Keep your URL changes to a minimum (preferably, just set it once and leave it) so that everyone knows how to get to your profile, especially search engines. (If you change your custom URL later, the previous custom URL is no longer valid.) Otherwise, you'll have different versions of your profile with different URLs in different places on the Internet.

4. **Scroll down the Profile Content section on the page and determine what parts of your LinkedIn profile you want available for public viewing.**

Pick which sections of your LinkedIn profile are public. To reveal a section on your public profile, simply select the check box next to that section, as shown in Figure 3-17. Your basic information is already selected for you by default, but you can decide whether to add your education, positions, groups, or any other indicated section. As you add sections, the preview of your profile page on the left side of the page is updated.

Figure 3-17: Decide what to add to your public LinkedIn profile, and the preview shows the changes instantly.

5. **Your changes are automatically saved as you select each section.**

   Click the Go Back to Home Page link (at the top right of the page, as shown in Figure 3-16) to go back to your main LinkedIn page, or click any of the links in the top navigation bar to go about your business.

 Whenever you're editing your public profile settings, you can scroll down and click the View Your Public Profile link to open a new browser window and see your public profile.

Checking your contact settings

You definitely want to make sure that you select the correct contact settings for your LinkedIn profile. After all, if you're looking for a new job, for example, you want to make sure the option for Career Opportunities has been checked. (I go into plenty of detail about the eight main contact settings in the earlier section "Determining the Contact Settings for Your Profile.")

When you're ready to check your contact settings, just follow these steps:

1. **Go to LinkedIn and log in. Hover your mouse over the Account & Settings button (a small version of your picture) in the top right corner of the screen, then click the Review link next to Privacy & Settings.**

   Your browser presents you with your Account Settings page.

2. **From the headers in the bottom left of your screen, click Communications. Then, in the middle of the screen, click the Select the Types of Messages You're Willing to Receive link.**

   This opens up a Types of Messages box, as shown in Figure 3-18.

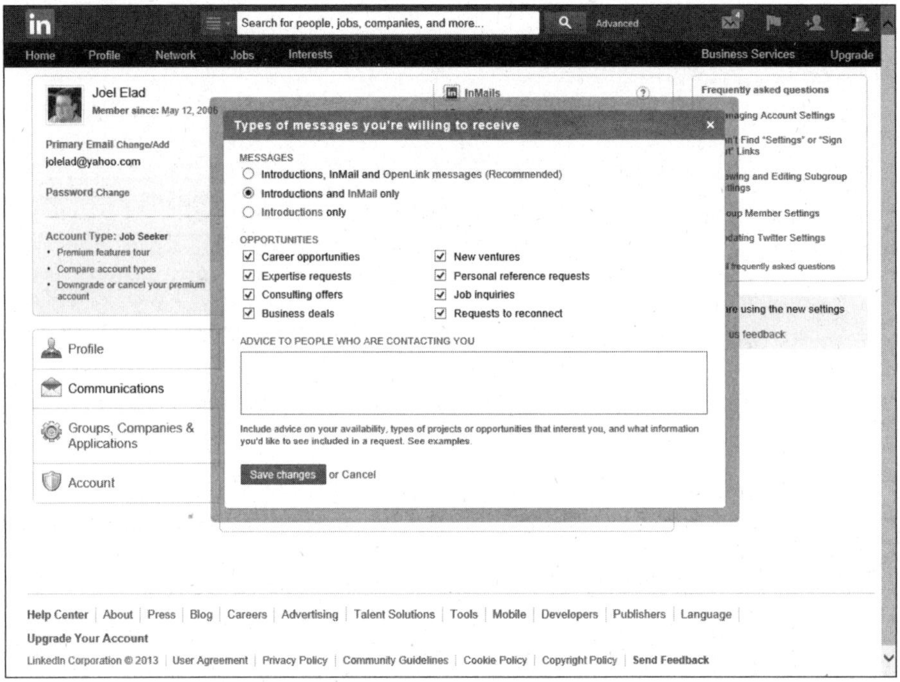

Figure 3-18:
Update your contact settings for your profile.

3. **Select your option(s) under the Messages header for what types of messages you wish to accept.**

   If you wish to receive mail through all of LinkedIn's different communication systems, select the Introductions, InMail, and OpenLink Messages option, so that people can contact you through any of those three methods.

If you only want to receive InMail e-mails from people who aren't direct connections in your network, but not anyone who's using LinkedIn's OpenLink system, select the Introductions and InMail Only option.

Otherwise, select the Introductions Only option to block anyone sending you InMail. Your first-degree connections can always send you a message through LinkedIn. (This is different from the InMail e-mails you can send any LinkedIn user, which you find out about in Chapter 5.)

4. **Select the correct options in the Opportunities section.**

   The items you select here appear as a bulleted list in your profile and limit (or allow) the ways in which other LinkedIn members can contact you. If you don't want to receive any InMail or introductions from other LinkedIn users, you can deselect those check boxes, and no options to contact you are displayed on your profile.

5. **(Optional) To give advice on how people can contact you, fill in that information in the indicated text box.**

   For example, if you require a few pieces of information from someone before you add him to your network, you can indicate that in this text box. You can also indicate whether this is a good time to contact you, or what projects or subject areas you're involved in.

6. **Click the Save Changes button.**

   You're taken back to your Account settings page.

Part II

Finding Others and Getting Connected

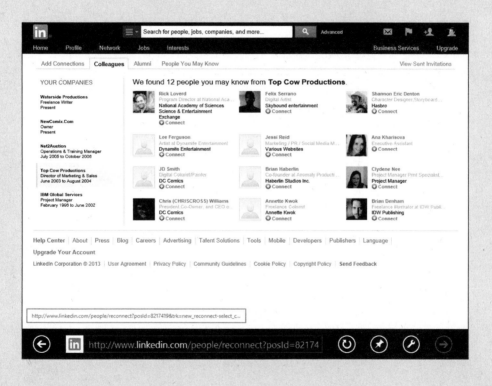

Learn how to upload your photo to your LinkedIn profile at www.dummies.com/extras/linkedin.

In this part...

- ✔ Search the database far and wide for people, groups, or companies.
- ✔ Manage the way you invite and introduce yourself to others on the LinkedIn site.
- ✔ Grow your network using the LinkedIn built-in tools.
- ✔ Keep track of your existing network with the LinkedIn Contacts system.
- ✔ Give and receive endorsements.

Chapter 4

Searching LinkedIn

*A*fter you sign up for LinkedIn and build your profile (see Chapters 2 and 3, respectively, for more on those topics), it's time to go forth and find connections! As you start searching your own immediate network of your first-degree connections, plus second- and third-degree network members, you can see just how valuable LinkedIn can be to you. LinkedIn is the embodiment of the Six Degrees of Separation concept because in most cases, you can connect to any other person in the network regardless of whether you already know that person.

In this chapter, I demonstrate the different ways you can search the LinkedIn network. By that I mean your ever-growing personal network and the greater LinkedIn member network. I talk about viewing your own network, searching within the second and third levels of your network, and performing searches on LinkedIn using different types of criteria or search terms.

Viewing Your Connections

I recall an old saying: "You have to know where you have come from to know where you are going." This holds true even for LinkedIn. Before you start searching throughout the network, it's helpful to understand the reach of your own immediate network and how your first-degree connections' networks add up to keep you connected with a lot of people. The first thing you should do is get familiar with your own LinkedIn network.

To view your LinkedIn network and also some nifty statistics about your network, just follow these steps:

1. **Log in to LinkedIn. From the top navigation bar, hover your mouse over the Network link and then click the Contacts link that appears.**

   This brings up a list of your current connections on the Contacts page, as shown in Figure 4-1. You can scroll through the list or hover your mouse over the Sort By link and then click the Last Name option (located below the tiled bar of potential contacts) to sort the list of connections in an alphabetical order.

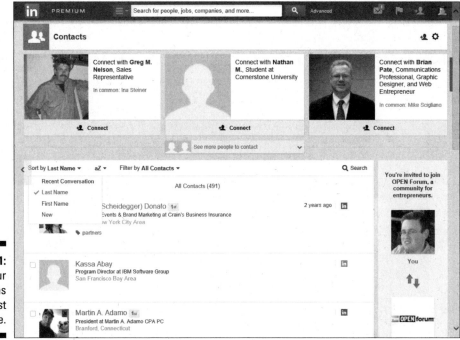

Figure 4-1:
Sort your connections by last name.

2. **Use the search box and drop-down arrow next to the Filter By link in the middle of the screen to filter your list of connections.**

   Enter any keyword into the search box or use one of the predefined filters (Tags, Companies, Locations, Industries, and Recent Activity) to display connections who, say, live in a greater metropolitan area of a certain city or work in a particular industry. You can also click the Advanced link at the top of the page to bring up all the filtering options.

The drop-down lists contain options only for your first-degree connections.

Suppose you're looking for Internet professionals. After clicking the Advanced link at the top of the page, you simply expand the Industry filter by clicking the triangle next to Industry (as shown in Figure 4-2) and then clicking Internet. LinkedIn can show you who in your network matches that request! If you're looking for an option in any of these filter lists (like Austin, TX, as a location) that doesn't appear on the filter list, none of your first-degree connections have that option defined in their profiles. (In this case, it would mean that none of your first-degree connections reside in Austin.)

Relationship	▲
☐ All	
✓ 1st Connections	(486)
☐ 2nd Connections	(285488)
☐ Group Members	(279168)
☐ 3rd + Everyone Else	(0)

Location	▼

Current Company	▼

Industry	▲
✓ All	
☐ Publishing	(51)
☐ Entertainment	(45)
☐ Marketing and Adverti...	(36)
☐ Internet	(35)
☐ Information Technolog...	(27)
✦ Add	

Past Company	▼

School	▼

Profile Language	▼

in Groups	▼

in Years of Experience	▼

in Function	▼

in Seniority Level	▼

Figure 4-2: Generate a targeted list of your connections based on a filter.

3. **Expand the Locations filter (as shown in Figure 4-3) to see a break-down of where the folks in your network are located.**

    LinkedIn shows you the numerical breakdown of which regions are the most popular in your network.

TIP

Click any region on this list, and LinkedIn automatically performs a search of your network with that criteria. So, to see your first-degree connections who live in the greater New York City area, click the Greater New York City Area link in the Locations list.

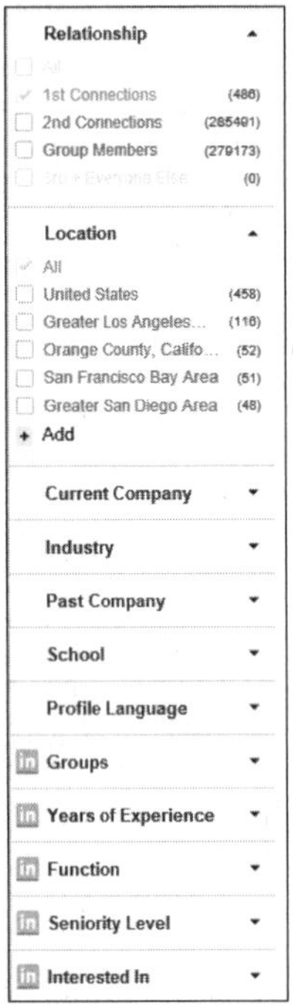

Relationship	▲
☐	
✓ 1st Connections	(486)
☐ 2nd Connections	(265401)
☐ Group Members	(279173)
☐	(0)
Location	▲
✓ All	
☐ United States	(458)
☐ Greater Los Angeles...	(116)
☐ Orange County, Califo...	(52)
☐ San Francisco Bay Area	(51)
☐ Greater San Diego Area	(48)
✦ Add	
Current Company	▼
Industry	▼
Past Company	▼
School	▼
Profile Language	▼
in **Groups**	▼
in **Years of Experience**	▼
in **Function**	▼
in **Seniority Level**	▼
in **Interested In**	▼

Figure 4-3:
See the region and industry breakdown of your network.

Searching the LinkedIn Network

When you're ready to find a specific person, use the LinkedIn search engine, with which you can scan the tens of millions of LinkedIn members, based on keywords. The two main ways to search the network are a basic search and an Advanced Search.

At the top of every page on LinkedIn is a simple search box, with which you can run a keyword search via the LinkedIn database. This is your go-to tool if you're searching for a specific name, employees of a particular company, or people with a specific job title. In fact, you'll get a lot of results with the basic search because you're searching each LinkedIn member's entire profile for your keywords, not just one field. For example, if you type **Mike Jones** in the basic search box (as opposed to searching by the name Mike Jones; see the upcoming section, "Searching by name"), you get a larger set of results because you see every profile where the words "Mike" and "Jones" were anywhere in the profile. (When you search by name, LinkedIn searches only everyone's Name field.) Keep this in mind when you do your search, and pick the method you want based on your goals.

In some situations, though, a simple search just doesn't cut it because you want to specify whether you're searching for someone's name, title, employer, industry, skills, location, or some combination thereof. In those cases, use the Advanced Search function:

- ✔ From almost any page on LinkedIn, click the Advanced link at the top of the page to bring up the search page. If you're using LinkedIn Jobs or LinkedIn Groups, clicking this link brings up the Job Search or Groups search page, respectively. In addition, on the Job Search page, for example, there is an Advanced Search link below the job search text box that expands and shows filters for searching jobs.

- ✔ Click the drop-down arrow next to the search box at the top of any LinkedIn page to bring up links to the Advanced searches for People, Jobs, Companies, Groups, Universities, or your messages Inbox, as shown in Figure 4-4.

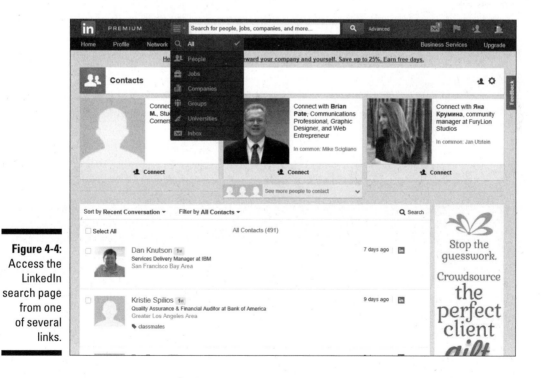

Figure 4-4:
Access the LinkedIn search page from one of several links.

- ✔ If you download the companion software (as discussed in Chapter 10), you can perform a search from the search box in that software program.

REMEMBER

The examples in the rest of this chapter assume that you're clicking the Advanced link. Of course, feel free to pick the method of search you're most comfortable with.

Searching by keyword

Quick, do you know someone who can write software code in PHP? Who do you know that enjoys mountain climbing or hiking? Do you know anybody who gives presentations on a regular basis? Well, with LinkedIn's search capabilities, you can find out when you search by keyword.

When you search by keyword, LinkedIn analyzes everyone else's profiles to find that matching word. You can put any sort of skill, buzzword, interest, or other keyword that would be present in someone's profile to see who in your network is a match. To search by keyword, just follow these steps:

1. **While logged in to LinkedIn, click the Advanced link at the top of the page.**

   You're taken to the Advanced People Search page.

2. **Enter the keyword(s) in the Keywords text box.**

   In Figure 4-5, I'm searching for "Six Sigma". If you enter multiple keywords like I did, LinkedIn looks for members who have all the keywords in their profile.

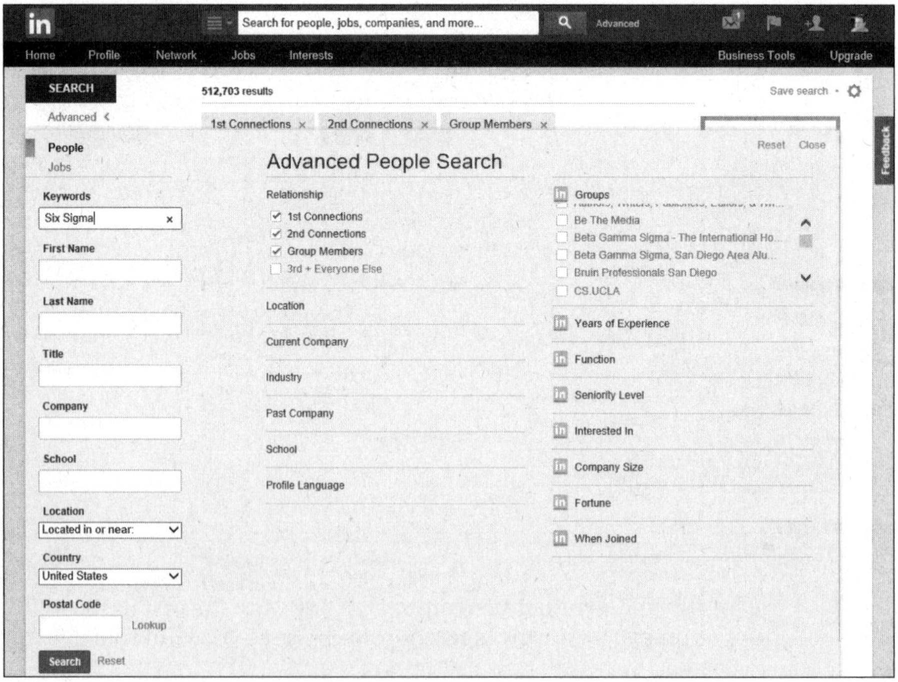

Figure 4-5: Search for people by the keywords in their profile.

I recommend tacking on additional search criteria, such as picking one or more industries, location information (country and ZIP/postal code), or perhaps a job title to get a more meaningful search result. Otherwise, your result list will be long and unhelpful.

If you're searching for a specific keyword phrase, put those words in quotation marks so LinkedIn searches for the exact phrase; for example, "Six Sigma". Otherwise, LinkedIn searches each individual word, and you might get a result like mine in Figure 4-6, where I have the words "six" and "Sigma" in different places in my profile. (Although it's not visible in the figure, I have the word "Sigma" as a keyword in my profile because I'm a member of Beta Gamma Sigma.) Because LinkedIn found both words in my profile, even though those words didn't appear together in one phrase, I came up on the search results page.

Figure 4-6:
Enclose
keyword
phrases in
quotes.

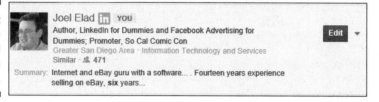

3. **Click the blue Search button.**

   You see the people in your extended network with those keywords in their profile.

4. **(Optional) Fine-tune your results with the filtering options.**

   You can expand the various filters along the left side of the Search Results screen and use them to refine your results by entering more information, such as keywords, job titles, user types, and location information, by selecting the check boxes provided. (See Figure 4-7.) As you select each filter, LinkedIn automatically updates the search results to give you a more precise search that narrows down the list. As of this writing, you can filter by Relationship (degree of connection), Location, Current Company (of the people you're searching), Industry, Past Company, School, Profile Language, LinkedIn Group membership, Years of Experience, Seniority Level, Interests, Company Size, and several more options.

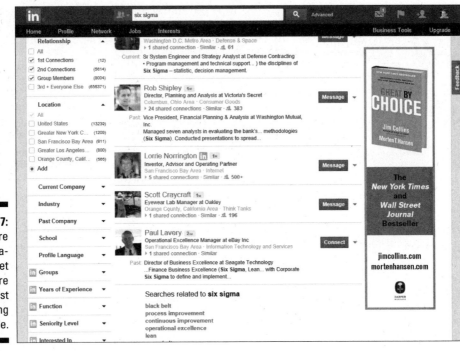

Figure 4-7:
Add more
informa-
tion to get
a more
targeted list
of matching
people.

Searching by name

When you want to find a specific person on LinkedIn, you can search by
name. LinkedIn has developed special First and Last Name Search fields to
help you find that person. When you search by name, you are required to
enter the last name; entering the first name is optional.

When you're ready to search by name, just follow these steps:

1. **While logged in to LinkedIn, click the Advanced link at the top
   of the page.**

   You're taken to the Advanced People Search page.

2. **Enter the last name (and first name, if you know it) into the Last
   Name and First Name text boxes. (See Figure 4-8.)**

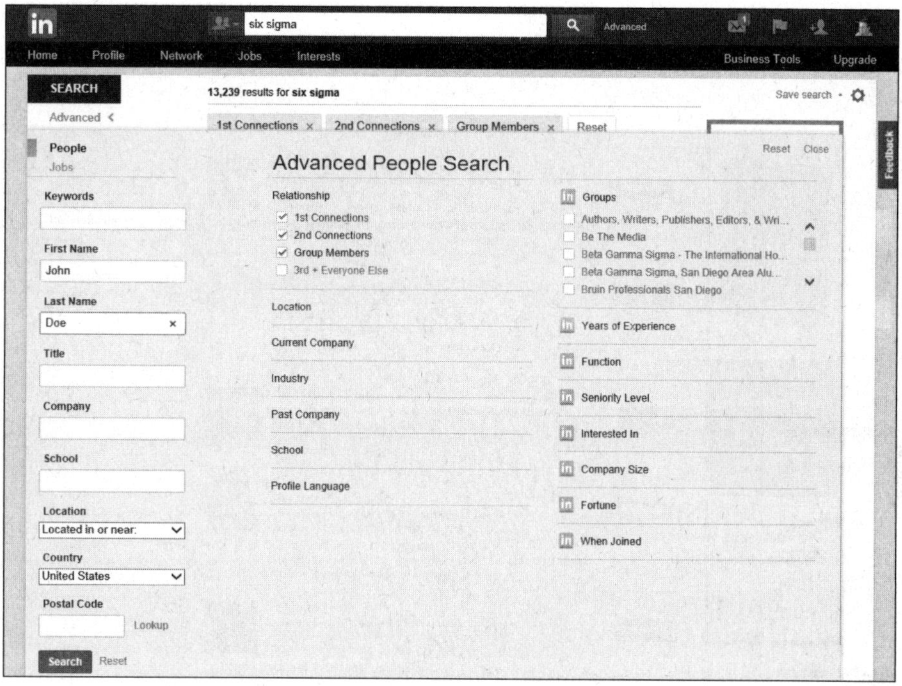

Figure 4-8:
Search
LinkedIn by
someone's
name.

3. **(Optional) Input additional information to help find the person you're looking for.**

   If you know a company where the person used to work or is currently employed, you can input a company name into the Company text box.

4. **(Optional) If you know the approximate location of this person, use the Location drop-down list to select the Located In or Near option. Then use the Country drop-down list and fill in the Postal Code text box.**

   Only after you select Located In or Near can you pick a country from the Country drop-down list and input a ZIP code in the box indicated, as shown in Figure 4-9.

5. Click the Search button.

You see a results list of people, sorted by the relevance of your name search and then by the degrees of connection in your overall LinkedIn network. (For example, people who are second-degree network members appear above people who are third-degree network members.)

6. (Optional) For better results, use filters in your search.

If you haven't already done so, you can add more keywords, a company name, or location information into the boxes provided on the left side of the Search Results screen. Then click the Search button. Also, you can scroll down and pick specific filters to refine your search results.

Searching by company

Sometimes, you might need to search by company. Maybe you're thinking of applying to a company, and you want to see who you know (or, rather, who is in your extended network) who works for that company so you can approach them to ask some questions or get a referral. Perhaps you're looking for a decision maker at a company who can help you with a deal, or you're curious how active a particular company's employees are on LinkedIn. You can also look for key thought leaders whom you might want to approach for an informational interview.

Whatever the reason, LinkedIn is an excellent place for searching detailed corporate profiles of specific companies. When you're ready to search by company, just follow these steps:

1. **While logged in to LinkedIn, click the Advanced link at the top of the page**.

   You're taken to the Advanced People Search page.

2. **Enter the name of the company in the Company text box (as shown in Figure 4-10).**

   If you want to search for only current employees of the company, change the drop-down list choice from the Current or Past option to just Current. If you don't change the default option, your search results will include all the people who ever worked for that company and included that job on their LinkedIn profiles.

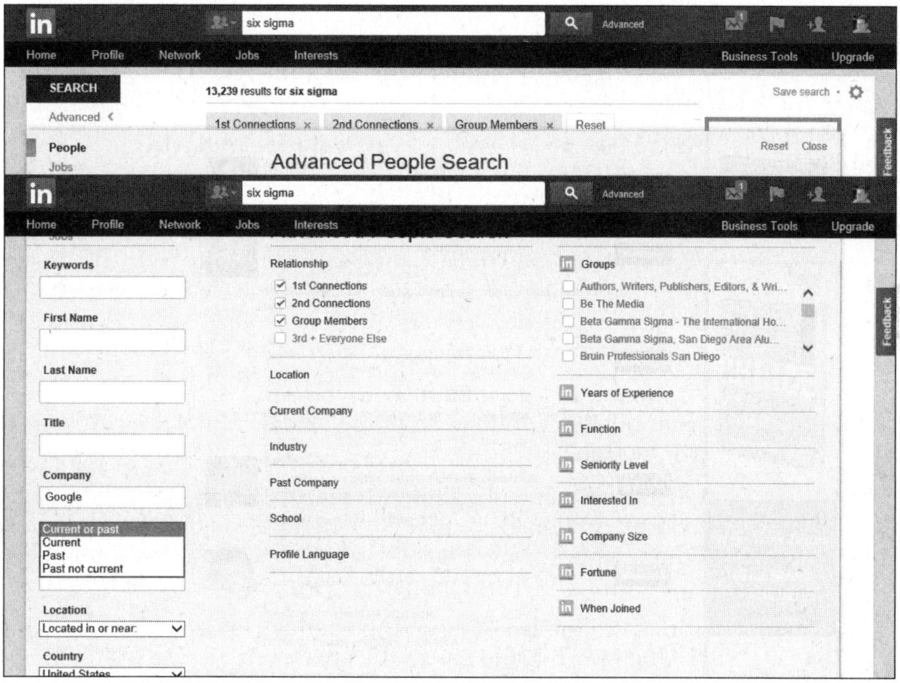

Figure 4-10: Search for people by the company where they work(ed).

3. **Click the Search button.**

   You see as many as 100 results that match your company and exist somewhere in your extended network. (If you've paid for a premium account, you see more results, depending on the level of your account.)

4. **(Optional) For better results, modify your search.**

   You can enter more information, such as job titles, user types, or location information, into the boxes provided on the left side of the Search Results screen. Then click the Search button. Also, you can scroll down and pick specific filters to refine your search results.

Searching by job title

Sometimes you might need to look for someone in a specific position rather than for a specific person. After all, who knows what you go through better than other people with the same job, right? Who better to give advice on a topic like search engine optimization (SEO) than someone whose job relates to SEO?

Therefore, LinkedIn gives you the ability to search by job title instead of person. When you're ready to search by job title, just follow these steps:

1. **While logged in to LinkedIn, click the Advanced link at the top of the page.**

   You're taken to the Advanced People Search page.

2. **Enter the job title in the Title box provided; Figure 4-11 shows Project Manager entered.**

   To search for only those people who currently have that title, change the drop-down list choice to Current. If you leave the default choice of Current or Past, your search results will include all the people who have ever defined that job title in one of the positions on their LinkedIn profiles.

3. **(Optional, but do it anyway if you can.) Select at least one Industry from the list provided so your search results are relevant to the job title search.**

   I highly recommend doing this step. After all, a Project Manager in Construction is completely different from a Project Manager in Computer Software. Click the word "Industry" in the center of the screen to bring up the list of industries you can select from.

   You can actually select multiple industries from the list. Simply scroll through the list and select the check box next to each industry you want to select.

4. **Click the Search button to see your results.**

   You see a set of results that match your job title request. You can use the filtering options on the left side of the Search Results screen and the middle of the screen, as shown in Figure 4-11, to add more information and get a more targeted list.

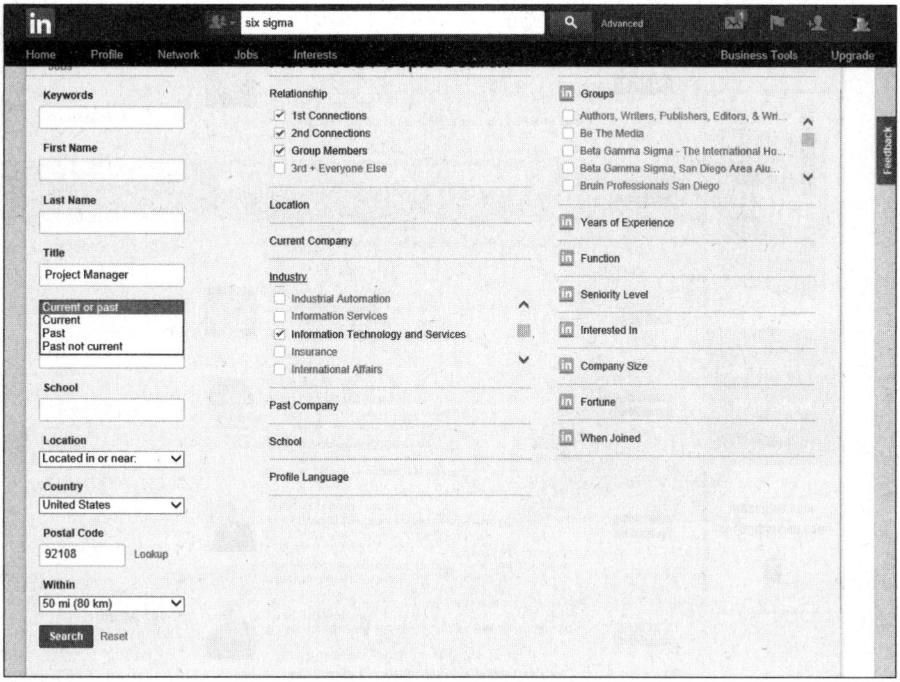

Figure 4-11:
Search for
people by
their current
or previous
job titles.

Performing a reference search

One of the benefits of being a LinkedIn premium member is that you can
search for someone who might have worked with someone you're researching.
Perhaps you're about to hire someone but would like to speak with someone
else who knows your potential candidate because they worked together. Say
you're deciding to hire a consultant for a project but want to contact someone
who has hired this consultant in the past to get a better idea of his work
quality. Or maybe you're about to enter a business deal and want some
information from someone who knows your potential new partner.

LinkedIn has created the reference search to give their premium users a
better window into the person or company. All you need is the company
name and the range of years someone has worked there, and LinkedIn
searches your network and shows you the people who match that search and
how closely they're connected to you.

To perform a reference search, just follow these steps:

1. **Click the word "Advanced" at the top right of the LinkedIn home page
   next to the search box.**

   You're taken to the Advanced People Search page.

2. **Click the cog near the top right of the page (next to the Save Search link) to bring up a drop-down list, then select Reference Search.**

   The Reference Search page is shown in Figure 4-12.

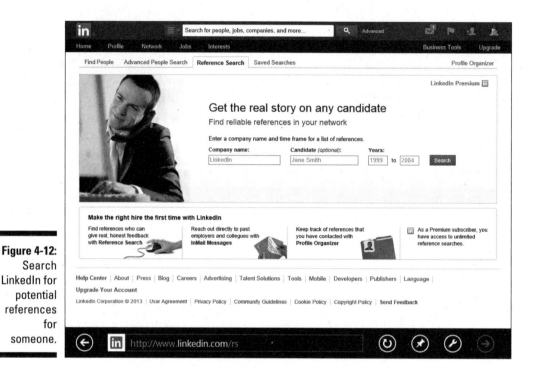

Figure 4-12:
Search
LinkedIn for
potential
references
for
someone.

3. **Enter the name of the company and a date range.**

   For example, suppose you have a job candidate who claims to have worked for Top Cow Productions from 2000 to 2002. You would enter that company name and date range into the text boxes provided.

4. **Click the Search button.**

   If you have the basic account, you see a Summary page like the one shown in Figure 4-13. This gives you an idea of how many potential connections exist and how many are available through LinkedIn's InMail system (see Chapter 5 for more information about InMail). If you have a premium account, you would see a list of people (like in a name or job title search) who worked at the designated company in that timeframe (as shown in Figure 4-14), *and* you'd have the ability to contact them. (For more on the different account types, take a gander at Chapter 1.)

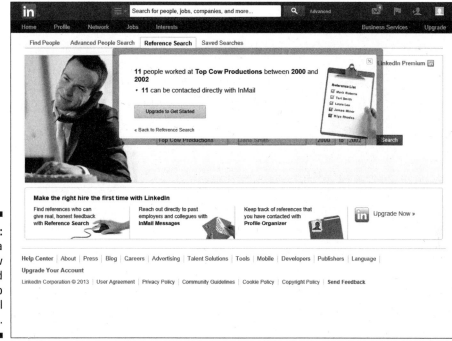

Figure 4-13:
Get an idea
of how
connected
you are to
potential
references.

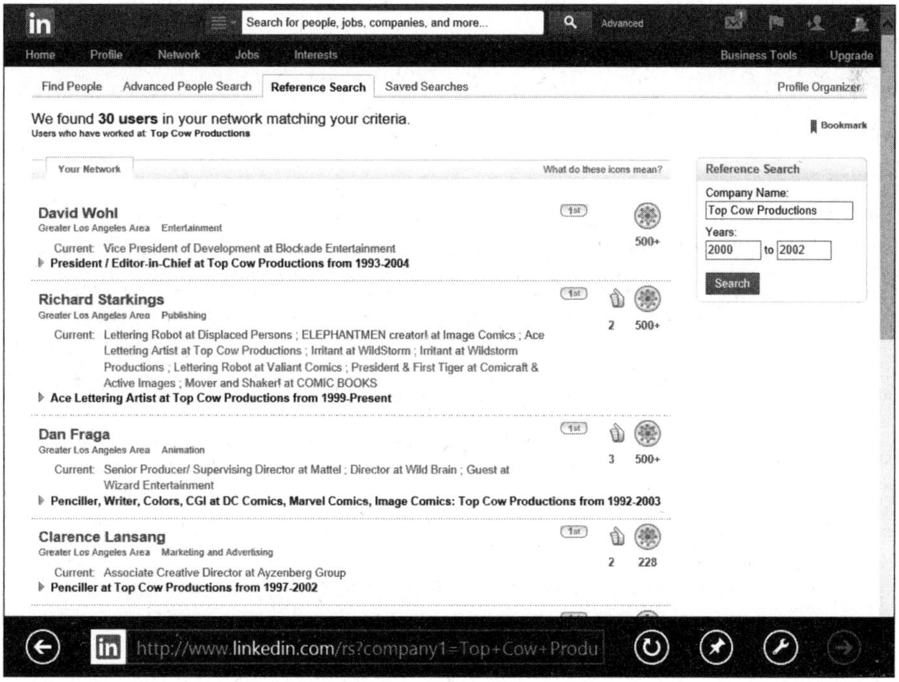

Figure 4-14:
With a
premium
account,
find exactly
who can
help you
verify a
reference.

Chapter 5

Managing Introductions and InMail

*O*ne of the goals of using LinkedIn is to expand your personal network of friends and colleagues by seeing who is connected to you at each degree level. When you can see the second and third degrees of your network, your next goal is to start interacting with these people and see how they might fit into your network, goals, or ambitions. However, the whole system of contacting people requires some order and decorum (otherwise, nobody would feel comfortable signing up for the site in the first place). Therefore, LinkedIn offers two methods for meeting and connecting with people outside your immediate network: introductions and InMail. Not so coincidentally, I cover introductions and InMail in this very chapter.

Introductions are simply where you ask to be introduced to a friend of a friend, and your friend can decide whether to pass along your introduction to the intended target. InMail allows you to directly communicate with anyone in the LinkedIn network through a private LinkedIn message. I also cover what to do when you get a request from a connection on LinkedIn.

InMail Versus Introductions

Your first question is most likely, "What's the difference between introductions and InMail?" (Figure 5-1 shows an InMail example at the top and an introduction at the bottom.) The answer depends on how involved your common friend or colleague is in connecting you with this new contact.

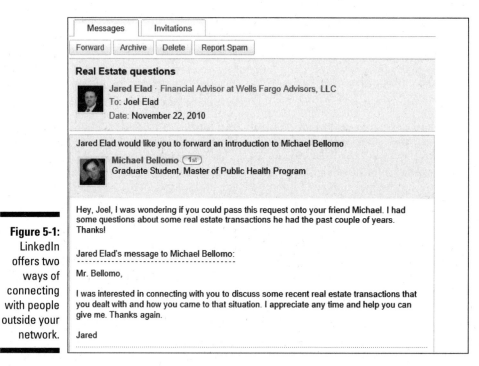

Figure 5-1:
LinkedIn
offers two
ways of
connecting
with people
outside your
network.

Every LinkedIn user decides on his own contact level, and a user can decline to allow any introduction or InMail to reach him, regardless of sender. If you don't want to receive any introductions or InMail, simply deselect all the Contact Settings options. (See Chapter 3 for the section on checking your contact settings.)

If you don't mind introductions but really don't want to have to deal with any InMail, just deselect the InMail option in the Contact Settings section and leave the Introductions option alone. Otherwise, leave the InMail option selected, since it is a valuable tool for sending and receiving communication with people who might become a valuable part of your network or help you with one of your professional goals.

Understanding introductions

Say you're at a party with your friend Michael, and you say to him, "You know, I'd really like to meet someone who can help me with some software tasks for my company." Michael looks around, sees his friend James, and introduces you to James by saying, "Hello, James. This is my entrepreneur friend from business school, [Your Name Here]. [Your Name Here], this is my old buddy James. He and I studied computer science together in college." After that, Michael might give some more background information about each person to the other.

On LinkedIn, an *introduction* is very similar to my real-world example. You send a request to someone in your immediate first-degree network (Michael) and ask that person to introduce you to someone in his network (James) by forwarding your request to the intended party. In some cases, if you're trying to reach someone in your third-degree network (maybe James has a programming buddy you should talk to), your introduction request would have to go to two different parties before reaching the intended recipient.

Here are some benefits of using introductions:

- ✔ **You're represented by someone close.** Instead of sending a random, unexpected e-mail to a stranger, you're introduced by somebody who knows the intended party, even if that introduction is done with an e-mail. That gives your introduction request a much higher chance of being read and getting a response.

- ✔ **You get your network involved.** When you ask people in your network to get involved, they learn more about you and your intentions, and sometimes you might find what you're looking for is closer than you think. In addition, when you ask them to pass along your introduction request, you can offer to facilitate an introduction on their behalf, which helps both parties.

✔ **You leverage the power of your network.** By using LinkedIn, you not only expand your network by using your first-degree connections to help you meet new people, but you can also decide who would make the introduction for you. I recommend that you read up on your friend's profile and your intended party's profile to see what they have in common.

✔ **You can have multiple introductions going on at one time.** With a LinkedIn free account, you can have up to five open introductions going at any one time. When you get introduced to your intended party, that spot opens up, and you can make another introduction request. InMail, in all cases, costs money, either on a per-mail basis or as part of a premium paid account. (That means even someone with a free basic account can use InMail, but it will cost you.)

You can get more introductions at one time by upgrading to a premium account. I discuss the different paid accounts in Chapter 1.

Getting to know InMail

Because everyone on LinkedIn has a profile and a secure message Inbox, communicating with other people online is easy. LinkedIn allows you to send InMail directly to an intended party, regardless of whether he is directly or indirectly connected with you. The e-mail gets immediately delivered to the recipient's Web-based Inbox on the LinkedIn site (and, if the recipient has configured his settings to get e-mails of all his InMail, in the Inbox at his e-mail address); the sender never learns the recipient's address, so each party has some privacy. The recipient can then read your profile and decide whether to respond.

The cost of using InMail depends on whether you subscribe to a premium account. You can purchase InMail credits (one credit allows you to send one message) at a cost of $10 per InMail message. Premium accounts, such as the Job Seeker account for $29.99/month, come with a set number of InMail credits per month that roll over to the next month if unused. The Business account gets 3 credits per month, the Business Plus account gets 10 credits per month, and the Executive account gets 25 credits per month.

Here are some benefits of using InMail:

✔ **Delivery is instant.** With InMail, you simply write your message or request and send it directly to the intended party. There's no delay as a request gets passed from person to person and waits for approval or forwarding.

✔ **You owe no favors.** Sometimes, you just want to reach somebody without asking your friends to vouch for you. InMail allows you to send a request to someone new without involving anyone else.

✔ **It's sure to be delivered.** With introductions, the party(ies) involved in the middle could choose to deny your request and not pass along the message. With InMail, you know that the intended party will get a copy of your message in his e-mail account and LinkedIn Inbox.

Setting Up an Introduction

When you want to bring two (or more) parties together, you usually need to apply some thought to the process, whether it's figuring out what both parties have in common, thinking up the words you'll use to introduce party A to party B, or coming up with the timing of exactly when and where you plan to make the introduction. On LinkedIn, you should do your best to make sure the intro-duction process goes smoothly — but don't worry, there's not nearly as much social pressure. The following sections give you tips and pointers for setting up an introduction.

Planning your approach to each party in the introduction

When you want to send an introduction request, spend some time planning your request before you log on to LinkedIn to generate and send it. Preparing a quality and proper introduction goes a long way toward keeping your network in a helpful and enthusiastic mood, and it increases your chances of making a new and valuable connection.

You need to prepare two messages: one for your intended recipient and one for your connection/friend. Each message needs to perform a specific objective. Start with the message to your friend, and keep the following tips in mind when you're writing it:

- ✔ **Be honest and upfront.** Say exactly what you hope to achieve so there are no surprises. If you tell your friend that you're hoping her contact will be a new bowling buddy for you, but when you reach that contact, you ask for funding for your new business plan, you're in trouble. Your friend will probably never forward another request again, and the contact, who expected one type of interaction and got another, will see you as untrust-worthy and be unlikely and/or unwilling to help on this request or any in the future. Even if your eventual goal is something big, such as asking someone for a job, start with an initial goal that is reasonable, such as asking for information or advice. Let the other person know that you would like to keep talking to see what possibilities might occur in the future.

- ✔ **Be polite and courteous.** Remember, you're asking your friend to vouch for you or back you up when your request goes to the intended party. So be polite when making your request and show your gratitude regardless of the outcome.

✔ **Be ready to give in order to get.** One of the best ways to go far with your network is to offer some sort of reciprocal favor when you want someone to do a favor for you. Perhaps you can introduce your friend to one of your other contacts in exchange for your friend accepting your introduction request.

✔ **Be patient.** Although you might be eager and under a deadline, your friends probably operate on different schedules driven by different levels of urgency. Some people are online all the time, other people log in to LinkedIn infrequently, and most people are completely disconnected at times, like when they're on vacation or behind on a project. Asking your friend every day whether she forwarded your request is an almost sure-fire way of getting that request bounced back to you.

When writing your message to your intended recipient, keep these tips in mind:

✔ **Be honest and upfront.** Just like with your friend, when you have a specific goal or request in mind, make it known in the message. The recipient is most likely busy and doesn't know you, so if he spends the time to talk to you and finds out that you have an ulterior motive, he feels like his time was wasted and that he was deceived, which are *not* good feelings to create when trying to get help from someone.

✔ **Be succinct.** You're asking someone for his time, resources, or advice, so don't beat around the bush. Introduce yourself in your first sentence or two. Then explain why you're contacting the recipient and how you hope he can help you.

✔ **Be original.** If you stick to the sample text that LinkedIn gives you, your message has an air of "Hey, I want to talk to you, but I don't want to spend a few seconds of effort to really tell you what I'm after." When you customize your message, you have a greater chance of capturing the other person's attention. If your intended recipient gets a lot of requests, you'll stand out if you show some effort to rise above the daily noise this person encounters.

✔ **Be ready to give in order to get.** You're asking for help of some sort, so again, be ready to give something, whether it's gratitude, a reciprocal favor, or something more tangible. Most people are eager to help, especially when they understand the situation, but having something to offer in exchange rarely hurts. Explain to your recipient how you might provide something useful in return.

Sending an introduction

When you've prepared your messages (one to your contact and one to the recipient) and you're all ready to send an introduction request, just follow these steps:

1. **While logged in to LinkedIn, search for the person you'd like to meet.**

   You can use the Search box at the top of any LinkedIn page, or you can click your Connections and search your friend's networks. (See Chapter 4 for the lowdown on searching LinkedIn.)

2. **From the list of search results, click the name of the person you want to contact. (If you didn't find the person you're looking for, try another search.)**

   This step takes you to the recipient's profile page, where, as you scroll down the page, you should see two things: a chart along the right side of the page showing how you're connected to this person and a link entitled Get Introduced. (If you don't have anyone in your network yet, you won't see the chart or the link.)

   Suppose I'm hoping to be introduced to Erin O'Harra, PR Associate over at LinkedIn. When I get to Erin's profile page, I see that I have a connection to her (see Figure 5-2) in the form of a business contact who I met through LinkedIn.

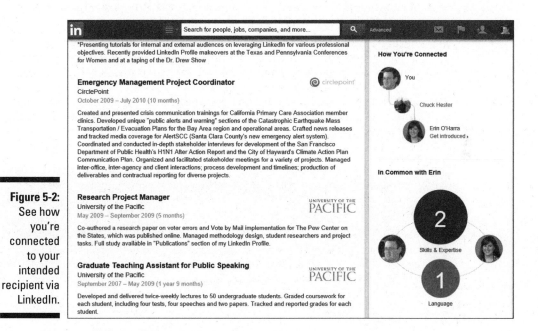

Figure 5-2: See how you're connected to your intended recipient via LinkedIn.

3. **On the person's profile page, click the Get Introduced link to start the introduction process.**

   You see a pop-up window that starts the introduction process, as shown in Figure 5-3. Select the shared connection who you'd like to have make the introduction. In cases like this example, where there is only one shared connection, you still have to select the person to continue the process.

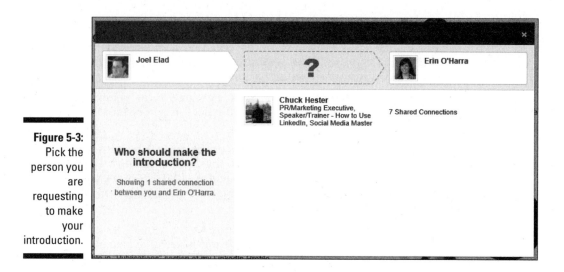

Figure 5-3:
Pick the person you are requesting to make your introduction.

4. **Write a subject line and add a message for the person who will be passing on your introduction.**

   Adding a note here is required (see Figure 5-4) so the *facilitator* (the person who receives the introduction request from you) knows why you want to reach the other party. After all, the facilitator is going to vouch for you when he sends this request to the intended party, so the more information you give, the better. (See the preceding section, "Planning your approach to each party in the introduction," for more about writing this message.)

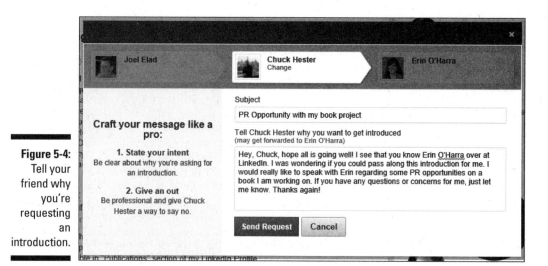

Figure 5-4:
Tell your friend why you're requesting an introduction.

5. Click the Send Request button.

You see a pop-up window message as you're taken back to the person's LinkedIn profile page telling you that your request has been sent, and your first-degree connection will receive this introduction request in his LinkedIn Inbox.

After that, your facilitator friend will accept or decline your request, and you'll get a notification about the facilitator's decision. You can always view your introduction request in your Sent Messages folder.

Keep in mind some LinkedIn members are inactive or may not respond, so try not to take it personally. Move on to another potentially helpful contact.

You might want to send an e-mail to your facilitator friend first before starting the introduction process, especially if you think he might not want to forward your request, you want to make sure the facilitator has kept in contact with the intended recipient well enough to make the introduction, or the intended recipient might be too busy to receive an introduction request. This also gives the facilitator a chance to let you know first that he is not interested or able in forwarding the introduction.

Sending InMail

If you're looking to connect with someone right away and you don't have an immediate or secondary connection with someone, you can use the InMail feature to send a message directly to another LinkedIn member without anyone else getting involved.

This feature is currently available to paid members of LinkedIn with available InMail credits. If you're using a free account, you have to pay for individual InMail credits to reach other members through InMail. Consult the LinkedIn Help Center for more information (http://linkedin.custhelp.com).

InMail is basically a private e-mail message that enables you to reach other members, but it protects those members' privacy and e-mail address information. If your message is accepted, you'll receive a message in your LinkedIn Inbox with the other party's name and e-mail address, and you can communicate further. In some cases, you see only the other person's professional headline first, and then you see the person's name after he accepts the InMail message.

When you're ready to send someone an InMail, just follow these steps:

1. While logged in to LinkedIn, search for the person you'd like to meet.

You can use the Search box at the top of any LinkedIn page, or you can click your Contacts and search your friend's networks. (Chapter 4 has all sorts of details for you about searching LinkedIn.)

2. **From the list of search results, click the name of the person you want to contact. (If you didn't find the person you're looking for, try another search.)**

   You're taken to the person's profile page.

3. **Click the Send InMail link.**

   For example, suppose that I want to connect with Lynn Dralle, the Queen of Auctions, who can not only teach you how to sell on eBay, but who sells more than $100,000 a year in antiques and collectibles herself. When I look at her profile (see Figure 5-5), I see the Send InMail button, which means she is open to receiving InMail. I would click the Send InMail button to send her a message.

   After you click that button, you can start filling out the Compose Your Message form.

Send InMail button

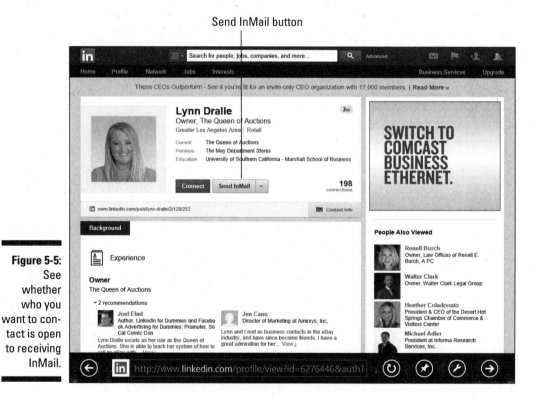

Figure 5-5: See whether who you want to contact is open to receiving InMail.

4. **In the Compose Your Message form, select or deselect the Include My Contact Information check box, depending on your preference.**

You're asked whether to provide contact information that your recipient can use to contact you, in the form of e-mail and/or a phone number. Simply select the Include My Contact Information check box (as shown in Figure 5-6) if you want to send contact information.

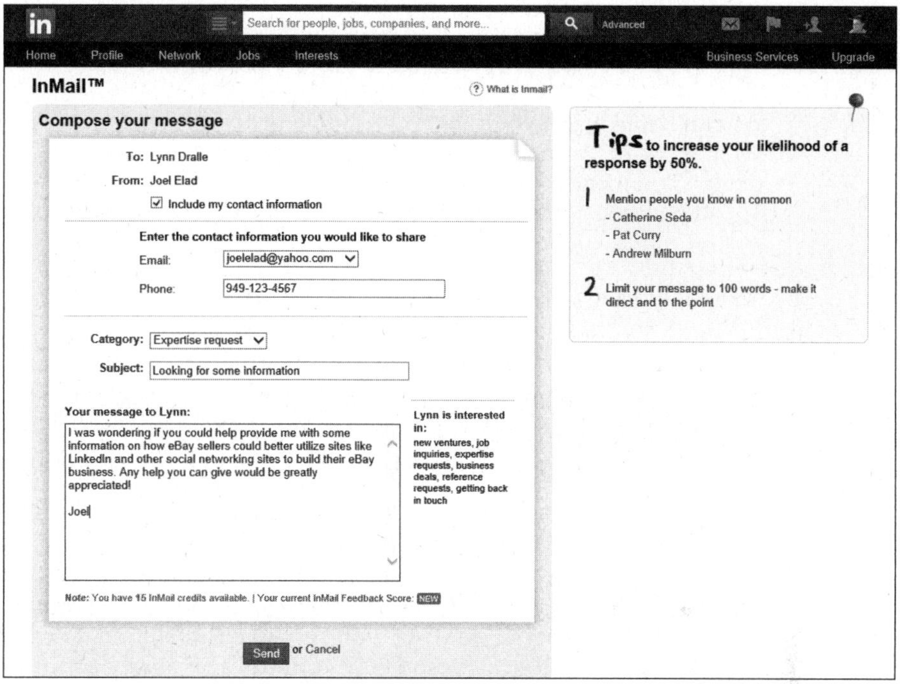

Figure 5-6:
Compose your InMail message.

5. **Complete the Category and Subject fields, and then type a message in the text box.**

   As with an introduction, keep your message focused on why you would like to talk with this person, and/or what information you were hoping to exchange. (The earlier section, "Planning your approach to each party in the introduction," contains advice about writing to an intended recipient that applies to InMail messages as well.) At the bottom of Figure 5-6, you can see how many InMail credits you have; remember that you need at least one credit to send this message.

   Be sure to proofread your message before sending it out. If you send a message with typos, it probably won't help your case at all.

6. **Click the Send button to send off your InMail.**

   Your recipient receives this InMail in her LinkedIn Inbox and can decide whether to accept it. (If she has configured LinkedIn to get immediate e-mails of her InMail messages, she will receive the InMail in her e-mail account Inbox as well.) If your message is accepted, it's up to the recipient to contact you in return. Be patient. While you're waiting, I recommend a game of Connect Four or Internet Chess.

Managing Introduction Requests

What if someone in your network is looking for your help to meet someone in your network? You can facilitate the introduction between your LinkedIn first-degree connections. Now that your reputation is on the line, too, you should spend some time thinking about and processing any and all introduction requests that come your way.

You really have only two options for handling an introduction request:

✔ Accept it and forward it on to the party it's intended for.

✔ Decline it (politely!).

I cover these two options in more detail in the following sections. However you decide to handle the request, keep these tips in mind:

✔ **Act or reply quickly.** The reason why LinkedIn works so well is that people are active with their networks and build upon their profile by answering questions, meeting new people, or joining groups. When you get an introduction request, you should either act on it or respond to the person with the reason why you won't act on it. Ignoring it isn't a productive use of the LinkedIn system and makes you look very unprofessional.

✔ **Don't be afraid to ask for clarification.** Sometimes you might need someone to remind you exactly how you're connected with her. Hopefully, in the note you get from this person, she includes some reminder or thought that helps you place her. If not, don't be afraid to shoot back a message and ask for clarification or a gentle reminder.

✔ **Read your friend's request before forwarding.** Chances are good that the person to whom you forward this request might come back to you and ask, "Hey, why did I get this?" or "What do you really think about this person?" If you don't know the details of your friend's request, the intended party might think you're a quick rubber-stamper who sends off stuff without offering to screen anything, and that lowers this person's impression of you. Knowing what your friend is requesting can help you decide how to promote and encourage the connection, perhaps by giving you an idea of how best to approach the intended party.

Accepting requests and forwarding the introduction

When you're ready to accept your friend's request and forward her introduction, follow these steps:

1. **Click the Messages button in the top navigation bar.**

   This brings up your Inbox of messages, as shown in Figure 5-7. When you're looking at all your messages, look for a drop-down arrow next to All Messages.

   If you receive copies of introductions in your e-mail and then click the link from the e-mail message, you've already completed Steps 1 and 2.

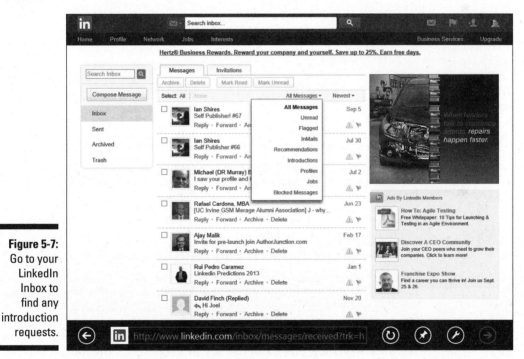

Figure 5-7:
Go to your LinkedIn Inbox to find any introduction requests.

2. **Click the drop-down arrow and select introductions from the list provided to see your requests.**

   This brings up your Introductions page, as shown in Figure 5-8. Here you can see introduction requests from fellow members, as well as the results from introductions you have requested yourself.

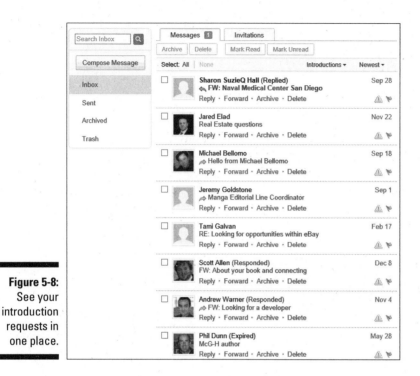

Figure 5-8:
See your
introduction
requests in
one place.

3. **Click the subject line of the request you're evaluating.**

In this example, I clicked Real Estate questions from Jared Elad, my brother. Doing so brings up the introduction request, as shown in Figure 5-9.

Read the full text before acting on the request. Don't just skim it — you might miss an important detail.

4. **If you accept the request, click the Forward button.**

A new window opens where you can compose your message to the recipient, as shown in Figure 5-10. The text box in the middle contains the note from your friend to you, which you can supplement with a note to the intended recipient. Be sure to add your own comments, in the place I indicated in Figure 5-10, to help connect the two people properly. You can also delete the first person's note to you, especially if that personal note was for your eyes only, not the intended recipient.

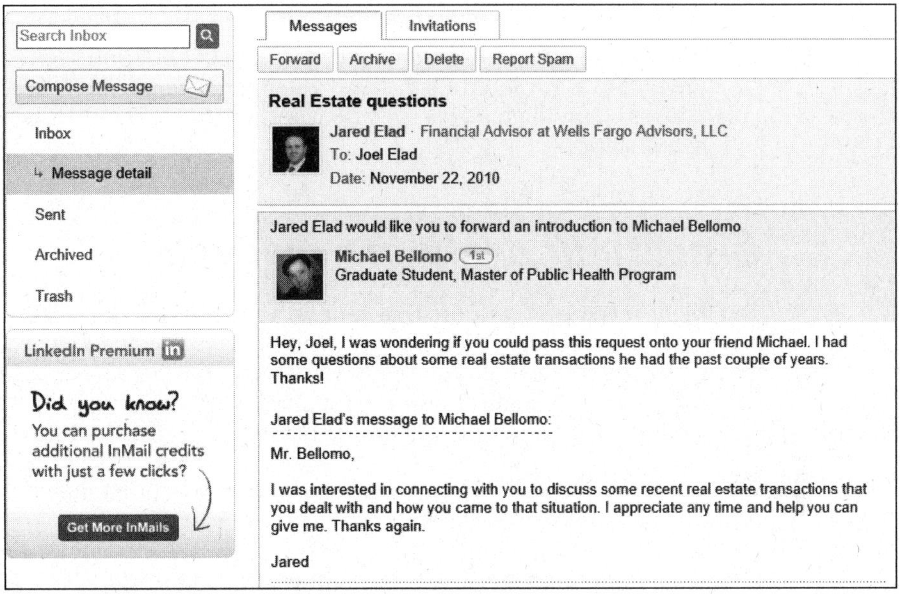

Search Inbox 🔍

Compose Message ✉

Inbox

↳ Message detail

Sent

Archived

Trash

LinkedIn Premium 💼

Did you know?
You can purchase additional InMail credits with just a few clicks?

[Get More InMails]

Messages | **Invitations**

Forward | Archive | Delete | Report Spam

Real Estate questions

Jared Elad · Financial Advisor at Wells Fargo Advisors, LLC
To: Joel Elad
Date: November 22, 2010

Jared Elad would like you to forward an introduction to Michael Bellomo

Michael Bellomo (1st)
Graduate Student, Master of Public Health Program

Hey, Joel, I was wondering if you could pass this request onto your friend Michael. I had some questions about some real estate transactions he had the past couple of years. Thanks!

Jared Elad's message to Michael Bellomo:

Mr. Bellomo,

I was interested in connecting with you to discuss some recent real estate transactions that you dealt with and how you came to that situation. I appreciate any time and help you can give me. Thanks again.

Jared

Figure 5-9:
Read the introduc-
tion request
from your
contact.

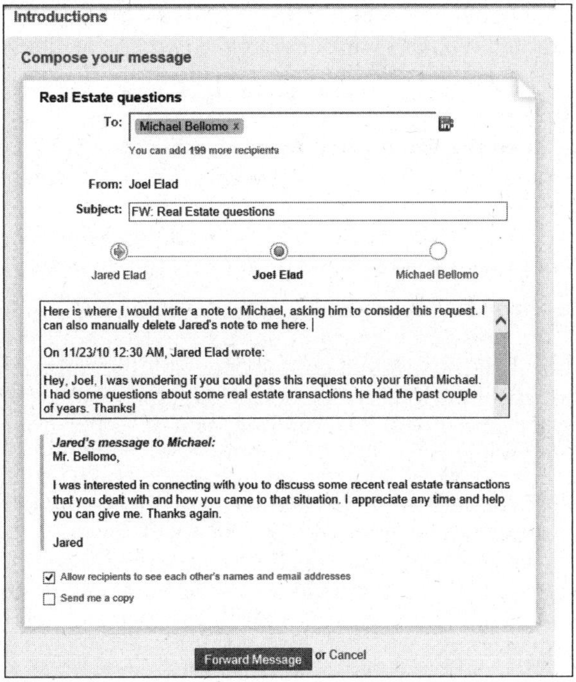

Introductions

Compose your message

Real Estate questions

To: [Michael Bellomo x]   💼
You can add 199 more recipients

From: Joel Elad

Subject: [FW: Real Estate questions]

⊕──────────●──────────○
Jared Elad   **Joel Elad**   Michael Bellomo

Here is where I would write a note to Michael, asking him to consider this request. I can also manually delete Jared's note to me here. |

On 11/23/10 12:30 AM, Jared Elad wrote:

Hey, Joel, I was wondering if you could pass this request onto your friend Michael. I had some questions about some real estate transactions he had the past couple of years. Thanks!

Jared's message to Michael:
Mr. Bellomo,

I was interested in connecting with you to discuss some recent real estate transactions that you dealt with and how you came to that situation. I appreciate any time and help you can give me. Thanks again.

Jared

☑ Allow recipients to see each other's names and email addresses
☐ Send me a copy

[Forward Message] or Cancel

Figure 5-10:
Compose a
message to
send to the
intended
recipient.

5. **Click the Forward Message button to send the request.**

   In this case, Michael Bellomo will get the introduction request from me on behalf of Jared Elad. Jared will never see Michael's direct e-mail address, and Michael can decide whether to reach out to Jared and form a connection.

Gracefully declining requests

You might receive an introduction request that you just don't feel comfortable sending to the recipient. Perhaps you don't know enough about your contact who made the request, or you're unclear about that person's true motivations. Or maybe your connection with the recipient isn't at the stage where you feel you can introduce other people to this person.

Whatever the reason, the best response is simply to gracefully decline the request. Here are some tips on how to respond:

- ✔ **It's not you, it's me.** The most common way to decline is to simply inform the initial contact that you're not that deeply connected with the intended recipient, and you really don't feel comfortable passing on a request to someone who isn't a strong contact. Often, you might have first-degree connections in your network who are "weak links" or people with whom you're acquainted but aren't particularly close to or tight with.

- ✔ **The recipient doesn't respond well to this approach.** You can respond that you know the intended recipient, and you know what she's going to say, either from past requests or other experiences with that person. Because you know or feel that the intended recipient wouldn't be interested, you would rather not waste anyone's time in sending the request.

- ✔ **I just don't feel comfortable passing along the request.** Be honest and simply state that you don't feel right passing on the request you've received. After all, if the original contact doesn't understand your hesitation, he'll probably keep asking, and LinkedIn will want you to follow up on any unresolved introduction. Just as in life, honesty is usually the best policy.

- ✔ **I think your request needs work.** Because you're vouching for this person, you don't want to pass along a shoddy or questionable request that could reflect badly on you. In this case, simply respond that you think the request needs to be reworded or clarified, and offer concrete suggestions on what should be said as well as what requests you feel comfortable forwarding.

When you're ready to decline the request, follow these steps:

1. **Click the Messages button in the top navigation bar, then click the drop-down arrow next to All Messages and select Introductions from the list.**

   This should bring up the list of introductions in your Inbox. If you receive copies of introductions in your e-mail and then click the link from the e-mail message, you've already completed Step 2.

2. **Click the subject line of the introduction request.**

   You see the introduction request. (Refer to Figure 5-9.)

3. **Click the Decline button at the bottom of the request.**

   The Not Interested in Forwarding page appears, as shown in Figure 5-11.

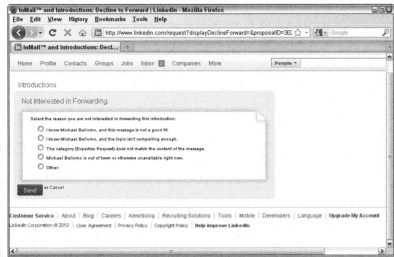

Figure 5-11: Describe why you're declining to forward the request.

4. **Pick a reason for not forwarding the request, or select the Other option and write a message why you're declining to forward.**

   If you pick any of the main options, like "I know X, and this message is not a good fit," you don't have to provide any additional message. Unless one of these options really states your case, you should probably select Other and write a custom message (or send a separate e-mail message giving more information).

5. **Click the Send button to decline the request.**

   The original contact receives an e-mail as well as a message in his LinkedIn Inbox.

Chapter 6

Growing Your Network

In This Chapter

▶ Discovering the keys to having a meaningful network

▶ Using the best strategies for expanding your network

▶ Sending connection requests to members and persuading nonmembers to join

▶ Knowing why you should *not* use canned invitations

▶ Weeding out connections you no longer want on your network

▶ Dealing with invitations you receive

Maybe by now, you've signed on to LinkedIn, created your profile, searched through the network, and started inviting people to connect to you — and you're wondering, what's next? You certainly shouldn't be sitting around on your hands, waiting for responses to your invitations. LinkedIn is designed to open doors to opportunities using the professional relationships you already have (and, with luck, by creating new ones). The best use of it, therefore, is to capture as much of your professional network as possible in the form of first-degree connections to your LinkedIn network so that you can discover those inside leads as well as those friends of friends who can help you.

In this chapter, I discuss how you can grow your LinkedIn network and offer some guidelines to keep in mind when growing your network. I also cover various search tools for you to use to stay on top of LinkedIn's growing membership and how others may relate to you.

Of course, to expand your network, you need to know how to send invitations as well as how to attract LinkedIn members and your contacts who haven't yet taken the plunge into LinkedIn membership. I cover all that here, too. And finally, this chapter helps you deal with the etiquette of accepting or declining invitations that you receive, and shows you how to remove connections that you no longer want to keep in your network.

An *invitation* is when you invite a colleague or friend of yours to join LinkedIn and stay connected to you as part of your network. An *introduction* is when you ask a first-degree connection to introduce you to one of her connections so you can get to know that person better. I cover introductions in more depth in Chapter 5, while invitations are covered right here.

Building a Meaningful Network

When you build a house, you start with a set of blueprints. When you start an organization, you usually have some sort of mission statement or guiding principles. Likewise, when you start to grow your LinkedIn network, you should keep in mind some of the keys to having and growing your own professional network. These guiding principles help decide who to invite to your network, who to search for and introduce yourself to, and how much time to spend on LinkedIn.

Undoubtedly, you've heard of the highly popular social networking sites Facebook and Twitter. LinkedIn is different from these sites because it focuses on business networking in a professional manner rather than encouraging users to post pictures of their latest beach party or tweet their latest status update. The best use of LinkedIn involves maintaining a professional network of connections, not sending someone a Super Hug.

That said, you'll find variety in the types of networks that people maintain on LinkedIn, and much of that has to do with each person's definition of a meaningful network:

✔ **Quality versus quantity:** As I mention in Chapter 1, some people use LinkedIn with the goal of gaining the highest number of connections possible, thereby emphasizing quantity over the quality of their LinkedIn connections. Those people are typically referred to as LinkedIn open networkers (LIONs). At the other end of the spectrum are people who use LinkedIn only to keep their closest, most tightly knit connections together without striving to enlarge their network. Most people fall somewhere in between these two aims, and the question of whether you're after quality or quantity is something to keep in mind every time you look to invite someone to join your network. LinkedIn strongly recommends connecting only with people you know, so its advice is to stick to quality connections. Here are some questions to ask yourself to help you figure out your purpose. Are you looking to

- Manage a network of *only* people you personally know?

- Manage a network of people you know or who might help you find new opportunities in a specific industry?

- Promote your business or expand your professional opportunities?

- Maximize your chances of being able to reach someone with a new opportunity or job offering, regardless of personal interaction?

✔ **Depth versus breadth:** Some people want to focus on building a network of only the most relevant or new connections — people from their current job or industry who could play a role in one's professional development in that particular industry. Other people like to include a wide diversity of connections that include anyone they have ever professionally interacted with, whether through work, education, or any kind of group or association, in hopes that anyone who knows them at all can potentially lead to future opportunities. For these LinkedIn users, it doesn't matter that most of the people in their network don't know 99 percent of their other connections. Most people fall somewhere in between these two poles but lean toward including more people in their network. Here are some questions to keep in mind regarding this question. Do you want to

- Build or maintain a specific in-depth network of thought leaders regarding one topic, job, or industry?

- Build a broad network of connections that can help you with different aspects of your career or professional life?

- Add only people to your network who may offer an immediate benefit to some aspect of your professional life?

- Add a professional contact now and figure out later how that person might fit with your long-term goals?

✔ **Strong versus weak link:** I'm not referring to the game show *The Weakest Link*, but rather to the strength of your connection with someone. Beyond the issue of quality versus quantity, you'll want to keep differing levels of quality in mind. Some people invite someone after meeting him once at a cocktail party, hoping to strengthen the link as time goes on. Others work to create strong links first and then invite those people to connect on LinkedIn afterward. This issue comes down to how much you want LinkedIn itself to play a role in your business network's development. Do you see your LinkedIn network as a work in progress or as a virtual room in which to gather only your closest allies? Here are some questions to keep in mind:

- What level of interaction needs to have occurred for you to feel comfortable asking someone to connect with you on LinkedIn? A face-to-face meeting? Phone conversations only? A stream of e-mails?

- What length of time do you need to know someone before you feel that you can connect with that person? Or, does time matter less if you have had a high-quality interaction just once?

- Does membership in a specific group or association count as a good enough reference for you to add someone to your network? (For example, say you met someone briefly only once, but he is a school alum: Does that tie serve as a sufficient reference?)

✔ **Specific versus general goals:** Some people like to maintain a strong network of people mainly to talk about work and job-related issues. Other people like to discuss all matters relating to their network, whether it's professional, personal, or social. Most people fall somewhere in between, and herein lies what I mean by the "purpose" of your network. Do you want to simply catalog your entire network, regardless of industry, because LinkedIn will act as your complete contact management system and because you can use LinkedIn to reach different parts of your network at varying times? Or do you want to focus your LinkedIn network on a specific goal, using your profile to attract and retain the "right kind" of contact that furthers that goal? Here are some more questions to ask yourself:

  - Do you have any requirements in mind for someone before you add him to your network? That is, are you looking to invite only people with certain qualities or experience?

  - Does the way you know or met someone influence your decision to connect to that person on LinkedIn?

  - What information do you need to know about someone before you want to add him to your network?

By the way, this isn't a quiz — there is no one right answer to any of these questions. You decide what you want to accomplish through your LinkedIn network, and how you want to go from there. Also keep in mind that although you might start LinkedIn with one goal in mind, as with most other things in life, your usage and experience might shift you to a different way of using the site. If that happens, just go with it, as long as it fits with your current goals.

After you establish why you want to link to other people, you can start looking for and reaching out to those people. In the next section, I point you to a number of linking strategies that can help you reach your goals for your network. When you start on LinkedIn, completing your profile (see Chapter 3) helps you get your first round of connections, and you're prompted to enter whatever names you can remember to offer an invitation for them to connect with you. Now you're ready to generate your next round of connections, and to get into the habit of making this a continual process as you use the site.

Checking for LinkedIn Members

When you fill out your LinkedIn profile, you create an opportunity to check for colleagues and classmates as well as import any potential contact and invite that person to connect with you and stay in touch using LinkedIn. However, that search happens only after you define your profile (and when you update or add to your profile). After that, it's up to you to routinely check the LinkedIn network to look for new members on the site who might want to connect with you or with whom you might want to connect. Fortunately, LinkedIn provides a few tools that help you quickly scan the system to see whether a recently joined member is a past colleague or classmate of yours. In addition, it never hurts to use your friends to check for new members, as I discuss in a little bit.

Finding newly added colleagues

If you've worked at least one job in a medium-size or large company, you're probably familiar with the concept of the farewell lunch. The staff goes out to lunch, reminiscences about the good old days, and wishes the departing employee well as that person gives out her e-mail address and phone number, and pledges to keep in touch. But as time goes on, jobs change, people move around, and it's easy to lose touch with that co-worker. Thankfully, LinkedIn allows you to stay connected regardless of moves.

Sometimes people you've fallen out of contact with have joined LinkedIn since the last time you checked, so do an occasional search to see whether you know any newly added colleagues.

When you want to search for colleagues (and add them to your network, if you choose), just follow these steps:

1. **While logged in to your LinkedIn account, go to** `www.linkedin.com/people/reconnect`.

2. **Pick an employer (current or past) from the list.**

   If there are no new connections, you see the message, "Sorry, we couldn't find any colleagues at Company X for you." Otherwise, you see potential new connections, as shown in Figure 6-1.

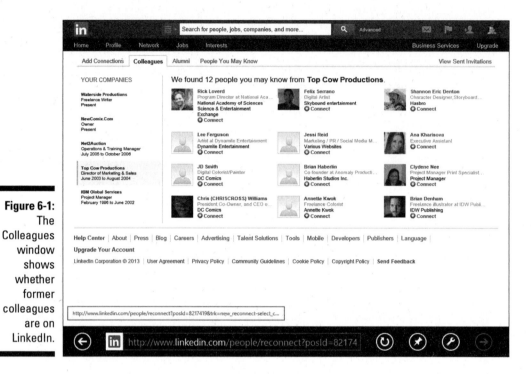

Figure 6-1:
The Colleagues window shows whether former colleagues are on LinkedIn.

3. Go through the list of names to see names you recognize or wish to connect with via LinkedIn.

Click a name to see the person's profile for more information. If you want to invite someone to your network, click the Connect link below the name to have LinkedIn send that person an automatic invitation. The screen updates and you see an "Invite Sent" confirmation message in place of the Connect link, as shown in Figure 6-2.

I encourage you to click the person's name, go to his profile, and then click the Connect button, so you can add a personal note with your invitation to help the contact remember who you are.

4. Check other employers to see if there are any new colleagues available.

You can repeat the process by clicking each employer from the list provided.

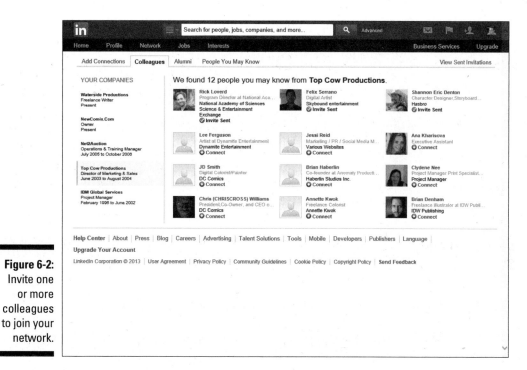

Figure 6-2:
Invite one
or more
colleagues
to join your
network.

Finding newly added classmates

No matter how much time goes by since I graduated from college, I still remember my school years well. I met a lot of cool and interesting people, folks I wanted to stay in contact with because of common goals, interests, or experiences. As time progressed and people moved on to new lives after graduation, it was all too easy to lose touch and not be able to reconnect.

Through LinkedIn, though, you can reconnect with former classmates and maintain that tie through your network, no matter where anyone moves on to. For you to find them to begin with, of course, your former classmates have to properly list their dates of receiving education. And, just as with the search for former colleagues, it's important to do an occasional search to see what classmates recently joined LinkedIn.

To search for classmates — and to add them to your network, if you want — just follow these steps:

1. **While logged in to your LinkedIn account, hover your mouse over the Network link from the top navigation bar, then click the Find Alumni link from the drop-down list that appears.**

2. **In the screen that appears, filter the results for a better list.**

   The Classmates window appears, as shown in Figure 6-3, if you've prefilled in at least one educational institution. You can click any of the classifications, like "Where they live" or "Where they work" to add extra filters and get a more precise list. You can also change the years of attendance in the boxes provided to see a different set of candidates, or search by a specific graduation date. If the screen is blank, you haven't yet added any education entries to your profile. (I discuss how to add education information to your profile in Chapter 3.)

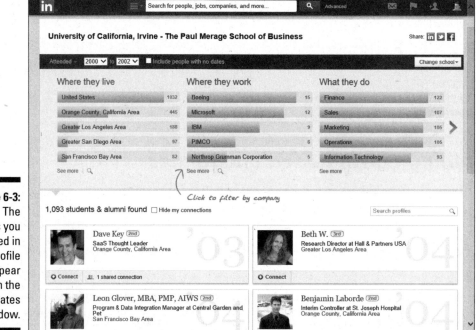

Figure 6-3: The schools you identified in your profile appear in the Classmates window.

3. **Look over the list of potential classmates and connect with any people you recognize.**

   You can always click the name of the classmate to see her profile first, or just click the Connect link below the name to send an invitation to connect. If there are any shared connections, you can click the words "X shared connections" to see what connections you have in common.

Before you invite people, click their name to read their profiles and see what they've been doing. Why ask them what they've been doing when you can read it for yourself? By doing your homework first, your invitation will sound more natural and be more likely to be accepted.

4. **Repeat the process for other schools by clicking the Change School button, as shown in Figure 6-4, and selecting another school from your educational history.**

When you select a new school, you see the same screen as shown in Figure 6-3, but for the newly selected school. You can filter those results and invite whomever you recognize.

Figure 6-4:
Check for classmates from other schools you attended.

University of California, Irvine - The Paul Merage School of Business   Share:

Attended ▾ 2000 ▾ to 2002 ▾ ☐ Include people with no dates		Change school ▾

You selected: Microsoft ✕   Clear Filters

Your schools
University of California, Irvine - Th..., 2000-2002
University of California, Los Angeles, 1991-1995
Booker T Washington HS, 1987-1991

Similar schools
Golden Gate University
University of North Carolina at Chape...
University of California, Irvine
California State University-Fullerton
University of California, Los Angeles...
Pepperdine University

Browse by name

Where they live		Where they work		Wr
United States	12	Boeing	15	Pr
Greater Seattle Area	8	Microsoft	12	Fi
Orange County, California Area	2	IBM	9	M
Reno, Nevada Area	1	PIMCO	6	O
San Francisco Bay Area	1	Northrop Grumman Corporation	5	Si
🔍		See more 🔍		See

I cover more about sending invitations later in this chapter, in the "Sending Connection Requests" section.

Browsing your connections' networks

Although it's helpful for LinkedIn to help you search the network, sometimes nothing gives as good results as some good old-fashioned investigation. From time to time, I like to browse the network of one of my first-degree connections to see whether he has a contact that should be a part of my network. I don't recommend spending a lot of your time this way, but doing a "spot check" by picking a few friends at random can yield some nice results.

Why is this type of research effective? Lots of reasons, including these:

- ✔ **You travel in the same circles.** If someone is a part of your network, you know that person from a past experience, whether you worked together, learned together, spoke at a conference together, or lived next door to each other. Whatever that experience was, you and this contact spent time with other people, so chances are you have shared connections — or, better yet, you will find people in that person's network who need to be a part of your network.

- ✔ **You might find someone newly connected.** Say that you've already spent some time searching all your undergraduate alumni contacts and adding as many people as you could find. As time passes, someone new may connect to one of your friends.

  One effective way to keep updated about who your connections have recently added is to review your Notifications (which I discuss in Chapter 1).

- ✔ **You might recognize someone whose name you didn't fully remember.** Many of us have that contact who we feel we know well, have fun talking to, and consider more than just an acquaintance, but for some reason, we can't remember that person's last name. Then, when you search a common contact's network and see the temporarily forgotten name and job title, you suddenly remember. Now you can invite that person to join your network. Another common experience is seeing the name and job title of a contact whose last name changed after marriage.

- ✔ **You might see someone you've wanted to get to know better.** Have you ever watched a friend talking to someone who you wanted to add to your network? Maybe your friend already introduced you, so the other person knows your name, but you consider this person a casual acquaintance at best. When you see that person's name listed in your friend's LinkedIn network, you can take the opportunity to deepen that connection. Having a friend in common who can recommend you can help smooth the way.

Looking through your friend's contacts list can be a cumbersome process if he has hundreds of contacts, so allow some time if you choose this technique.

To browse the network of one of your connections, follow these steps:

1. **Click the Network link from the top navigation bar, and then choose Contacts from the menu that appears to bring up your network.**

2. **Click the name of a first-degree connection.**

   Alternatively, search for the name via the search box on the home page. Then, on the search results page, click the name you want.

When perusing the person's profile, look for a link on a number above the word Connections, which should be next to the name and below the professional headline: something like "174 connections." If you see the number of connections but that word isn't hyperlinked, you can't proceed with this process because that person has chosen to make her connection list private. If that's the case, you need to select a different first-degree connection.

3. **Click the Connections link of the first-degree connection.**

   For the example in these steps, I picked a friend and associate, Michael Wellman, of the Comic Bug in Redondo Beach, California. His connection list is shown in Figure 6-5.

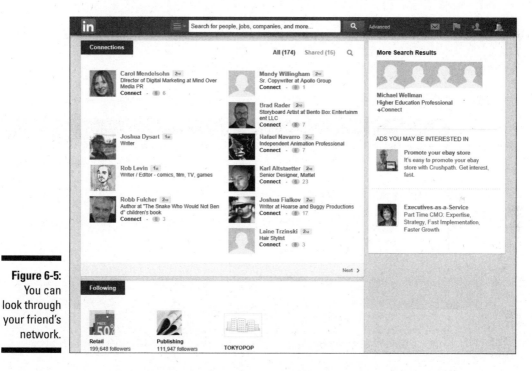

Figure 6-5:
You can look through your friend's network.

4. **Look through the list to see whether you'd like to send an invitation to anyone. If so, click the person's name to pull up his profile.**

   When I scan through Mike's list, I notice that his wife, Carol Mendelsohn, is in his network. I spoke with her once about some questions she had regarding search engine optimization (SEO), so I clicked her name to bring up her profile, which is shown in Figure 6-6.

5. **Click the Connect button, which appears in the middle of the page.**

   The Invitation page appears, as shown in Figure 6-7.

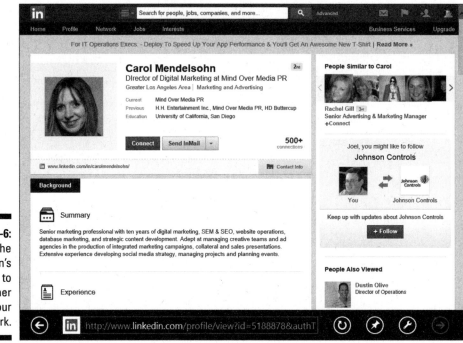

Figure 6-6:
Pull up the person's profile to add her to your network.

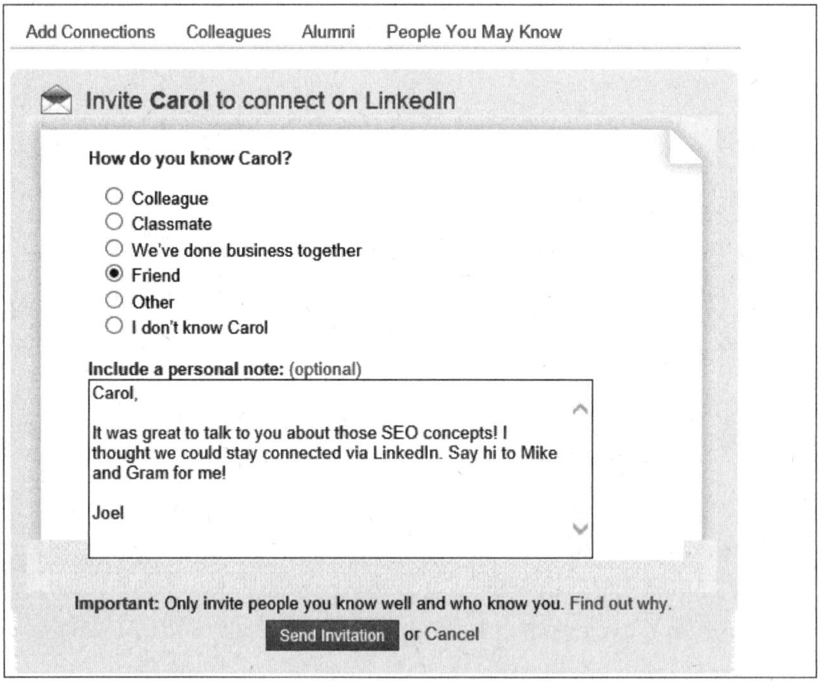

Add Connections   Colleagues   Alumni   People You May Know

✉ **Invite Carol to connect on LinkedIn**

How do you know Carol?

○ Colleague
○ Classmate
○ We've done business together
◉ Friend
○ Other
○ I don't know Carol

Include a personal note: (optional)

Carol,

It was great to talk to you about those SEO concepts! I thought we could stay connected via LinkedIn. Say hi to Mike and Gram for me!

Joel

Important: Only invite people you know well and who know you. Find out why.

Send Invitation   or Cancel

Figure 6-7:
Send a custom invitation to your new contact.

6. **Select the option that best describes your connection to this person or provide the person's e-mail address.**

   In some cases, you might have to input the person's e-mail address to help prove that you actually know the person. In other cases, like in Figure 6-7, you simply have to indicate whether you're a colleague, classmate, business partner, or friend, or have another association with this person. It's a good idea to enter some text in the Include a Personal Note field. This text customizes your invitation, and you can use it to remind the person who you are and why you'd like to connect.

7. **Click the blue Send Invitation button.**

   Presto! You're all done.

Sending Connection Requests

You can check out previous sections of this chapter to find out how to use LinkedIn to search the entire user network and find people you want to invite to join your personal network. In the following sections, I focus on sending out the invitation, including how to go about inviting people who haven't yet decided to join LinkedIn.

Sending requests to existing members

When you're on a LinkedIn page and spot the name of a member who you want to invite to your network, you can follow these steps to send that person a connection request:

1. **Click the person's name to go to his profile page.**

   You might find people to invite using one of the methods described in the "Checking for LinkedIn Members" section earlier in this chapter. You might also find them while doing an advanced people search, which I cover in Chapter 4. Figure 6-8 shows the profile page of a LinkedIn member.

2. **Click the blue Connect button to start the connection request.**

   The Invitation page appears, as shown in Figure 6-9.

Figure 6-8:
Add a
person
to your
network
from that
person's
profile page.

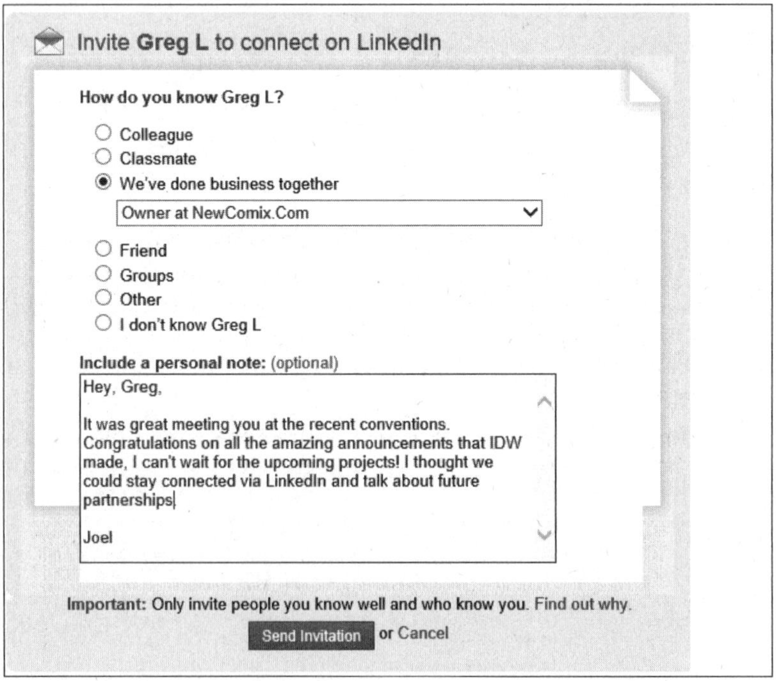

Figure 6-9:
Here is
where you
can invite
someone
to connect
with you.

3. **From the list of connection reasons, choose the option that best describes your relationship to this person.**

   You might have to input the person's e-mail address to help prove that you actually know the person. If you select the I Don't Know *Person's Name* option, LinkedIn denies the request, so keep that in mind. If you pick a category such as Colleague or Classmate, LinkedIn displays a drop-down list of options based on your profile. For example, if you pick Colleague, LinkedIn displays a drop-down list of your positions. You need to pick the position you held when you knew this person.

4. **Enter your invitation text in the Include a Personal Note field.**

   I highly recommend that you compose a custom invitation rather than use the standard text, "I'd like to add you to my professional network on LinkedIn." In my example in Figure 6-9, I remind the person how we recently met, acknowledge one of his achievements, and ask him to connect.

5. **Click the blue Send Invitation button.**

   You'll be notified by e-mail when the other party accepts your connection request.

Why you shouldn't use canned invitations

You might be tempted to look at the "canned" invitation that LinkedIn displays when you go to the Invitation Request page, especially if you're having a rough or busy day, and just send off the invitation without adding to or replacing the canned invitation with some custom text. We all have things to do and goals to accomplish, so stopping to write a note for each invitation can grow tedious. However, it's becoming increasingly important, for the following reasons, to replace that text with something that speaks to the recipient:

✔ **The other person might not remember you.** Quite simply, your recipient can take one look at your name, see no additional information in the note that accompanied it, and think, "Who is that guy (or gal)?" A few might click your name to read your profile and try to figure it out, but most people are busy and won't take the time to investigate. They are likely to ignore your request. Not good.

✔ **The other person could report you as someone he doesn't know.** Having someone ignore your request isn't the worst possibility, though. Nope, the worst is being declined as unknown. Recipients of your invitation see an I Don't Know This Person button. If several people click this button from an invitation you sent, LinkedIn will consider you a spammer and will suspend you — and possibly even remove your profile and account from the site!

✔ **You offer no motivation for a mutually beneficial relationship.** When people get an invitation request, they understand pretty clearly that you want something from them, whether it's access to them or to their network. If you've sent a canned invitation, they can't answer the question, "What is in it for me?" A canned invitation gives no motivation for or potential benefit of being connected to you. A custom note explaining that you'd love to swap resources or introduce that person to others is usually enough to encourage an acceptance.

✔ **A canned invitation implies you don't care.** Some people will look at your canned invitation request and think, "This person doesn't have 30 to 60 seconds to write a quick note introducing herself? She must not think much of me." Worse, they may think, "This person just wants to increase her number of contacts to look more popular or to exploit my network." Either impression will quickly kill your chances of getting more connections.

Sending requests to nonmembers

Only members of LinkedIn can be part of anyone's network. Therefore, if you want to send a connection request to someone who hasn't yet joined LinkedIn, you must invite that person to create a LinkedIn account first. To do so, you can either send your invitee an e-mail directly, asking him to join, or you can use a LinkedIn function that generates the e-mail invitation that includes a link to join LinkedIn.

Either way, you need to have the nonmember's e-mail address, and you'll probably have to provide your invitee with some incentive by offering reasons to take advantage of LinkedIn and create an account. (I give you some tips for doing that in the next section.)

When you're ready to send your request using LinkedIn, just follow these steps:

1. **Click the Add Connections button at the top right of the LinkedIn home page.**

   The Add Connections window appears.

2. **Click the Any Mail button. In the middle of the page, under the header "More ways to connect," click the Invite by individual e-mail link.**

   This brings up a text box, as shown in Figure 6-10. Fill in the e-mail addresses of the people you want to invite to LinkedIn in the box provided.

Because you can't personalize the invitation request to nonmembers, you may want to contact those people via e-mail or phone first to let them know this request is coming and encourage them to consider joining LinkedIn.

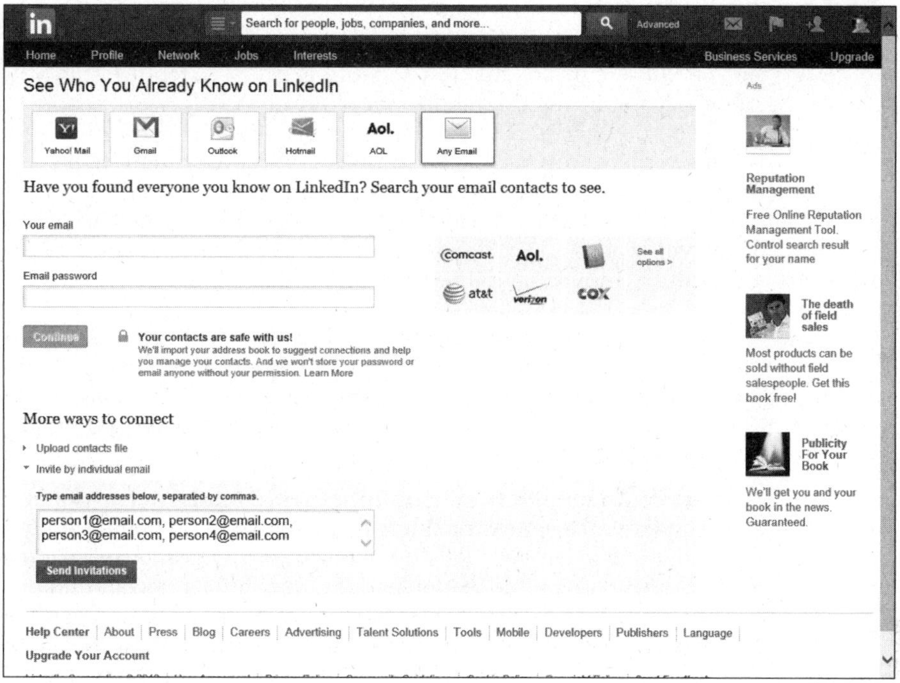

Figure 6-10:
Fill in the
e-mail
addresses
of anyone
you want to
invite to join
LinkedIn.

3. **Click the blue Send Invitations button.**

You're returned to the Add Connections page, where you see a confirmation message. You can repeat the process at any time to invite additional people to join LinkedIn and be added to your network.

Communicating the value of joining LinkedIn

So you want to add some people to your LinkedIn network, but they haven't yet taken the plunge of signing up for the site. If you want them to accept your request by setting up their account, you might need to tout the value of LinkedIn to your contacts. After all, recommendations are one of the most powerful sales tools, which is why all types of businesses — from e-commerce stores and retail businesses to service directories and social networking

Web sites — use recommendations so often. Offering to help them build their profile or use LinkedIn effectively wouldn't hurt either.

Because LinkedIn (as of this writing) does not allow you to personalize your invitation to nonmembers, you will need to make this pitch either via e-mail or directly with the person you are recruiting.

So, how do you make the "sale"? (I use that term figuratively, of course. And as you know, a basic LinkedIn account is free — a feature that you should definitely not neglect to mention to your invitees!) If you send a super-long thesis on the merits of LinkedIn, it'll most likely be ignored. If you send a simple "C'mon! You know you wanna . . . ." request, that might or might not work. (You know your friends better than me.) You could buy them a copy of this book, but that could get expensive. (But I would be thrilled! C'mon! You know you wanna . . . .) The simplest way is to mention some of the benefits they could enjoy from joining the site:

- ✔ **LinkedIn members always stay in touch with their connections.** If people you know move, change their e-mail addresses, or change jobs, you still have a live link to them via LinkedIn. You'll always be able to see their new e-mail addresses if you're connected (assuming that they provide it, of course).

- ✔ **LinkedIn members can tap into their friends' networks for jobs or opportunities, now or later.** Although someone might not need a job now, she may eventually need help, so why not access thousands or even millions of potential leads? LinkedIn has tens of millions of members in all sorts of industries, and people have obtained consulting leads, contract jobs, new careers, and even startup venture capital or funding for a new film. After all, it's all about "who you know."

- ✔ **LinkedIn can help you build your own brand.** LinkedIn members get a free profile page to build their online presence, and can link to up to three of their own Web sites, such as a blog, personal Web site, or e-commerce store. The search engines love LinkedIn pages, which have high page rankings — and this can only boost your online identity.

- ✔ **LinkedIn can help you do all sorts of research.** You might need to know more about a company before an interview, or you're looking for a certain person to help your business, or you're curious what people's opinions would be regarding an idea you have. LinkedIn is a great resource in all these situations. You can use LinkedIn to get free advice and information, all from the comfort of your own computer.

- ✔ **Employers are using LinkedIn every day.** Many employers now use LinkedIn to do due diligence on a job seeker by reviewing her LinkedIn profile before an interview. If you are not on LinkedIn, an employer may see this as a red flag and it could affect your chances of getting the job.

- ✔ **A basic LinkedIn account is free, and joining LinkedIn is easy.** There are a lot of misconceptions that users have to pay a monthly fee or spend a lot of time updating their LinkedIn profiles. Simply remind people that joining is free, and after they set up their profiles, LinkedIn is designed to take up very little of their time to keep an active profile and to benefit from having an account.

Removing people from your network

The day might come when you feel you need to remove someone from your network. Perhaps you added the person in haste, or he repeatedly asks you for favors or introduction requests, or sends messages that you don't want to respond to. Not to worry — you're not doomed to suffer forever; simply remove the connection. When you do so, that person can no longer view your network or send you messages, unless he pays to send you an InMail message.

To remove a connection from your network, just follow these steps:

1. **While logged in to your LinkedIn account, click the Network link from the top navigation bar, and then choose Contacts from the menu that appears to bring up your list of connections.**

2. **Scroll through the list to find the connection you wish to remove. When you hover your mouse over the connection's name, you see the Tag, Message, and More links appear below the person's name and headline as shown in Figure 6-11.**

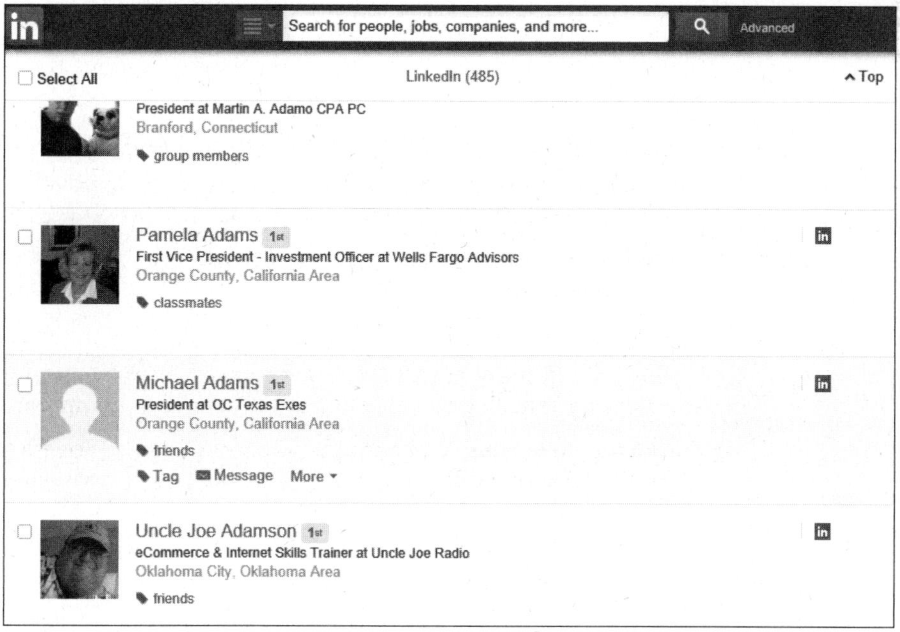

Figure 6-11: Find the connection you wish to remove.

3. **Click the drop-down arrow next to the More link, and then select Remove Connection from the drop-down list that appears, as shown in Figure 6-12.**

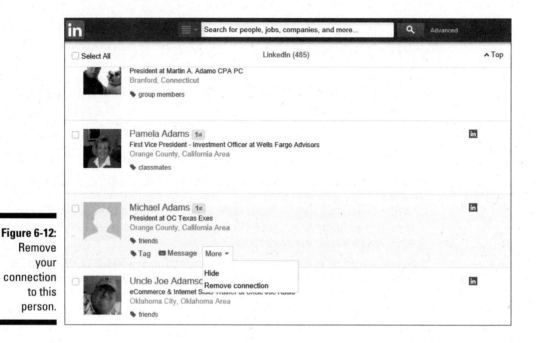

Figure 6-12: Remove your connection to this person.

A pop-up box appears, warning you of what abilities you'll lose with this removal and asking you to confirm you want to remove the connection, as shown in Figure 6-13.

4. **Click the Remove button to remove this person from your network.**

Your removed connection won't be notified of the removal.

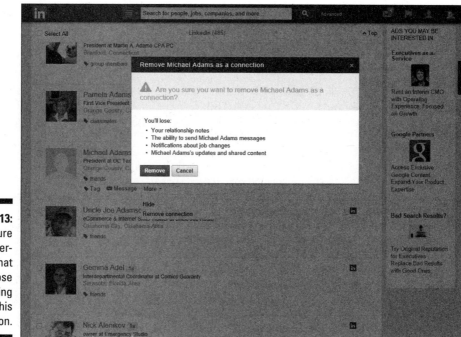

Figure 6-13:
Make sure
you under-
stand what
you'll lose
by removing
this
connection.

Accepting Invitations (or Gracefully Declining)

In this chapter, I talk a lot about how and why you might send invitations and add people to your network, and even cover what to do when you need to remove someone from your network. But what about the flip side of that coin — that is, being the invitee? In this section, I offer some guidance on what to do when you're faced with an invitation, and you have to decide whether to happily accept or gracefully decline it.

When you receive an invitation to join someone's network of connections and you're not sure whether to accept or decline the invitation, ask yourself these questions:

✔ **How well do you know this person?** With any luck, the inviter has included a custom message clueing you in to who she is, in case you don't remember. You can, of course, click the name to read that person's profile, which usually helps trigger your memory. If you don't know or remember this person, you probably don't want to add him to your network just yet. If you do know him, you need to consider whether he's worth adding to your network.

✔ **Does this person fit with the goals of your network?** As I mention early in this chapter, it's easier to put together a network when you've established a sense of the purpose you want it to serve. When you're looking at this invitation, simply ask yourself, "Does accepting this invitation help further my goals?"

✔ **Is this someone with whom you want to communicate and include in your network?** If you don't like someone or don't want to do business with him, you should certainly not feel obligated to accept the invitation. Keep in mind that these people will have access to your network and can hit you up with introduction and recommendation requests (see Chapters 5 and 8, respectively).

If you're thinking of declining an invitation, here are some tips to help you do so gracefully:

✔ **Respond quickly.** If you wait to respond to the invitation and then decide to go ahead and decline the invite, the other person might be even more offended and confused. Respond quickly so that this issue isn't hanging over anyone's head.

✔ **If necessary, ask for more information.** If you feel uncomfortable because you don't know the person well but want to consider the invitation before you decline, respond with a request for more information, such as, "I appreciate your interest, but I am having trouble placing our previous meetings. What is your specific interest in connecting with me on LinkedIn? Please let me know how we know each other and what your goals are for LinkedIn. Thanks again."

✔ **Respond politely but with a firm no.** You can simply write something along the lines of, "Thank you for your interest; I appreciate your eagerness. Unfortunately, because I'm not familiar with you, I'm not interested in connecting with you on LinkedIn just yet." Then, if you want, you can spell out the terms in which you might be interested in connecting, such as if the opportunity ever arises to get to know the person better or if he is referred to you by a friend.

Chapter 7

Connecting With and Endorsing Your Network

In This Chapter

▶ Organizing your LinkedIn contacts

▶ Storing conversations and notes about your first-degree connections

▶ Understanding LinkedIn endorsements

▶ Giving your network endorsements

▶ Approving and displaying others' endorsements of you

*L*et's look inward for a moment and think about the basic building block of your LinkedIn network — your relationship with each of your first-degree connections. Each of these relationships has a different identity, from the colleague you just met and added to your network, to a lifelong friend. LinkedIn wants to help you manage the qualities of that relationship, not just the fact that you know that person. This way, LinkedIn becomes more of your hub for managing your professional network and building your own brand and/or business.

In this chapter, I discuss how to properly use two of LinkedIn's newer functions, Contacts and Endorsements. I start by discussing how LinkedIn displays and organizes your contacts, and then I walk you through how you can use Contacts as your own personal "Customer Relationship Management" (CRM) system to store notes, tags, and information about how you relate to each contact. Then, I shift gears and focus on LinkedIn Endorsements, where you can give and receive endorsements of others' skills, and how they differ from recommendations. You find out how to endorse your first-degree connections, review the endorsements they give you, and add those endorsements to your profile.

Interacting with Your Network with LinkedIn Contacts

The goal of LinkedIn Contacts is to give users "a smarter way to stay in touch." LinkedIn Contacts lets you sync your address books, e-mails, and calendar entries with your LinkedIn contact information, so LinkedIn can organize your communication with your colleagues and professional friends. By knowing all the information you keep in these various systems (address book, calendar, e-mail, LinkedIn), it can sort that information, by the other person, and show you a comprehensive history starting with how you met or linked to each person, plus a history of your interactions with each person up until the last conversation, an inventory of mutual friends and colleagues, and updates of their career events and LinkedIn activities. Finally, LinkedIn gives you the power to add and store your own private notes for each contact and schedule follow-up or regular interactions with those contacts.

LinkedIn Contacts is a tool to help you manage your professional relationships en masse while still being personal. Here are some of the advantages of using this system:

 ✔ **It stores your contact history.** For each contact, LinkedIn shows you when you connected with that person, and logs each conversation with that person you did through LinkedIn. If you synced other systems (like your e-mail), LinkedIn Contacts shows you a chronological history of those conversations as well.

 ✔ **It shows mutual connections.** When you communicate with other colleagues, sometimes it's helpful to know at a glance which connections you share with that person. Perhaps you need a favor and must decide who among your network can help you make your case to the other person. LinkedIn Contacts displays, for each contact, who you and that person both have as first-degree connections, which is perfect for you to know who to enlist when it's time to ask for help or an opinion.

 ✔ **It encourages new and ongoing communication.** Since professionals use LinkedIn to record their career accomplishments, from new jobs and promotions to receiving awards and certifications, LinkedIn Contacts notifies you when someone in your network has a career "event" (for example, a promotion or work anniversary) and encourages you to reach out and communicate, whether it's to say "Congrats" or connect with a common friend who just joined LinkedIn. Contacts also allows you to set reminders so you can follow up with someone at a later date. By encouraging regular communication, LinkedIn helps reduce the awkwardness when you need to reach out to a contact.

✔ **It's available at your fingertips.** LinkedIn made sure that the Contacts feature is robust and available not just on its website, but also through mobile applications. You can download and install a LinkedIn Contacts app for your Apple or Android OS system and have the same information at your fingertips, in case you're not in front of your computer.

✔ **You can add your own notes.** After LinkedIn catalogs your past and current interactions, it allows you to record your own notes for each person, visible only to you. Your notes are stored on LinkedIn and available anytime. In addition, you can create tags for each contact, allowing you to create your own virtual "groups" of people that you can manage or change at any time.

Understanding how LinkedIn Contacts is structured

The good news is there is nothing to install or pay for in order to use LinkedIn Contacts. Any LinkedIn member, whether he has a free or paid account, sees the same LinkedIn Contacts screen and has access to all the LinkedIn Contacts functions. This capability is available from the moment you join LinkedIn and start adding connections, and it's free to sync any of your other accounts to LinkedIn to store additional information. As of this writing, LinkedIn is able to sync with major e-mail providers such as Gmail, Yahoo! Mail, and Outlook, along with address books like Google Contacts, Yahoo! Address Book, Outlook Address Book, and the iPhone Address Book. In addition, you can sync information with systems such as CardMunch, Evernote, and TripIt.

To get started, you can either hover your mouse over the Network link in the top navigation bar and then click Contacts, or go directly to contacts.linkedin.com. You should see the Contacts screen, as shown in Figure 7-1.

Along the top of the screen, LinkedIn displays a tiled bar of contacts who have either reported a new event or potential new contacts of someone in your network. Each element in that bar has a suggested action, such as "Say Congrats" or "Connect," that you can click, which encourages some interaction with that person. You can also click the Skip link at the bottom right of each tile area to bring up another potential contact, or click the See More People to Contact link to bring up another row of contact tiles.

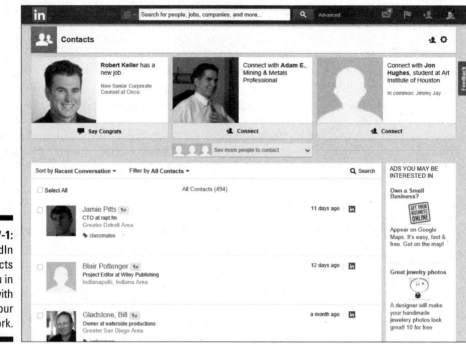

Figure 7-1:
LinkedIn
Contacts
keeps you in
touch with
your
network.

Below that bar is your list of contacts, sorted by Recent Conversation by default. This way, you see the LinkedIn contacts you've most recently talked to, and next to each name, LinkedIn shows the length of time that has passed since your last interaction.

You can click the drop-down arrow next to Sort By to change the sort order of your contacts. As of this writing, your choices for sorting are:

- ✔ **Recent Conversation**
- ✔ **Alphabetical** (based on each contact's first or last name)
- ✔ **New** (starting with the newest connections to your network)

Next to the Sort By option is the Filter By option, which is useful if you want to see a certain subset of your contacts list. By default, it's set to All Contacts, but if you click the drop-down arrow, you can set a filter to see only the list of contacts from a certain Company, Location, Job Title, or self-created Tag, instead of the list of All Contacts.

To the right of the Filter By option is a Search link. When you click it, a text box appears that you can use to search your contact list. Simply type the desired keywords in the box and then press Enter to run the search.

Using LinkedIn Contacts

When you're ready to use all of LinkedIn Contact's capabilities, just follow these steps:

1. **From the LinkedIn Contacts screen, click the wheel icon on the top right of your screen, as shown in Figure 7-2.**

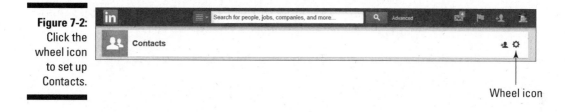

Figure 7-2:
Click the wheel icon to set up Contacts.

Wheel icon

You are taken to the Contacts Settings page, as shown in Figure 7-3.

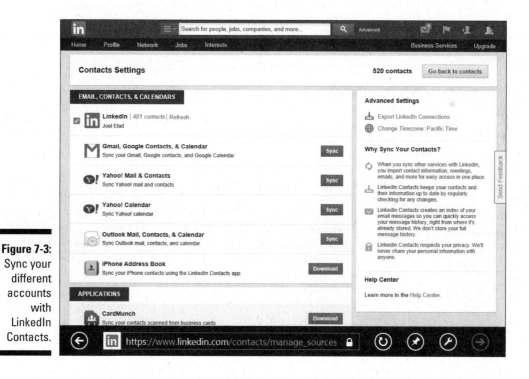

Figure 7-3:
Sync your different accounts with LinkedIn Contacts.

2. **Click Sync next to the name of your e-mail system and/or address book to sync your e-mail messages with the LinkedIn Contacts system.**

   If you've got Gmail, Yahoo! Mail, or Outlook, click the appropriate blue Sync button to start the sync process. In this example, I sync my Gmail and Google accounts.

3. **Follow the prompts to sync your other accounts.**

   In this example, I am prompted to log into my Google account, as shown in Figure 7-4. After I do, I get a Permissions screen, as shown in Figure 7-5, where I click the blue Allow Access button to give LinkedIn the ability to sync with my Google account.

Figure 7-4:
Log into
your other
accounts.

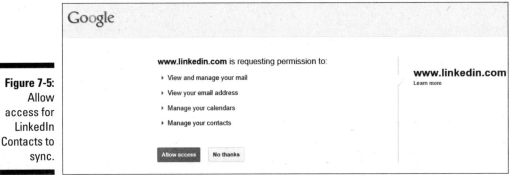

Figure 7-5:
Allow
access for
LinkedIn
Contacts to
sync.

4. **Repeat Steps 2 and 3 for any other accounts you wish to sync with LinkedIn Contacts.**

   After each sync, you are returned to the LinkedIn Contacts Settings page, where you can pick another e-mail, contacts, calendar, or application provider. In addition, you can import your Outlook, Yahoo! Mail, or Mac Address Book contacts by importing a .CSV (comma-separated values) file created by those applications.

LinkedIn Contacts stores more information than just your first-degree connections. You can also add someone who's not yet a LinkedIn member.

5. **From the Contacts Settings page, click the gray Go Back to Contacts button and pick an individual contact by clicking her name from the Contacts screen.**

To use the Contacts functions for any particular first-degree connection, you need to pull up the person's profile information by clicking his name on the Contacts screen. When you reach a contact's profile page, you should see a box with the Relationship and Contact Info tabs, as shown in Figure 7-6. LinkedIn has already populated this box with any LinkedIn messages you've sent to each other.

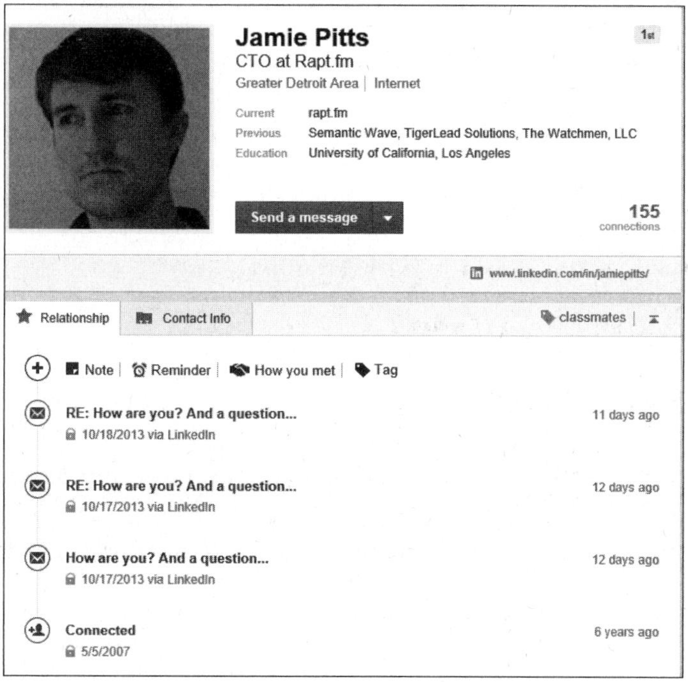

Jamie Pitts
CTO at Rapt.fm
Greater Detroit Area | Internet

Current   rapt.fm
Previous   Semantic Wave, TigerLead Solutions, The Watchmen, LLC
Education   University of California, Los Angeles

Send a message ▼

155 connections

www.linkedin.com/in/jamiepitts/

★ Relationship   Contact Info   🏷 classmates | ⚏

(+)   📋 Note | ⏰ Reminder | 💬 How you met | 🏷 Tag

(✉)   **RE: How are you? And a question...**   11 days ago
🔒 10/18/2013 via LinkedIn

(✉)   **RE: How are you? And a question...**   12 days ago
🔒 10/17/2013 via LinkedIn

(✉)   **How are you? And a question...**   12 days ago
🔒 10/17/2013 via LinkedIn

(+👤)   **Connected**   6 years ago
🔒 5/5/2007

Figure 7-6: LinkedIn Contacts shows the Relationship elements.

6. **(Optional) Click the Note link to add a note to yourself pertaining to this contact.**

Think of the Note function as a way for you to record any thoughts about this contact, remind yourself of information that was mentioned in past conversations, or jot down any questions you need to ask this person. When you click the Note link, a text box opens where you can type the note, as shown in Figure 7-7. When you're done, click the blue Save button and the note is added to the log of communications for that contact, as shown in Figure 7-8.

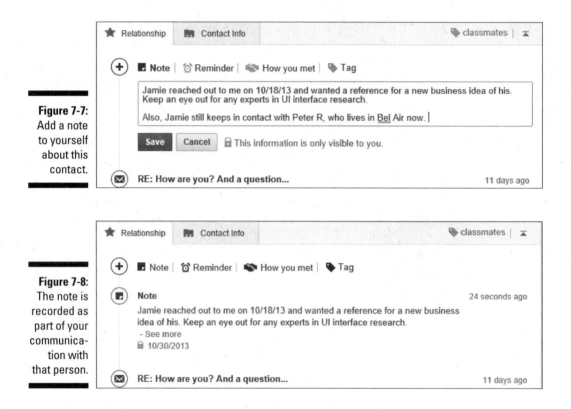

Figure 7-7:
Add a note to yourself about this contact.

Figure 7-8:
The note is recorded as part of your communica-tion with that person.

7. **(Optional) Click the Reminder link to set up a reminder message from LinkedIn pertaining to this contact.**

When you click the Reminder link, a text box opens where you can type the subject of the reminder message that LinkedIn will send you, as shown in Figure 7-9. Using the radio buttons below that text box, decide when you want the reminder message sent to you. Click the blue Save button to create the reminder, and in the designated time frame, LinkedIn sends you a reminder message with the subject line you just entered.

8. **(Optional) Click the How You Met link to record how you met this contact.**

Clicking the How You Met link opens a text box where you can record the details of how you met this contact. When you click the blue Save button, LinkedIn creates an entry entitled "How you met" and puts it at the bottom of the Relationship box, as shown in Figure 7-10. This way, this information is always available to you.

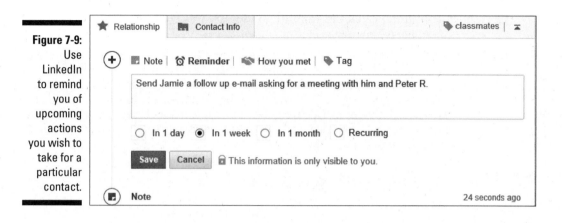

Figure 7-9:
Use
LinkedIn
to remind
you of
upcoming
actions
you wish to
take for a
particular
contact.

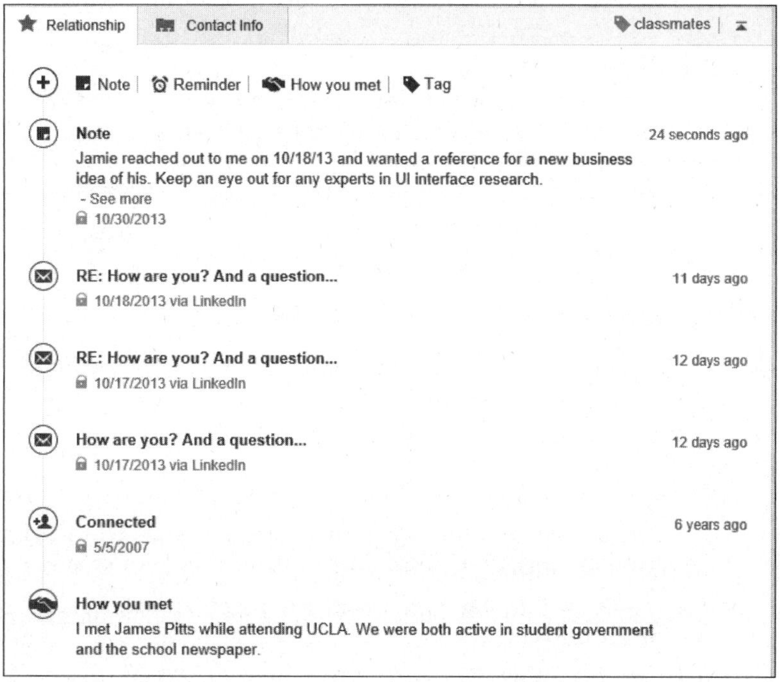

Figure 7-10:
Record the
details of
how you
met this
contact.

The information you add with these functions is visible only to you and nobody else, so you can type these notes without the other person (or anybody else) seeing this information.

9. (Optional) Click the Tag link to identify this contact with your own "category" name.

Let's say that you want to tag your LinkedIn connections with whom you shared a certain group in college, in case you want to send messages to only this group regarding a reunion or something similar. Click the Tag link to generate a drop-down list of tags to choose from. You can select the check box next to a pre-determined tag, like colleague or classmate, or click the Add a Tag link to generate a text box to write your own tag, as shown in Figure 7-11.

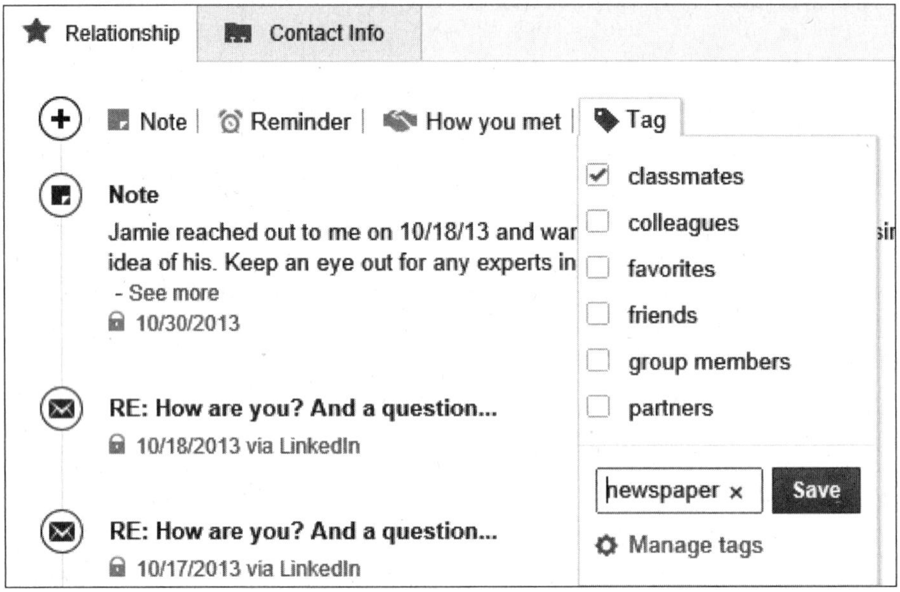

Figure 7-11:
Create your own tags to identify the different contacts in your network.

★ Relationship	📷 Contact Info

(+) 📝 Note | 🕐 Reminder | 🤝 How you met | 🏷️ Tag

☑ classmates
☐ colleagues
☐ favorites
☐ friends
☐ group members
☐ partners

newspaper ✕ **Save**

📝 **Note**
Jamie reached out to me on 10/18/13 and war ...
idea of his. Keep an eye out for any experts in ...
- See more
🔒 10/30/2013

⚙ Manage tags

📧 **RE: How are you? And a question...**
🔒 10/18/2013 via LinkedIn

📧 **RE: How are you? And a question...**
🔒 10/17/2013 via LinkedIn

You can assign multiple tags to the same person — if the same person is involved in more than one category in your life, for example.

10. Repeat Steps 6 to 9 for any contacts where you want to record any of this information.

You can add this information whenever you want, it doesn't have to be done all at once. As you use LinkedIn, be aware that these options exist, especially when you're looking at someone's profile page. Make notes while they're still fresh in your mind, or after receiving an e-mail or notification from someone.

Giving and Receiving Endorsements on LinkedIn

Although many people believe "It's not what you know, it's who you know," which is one of the main reasons why LinkedIn is so valuable, many folks (recruiters, hiring managers, CEOs, investors, and more) are very interested in what you know. Logically, the people who know you best are the people in your network, who have observed your work firsthand and can speak to the quality and degree of your skill set. LinkedIn came up with an easier way for users to identify what skills they think their contacts have, and this system is called LinkedIn Endorsements.

Initially, LinkedIn offered this ability through its Recommendations system (which I cover in the next chapter), but it wanted to offer a way for users to identify skills in their contacts that was easier to use and less comprehensive (and time-consuming) than its Recommendations system, which is how the Endorsements function was created. Endorsements had only been available a short time when, LinkedIn announced more than 2 billion endorsements had been given on its site, signaling a widespread adoption of this new functionality. So why is LinkedIn Endorsements important to understand and use? Here are a few reasons to consider:

- ✔ **Endorsements are an easier way to recognize someone's skill set.** While a recommendation can be a thorough and positive review of someone's job, endorsing a particular skill can show the community very quickly what skills someone possesses.

- ✔ **Endorsements are a great way for you to highlight important skills.** When you're looking for a job or thinking about your career, having your key skill set show up as endorsements on your profile signals to recruiters and hiring managers that not only do you have the skills to do that job, but other people believe in your skills enough to endorse you. Just like with recommendations, people are more likely to believe other people's testimony about your skills than your own assertions.

- ✔ **Endorsements are independent of any specific position.** When you write a recommendation for someone on LinkedIn, it is tied to one position. When you endorse someone's skill, it's tied to that person's entire profile, not just one job that was held any number of years ago.

- ✔ **Endorsements are faster and more specific.** It's much easier and more precise for your contacts to endorse your specific skills than to write an entire recommendation. Many of your contacts can only speak to certain skills anyway, and with LinkedIn Endorsements, they can "give kudos with just one click."

Because of the ease and speed of endorsing someone's skills, coupled with the fact that LinkedIn offers lots of prompts for you to endorse people's skills, there is a very real trap you need to avoid: blindly endorsing skills the other person may not possess (and others endorsing skills of yours they can't verify you possess). It's important that your endorsements are authentic, so put some thought into giving and managing your endorsements.

Each LinkedIn user can have up to 50 skills that can be endorsed by his network, and the top 10 endorsed skills appear on your profile page, under the Skills & Expertise section, as shown in Figure 7-12. The profile pictures of the people who endorsed those skills appear to the right of each skill. While many of the skills that appear on the Endorsements list come from what you entered as your skills and experience on your profile, your contacts can add skills you may not have identified yet. (For example, in Figure 7-12, someone endorsed me for Books and Cloud Computing, which were skills I had not yet defined in my profile.)

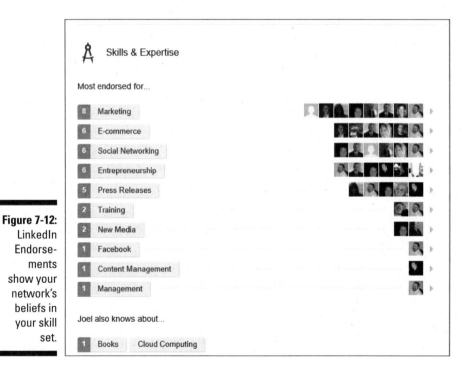

Figure 7-12:
LinkedIn Endorse-ments show your network's beliefs in your skill set.

Endorsing someone on LinkedIn

As you use LinkedIn, you should notice that the system often prompts you to endorse your contacts for specific skills on their profile. LinkedIn built this into its system to make it as easy and automatic as possible to endorse your contacts without you looking for a particular screen or function.

You might see a screen where you are prompted with the option to endorse four different contacts for a particular skill (as shown in Figure 7-13). When you see that box, you have several options:

- ✔ **If offered, you can click the Endorse All 4 button to endorse all four contacts at once.** In some cases, you can click the View More button to see a new screen of four contacts with a skill to endorse for each one.

- ✔ **You can click individual Endorse links (below each profile picture) to select which of the four endorsements you want to give.** Each time you click Endorse, a new skill and contact pops up in that box for you to consider.

- ✔ **You can click the X in the top right corner of each box to close that option.** That box is repopulated with a new contact and a new skill to endorse for that contact.

- ✔ **You can click the Close button (the X in the top right corner of the big blue box) to stop the process.**

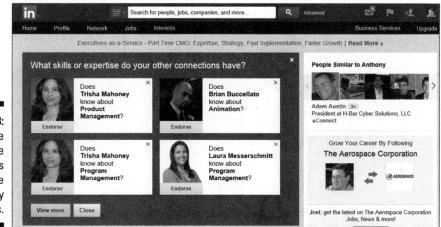

Figure 7-13: Endorse multiple contacts for the skills they possess.

When you are looking at any particular contact's profile, you may be presented with a blue box asking you to endorse multiple skills for that contact (as shown in Figure 7-14). You can also bring up this box by clicking the drop-down arrow next to the Send a Message button and selecting Endorse Skills & Expertise.

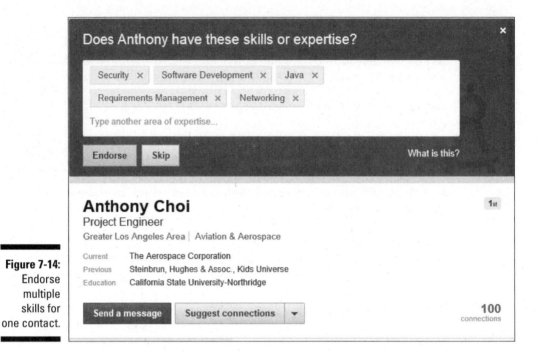

Figure 7-14:
Endorse
multiple
skills for
one contact.

When you see this box, you have several options:

- ✔ **You can click the yellow Endorse button to endorse all the skills listed in the box.**

- ✔ **To remove an individual skill from the list before clicking Endorse, click the X next to the skill name.**

- ✔ **To add an individual skill to the list before clicking Endorse, simply start typing in the Type another area of expertise** area. LinkedIn prompts you with possible skill names that you can click (as shown in Figure 7-15), or finish typing to add that skill to the list.

- ✔ **You can click the Skip button (or the X in the top right corner of the blue box) to stop the process.** The box disappears and you see the contact's profile page.

After you click Endorse or Skip, the process is concluded for that particular contact. When you visit another contact's profile page, the process begins again for that contact.

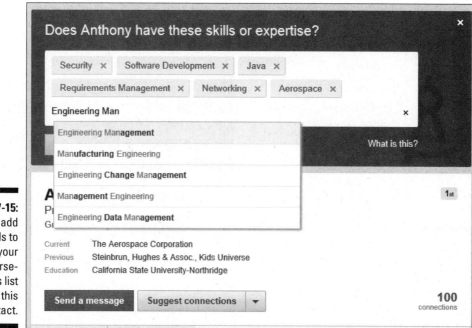

Figure 7-15:
You can add skills to your endorsements list for this contact.

Think carefully about which skills you can honestly endorse for another person, as you should only endorse skills you truly believe the other person has or that you have witnessed in action. You may also want to consider what skills the other person wants highlighted on her profile, which can be evident from the most endorsed skills she has currently. You should never feel compelled to endorse someone's skill just because LinkedIn prompts you for one particular skill.

If you want to give endorsements for someone's skills without being prompted, simply go to her profile page and scroll down to her Skills & Expertise section, where you can see her identified skills. When you see an individual skill you want to endorse, hover your mouse over the + sign next to the skill name (as shown in Figure 7-16) and click the Endorse link that appears. You can repeat the process to endorse as many skills as you wish.

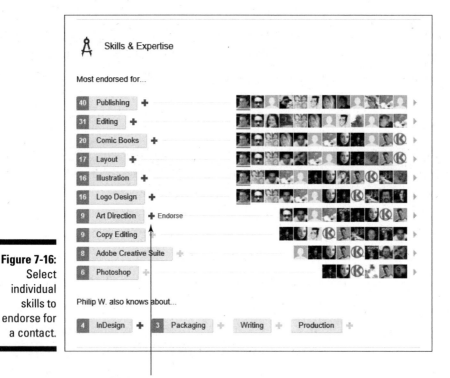

Figure 7-16:
Select individual skills to endorse for a contact.

Click the + sign to
bring up the Endorse link.

Any skills you have already endorsed appear with a blue filled in + sign next to the skill name, and your profile picture is underlined to the right of the skill name. If you want to remove a particular endorsement, hover your mouse over that blue + sign and click the Remove Endorsement link that appears.

You can always go back and add more skill endorsements at any time, even after you initially endorse someone's skills.

Accepting endorsements on LinkedIn

LinkedIn does not automatically add any incoming endorsements to your profile; you must accept those endorsements first.

When you receive an endorsement, it appears in your Notifications list at the top right corner of the LinkedIn screen (as shown in Figure 7-17), and you also receive an e-mail (depending on your e-mail settings) letting you know who endorsed you and for what skills.

The easiest way to accept (or reject) these endorsements is to edit your LinkedIn profile. Hover your mouse over the Profile link in the top navigation bar, and then click Edit Profile from the drop-down list that appears. You can also respond to the Notification message that LinkedIn sends you, which takes you to the Edit Profile screen, too. When your profile comes up for editing, you should see a blue box indicating that your connections have endorsed you for skills and expertise, as shown in Figure 7-18.

Figure 7-17:
LinkedIn notifies you when someone endorses your skills!

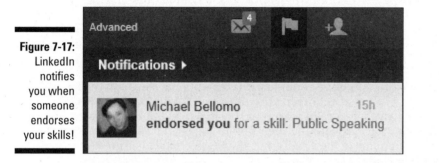

Figure 7-18:
LinkedIn asks you to add new endorsements to your profile.

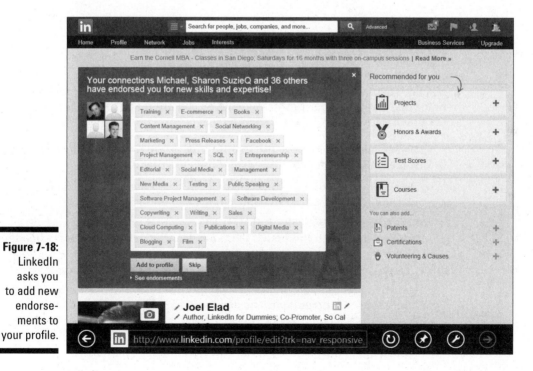

When you see this box, you have several options:

✔ **Click the yellow Add to Profile button to add all the incoming endorsements to your profile.** (You can manage your endorsements later, which I discuss in the next section.)

✔ **Click the gray Skip button, or the X in the top right corner of the blue box, to ignore this and deal with it later.**

✔ **Click the See Endorsements link to see who endorsed which skills.**

If you decide to add these endorsements to your profile, LinkedIn offers you the chance to give endorsements to people in your network, similar to Figure 7-13 from the previous section.

After you've accepted the endorsements, an optional step is to contact the person or people that endorsed you with a quick note to say thanks. Not only does it give you a valid reason to stay in touch, but it helps cultivate the relationship. You can also visit their profile page and decide to reciprocate by endorsing some of their skills, but staying in contact is a great networking chance that shouldn't be missed.

Managing your endorsements

Now that you've added endorsements to your profile, you may want to manage them and make sure you are happy with the ones you've received being displayed on your profile. Whenever you are ready to manage your endorsements, simply follow these steps:

1. **Hover your mouse over the Profile link in the top navigation bar and select Edit Profile from the drop-down list that appears.**

   This allows you to edit your LinkedIn profile, which is necessary when you want to manage your skills listings and endorsements.

2. **Scroll down to the Skills & Expertise section of your profile and click the Edit link (with the pencil icon) next to the Skills & Expertise header.**

   This opens up a new section below the Skills & Expertise header to help you manage your skills listings and endorsements of those skills, (as shown in Figure 7-19. There are two options: Add & Remove and Manage Endorsements. By default, you see the Add & Remove options first.

3. **If you want to add a skill to your list (so people can endorse it later) simply type in the name of the new skill and then click Add. When you're done, click the Save button to save your changes.**

   You must click the Save button before doing anything else, like managing your endorsements. Otherwise, any skills you add won't be saved to your profile.

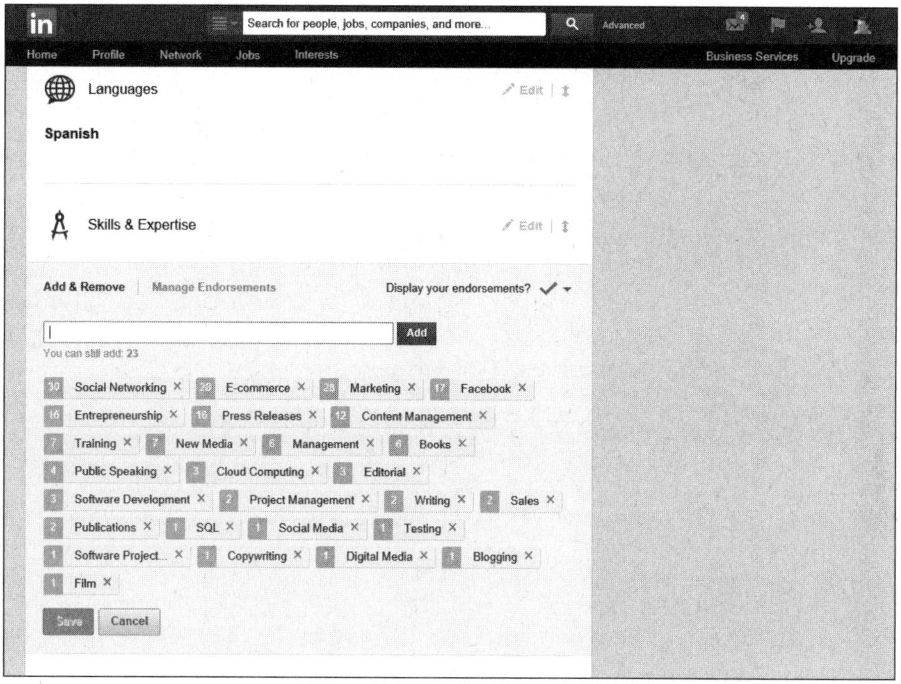

Figure 7-19:
Add skills to
be endorsed
later.

As you start typing the name of your skill, LinkedIn automatically prompts you with possible skill names based on other users' profiles, as shown in Figure 7-20. You can click the option that best matches what you want, or finish typing your own skill name.

You don't have to accept what LinkedIn prompts you for, especially if you are trying to ensure the right keywords come up for your skills profile when other people review it.

4. **To manage your endorsements, click the Manage Endorsements link. Click the name of the skill that was endorsed and then click any person's name to deselect the check box, effectively hiding that person's endorsement from your profile.**

On the Manage Endorsements screen that appears, your skills are sorted by the number of endorsements you've received for each skill, from highest to lowest, as shown in Figure 7-21. Click the arrows next to the number of endorsements to scroll up and down the list of skills, and use the scroll bar on the right side to scroll through the names of your connections that endorsed the highlighted skill.

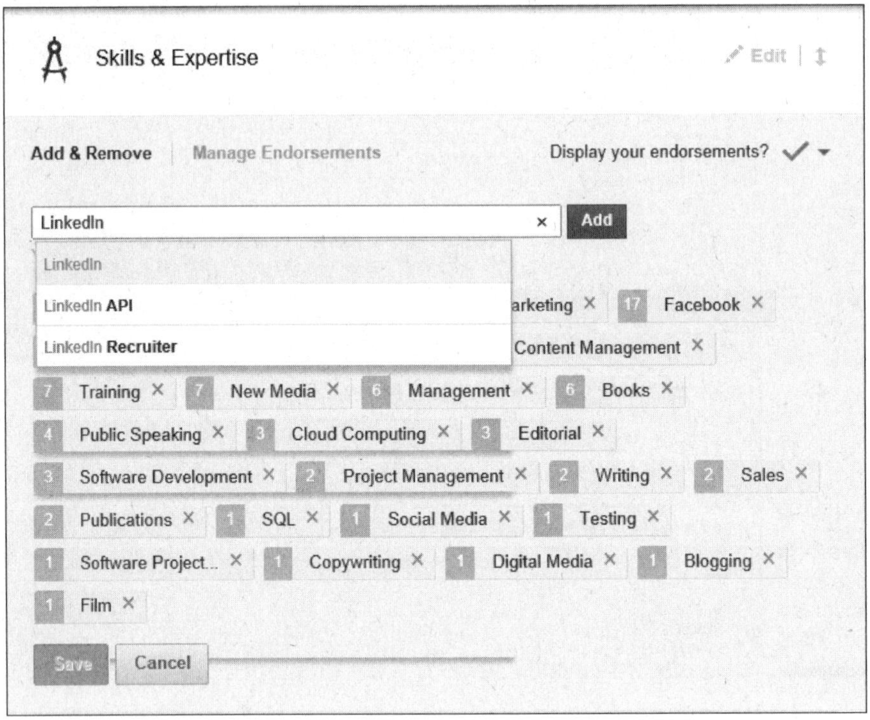

Figure 7-20:
LinkedIn
prompts you
for new skill
names.

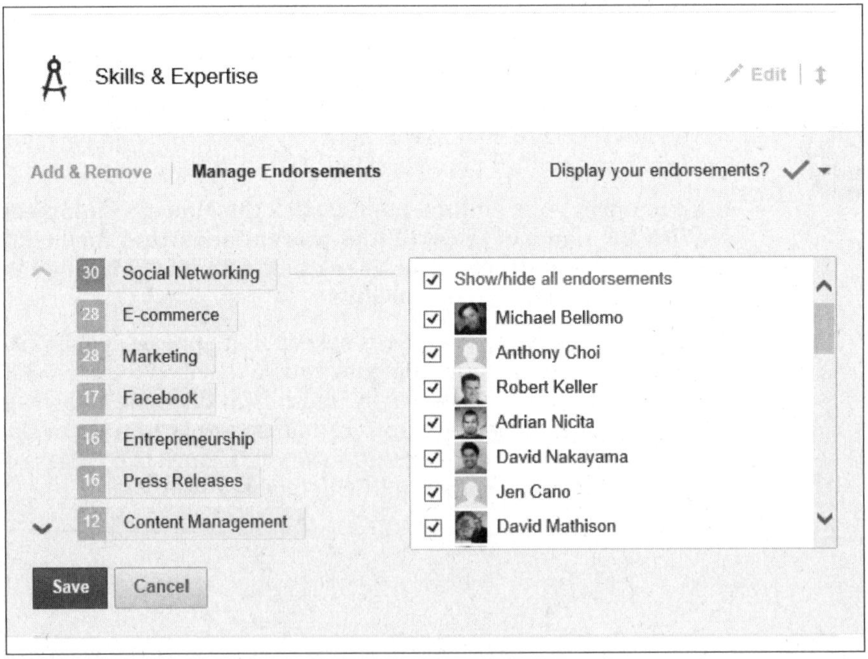

Figure 7-21:
You
can hide
someone's
skill
endorse-
ment from
appearing
on your
profile.

If you want to remove all the endorsements for any given skill, simply deselect the Show/Hide All Endorsements check box.

5. **Repeat Step 4 for any other endorsements you want to hide from your profile. When you're done, click the Save button to save your changes.**

After you finish with your changes, you see the Skills list again and the number of endorsements for your skills is updated based on the changes you made.

Part III
Growing and Managing Your Network

Joel Elad
Member since: May 12, 2006

Primary Email Change/Add
jolelad@yahoo.com

Payment
- Manage Billing Information
- View purchase history

InMails ?
15 available Purchase
Next grant: 5 credits on October 20, 2013

Password Change

Introductions ?
14 of 15 available Upgrade

OpenLink ?
Not accepting messages Change

Account Type: Job Seeker
- Premium features tour
- Compare account types
- Downgrade or cancel your premium account

Get More When You Upgrade!
- More communication options
- Enhanced search tools

Upgrade

Show more items

Profile

Communications

Groups, Companies & Applications

Account

Emails and Notifications
Set the frequency of emails
Set push notification settings

Member Communications
Select the types of messages you're willing to receive
Select who can send you invitations

LinkedIn Communications
Turn on/off invitations to participate in research
Turn on/off partner InMail

Learn how to interact with people through their status updates at www.dummies.com/extras/linkedin.

In this part...

- Learn the ins and outs of the LinkedIn Recommendations feature, which can help you earn trust and even find a new job.

- Stay up to date with all communications.

- Send and receive invitations.

- Integrate your LinkedIn activities with other programs, like your e-mail program or Internet browser.

Chapter 8

Exploring the Power of Recommendations

*E*ndorsements and testimonials have long been a mainstay of traditional marketing. But really, how much value is there in reading testimonials on someone's own Web site, like the following:

> *Maria is a great divorce attorney — I'd definitely use her again.*
>
> Elizabeth T. London

or

> *Jack is a fine lobbyist — a man of impeccable character.*
>
> Emanuel R. Seattle

Without knowing who these people are, anyone reading the testimonials tends to be highly skeptical about them. At the very least, the reader wants to know that they're real people who have some degree of accountability for those endorsements.

The reader is looking for something called *social validation*. Basically, that's just a fancy-shmancy term meaning that a person feels better about his decision to conduct business with someone if other people in his extended network are pleased with that person's work. The reader knows that people are putting their own reputations at stake, even if just to a small degree, by making a public recommendation of another person.

As this chapter shows you, the LinkedIn Recommendations feature offers you a powerful tool for finding out more about the people you're considering doing business with, as well as a means to build your own reputation in a way that's publicly visible. I walk you through all the steps needed to create a recommendation for someone else, request a recommendation for your profile, and manage your existing recommendations.

Understanding Recommendations

The LinkedIn Recommendation process starts in one of three ways:

✓ **Unsolicited:** When viewing the profile of any of your first-degree connections, a Recommend link is displayed when you click the drop-down arrow next to the Send a Message button in the middle of that person's profile, as shown in Figure 8-1. (For more information on connections, see Chapter 5.) By clicking that link, you can give an unsolicited recommendation.

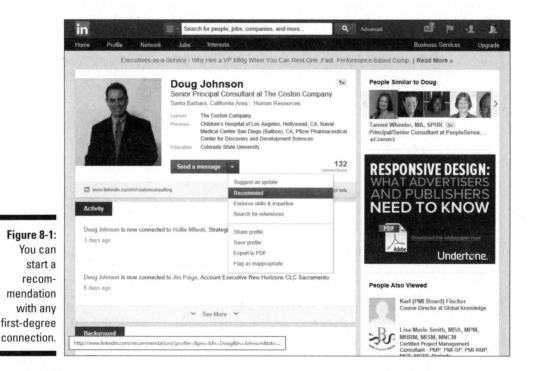

Figure 8-1: You can start a recommendation with any first-degree connection.

✔ **Requested:** You can request recommendations from your first-degree connections. You might send such a request at the end of a successful project, for example, or maybe ask for a recommendation from your boss before your transition to a new job.

✔ **Reciprocated:** Whenever you accept a recommendation from someone, LinkedIn gives you the option of recommending that person in return. Some people do this as a thank you for receiving the recommendation, other people reciprocate only because they didn't realize they could leave a recommendation until someone left them one, and some people don't feel comfortable reciprocating unless they truly believe the person deserves one. You decide in each circumstance whether to reciprocate, because there are circumstances where that might be awkward, such as if you get a recommendation from a supervisor or boss.

After the recommendation is written, it's not posted immediately. It goes to the recipient for review, and he has the option to accept it, reject it, or request a revision. So even though the majority of recommendations you see on LinkedIn are genuine, they're also almost entirely positive because they have to be accepted by the recipient.

LinkedIn shows all recommendations you've received as well as links to the profiles of the people who recommended you. (See Figure 8-2.) This provides that social validation you want by allowing people to see exactly who is endorsing you.

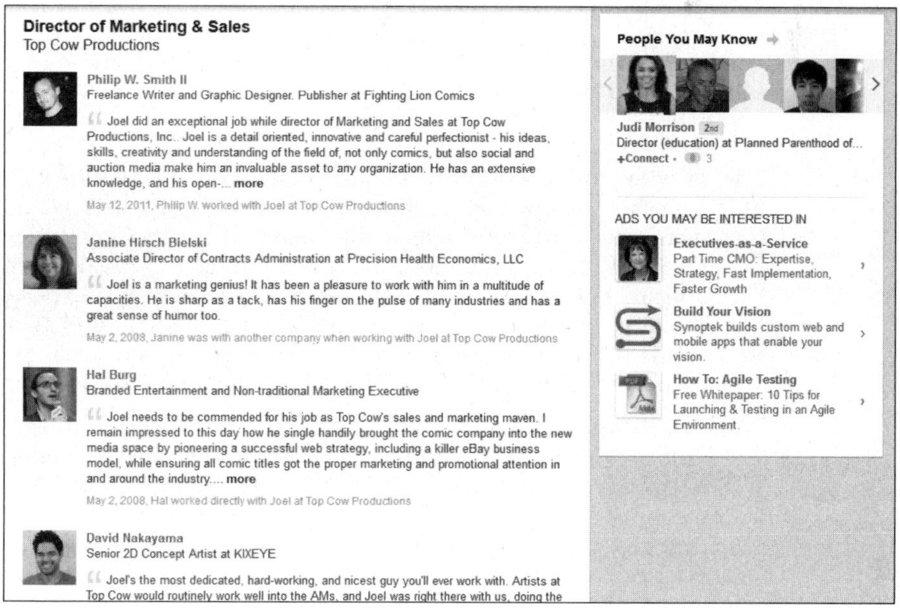

Director of Marketing & Sales
Top Cow Productions

Philip W. Smith II
Freelance Writer and Graphic Designer. Publisher at Fighting Lion Comics

❝ Joel did an exceptional job while director of Marketing and Sales at Top Cow Productions, Inc.. Joel is a detail oriented, innovative and careful perfectionist - his ideas, skills, creativity and understanding of the field of, not only comics, but also social and auction media make him an invaluable asset to any organization. He has an extensive knowledge, and his open-... **more**

May 12, 2011, Philip W. worked with Joel at Top Cow Productions

Janine Hirsch Bielski
Associate Director of Contracts Administration at Precision Health Economics, LLC

❝ Joel is a marketing genius! It has been a pleasure to work with him in a multitude of capacities. He is sharp as a tack, has his finger on the pulse of many industries and has a great sense of humor too.

May 2, 2008, Janine was with another company when working with Joel at Top Cow Productions

Hal Burg
Branded Entertainment and Non-traditional Marketing Executive

❝ Joel needs to be commended for his job as Top Cow's sales and marketing maven. I remain impressed to this day how he single handily brought the comic company into the new media space by pioneering a successful web strategy, including a killer eBay business model, while ensuring all comic titles got the proper marketing and promotional attention in and around the industry.... **more**

May 2, 2008, Hal worked directly with Joel at Top Cow Productions

David Nakayama
Senior 2D Concept Artist at KIXEYE

❝ Joel's the most dedicated, hard-working, and nicest guy you'll ever work with. Artists at Top Cow would routinely work well into the AMs, and Joel was right there with us, doing the

People You May Know

Judi Morrison 2nd
Director (education) at Planned Parenthood of...
+Connect · 3

ADS YOU MAY BE INTERESTED IN

Executives-as-a-Service
Part Time CMO: Expertise,
Strategy, Fast Implementation,
Faster Growth

Build Your Vision
Synoptek builds custom web and
mobile apps that enable your
vision.

How To: Agile Testing
Free Whitepaper: 10 Tips for
Launching & Testing in an Agile
Environment.

Figure 8-2:
Recommen-
dations
shown on a
profile page.

The quality of the recommendations matters as well as who they're from. Five very specific recommendations from actual clients talking about how you helped them solve a problem are worth more than 50 general recommendations from business acquaintances saying, "I like Sally — she's cool," or "Hector is a great networker." And any recommendations that heartily endorse the number of cocktails you had at the last formal event probably need revision. Check out the later section, "Gracefully Declining a Recommendation (Or a Request for One)," if you're receiving those kinds of statements.

Writing Recommendations

I suggest you practice making some recommendations before you start requesting them. Here's the method to my madness: When you know how to write a good recommendation yourself, you're in a better position to help others write good recommendations for you. And the easiest way to get recommendations is to give them. Every time you make a recommendation and the recipient accepts it, she is prompted to give you a recommendation. Thanks to the basic desire that most people want to be fair when dealing with their network, many people will go ahead and endorse you in return.

Choose wisely, grasshopper: Deciding who to recommend

Go through your contacts and make a list of the people you want to recommend. As you build your list, consider recommending the following types of contacts:

- ✔ **People you've worked with:** I'm not going to say that personal references are completely worthless, but standing next to specific recommendations from colleagues and clients, they tend to ring pretty hollow. Business recommendations are much stronger in the LinkedIn context. Your recommendation is rooted in actual side-by-side experience with the other party, you can be specific on the behavior and accomplishments of the other party, and the examples you give are most likely to be appreciated by the professional LinkedIn community at large.

- ✔ **People you know well:** You may choose to connect with casual acquaintances or even strangers, but reserve your personal recommendations for people you have an established relationship with (and by that, I mean friends and family). Remember, you're putting your own reputation on the line with that recommendation. Are you comfortable risking your rep on them?

Recommend only those people whose performance you're actually happy with. I can't say it enough: Your reputation is on the line. Recommending a real doofus just to get one recommendation in return isn't worth it! Here's a great question to ask yourself when deciding whether to recommend someone: Would you feel comfortable recommending this person to a best friend or family member? If not, well, then, you have your answer.

When you complete your To Be Recommended list, you're probably not going to do them all at once, so I suggest copying and pasting the names into a word processing document or spreadsheet so that you can keep track as you complete them.

Look right here: Making your recommendation stand out

Here are a few things to keep in mind when trying to make your recommendation stand out from the rest of the crowd:

- ✔ **Be specific.** Don't just say the person you're recommending is great: Talk about her specific strengths and skills. If you need help, ask the person you're recommending if there's any helpful elements they think you could highlight in your recommendation.

- ✔ **Talk about results.** Adjectives and descriptions are fluff. Clichés are also pretty useless. Tell what the person actually did and the effect it had on you and your business. It's one thing to say, "She has a great eye," and another to say, "The logo she designed for us has been instrumental in building our brand and received numerous positive comments from customers." Detailed results make a great impression, from the scope of difficulty of a project to the degree of challenge the person faced.

- ✔ **Tell how you know the person.** LinkedIn offers only the very basic categories of colleague, service provider, business partner, and student. If you've known this person for 10 years, say so. If she's your cousin, say so. If you've never met her in person, say so. Save it for the end, though. Open with the positive results this person provided, or the positive qualities the person exhibited in your interaction; then qualify the type of interaction.

- ✔ **Reinforce the requestor's major skills or goals.** Look at her profile. How is she trying to position herself now? What can you say in your recommendation that will support that? That will be far more appreciated by the recipient. For example, if you read her profile and see that she's really focusing on her project management skills as opposed to her earlier software development skills, your recommendation should reinforce *that* message because that's what she's trying to convey on her profile.

✔ **Don't gush.** By all means, if you think someone is fantastic, exceptional, extraordinary, or the best at what she does, say so. Just don't go on and on about it, and watch the overly clichéd adjectives.

✔ **Be concise.** Although LinkedIn has a 3,000-character limit on the length of recommendations, you shouldn't reach that limit. That should be more than enough to get your point across. Make it as long as it needs to be to say what you have to say, and no longer.

Don't be afraid to contact the requestor and ask for feedback on what you should highlight in your recommendation of that person. He knows his own brand better than anyone, so go right to the source!

Creating a recommendation

Now you're ready to write your first recommendation. To create a recommendation, first you need to pull up the person's profile:

1. **Hover your mouse over the Network link from the top navigation bar of any page and then click the Contacts link from the drop-down list that appears.**

2. **Select the person you're recommending from the connections list that appears.**

Your recommendation goes directly to that person, not prospective employers. Any prospective employer who wants a specific reference can request it through doing a reference search on LinkedIn, which I cover in greater detail in Chapter 11.

3. **Visit the profile of the person you want to recommend.**

Before you write up your recommendation, review the person's experience, summary, professional headline, and other elements of his profile. This helps you get a sense of what skills, attributes, or results should be reflected in your recommendation of that person. After all, if the person you want to recommend is trying to build a career as a finance executive, your recommendation will serve him better if you focus on finance instead of his event planning or writing skills, for example.

After you inform yourself a bit more about the person you're going to recommend and have thought about what you are going to say, you can get your recommending groove on. Follow these steps:

1. **Click the drop-down arrow next to the Send a Message button in the middle of his profile page, and then click the Recommend link from the drop-down list that appears.**

2. Select a category for that person.

As soon as you click the Recommend link, you're prompted to choose an option describing how you know this person, as shown in Figure 8-3.

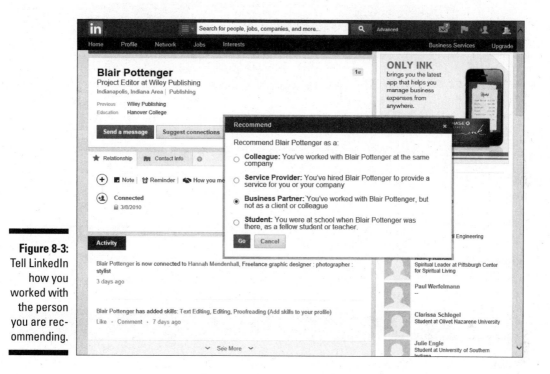

Figure 8-3:
Tell LinkedIn how you worked with the person you are recommending.

Your four choices are

- *Colleague:* You worked together at the same company. This also includes situations where you or the other person was the boss.

- *Service Provider:* You hired the person to provide a service to you or your company.

- *Business Partner:* You worked with the person but not as a client or colleague. (Of course, common usage of "business partner" traditionally means that you're partners in a business together, but that isn't what this means. If you work in the same company as the other party, choose Colleague, even if you're both owners and not manager or employee.)

- *Student:* You went to school with the person, either as a fellow student or as a teacher.

As of this writing, there is no option for a personal relationship nor for you being a service provider to the person. In these cases, I recommend that you select Business Partner.

3. **Click the Go button.**

   The Create Your Recommendation page appears, as shown in Figure 8-4.

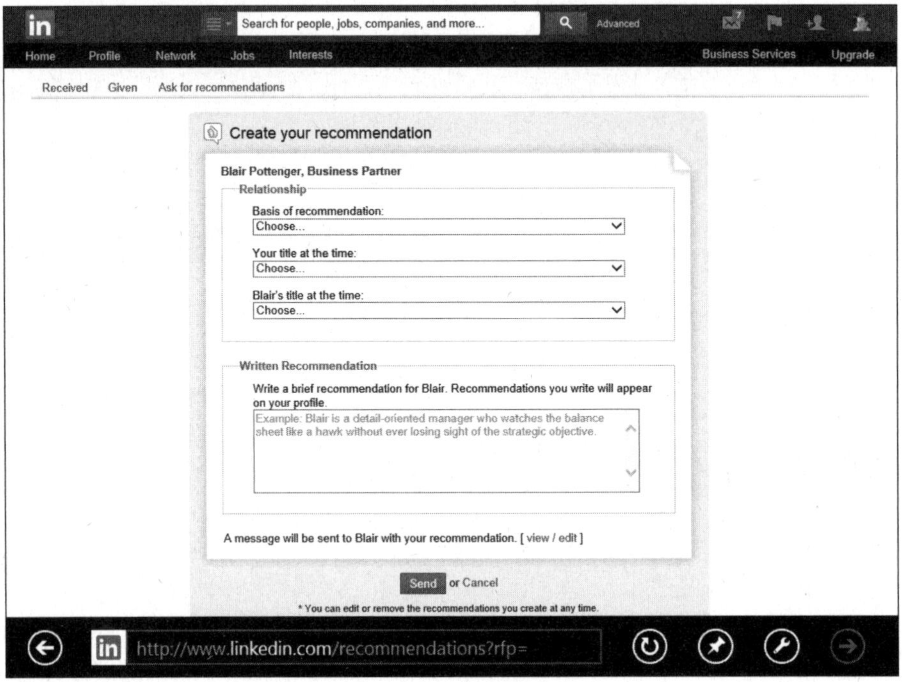

Figure 8-4:
Create your recommen-
dation here.

4. **Define your relationship with the person you're recommending by answering a few questions.**

   Each of the three drop-down boxes asks you to pick an answer from a predefined list. Specifically, you will be asked to

   a. *Define the basis of the recommendation.*

      If you're a colleague of the person, LinkedIn wants to know whether you managed or worked side by side with the other party, or whether that person was the manager or senior official. If you're a business partner, LinkedIn wants to know whether you worked at a different company from the other person or whether the person was a client of yours.

   b. *Define your title at the time.*

      Identify which position you held when you worked with or knew the other person you're recommending. This list is generated from the positions you defined in your LinkedIn profile. If your experience overlaps multiple positions, pick the position that best defines your relationship with the other party.

c. *Define the other person's title at the time.*

You have to select at least one position that the other party held to associate the recommendation. You can enter only one recommendation per position, but you can recommend the other party on multiple positions.

By answering these questions, you inform anyone reading the recommendation about how you know the person you're recommending. Perhaps you were the person's manager at one time.

5. **Write the recommendation in the Written Recommendation field.**

In earlier chapters, I stress staying specific, concise, and professional while focusing on results and skills. Keep in mind that recommendations you write that end up getting accepted by the other party also appear in your own profile in a tab marked Recommendations. Believe it or not, people judge you by the comments you leave about others, not just what they say about you. So, read your recommendation before you post it and look for spelling or grammatical errors. (You may want to prepare your recommendation in a word processing program like Microsoft Word, use its Spelling & Grammar check, and then cut and paste your newly pristine prose into the Written Recommendation field.)

6. **(Optional) Include a note in the Personalize This Message text box.**

When you send your recommendation, you have the option to also attach a personal note. Simply click the View/Edit link next to the line `A message will be sent to Name with your recommendation.` If it's someone you're in recent contact with, the note is probably unnecessary — the endorsement should speak for itself. But if it's someone you haven't spoken to in a while, take advantage of the opportunity to reconnect with a brief note. (See Figure 8-5.) You can keep the boilerplate text, "I've written this recommendation of your work to share with other LinkedIn users," or you can write your own note, like I did in Figure 8-5. Let the person know why you are writing the recommendation, whether it's because you admire her work, enjoyed working with her, or wanted to recognize her for a job well done.

7. **Click Send.**

The recommendation is sent to the recipient.

After you send your recommendation, the other person has to accept it before it's posted. Don't take it personally if she doesn't post it, or at least not right away. After all, it's a gift, freely given. The primary value to *you* is in the gesture to the recipient, not the public visibility of your recommendation. And if she comes back with requested changes to the recommendation, by all means accommodate her as long as it's all true and you feel comfortable with it. It's a service to her, not you.

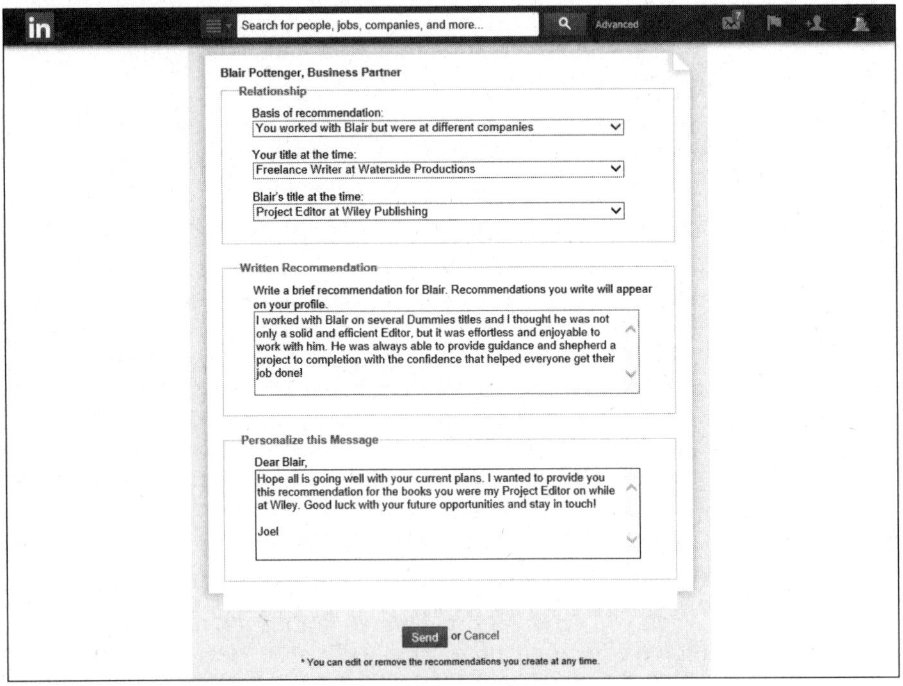

Figure 8-5:
Sending a personal note with a recommendation is a good idea.

Requesting Recommendations

In an ideal world, you'd never request a recommendation. Everyone who's had a positive experience working with you would just automatically post a raving recommendation on LinkedIn. But the reality is that most likely only your raving fans and very heavy LinkedIn users are going to make unsolicited recommendations. Your mildly happy customers, former bosses whose jokes you laughed at consistently, and co-workers who you haven't seen in five years could all stand a little prompting.

Be prepared, though: Some people feel that recommendations should only be given freely, and they may be taken aback by receiving a recommendation request. So it's imperative that you frame your request with a personal message, not just a generic message from LinkedIn.

Don't be afraid to consider off-line methods of requesting a recommendation, such as a phone call or a face-to-face meeting, to make the request more personal and more likely for the person to say yes.

Choosing who to request recommendations from

Request recommendations from the same people you might write them for: colleagues, business partners, and service providers. The only difference is that you're looking at it from his point of view.

Relationships aren't all symmetrical. For example, if someone hears me speak at a conference and buys this book, that person is my customer. My customers know my skills and expertise fairly well — perhaps not on the same level as a consulting client, but still well enough to make a recommendation. I, on the other hand, might not know a customer at all. I'm open to getting to know him, and I'm willing to connect, but I can't write a recommendation for him yet.

Creating a polite recommendation request

When you identify the person (or people) you want to write your recommendations, you're ready to create a recommendation request. To get started on authoring your request, follow these steps:

1. **Click the Profile link from the top navigation bar to bring up your profile. Click the drop-down arrow next to the Edit button (in your Summary box) and click the Ask to Be Recommended link.**

2. **After the Ask for Recommendations page loads, click the drop-down arrow (right there at Step 1 — see Figure 8-6) to choose what you want to be recommended for from the list provided.**

   LinkedIn ties this recommendation to a particular position or school attended from your profile, so you need to select the position (or school you were attending) where the recommender observed you and is providing his recommendation.

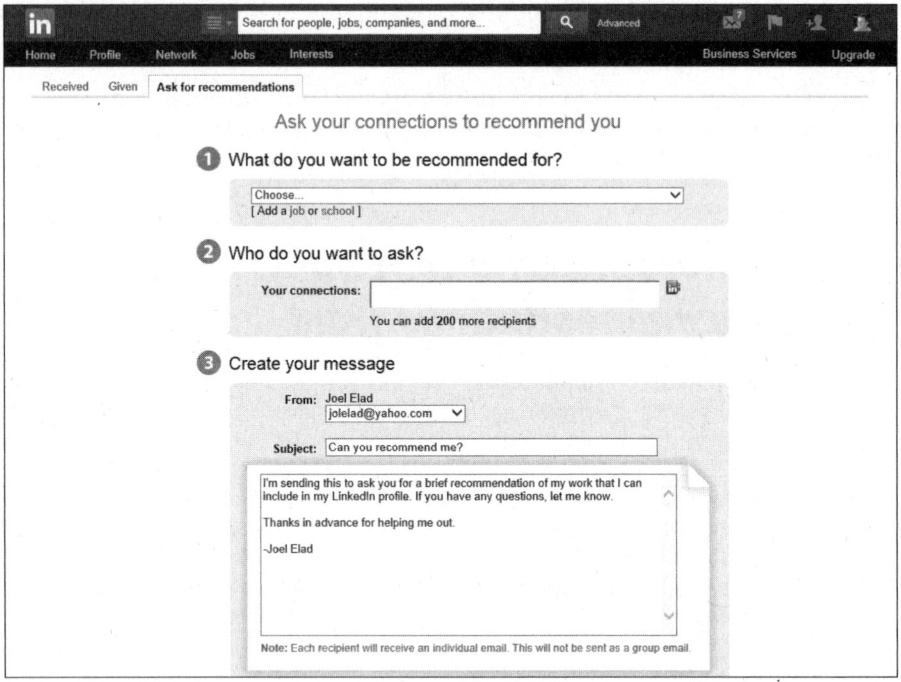

Figure 8-6:
Select the position to be associated with your requested recommendation.

The figure shows a LinkedIn screen:

Search for people, jobs, companies, and more... | Advanced | Business Services | Upgrade

Home Profile Network Jobs Interests

Received Given **Ask for recommendations**

Ask your connections to recommend you

1. What do you want to be recommended for?

Choose...
[Add a job or school]

2. Who do you want to ask?

Your connections:
You can add 200 more recipients

3. Create your message

From: Joel Elad
jolelad@yahoo.com

Subject: Can you recommend me?

I'm sending this to ask you for a brief recommendation of my work that I can include in my LinkedIn profile. If you have any questions, let me know.

Thanks in advance for helping me out.

-Joel Elad

Note: Each recipient will receive an individual email. This will not be sent as a group email.

3. **Under the Who do you want to ask? header, type the name of the person you want to request a recommendation from into the Your Connections text field.**

You can add the names of up to 200 people in this text field, and all will get a recommendation request.

If you click the little blue In icon to the right of the text box, LinkedIn opens up a new window containing the list of your connections, which you can select by selecting the check box next to someone's name in the window.

As you start typing the name of the person, you should see that name pop up, as shown in Figure 8-7. Clicking the name adds it to the list of names visible in the Your Connections field. You can now type in another name if you would like to send this recommendation request to more than one person.

4. **Type your message in the field provided, as shown in Figure 8-8.**

The same etiquette is recommended here as in other requests: Don't just accept the boilerplate text that LinkedIn fills in, but rather customize it to create a personal note, like I did in Figure 8-8. You can customize not only the body of your message, but the subject line as well.

Don't forget to thank the person for the time and the effort in leaving you a recommendation!

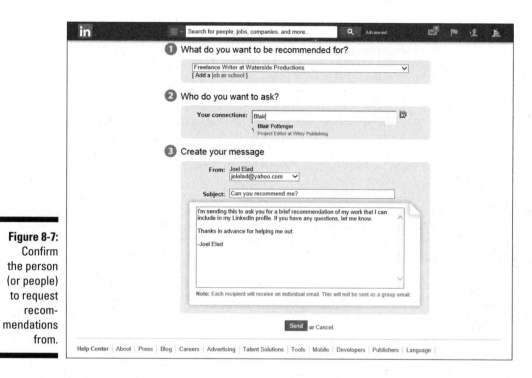

Figure 8-7:
Confirm the person (or people) to request recommendations from.

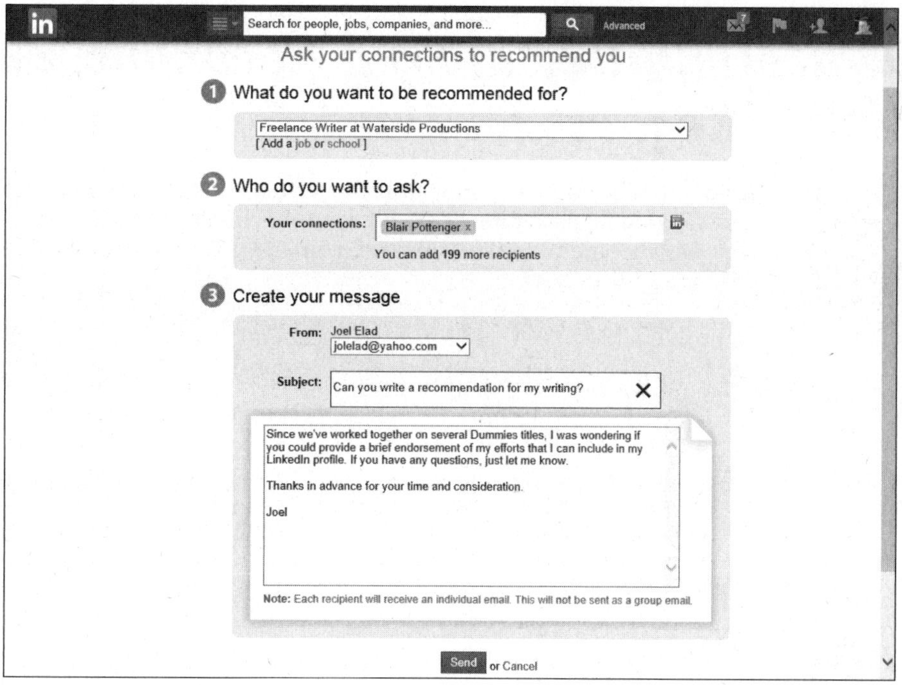

Figure 8-8:
A customized recommendation request.

5. **Check your spelling and grammar.**

   You can write your message first using a program like Microsoft Word, run the Spelling & Grammar check, then cut and paste your message into the space provided, if you like.

6. **Click Send.**

   The recommendation request is sent to the intended recipient.

Giving people some context as to why you're making the request helps motivate them more effectively, especially if they're nervous or unaware about how to use LinkedIn. Let them know you're available for any technical or follow-up help. Also, even though you should be asking only people who would be comfortable recommending you (you are, aren't you?), you still want to give them a gracious way to decline. After all, you're asking a favor. The person you're contacting is in no way obligated, so don't expect anything, and you won't be disappointed.

There's really no such thing as too many recommendations as long as the quality is good. Once you start accepting mediocre recommendations, though, on the assumption that "something is better than nothing," people will start to think that a lot of them are fluff. LinkedIn doesn't give you control over the display order, either, so you have all the more reason to make sure the recommendations displayed are good quality.

Gracefully Declining a Recommendation (Or a Request for One)

Unfortunately, not everyone naturally writes good recommendations, and all your LinkedIn connections haven't read this book, so it's bound to happen eventually: Someone will write a recommendation that you don't want to show on your profile.

No problem. Just politely request a replacement when you receive it. Thank him for thinking of you, and give him the context of what you're trying to accomplish:

Wei:

Thank you so much for your gracious recommendation. I'd like to ask a small favor, though. I'm really trying to position myself more as a public speaker in the widget industry, rather than as a gadget trainer. Since you've heard me speak on the topic, if you could gear your recommendation more toward that, I'd greatly appreciate it.

Thanks,

Alexa

If he's sincerely trying to be of service to you, he should have no problem changing it. Just make sure you ask him for something based on your actual experience with him.

You may also receive a request for a recommendation from someone you don't feel comfortable recommending. If it's because she gave you poor service or was less than competent, you have to consider whether you should even be connected to her at all because, after all, LinkedIn is a business referral system. I discuss how to remove a connection in Chapter 6.

Perhaps you don't have sufficient experience with her services to provide her a recommendation. If that's the case, just reply to her request with an explanation:

Alexa:

I received your request for a recommendation. While I'm happy to be connected to you on LinkedIn, and look forward to getting to know you better, or even work together in the future, at this point in time I just don't feel like I have enough basis to give you a really substantive recommendation.

Once we've actually worked together on something successfully, I'll be more than happy to provide a recommendation.

Thanks,

Wei

Managing Recommendations

Relationships change over time. Sometimes they get better, occasionally they get worse, and sometimes they just change. As you get more recommendations, you might decide that you don't want to display them all, or that you would like some of them updated to support your current branding or initiatives.

Fortunately, neither the recommendation you give nor those you receive are etched in stone (or computer chips, as the case may be). You can edit or remove the recommendations you've written at any time, and you can hide or request revisions to those you receive.

Editing or removing recommendations you've made

To edit or remove a recommendation you've made, follow these steps:

1. **Hover your mouse over the Profile link from the top navigation bar and then choose Edit Profile from the Profile drop-down list that appears.**

2. **Scroll down to the Recommendations section and click the Edit (pencil icon) link.**

   Doing so brings up the Your Recommendations header along the right side of the page.

3. **Click the Manage Visibility link to bring up the Recommendations page. Then click the page's Given tab.**

   All the recommendations you've made are listed in reverse chronological order, as shown in Figure 8-9. You can narrow the list down by clicking the link for Colleagues, Service Providers, Business Partners, or Students below the Manage Recommendations You've Sent header.

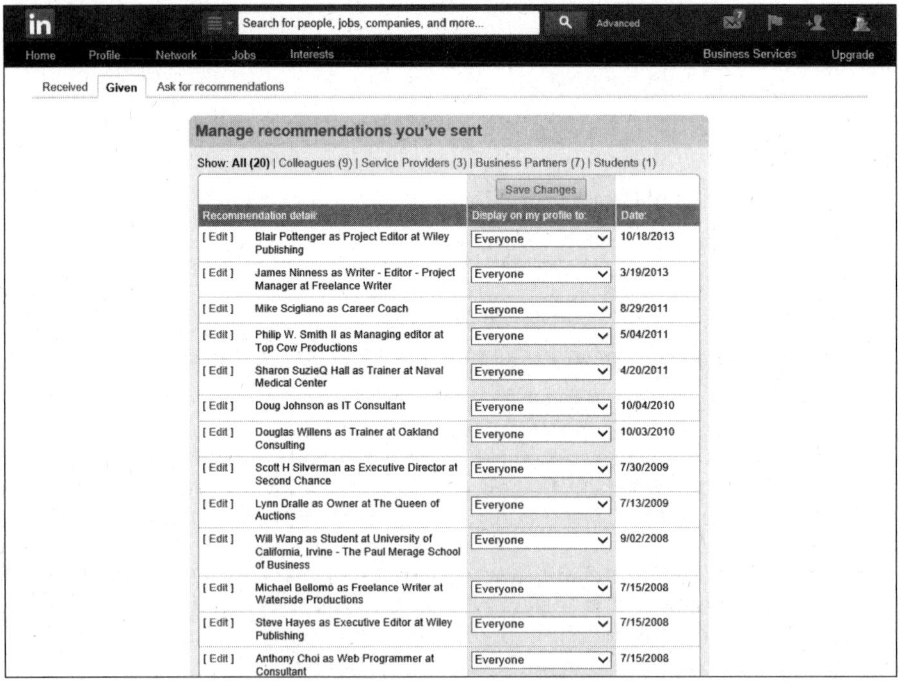

Figure 8-9: Pick the recommendation you want to edit or delete.

4. **Click the Edit link next to the recommendation you want to change or remove.**

You're taken to the Edit Your Recommendation screen, as shown in Figure 8-10.

- *Edit:* You can update some of the Relationship choices, such as Basis of Recommendation, or update your Written Recommendation text. When you're done, click Send at the bottom of the screen.

- *Remove:* Simply click the Withdraw This Recommendation link to ditch the recommendation completely. This link can be found at the top of the page, between the person's name and the Relationship header.

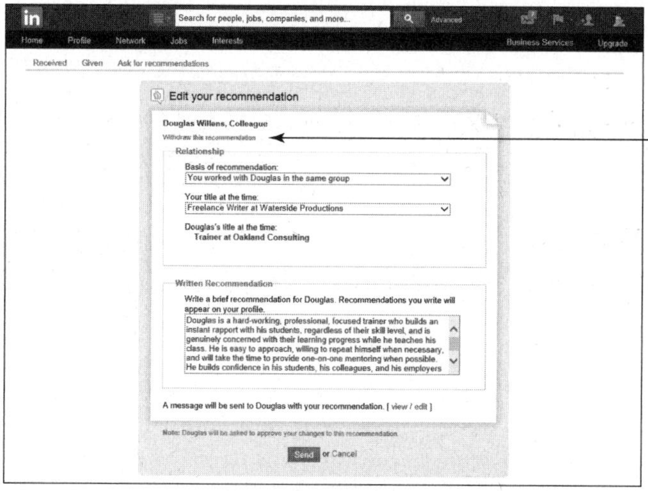

Figure 8-10: Make changes to your recommendation or withdraw it altogether.

Withdraw This Recommendation link

An edited recommendation is submitted to the recipient again for approval. If you remove it, it comes off immediately, and the recipient (or is that the *un*recipient?) doesn't receive any notification.

You can change the Basis of Recommendation field, which describes the exact relationship, such as whether you worked in the same department, or one of you was subordinate to the other. However, you can't change the type of recommendation; for example, Colleague versus Service Provider versus Business Partner. If you need to do so, you have to remove the current recommendation and write a new one, choosing the appropriate option.

Handling new recommendations you've received

Every time you receive a recommendation from someone else, you see a message in your LinkedIn Inbox, as shown in Figure 8-11.

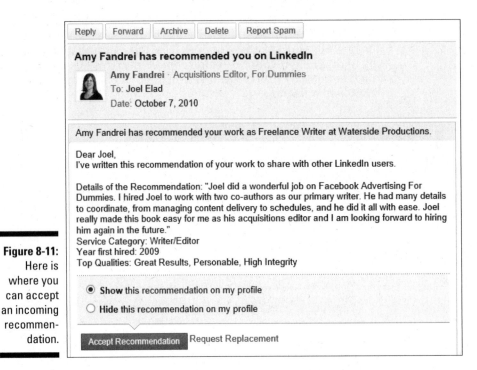

Reply | Forward | Archive | Delete | Report Spam

Amy Fandrei has recommended you on LinkedIn

Amy Fandrei · Acquisitions Editor, For Dummies
To: Joel Elad
Date: October 7, 2010

Amy Fandrei has recommended your work as Freelance Writer at Waterside Productions.

Dear Joel,
I've written this recommendation of your work to share with other LinkedIn users.

Details of the Recommendation: "Joel did a wonderful job on Facebook Advertising For Dummies. I hired Joel to work with two co-authors as our primary writer. He had many details to coordinate, from managing content delivery to schedules, and he did it all with ease. Joel really made this book easy for me as his acquisitions editor and I am looking forward to hiring him again in the future."
Service Category: Writer/Editor
Year first hired: 2009
Top Qualities: Great Results, Personable, High Integrity

⦿ **Show** this recommendation on my profile
○ **Hide** this recommendation on my profile

[Accept Recommendation] Request Replacement

Figure 8-11: Here is where you can accept an incoming recommendation.

When you receive a recommendation, you have these options:

- ✔ **Accept and show it on your profile.** Click the Accept Recommendation button but also make sure the Show This Recommendation on My Profile option is selected.

- ✔ **Accept and hide it.** You might choose this option if you don't want to decline the person's recommendation, but for some reason you don't want to display it (see the following section). Here, just make sure the Hide This Recommendation option is selected before you click the Accept Recommendation button.

✔ **Request replacement.** If you aren't completely happy with the person's recommendation, click the Request Replacement link to be given the opportunity to send him a brief note explaining what you would like changed.

✔ **Archive it.** This removes the recommendation message from your LinkedIn Inbox. It is available for later retrieval, just not as easily as if you choose the Hide option. You simply have to click the Show Archived Messages link when looking at your LinkedIn Inbox for recommendations; I cover the Inbox in detail in Chapter 10.

Removing a recommendation or requesting a revision

To remove a recommendation you've received or to request a revision, here's what you do:

1. **Hover your mouse over the Profile link from the top navigation bar and then choose Edit Profile from the menu that appears.**

2. **Scroll down to the Recommendations section and click the Edit link. When the Your Recommendations header appears on the right side of the screen, click the Manage Visibility link underneath that header.**

   Doing so takes you to the Manage Recommendations You've Received page, as shown in Figure 8-12.

3. **Pick the position from your Experience list that the recommendation is tied to, and click the Manage link below that title to bring up all the recommendations for that position, as shown in Figure 8-13.**

4. **To remove a recommendation, deselect the Show check box. Then scroll down and click the Save Changes button to hide your recommendation.**

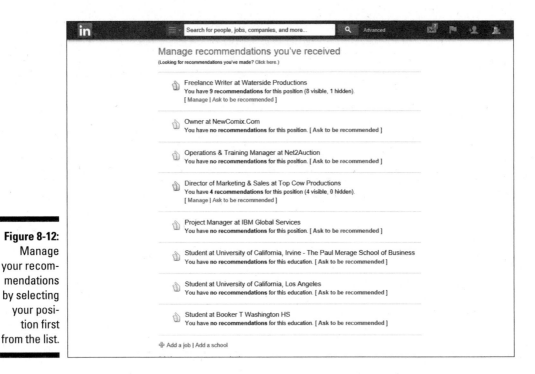

Figure 8-12:
Manage your recommendations by selecting your position first from the list.

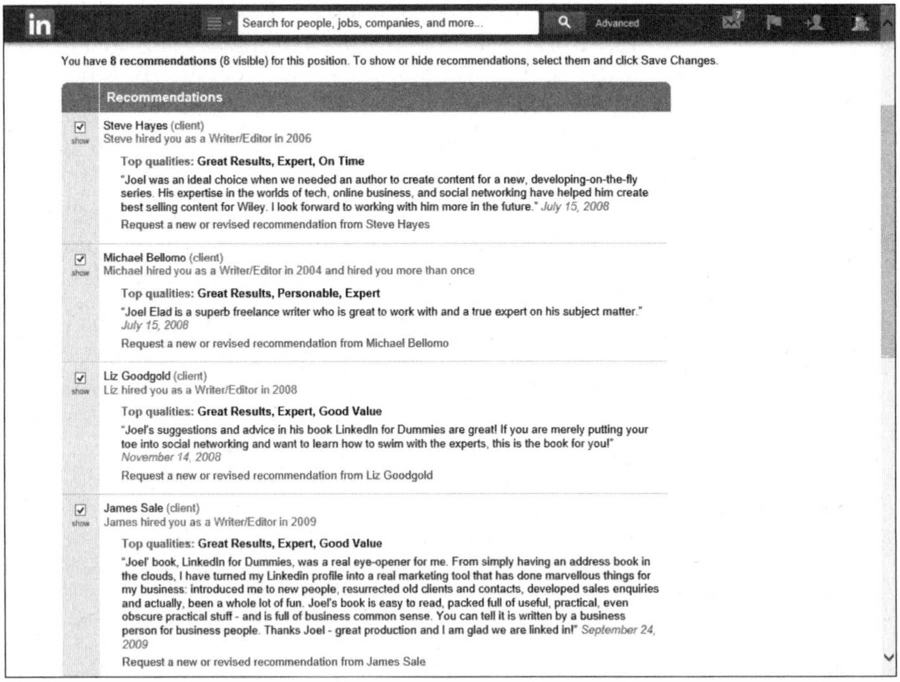

Figure 8-13:
Remove a recommendation or request a revision here.

5. **To request a new or revised recommendation, click the Request a New or Revised Recommendation From *Name* link.**

   This takes you back to the Request Recommendation screen (which I cover in the earlier section, "Creating a polite recommendation request"), where you should write a brief note explaining why you're requesting a change.

6. **Click Send.**

Negotiating the social graces around recommendations might feel a little awkward at first, but with some practice, you'll quickly become comfortable. By both giving and receiving good recommendations, you'll build your public reputation, increase your social capital with your connections, and have a good excuse for renewing some of your relationships with people you haven't contacted recently.

Chapter 9

Keeping Track of Your LinkedIn Activities

● ●

In This Chapter

▶ Using LinkedIn as your command console

▶ Reading your network updates

▶ Understanding your Inbox

▶ Tracking InMail and introductions

▶ Tracking sent and received invitations

● ●

I talk a lot about the different functions available on LinkedIn for you to use, and hopefully you've started to set aside some time on a regular basis to keep track of various tasks as you build up your profile and network. Because of the growing number of functions available on LinkedIn, you should take a look around the site to see how you can manage this new set of tasks most effectively.

In this chapter, I detail the different ways you can access the LinkedIn functions as well as how you can keep track of incoming mail, invitations, and other messages that require your input or approval. I discuss the functions that you can access from the top navigation bar on the LinkedIn home page. I also discuss the LinkedIn Inbox, where all your messages, invitations, answers, and communication are received. Then, I go over some ways you can set up LinkedIn to communicate with you through e-mail and keep you informed of communication from other LinkedIn users, whether those are Invitations, Introductions, Recommendations, Answers, or other LinkedIn functions.

Using the LinkedIn Home Page as Your Command Console

The LinkedIn home page is, by default, full of information about how you use the site. Think of the home page as your command console for working with LinkedIn. You can get to the home page at any time by clicking the LinkedIn logo or the Home link in the top-left corner of every LinkedIn Web page. The home page holds a variety of information. Of course, your home page is unique to your LinkedIn identity, so it will look different from mine (shown in Figure 9-1) or any other user on LinkedIn. And remember that your home page is based on the first-degree connections in your network, the pending messages in your Inbox, and the level of participation with functions, such as LinkedIn Groups or Recommendations, or applications like SlideShare or the Amazon Reading List.

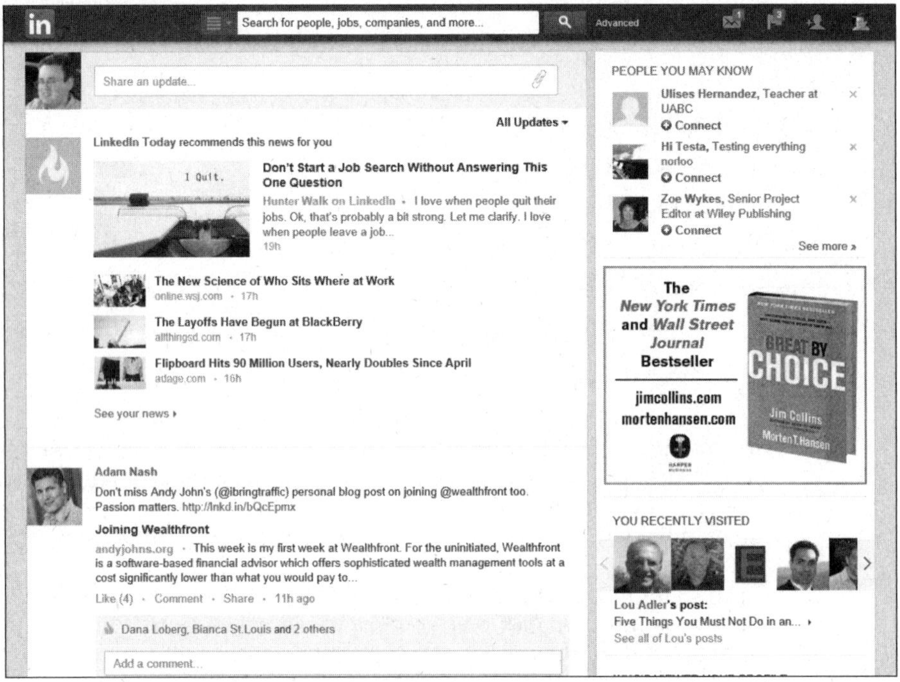

Figure 9-1:
Coordinate all your LinkedIn activities through the home page.

First off, check out the menu along the top of the site. As I mention in Chapter 1, I refer to this menu as the top navigation bar. This bar has all the major categories for checking your activities on LinkedIn. Just hover your mouse over each function to expand the menu item to see more options. Figure 9-2 shows an expanded Interests menu.

The number of unanswered messages or invitations in your Inbox is shown in an orange box next to the Inbox menu option, along the top right of the page. Just hover your mouse over the Inbox link and click a category to go straight to the Inbox. To the right of the Inbox link is a notifications flag, and the number of new notification items is shown in an orange box next to that flag, similar to other social media sites such as Facebook.

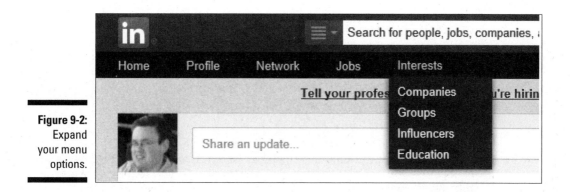

Figure 9-2:
Expand
your menu
options.

Scroll down your LinkedIn home page to see modules of other aspects of LinkedIn, such as LinkedIn Pulse, Jobs, and Network Activity. Based on your profile, positions, and whether you participate in functions like LinkedIn Groups, the site provides a default configuration for your home page and includes the modules it thinks are most useful to you. When you want to change any of the settings of your account, simply hover your mouse over your photo (in the top-right corner of the screen) and click the Review Privacy & Settings link to bring up your settings page, as shown in Figure 9-3. Later on this chapter, I discuss the different categories on this page.

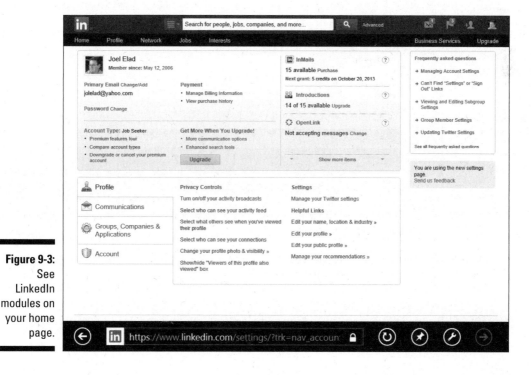

Figure 9-3:
See
LinkedIn
modules on
your home
page.

Reading your network activity

One way to stay involved with your LinkedIn network is to keep up to date on how your first-degree connections are using LinkedIn. (For more on connection degrees, see Chapter 1.) To that end, the Network Activity section (now called LinkedIn Pulse) summarizes all the activity within your immediate LinkedIn network.

Figure 9-3 gives you an idea of what this Network Activity section can contain. (Typically, it contains the most recent 25 items. I discuss how to change the number of items in a few paragraphs.) If you're looking at the Network Activity section of your LinkedIn home page, you can click the All Updates link (these words are a link) to filter your items, as shown in Figure 9-4. You can pick a subcategory, such as Connections (to see who in your network has new connections), Shares (to see what information your connections are sharing with you), Profiles (to see what profile updates your connections are making), Groups (to see any group updates), Companies (to see any updates from companies you're following), Jobs (to see any updates or activities regarding your job search), or Your Updates (to see a list of the network updates you've made on LinkedIn).

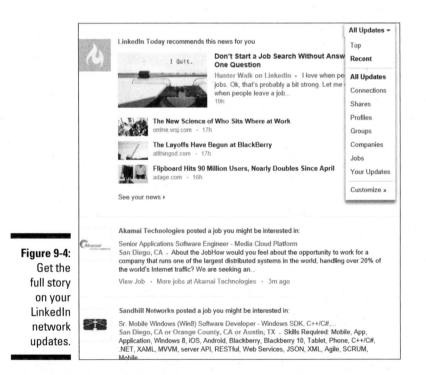

Figure 9-4: Get the full story on your LinkedIn network updates.

Because you can customize the network updates you see in your section, you need to decide which of the following events are worth keeping track of:

- ✔ Posts (status updates) shared from your first-degree connections
- ✔ Job opportunities
- ✔ Trending news
- ✔ Profile updates your connections make to their profiles
- ✔ New connections in your extended network (meaning any new connections your first-degree connections made)
- ✔ Updates from your extended network
- ✔ Updates from companies you are following
- ✔ Updates from any LinkedIn applications
- ✔ Groups that a first-degree connection of yours has joined
- ✔ Discussions from any of your LinkedIn groups

As a default, each of these categories is set up to show in your Network Activity section, and 25 updates appear on your home page. To customize the criteria of your Network Activity section, just follow these steps:

1. **Hover your mouse over the All Updates link in the top-right corner of the LinkedIn Pulse section of your page, then click the Customize link.**

   The Updates You See on Your Home Page pop-up window appears, as shown in Figure 9-5. By default, all the criteria shown on this page should be selected.

2. **To remove any criteria from the list, deselect the check box for that feature.**

   Additionally, you can change the number of network updates displayed on your home page by picking a number from the drop-down list near the bottom. (The default is 25; you can choose between 10 and 25.)

3. **Click the Save Changes button.**

   You're taken back to the Account & Settings page.

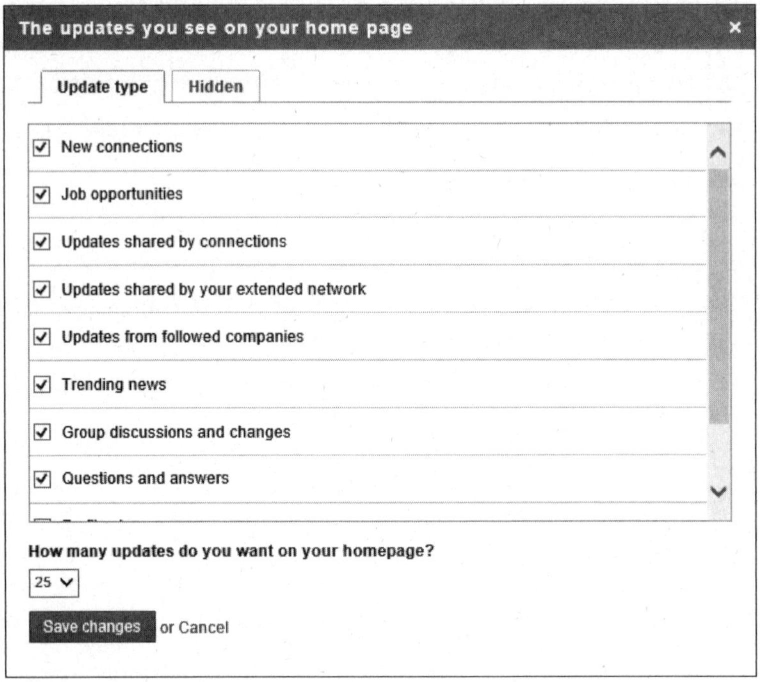

The updates you see on your home page ✕

| Update type | Hidden |

☑ New connections

☑ Job opportunities

☑ Updates shared by connections

☑ Updates shared by your extended network

☑ Updates from followed companies

☑ Trending news

☑ Group discussions and changes

☑ Questions and answers

How many updates do you want on your homepage?

25 ▼

Save changes or Cancel

Figure 9-5:
Decide what
network
updates you
want to see.

Having LinkedIn automatically contact you

Sure, you can do all the footwork by going to the LinkedIn home page and looking around to see what messages or changes have occurred. The true power of staying connected, however, is having LinkedIn automatically contact you with the information you need to stay informed.

As I mention in the preceding section, clicking the Review link next to Privacy & Settings (after hovering your mouse over your photo button from the home page) takes you to the settings page, which contains information about your account and your LinkedIn settings. Click the Communications header on the left side of the screen to bring up the Communications settings, as shown in Figure 9-6. This is your hub for controlling how you interact with LinkedIn and how the site communicates with you.

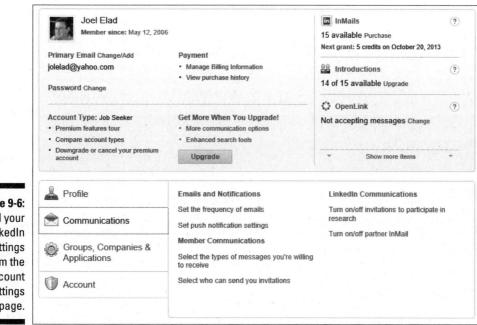

Figure 9-6:
Control your
LinkedIn
settings
from the
Account
& Settings
page.

Start by setting preferences in the Emails and Notifications section by deciding when LinkedIn should send you an e-mail to your e-mail account on file with LinkedIn:

1. **On the Account & Settings page, click the Set the Frequency of Emails link in the Emails and Notifications section.**

   You're taken to the Email Frequency page. For each section, like Messages from Other Members, click the pencil icon on the right side to expand the list of options, as shown in Figure 9-7.

2. **Review the list of options and decide how you want to receive your e-mails. Click the drop-down arrow for each row to select:**

   • *Individual Email:* As soon as something occurs in a given category, like introductions, invitations, or job notifications, LinkedIn sends you an e-mail with that one item in the e-mail.

   • *Weekly Digest Email or Daily Digest Email:* Instead of individual e-mails, LinkedIn groups activities in a given category and sends you one e-mail in a digest format, with a summary at the top of the e-mail and the detailed activities below the summary. Note that Daily Digests are for Group updates, while Weekly Digests are available for General and Group updates.

   • *No Email:* Turn off e-mail notification. You can read the message, though, when logged in to the LinkedIn site.

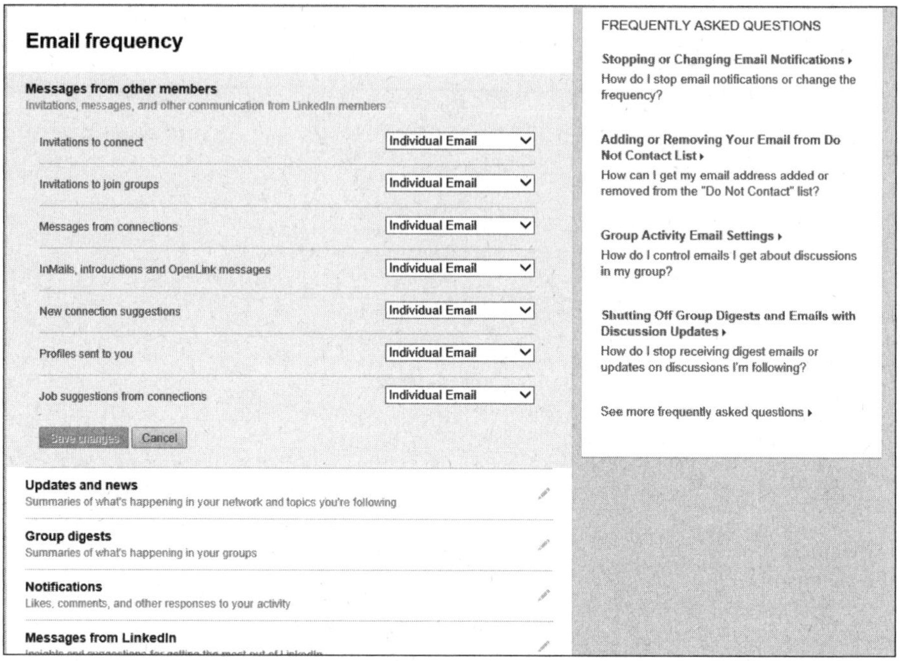

Email frequency

Messages from other members
Invitations, messages, and other communication from LinkedIn members

Invitations to connect   Individual Email

Invitations to join groups   Individual Email

Messages from connections   Individual Email

InMails, introductions and OpenLink messages   Individual Email

New connection suggestions   Individual Email

Profiles sent to you   Individual Email

Job suggestions from connections   Individual Email

Save changes   Cancel

Updates and news
Summaries of what's happening in your network and topics you're following

Group digests
Summaries of what's happening in your groups

Notifications
Likes, comments, and other responses to your activity

Messages from LinkedIn
Insights and suggestions for getting the most out of LinkedIn

FREQUENTLY ASKED QUESTIONS

Stopping or Changing Email Notifications ›
How do I stop email notifications or change the frequency?

Adding or Removing Your Email from Do Not Contact List ›
How can I get my email address added or removed from the "Do Not Contact" list?

Group Activity Email Settings ›
How do I control emails I get about discussions in my group?

Shutting Off Group Digests and Emails with Discussion Updates ›
How do I stop receiving digest emails or updates on discussions I'm following?

See more frequently asked questions ›

Figure 9-7:
Decide what e-mails you want to get from LinkedIn and how often.

3. **(Optional) Click the pencil icon next to the Messages from LinkedIn header, and select Individual Email for the Announcements, Tips, and Insights into New Products and Features option to receive information from LinkedIn.**

4. **Scroll down to the bottom of the page and click the Save Changes button.**

   You return to the Account & Settings page.

Understanding Your Inbox

The best hub for your communications is the LinkedIn Inbox, which you can access by clicking the Inbox link in the top navigation bar. In most cases, you go to the action items (or new messages that require your attention) in your Inbox, as shown in Figure 9-8.

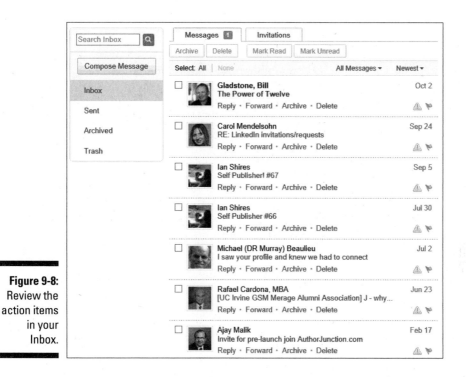

Figure 9-8:
Review the
action items
in your
Inbox.

Here are some things to keep in mind when navigating your Inbox:

- ✔ **Using the links on the left:** You can click any of the links along the left side to see your Inbox, sent items, archived items, or your trash.

- ✔ **Using the filters:** By default, when you're looking at your Inbox, you see all messages. If you click the drop-down arrow next to the All Messages heading (above your first item), you can pick a specific category (such as InMail, Introductions, Jobs, Unread Messages, Forwarded Profiles, or Recommendations).

- ✔ **Archiving:** After you read your message, you can archive the message for later viewing. However, unlike other e-mail systems, you can't (as of this writing) create your own folders within your LinkedIn Inbox. Instead, you simply archive a message into a general archive. From within the message, or in the list of messages in your Inbox, just click the Archive link to move the item from your Inbox to your Archived folder.

  To view your archived messages, click the Archived link on the left side of your screen when looking at your Inbox. Your archived messages appear in the same place where your Inbox messages appeared. You can also filter your archived messages the same way you filter your Inbox messages.

- ✔ **Deleting:** If you don't want to keep a message, click the Delete link.

Tracking Your InMail and Introductions

Although many of your communications with immediate first-degree LinkedIn connections take place through your own e-mail system, communications with people *outside* your network of first-degree connections need to be tracked and responded to via LinkedIn. So take a look at how you can track InMail and introductions through your LinkedIn Inbox.

To go directly to your list of InMail messages or introductions, click the InMail link or the Introductions link from the All Messages filter in your Inbox. For example, when I click the InMail link, I go to the InMails page shown in Figure 9-9. In addition, if you want to switch between received and sent InMails, click the Sent link and then filter all the Sent messages by using the All Messages filter to select only InMail.

Your Introductions message list uses a similar setup, like the one shown in Figure 9-10. The third introduction in this example, Michael Bellomo, has been accepted. The fourth introduction, from Jeremy Goldstone, has also been acted upon. You can tell because both items have a green arrow next to the subject line.

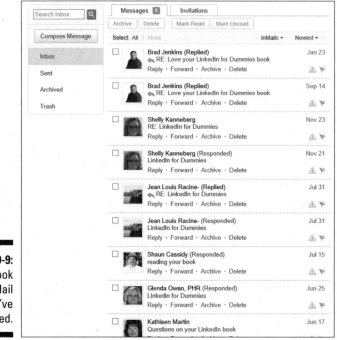

Figure 9-9:
Take a look at the InMail you've received.

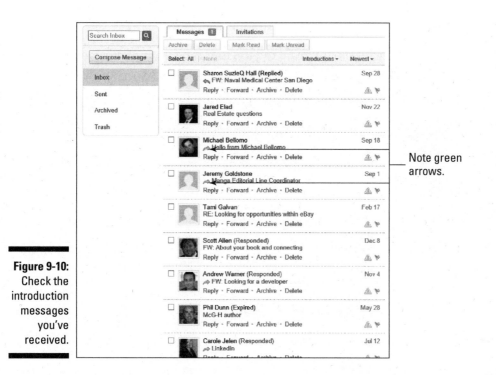

Note green arrows.

Figure 9-10:
Check the introduction messages you've received.

The process is similar for tracking any recommendations you've received. Turn to Chapter 8 for more info on recommendations.

Tracking Invitations

As you grow your network, you need to keep track of the invitations you sent to your connections as well as any incoming invitations. I cover invitations in Chapter 2, and I talk about setting up your notifications for receiving e-mail about invitations in the section "Having LinkedIn automatically contact you," earlier this chapter. The following sections tell you about monitoring your invitations on the LinkedIn Web site.

Tracking sent invitations

The last thing you want to do is send repeat invitations to the same person because you didn't monitor your sent invitations. Also, you might want to review your sent invitations to see whether someone has responded; if not, you can send that person a follow-up e-mail either through LinkedIn or via your own e-mail account. As of this writing, there is no running list, so you have to go through your Inbox to see which sent invitations have been accepted or not.

Here's how to track your sent invitations:

1. **Click the Inbox link from the top navigation bar of any LinkedIn page.**

   This opens the screen for viewing all your incoming messages and invitations, as shown in Figure 9-11.

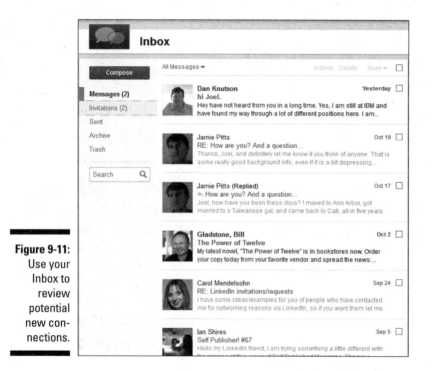

Figure 9-11:
Use your
Inbox to
review
potential
new con-
nections.

2. **Click the Sent link to pull up your sent invitations and messages.**

   You see the Sent page, as shown in Figure 9-12. The status of each invitation depends on whether (Accepted) appears next to each name. If so, that invitation was accepted. If not, the invitation has merely been sent. Be sure to ignore any messages that aren't related to an invitation.

3. **To view an invitation, click its Subject line.**

   You see a copy of your invitation, like the one shown in Figure 9-13. In this particular case, the Resend and Withdraw buttons appear because the recipient hasn't yet acted on the invitation.

   • *Resend:* Send a reminder to this person.

   • *Withdraw:* Delete your invitation request.

   When you withdraw the request, no message is sent to the other person.

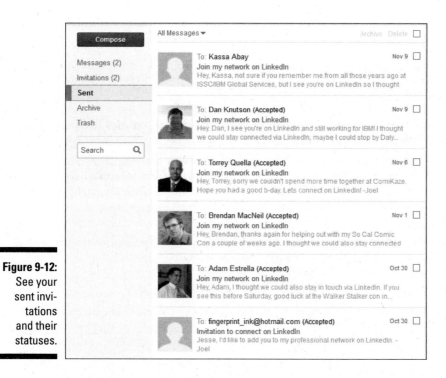

Figure 9-12:
See your sent invitations and their statuses.

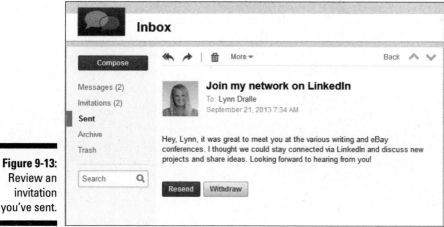

Figure 9-13:
Review an invitation you've sent.

Tracking received invitations

When growing your LinkedIn network, you should be responsive to others who want to add you to their LinkedIn connections lists. To review your received invitations, follow these steps:

1. **Click the Inbox link from the top navigation bar and then click the Invitations link on the left side of the screen.**

   You're taken to a list of your received invitations, as shown in Figure 9-14. You can hover your mouse over the person's name to see shared connections, and, with a click of the mouse, see his profile.

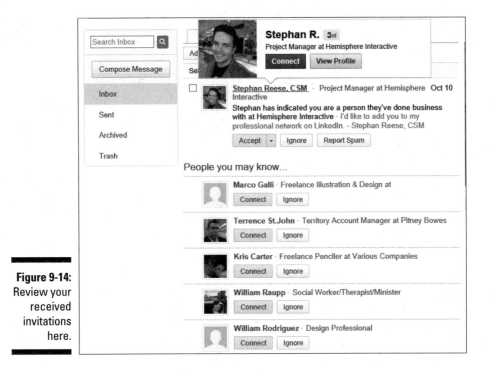

Figure 9-14: Review your received invitations here.

2. **To accept a pending invitation, click the Accept button.**

   If you want to reply to the person without immediately accepting that invitation (say, to get clarification in case you don't recognize the person), click the drop-down arrow next to the Accept button and then select Reply (Don't Accept Yet) to open a new message to that person. You can also click the Ignore button to remove this invitation from your Inbox. (See Chapter 6 for tips on growing your network.)

   After you click Accept, Reply, or Ignore, that invitation disappears from your view.

3. **Continue to act on each invitation in your list until there are no more new invitations.**

Chapter 10

Using LinkedIn with Your E-Mail and Browser

In This Chapter

▶ Importing contacts from Microsoft Outlook

▶ Importing contacts from a Web-based e-mail program

▶ Exporting your LinkedIn contacts to Outlook and other programs

▶ Enhancing your Outlook e-mail program with the LinkedIn Outlook Social Connector

▶ Creating e-mail signatures

*T*his chapter delves in to how you can use LinkedIn as a part of your over-all presence on the Internet, especially when it comes to communication. Specifically, I focus on two aspects of your Internet experience: your e-mail account with and without your Internet Web browser.

LinkedIn makes it convenient for you to exchange information between your e-mail program and your LinkedIn profile and to enhance your World Wide Web browsing experience with specialized LinkedIn functions. LinkedIn offers the capability to import your contacts list from programs such as Microsoft Outlook. You can also do the reverse: Export your LinkedIn contacts list to a variety of e-mail programs, including the Mail program that's part of Mac OS X. Other neat features in LinkedIn include a social Connector tool for use with Microsoft Outlook. For example, with the Outlook Social Connector, you can access certain LinkedIn information while writing e-mails in Outlook. I cover all these cool features in this chapter.

I also tell you about a nifty tool that LinkedIn offers to create an e-mail signature block for you that helps you promote your LinkedIn profile.

Importing Contacts into LinkedIn

One of the most popular (and necessary) activities people use the Internet for is e-mail. Your e-mail account contains a record of e-mail addresses of everyone you regularly communicate with via e-mail. And from your established base of communications, LinkedIn offers a way for you to ramp up your network by importing a list of contacts from your e-mail program. Importing your e-mail contacts into LinkedIn eliminates the drudgery of going through your address book and copying addresses into LinkedIn. The next sections show you how to generate a list of contacts and import that list into LinkedIn to update your connections.

Importing a contacts list from Outlook

Microsoft Outlook is one of the most popular e-mail programs out there. This section shows you how to import your Microsoft Outlook contacts list into LinkedIn. To do so, follow these steps:

1. **On the main Outlook screen, click Contacts to bring up your contacts list (similar to that shown in Figure 10-1).**

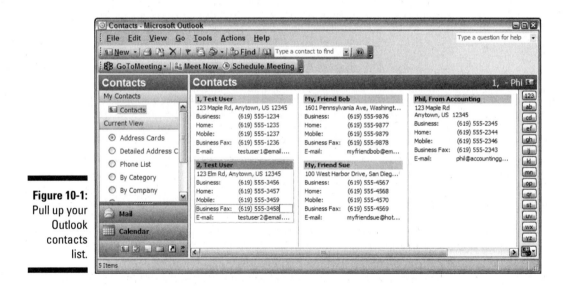

Figure 10-1:
Pull up your Outlook contacts list.

2. **Choose File⇨Import and Export.**

   The Import and Export window appears.

3. **Select the Export to a File option, click the Next button, and then select a file type in the Export to a File window.**

   You see a list of options, including Comma Separated Values (DOS), Comma Separated Values (Windows), Microsoft Access, and so on.

4. **Select the Comma Separated Values (Windows) option and then click Next.**

   The Export to a File window appears. Here, you're asked to pick a folder that you want to export, as shown in Figure 10-2. Look for the contacts folder, which contains your list of contacts through Microsoft Outlook.

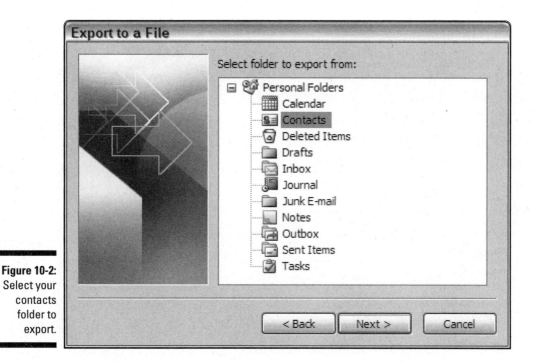

Figure 10-2:
Select your
contacts
folder to
export.

5. **Select the contacts folder to export and then click Next.**

If you created categories within your Outlook contacts list, you can select one of those subcategories under the main contacts folder and export just those contacts.

6. **In the next Export to a File window that appears, enter a suitable filename, click the Browse button to locate a folder for storing the new (exported) file, and then click Next.**

In the Export to a File window, Outlook displays the action it's about to take, as shown in Figure 10-3.

Note the filename and location of your exported contacts file because you need this information in a few steps. Pick a memorable name and save the file to a commonly used folder on your computer.

7. **Click Finish to start the export of your Outlook contacts file.**

Depending on the size of your contacts list, the export process might take a few minutes. When the export is complete, the status indicator disappears, and you're ready to go to the next step.

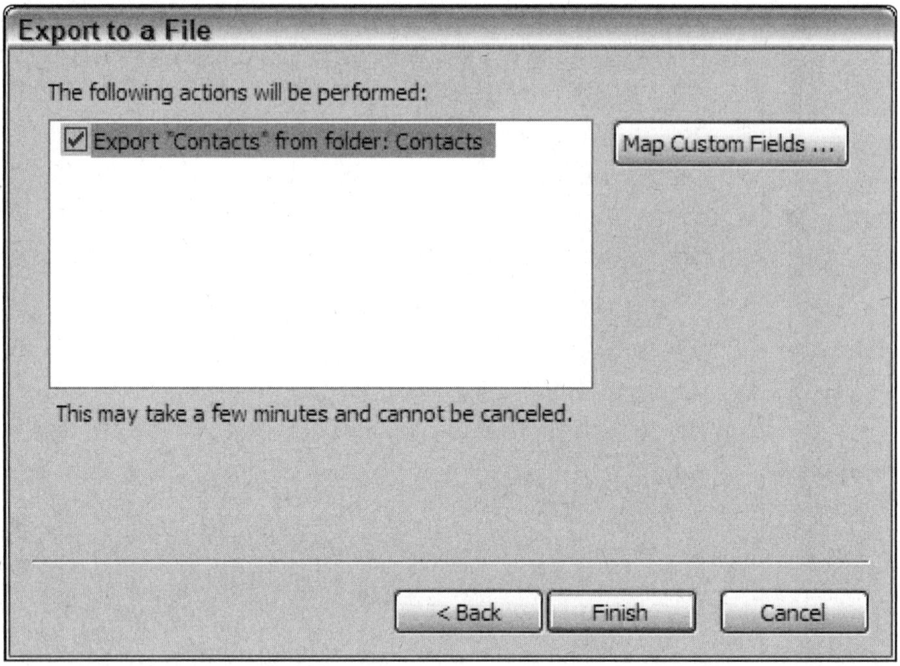

Export to a File

The following actions will be performed:

☑ Export "Contacts" from folder: Contacts | Map Custom Fields ... |

This may take a few minutes and cannot be canceled.

| < Back | Finish | Cancel |

Figure 10-3:
Outlook
verifies
the export
action.

8. **Using your Web browser, go to LinkedIn and log in to your account; then, on the top of the page, click the Network link, and then click the Add Connections link that appears from the drop-down list.**

9. **On the new page that appears, click the Any Mail button. When that page appears, look for the More Ways to Connect header and click the Upload Contacts File link.**

   The upload contacts instructions appears onscreen, as shown in Figure 10-4.

10. **Click the Browse button to locate the contacts file you just exported from Microsoft Outlook. When you locate that file, click the Upload File button to start the process.**

    After LinkedIn reads your entire contacts list, it displays the names of contacts from your list, as shown in Figure 10-5; and then, below those names where the person is already on LinkedIn, it shows how long they've been a member of LinkedIn.

    When LinkedIn imports the list, it usually drops the middle name from each person's full name when creating the imported contacts. You might need to edit your contacts to add the appropriate information.

11. **Review the names, deselect any check box for someone you don't wish to invite, and then click the Send Invitations button to complete the process.**

    If the names you see on the screen aren't correct (perhaps LinkedIn did not read the file properly and everyone's first and last names are reversed, for example), you can click Cancel to abandon the process.

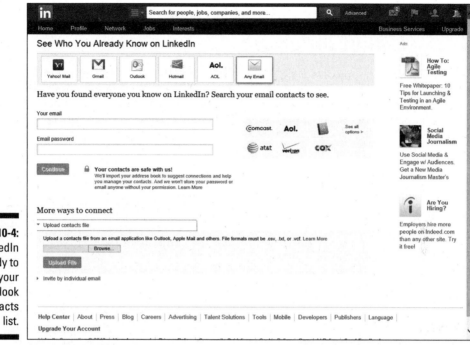

Figure 10-4:
LinkedIn
is ready to
accept your
Outlook
contacts
list.

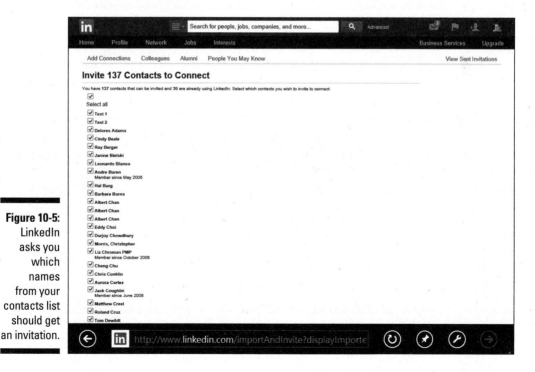

Figure 10-5:
LinkedIn
asks you
which
names
from your
contacts list
should get
an invitation.

Importing contacts from a Web-based e-mail program

Many people use a Web-based program (*Webmail*) to send and receive e-mail. Gmail (from Google), Yahoo! Mail, and Hotmail are among the most popular of these programs. Just like Outlook, you can import your Webmail program contacts list and feed it into LinkedIn to expand your network. For the example in this section, I use Yahoo! Mail, but the other systems work similarly for importing contacts.

To import a Webmail contacts list, just follow these steps:

1. **Using your Web browser, go to LinkedIn and log in to your account.**

2. **Click the Network link at the top of any LinkedIn page, and then click Add Connections from the drop-down list to bring up the Add Connections window.**

   The See Who You Already Know on LinkedIn page appears, as shown in Figure 10-6.

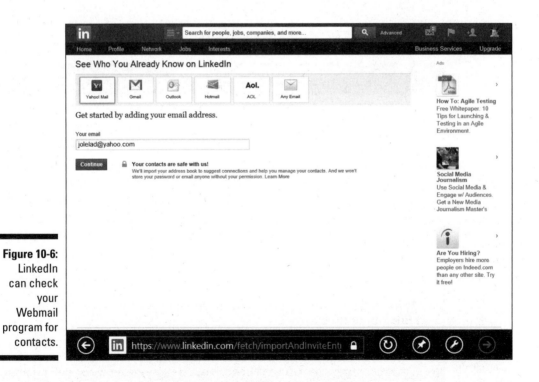

Figure 10-6: LinkedIn can check your Webmail program for contacts.

3. **Click the appropriate Webmail button, enter your e-mail address into the Email text box (and your password, when prompted), and then click the Continue button.**

   LinkedIn opens a new window in which you can connect with your Webmail program. (You are asked for your Webmail e-mail password, so LinkedIn can log in to your account for you.)

4. **Follow the instructions to access your Webmail account.**

   For this example, I used my Yahoo! account, which took me to the Yahoo! login screen. After I was logged in to my account, Yahoo! requested my permission to let LinkedIn access my Yahoo! contacts, as shown in Figure 10-7. You must click the Agree button if you want LinkedIn to import your contacts. After you do, LinkedIn automatically goes into the account and starts importing contacts, and you're returned to the LinkedIn Web site.

YAHOO!   Joel   Help

Click "Agree" to sign in to www.linkedin.com using your Yahoo! ID and allow sharing of Yahoo! info.

You are sharing the following:

joelelad@yahoo.com

You are authorizing access to:

Yahoo! Contacts

Agree

By clicking Agree you are agreeing to the Yahoo! Additional Terms of Service.

Copyright © 2013 Yahoo! Inc. All rights reserved.
Copyright/IP Policy | Terms of Service | Guide to Online Security | Privacy Policy

Figure 10-7: You need to allow LinkedIn to read your Webmail address book.

5. **Review the imported contacts and who you want to invite to your LinkedIn network.**

   LinkedIn may select all your contacts who aren't yet connected to you via LinkedIn and offer to send them an invitation, as shown in Figure 10-8. If that is the case, deselect the check box next to each person you don't want to invite. For some e-mail systems, you will see your imported contacts and have to manually select which contacts you want to invite by selecting the check box next to each person you want to invite. When you are ready, click the Add to Network button to send invitations to the contacts you wish to add to your network.

6. **When you're done, close the newly opened window that was created back in Step 3 when you started the import process.**

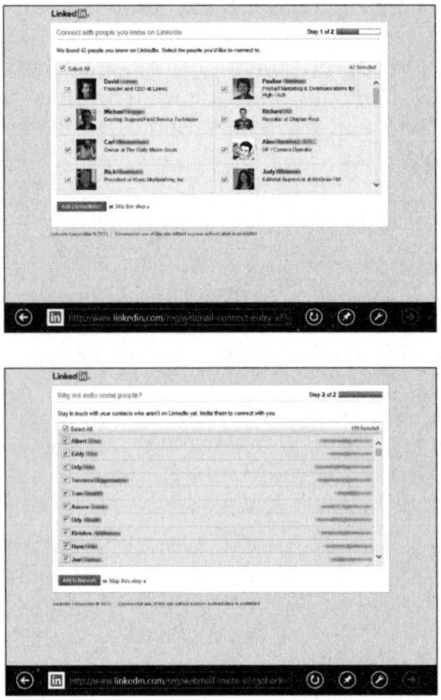

Figure 10-8:
From your imported address book, decide who gets invited to your network, or who gets invited to LinkedIn and then your network.

Exporting Contacts from LinkedIn to Your E-Mail Application

As you use LinkedIn and build up your contacts network, you might end up with more contacts "on file" in your LinkedIn network than stored away in your e-mail program. However, you may want to use your own e-mail system to communicate with all your LinkedIn first-degree connections instead of relying on LinkedIn's message system. Adding these people one by one to your e-mail address book could take a while. Thankfully, LinkedIn has a function to make this easier.

In essence, your list of LinkedIn connections is similar to a list of names in any e-mail program's address book. And just like you can import contacts from an e-mail program into LinkedIn, you can export your LinkedIn contacts to your e-mail program. Exporting is a simple process that amounts to the following:

1. You export your LinkedIn connections into a contacts file.

2. You import the contacts file into your main e-mail program.

You can always pick and choose which contacts to export, and your e-mail program should be able to detect any duplicates — meaning that if you try to import any names that already exist, you should get a warning message. I walk you through the process of exporting your LinkedIn contacts in the next few sections.

Creating your contacts export file in LinkedIn

First, you need to generate your exported file of contacts from LinkedIn. To do so, follow these steps:

1. **On any LinkedIn page, hover your mouse over the Network link in the top navigation bar, choose Contacts from the menu that appears, and then click the wheel icon to load the Settings page.**

2. **Click the Export LinkedIn Connections link.**

   You'll be taken to the Export LinkedIn Connections page, as shown in Figure 10-9. From the drop-down list provided, pick the e-mail program to which you want to export your contacts.

3. **Click the Export button to generate your contacts file.**

   First, you are asked to enter the text of a security image into the box provided. Then, the File dialog box appears, asking whether you want to open or save the file. Click Save to save the file to your computer. Give it a custom name, if you like, but remember the filename and location because you need that information when you load this file into your e-mail program, which I discuss in the next sections.

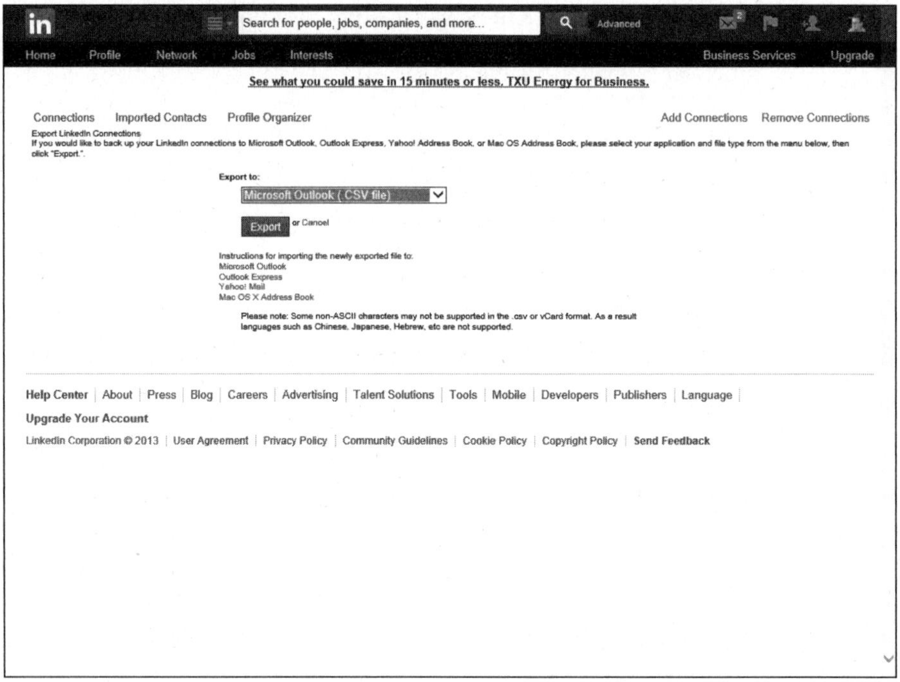

Figure 10-9:
Pick your
e-mail
program
and create
an exported
file of
contacts.

Exporting contacts to Outlook

Now that you've created your contacts file, it's time to import it into your e-mail program. For my first example, I'm going to use Microsoft Outlook, but the procedure is similar with other e-mail clients. The next few sections give you an idea of how to handle other e-mail clients.

After you create your LinkedIn export file and are ready to export your LinkedIn contacts to Microsoft Outlook, just follow these steps:

1. **On the main Outlook screen, choose File⇨Import and Export.**

   The Import and Export window appears.

2. **Select the Import from Another Program or File option and then click Next.**

3. **When Outlook asks you to select a file type to import from, select the Comma Separated Values (Windows) option and then click Next.**

4. **When Outlook asks you for the file to import, enter the path and file- name of your exported file, or click the Browse button to find the file on your computer. Be sure to select the Do Not Import Duplicate Items option and then click Next.**

If you don't select the Do Not Import Duplicate Items option, you risk flooding your Outlook account with multiple e-mail addresses and names for the same people, which will make your life more difficult and flood your connections with unnecessary e-mail messages.

5. **When Outlook asks you to select a destination folder, click the contacts folder and then click Next.**

6. **Verify that you're importing your contacts file into Outlook and then click Finish to start the process.**

Exporting contacts to Outlook Express

If you prefer Outlook Express to the full Outlook program, you're in luck: Your LinkedIn contacts can go live there just as easily as they can elsewhere. After you create your export file (as described earlier, in the "Creating your contacts export file in LinkedIn" section), you can export your connections to Outlook Express by following these steps:

1. **On your main Outlook Express screen, choose File⇨Import.**

2. **In the Import window that opens, select the Other Address Book option and then click Next.**

3. **When Outlook Express asks you to select a file type to import from, select the Text File (Comma Separated Values) option and then click the Import button.**

4. **When Outlook Express asks you for the file to import, enter the path and filename of your exported file, or click the Browse button to find the file on your computer. Click Next.**

5. **Verify the fields that you're importing into Outlook Express (click the Change Mapping button if you want to change how the information is being imported) and then click Finish to start the process.**

Exporting contacts to Yahoo! Mail

If you're using a Web-based mail program, like Yahoo! Mail, you can follow this basic procedure to export your LinkedIn contacts into your Webmail program. After you create your export file (as described earlier, in the

"Creating your contacts export file in LinkedIn" section), you can export your connections to Yahoo! Mail by following these steps:

1. **Using your Web browser, go to Yahoo! Mail and log in. Click the Contacts tab to go to the Yahoo! Contacts page.**

   You see a page similar to that shown in Figure 10-10.

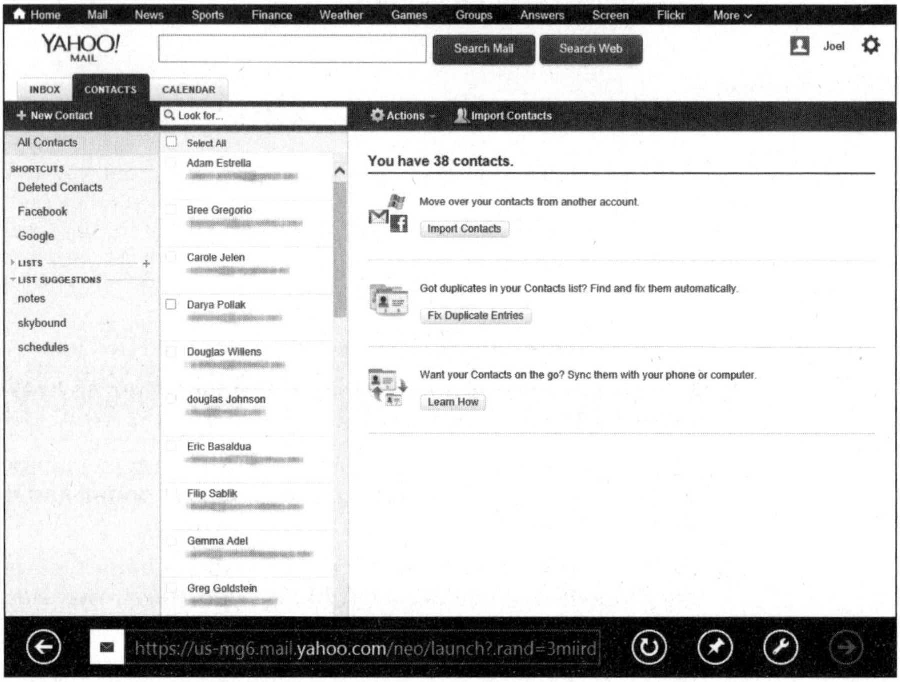

Figure 10-10: Start at your Yahoo! Contacts page.

2. **Click the Import Contacts button.**

   A new screen appears, as shown in Figure 10-11.

3. **Click the From File button.**

   The Upload from File screen appears.

4. **Click the Browse button to find the file on your computer, as shown in Figure 10-12.**

5. **Click the Upload button to send the LinkedIn contacts file to your Yahoo! account.**

On the next screen, you see a summary page of the number of contacts that were successfully imported or not imported, and the number of duplicate contacts that were found. Click the View Contacts button to see your new contacts list, or click the Done button to finish the process.

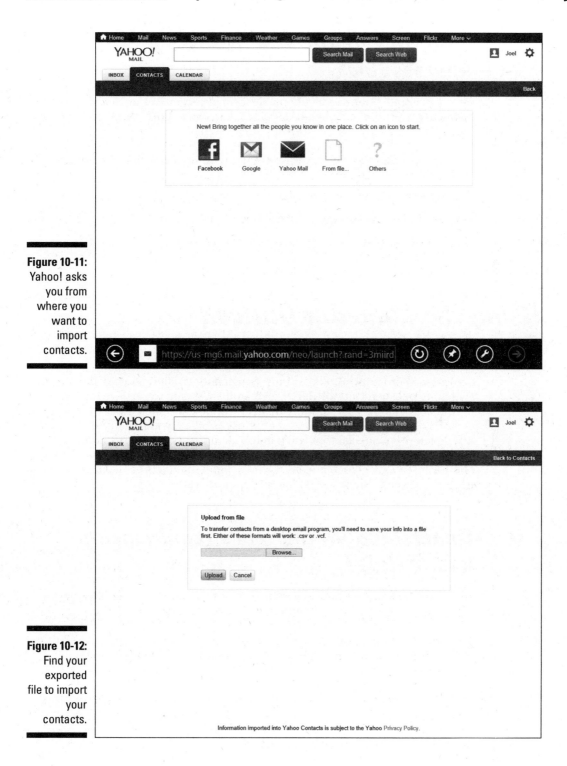

Figure 10-11:
Yahoo! asks you from where you want to import contacts.

Figure 10-12:
Find your exported file to import your contacts.

Exporting contacts to Mac OS X Address Book

After you create your export file (as described earlier, in the "Creating your contacts export file in LinkedIn" section), you can export your connections to Mac OS X Address Book by following these steps:

1. **Locate your Mac OS X Address Book icon in either the Dock or the Applications folder.**

2. **Look for the contacts file you created in the previous section.**

3. **Drag this file onto the Address Book icon.**

   This should start the importing of contacts from your LinkedIn contacts file.

Using the LinkedIn Outlook Social Connector

If you use Microsoft Outlook for your e-mail and you find yourself constantly switching between Outlook and the LinkedIn Web site to retrieve information, send e-mail to your connections via Outlook and then screen incoming e-mail by jumping to LinkedIn to read those profiles, you're in luck! LinkedIn has developed a special tool you can install in your system that automatically ties into its Web site. This Social Connector tool appears as part of your Microsoft Outlook screen and gives you several functions to make the connection between Outlook and LinkedIn smoother.

Understanding the tool's requirements and features

To use the LinkedIn Outlook Social Connector tool, you need to have certain levels of software on your computer for the tool to work correctly:

✔ Your operating system needs to be either Microsoft Windows 7, XP or Vista for the 32-bit version, or Windows 8 for the 64-bit version.

✔ Your Microsoft Outlook program should be the 2003, 2007, or 2010 version.

✔ You should have at least 5–10MB of free space on your hard drive before installing this program.

Here are the main benefits you can enjoy after installing this function:

✔ **It suggests sending an invitation to someone to join your network based on the number of times you e-mail that person.** The higher the "e-mail frequency," the more likely you should add him to your LinkedIn network.

✔ **It allows you to send invitations with one click, instead of having to find the person's profile on LinkedIn and clicking through the Invite process.** You can also pull up the LinkedIn Web site with one click using the tool.

✔ **It automatically displays a LinkedIn "mini-profile" of someone when you read an e-mail from that person using Outlook.** This way, you can get more information about the sender in the form of an instant pop-up, rather than manually going to LinkedIn to research the person.

✔ **Your Outlook contact information for a LinkedIn connection is automatically updated with that connection's profile information.**

✔ **You can receive e-mail notifications when someone in your LinkedIn network updates her profile information.**

✔ **You can access a LinkedIn "dashboard" to get a snapshot of your LinkedIn network and the status of your connections.**

Installing the Outlook Social Connector

To install Outlook Social Connector, just follow these steps:

1. **Go to the LinkedIn home page, scroll to the bottom of the page and click the Tools link.**

2. **From the Tools screen that appears, click the Outlook Social Connector tab.**

   The Outlook Social Connector screen appears, shown in Figure 10-13.

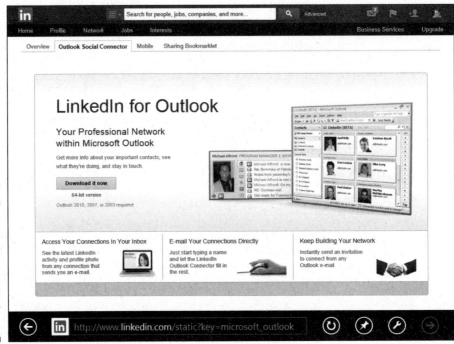

Figure 10-13:
Install the
Microsoft
Outlook
LinkedIn
Social
Connector
tool here.

3. **Click the Download It Now button. When the LinkedIn Outlook Connector Setup Wizard opens, click Next.**

4. **Review the License Agreement on the page that appears and then click the I Agree button.**

5. **In the Choose Install Location screen that appears, accept the default location (recommended) or pick a new directory to install the toolbar program; then click Install to start the process.**

   LinkedIn installs all the necessary files for the Connector tool onto your computer. Allow at least a few minutes for this process to be completed. When the tool is installed, and you've restarted Microsoft Outlook, a Build Network Wizard window appears.

6. **Click the Start button and follow the steps to have the Social Connector tool scan your Outlook program for contacts.**

   You can send an invitation to these contacts to join your LinkedIn network.

If you already imported your Microsoft Outlook Address Book into LinkedIn, going through the Build Network Wizard might not result in a lot of new contacts, but this process can find contacts you might not have saved to your Outlook Address Book.

Creating E-Mail Signatures

One of the best ways to communicate your presence on LinkedIn is to add your LinkedIn profile to your e-mail signature, if you've created one. Every time you send an e-mail, you can have text appear automatically at the end of your message similar to a written signature you would put at the end of a letter. Some people just sign their name; others use this space as an opportunity to put their name and some contact information, such as phone numbers, e-mail addresses, physical addresses, and, more recently, Web site addresses. Some LinkedIn members include their profile URL, so anyone getting an e-mail from them can take a look at their personal profile and learn more about them.

LinkedIn developed a cool tool with which you can build your own advanced e-mail signature using the LinkedIn Web site. You can decide what information you want to include in your signature, and LinkedIn helps you with formatting and graphics — the entire "look and feel" of your signature.

Access the e-mail signature tool by clicking the Tools link at the bottom of the LinkedIn home page. When you get to the Tools page, skip down below the Outlook Connector section and look for the Email Signature section (shown in Figure 10-14).

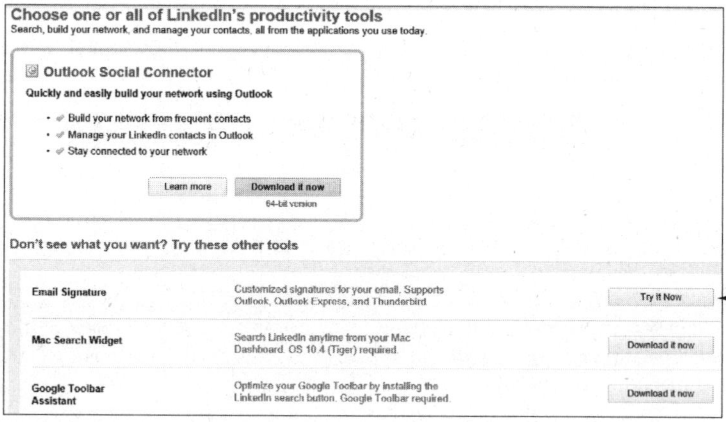

Figure 10-14:
Access the Email Signature tool from the Tools page.

When you're ready to create your e-mail signature, just follow these steps:

1. **Log in to LinkedIn, scroll to the bottom of the page, and click the Tools menu bar item.**

2. **On the Tools Overview page, scroll down to the Email Signature section and click the gray Try It Now button.**

   LinkedIn takes you to a special profile page: Create Email Signature.

3. **On your profile page, click the drop-down arrow next to Select Layout to choose the layout option you want.**

   You have multiple options to select from. Some (such as Ingot or Plastic Curve) add a graphical look; the Simple option lists your information as text; and the Executive layout presents your information in a more professional manner.

   Click around and pick a few layouts to see the automatic preview of that layout on your screen. This gives you an idea which layout and color scheme you like. You may want to revisit this step after you enter all your information so that you know how your finished signature will appear.

4. **After you pick your layout style, enter the contact information you want to appear in your signature.**

   You can input as much or as little as you'd like (see Figure 10-15), and that information will be reflected in your signature file (see Figure 10-16).

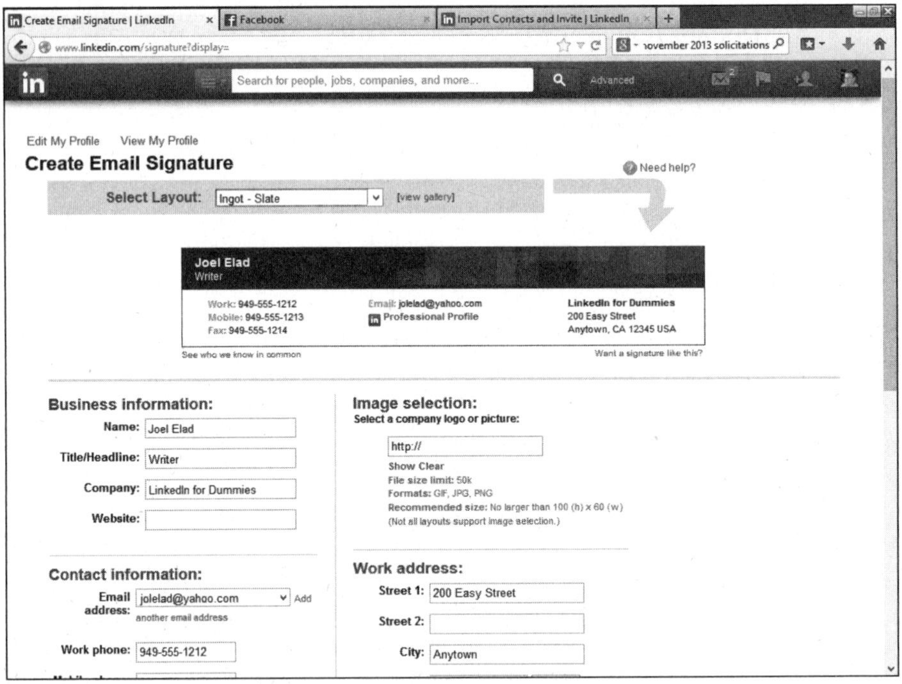

Figure 10-15:
Enter your
contact
information.

5. **(Optional) Add a picture to your signature by entering the URL of that picture's location in the Image Selection field.**

If you already uploaded a picture of yourself for your LinkedIn profile, you can include it here as well.

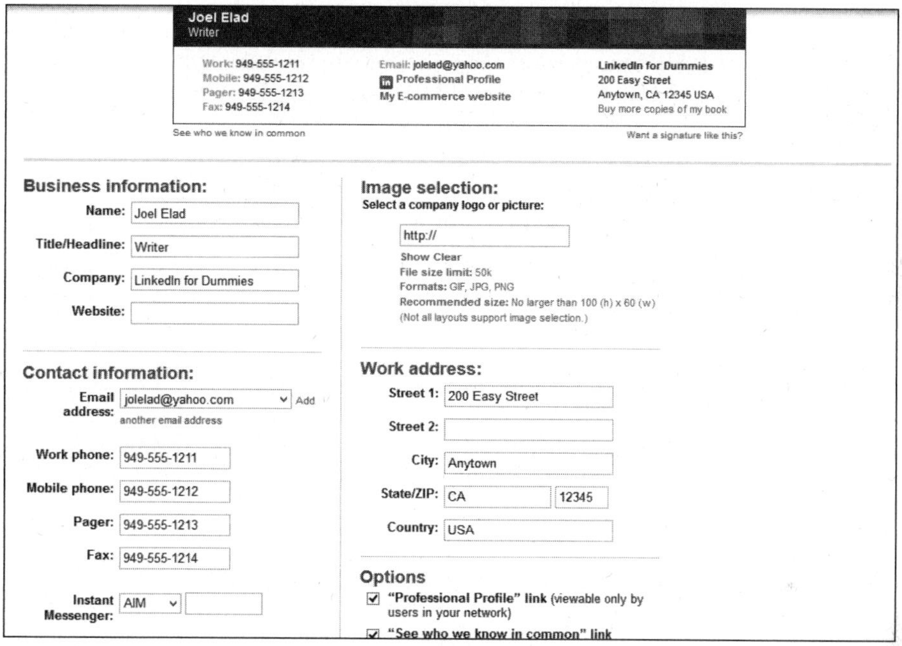

Figure 10-16:
Preview
how your
info looks in
your e-mail
signature.

6. **Scroll down to the Options section (below Work Address) and decide which of three links can appear as part of your signature by selecting the appropriate check box(es):**

   • *Professional Profile:* Creates a URL link to your LinkedIn profile page.

   • *See Who We Know in Common:* Creates a link to LinkedIn that, when clicked by a LinkedIn member, shows other LinkedIn members who are connected to you and that person.

   • *We're Hiring:* Creates a link that takes someone back to LinkedIn and starts a Job Search query for job openings in the company you've listed in your LinkedIn profile.

I highly recommend enabling the Professional Profile option. The other two links are fine to enable as well, especially if you want to promote job listings at your own company.

7. **Near the bottom of the page, click the Click Here for Instructions link under the Save Your Email Signature header to create and save your e-mail signature (see Figure 10-17).**

A pop-up window appears with your e-mail signature information. If you have a pop-up blocker on your Web browser, you may want to deactivate it temporarily before performing this step, or be ready to temporarily allow pop-ups from LinkedIn.com.

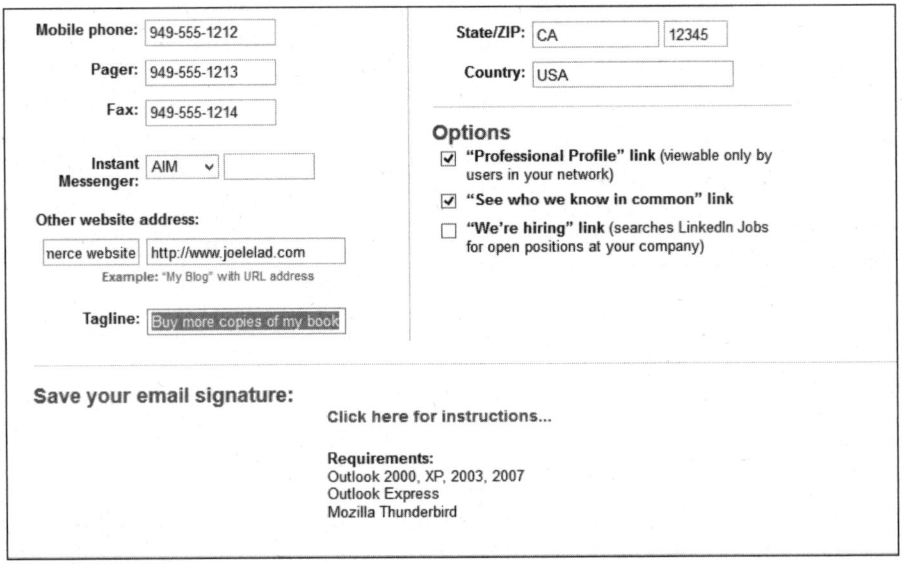

Mobile phone:	949-555-1212
Pager:	949-555-1213
Fax:	949-555-1214

Instant Messenger: AIM

Other website address:

nerce website | http://www.joelelad.com

Example: "My Blog" with URL address

Tagline: Buy more copies of my book

State/ZIP: CA 12345

Country: USA

Options

☑ **"Professional Profile" link** (viewable only by users in your network)

☑ **"See who we know in common" link**

☐ **"We're hiring" link** (searches LinkedIn Jobs for open positions at your company)

Save your email signature:

Click here for instructions...

Requirements:
Outlook 2000, XP, 2003, 2007
Outlook Express
Mozilla Thunderbird

Figure 10-17:
Click this link to generate your e-mail signature.

8. **When the page appears with the pop-up window containing the "code" of your e-mail signature, as shown in Figure 10-18, simply select all that text and then paste it into your favorite e-mail program, or you can scroll down and follow the instructions.**

   LinkedIn provides instructions for the most popular e-mail programs, such as Outlook and Yahoo! Mail. Click the drop-down arrow to bring up your e-mail program, and instructions appear at the bottom of the window. Instructions for Outlook Express are shown in Figure 10-18.

Figure 10-18:
Your e-mail signature is created. Copy and paste it into your e-mail program.

Inside the figure:

Import Your Signature | LinkedIn - Mozilla Firefox

www.linkedin.com/signature?display=

Your signature has been created and is ready to use.

Save Your Signature

Signature code:

"Select all" + "copy" then paste into your respective email client

```
<table border=0 cellpadding=0
cellspacing=0 width=600
style="background: #FFF; font: 11px
arial,sans-serif">    <tr
bgcolor="#333333">      <td width=330
style="border-top: 1px solid #333;
border-left: 1px solid #333; padding-left:
15px; color: #FFF">      <b
style="font-size: 14px;">Joel
Elad</b><br>      <span
style="font-size: 12px;">Writer
```

To add the signature to your email:

Choose your email client:
Microsoft Outlook Express

Don't see your email program listed? If your email program supports HTML signatures, please let us know .

To add an email signature to Microsoft Outlook Express:

1. Copy the email signature HTML text, paste it into Notepad, and save the file as "linkedin.html" in My Documents
2. Open Microsoft Outlook Express
3. Select Tools > Options
4. Select the Signatures tab
5. Click "New"
6. Select the "Add signatures to all outgoing messages" checkbox
7. Click "File" under the "Edit Signature" section (near the bottom)
8. Click "Browse" and select "linkedin.html"
9. Click "Apply" (near bottom right)
10. Compose a new message and verify the new signature is in place

Part IV
Finding Employees, Jobs, and Companies

In this part...

✔ Use LinkedIn to post a job listing and hire employees.

✔ Leverage your connections in your job search.

✔ Apply for jobs on LinkedIn as an active or passive job seeker.

✔ Search LinkedIn Company pages to see how you're connected to companies through your own network.

Chapter 11

Finding Employees

*W*hen you have a handle on the key elements of improving your LinkedIn profile and experience, it's time to look outward toward the LinkedIn network and talk about some of the benefits you can reap from a professional network of tens of millions of people.

Whether you're an entrepreneur looking for your first employee, a growing start-up needing to add a knowledgeable staffer, or a part of a Fortune 500 company filling a recent opening, LinkedIn can provide a rich and powerful pool of potential applicants and job candidates, including the perfectly skilled person who isn't even looking for a job! When it comes to looking for an employee, one of the benefits of LinkedIn is that you aren't limited to an applicant's one- or two-page resume and cover letter. Instead, you get the full picture of the applicant's professional history, coupled with recommendations and his knowledge and/or willingness to share information. Even if you find your candidate outside LinkedIn, you can use the site to perform reference checks and get more information about him. This information can augment what you learn from the candidate during the hiring process and from the references he provides. LinkedIn cannot replace your hiring process, but it can help you along the way.

In this chapter, I cover the basics of using LinkedIn to find an employee for your company or start-up. I begin with the basics of how you can post your job listing on LinkedIn and review your applicants. I then move on to the Reference Search function, where you can use LinkedIn to screen potential candidates, and I finish the chapter with search strategies you should employ to find the right person.

Managing Your Job Listings

LinkedIn offers a Talent Solutions page for companies to manage their job listings. Hover your mouse over the Business Services link on the top navigation bar on the home page, and select Talent Solutions from the drop-down list that appears to see the Talent Solutions home page, as shown in Figure 11-1. This is where you start the process of creating a job listing, reviewing the applicants you get, and paying LinkedIn to post the listing.

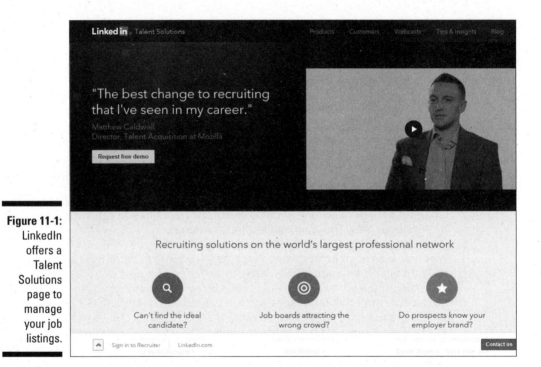

Figure 11-1:
LinkedIn offers a Talent Solutions page to manage your job listings.

As of this writing, it costs $195 for one standard, 30-day job listing on LinkedIn. LinkedIn also offers packs of five or ten job credits (one job credit allows you to post one job listing) that reduce the per-listing cost by up to 35 percent or so. You can pay for your job listing with a major credit card such as Visa, MasterCard, American Express, or Discover.

If you know you're going to need multiple or ongoing job postings on LinkedIn, you might want to consider LinkedIn Corporate Recruiting Solutions to get discounts on multiple credits for job postings and InMail. You can get more information by completing a request at `http://business.linkedin.com/talent-solutions`.

You can choose to renew your listing at the end of the 30-day window. Your *date posted* (the date you set up the job listing) is updated with the renewal date instead of the original posting date, so the listing appears at the top of search results. The cost for renewing a job listing is the same as the initial job posting cost.

You can advertise only one open position per job listing. If you solicit applications for more than one position within a single job listing, LinkedIn removes your listing or requires you to purchase multiple job credits.

Posting a job listing

To post your job opening, follow these steps:

1. **Hover your mouse over the Business Services link on the top navigation bar, and select Post a Job from the drop-down list that appears.**

   You see the Build your Job Posting screen, as shown in Figure 11-2.

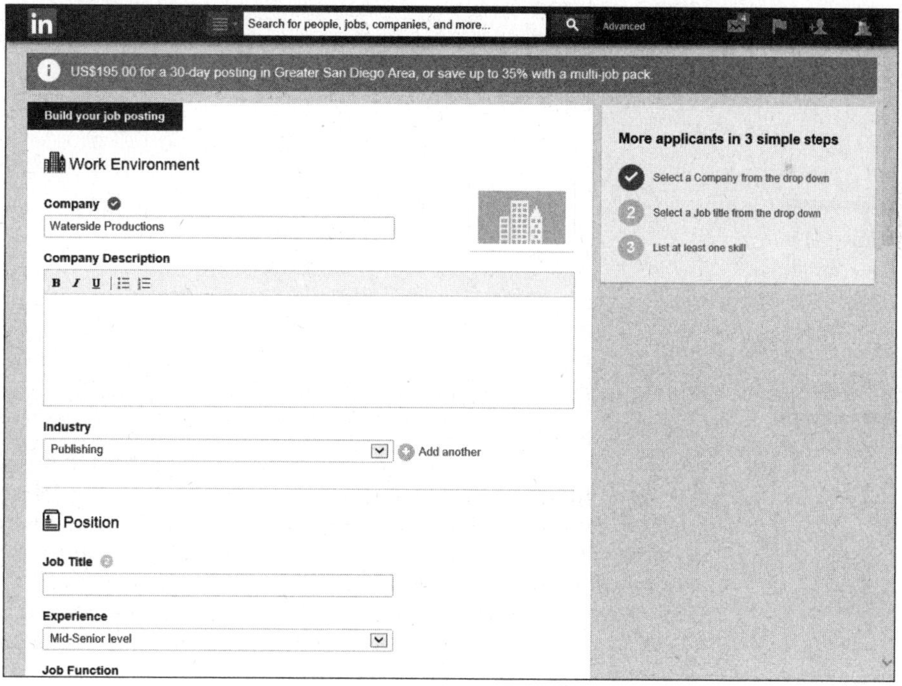

Figure 11-2:
Start com-
posing your
job posting
here.

2. **Using the text boxes and lists provided, enter the required information about your company and the job you're offering.**

   When it comes to your company, LinkedIn asks for your company name, a description, and the industry your company represents. As for the job posting itself, you need to specify the job title, employment type, experience level, and function. When you're done with that, you can scroll down and compose your job description and desired skills and expertise in the text boxes provided (see Figure 11-3) or copy the description from another source and paste it into the box. Just make sure any formatting (spacing, bullet points, font size, and so on) is correct after you paste the text.

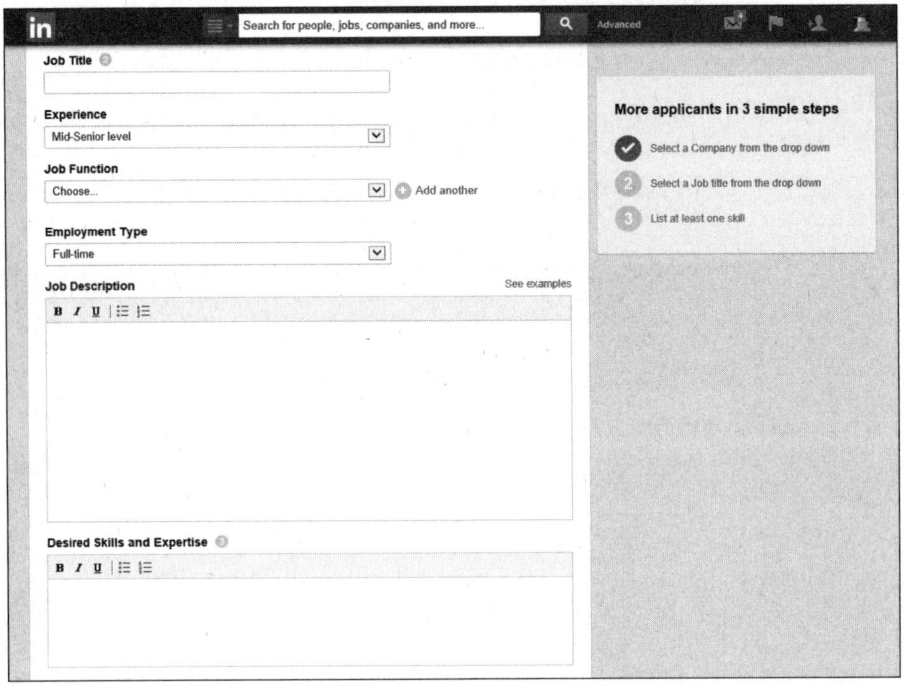

Figure 11-3: Enter the job description in the text box provided.

If your company isn't that well known, you should include some details about the company in the Company Description field. If the job title seems a bit ambiguous, you can elaborate a bit by filling out the skills required for the job title in the Desired Skills and Expertise field. LinkedIn recommends adding at least one skill to the job posting.

3. **Scroll down and fill in the How Candidates Apply and Job Location sections, as shown in Figure 11-4.**

   LinkedIn automatically offers you the ability to receive applications at one of your existing e-mail addresses, but you can decide which e-mail address should receive applications, or whether applicants should use a direct URL to apply to your job position.

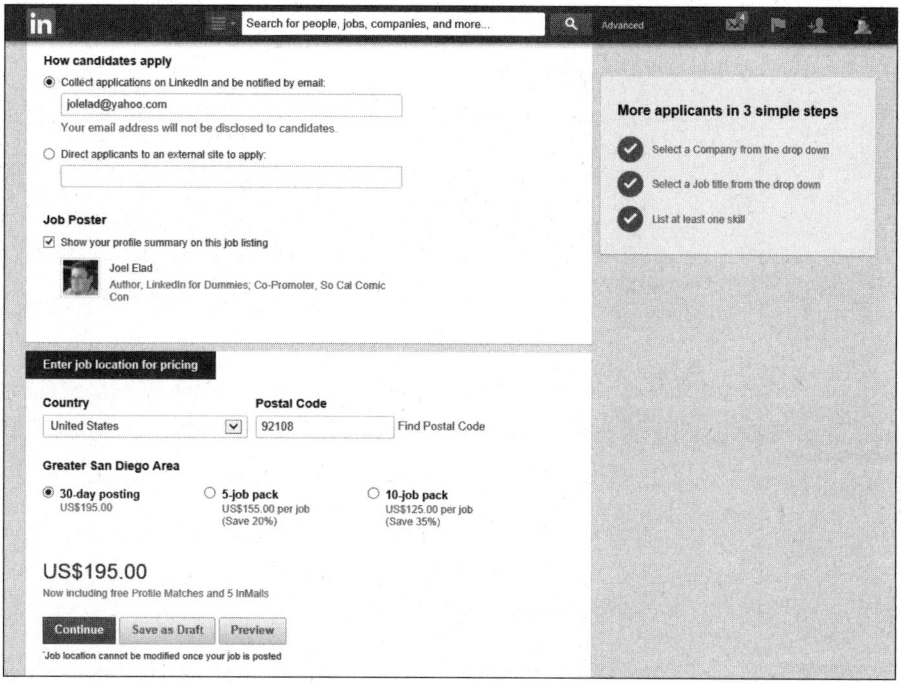

Figure 11-4:
Set your
informa-
tion for
candidate
routing and
job location
here.

4. **Click the Continue button to proceed to the next step, Billing Verification, as shown in Figure 11-5.**

   LinkedIn analyzes your job listing and looks for matches, but first, it needs your billing information. Even if you are using a pre-paid job credit, you still need to have a credit card on file for verification purposes. Complete all the fields required and click the Review Order button. Review all the info on the next screen and then click the yellow Review Order button to post your listing.

That's it! You have completed the all-important first step: You posted your job listing, as shown in Figure 11-6. This listing is available through LinkedIn's Jobs Home page, which you can get to by clicking the Jobs link (in the top navigation bar) and doing a search in the search box provided.

After your job listing is posted, LinkedIn pops up a window over the screen (as shown in Figure 11-6), asking if you want to restrict any applicants that don't live in your home country. Simply select the box if you want to limit your applicant pool, and click the Save button when you're done. LinkedIn brings you to your job posting page, which I cover in detail in the next section.

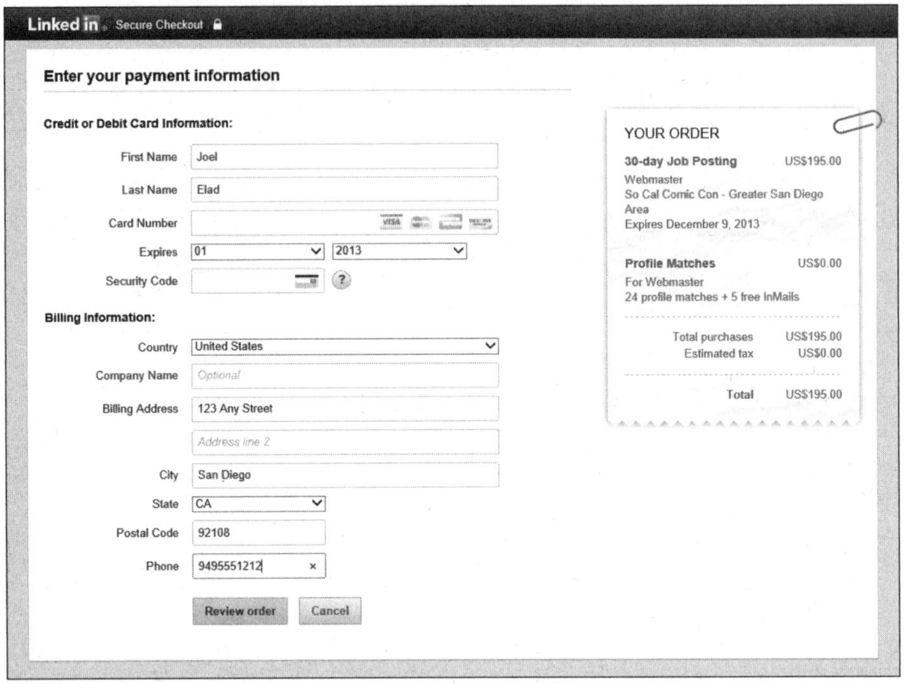

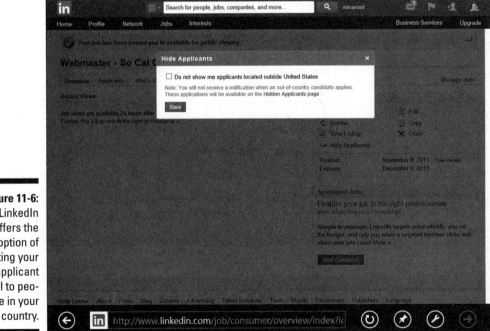

Figure 11-5:
Fill out
the billing
information
for your job
listing.

Figure 11-6:
LinkedIn
offers the
option of
limiting your
applicant
pool to peo-
ple in your
country.

Advertising your job listing to your network

Traditionally, when someone posted a job opening on the Internet using one of those ubiquitous job search sites, that person would hope the extensive pool of job seekers would find the posting and the appropriate parties would submit their resumes and cover letters. When you use LinkedIn to fill a job, however, you still benefit from the pool of job seekers who search LinkedIn's Jobs page, but you have a distinct advantage: *your own network.* You're connected to people who you know and trust, people who you have worked with before so you know their capabilities, and most importantly, people who know you and (hopefully) have a better idea than the average person as to what kind of person you would hire.

LinkedIn offers you the chance to "Share" your job listing using social networking sites like Facebook and Twitter, and it allows you to send all or some of the people in your network a message, letting them know about your job opening and asking them if they, or anyone they know, might be interested in this job. When you're ready to advertise your job listing, follow these steps:

1. **Hover your mouse over the Account & Settings button (on the top navigation bar on the right) and select Manage (next to Job Posting) from the drop-down list that appears.**

   After you've posted your job, you should see the position listed in the Manage Jobs window under Open Jobs. Click that job title to bring up the Job Status window for that job listing, as shown in Figure 11-7.

2. **Click the Share link (under the Actions for this job header) to generate a LinkedIn message.**

   LinkedIn automatically generates a Share box, as shown in Figure 11-8, that you can send to your network in a variety of ways. You can generate an automatic network update by selecting the LinkedIn check box. If you want to send out a Facebook update, select the Facebook check box. If you have an active Twitter following and your Twitter account is defined in your LinkedIn profile, you can send out a Twitter message by selecting the Twitter check box. If you belong to a LinkedIn group that might be right for this job, select the LinkedIn Groups check box and specify the LinkedIn group(s) to be notified. You can also select the Send to Individuals check box. Feel free to edit the text in the message box to make it sound like it's coming from you, or just leave the default message in place.

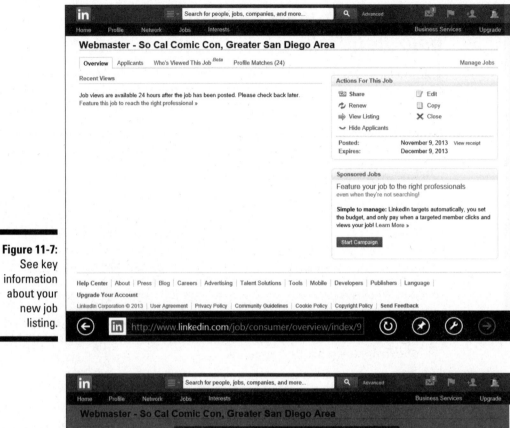

Figure 11-7:
See key information about your new job listing.

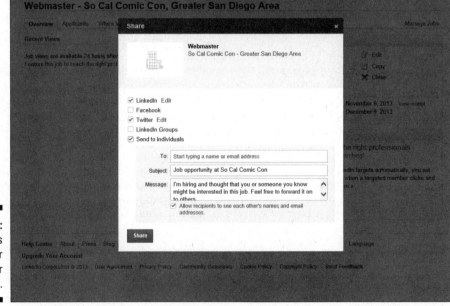

Figure 11-8:
LinkedIn lets you ask your network for help.

3. **If you select the Send to Individuals check box to forward this job listing to your connections, start typing names in the To: box to decide who will get this message from you.**

   As you start typing the name of a first-degree connection, LinkedIn automatically displays its best guesses as to the correct name and headline right there below the To box. When you see the name you want, click it, and it appears in the To box. Continue to type additional names, up to a maximum of ten people.

4. **Look over the subject line and text in the window again, make sure you have the right people selected, and when you're ready, click the Share button as shown in Figure 11-9.**

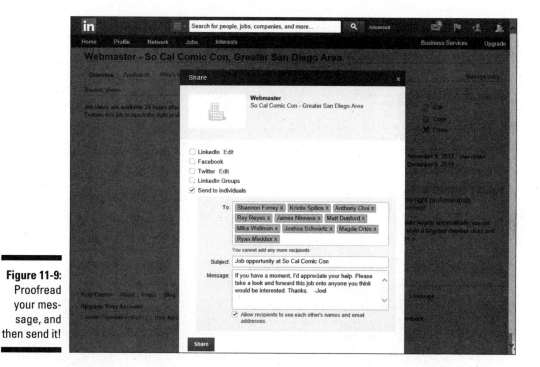

Figure 11-9:
Proofread your message, and then send it!

Your LinkedIn connections will receive a message in their LinkedIn Inboxes and, depending on their notification settings, an e-mail with this message as well. They can click a link from the message to see the job listing and either apply themselves or forward it to their contacts for consideration.

Reviewing applicants

After you've posted your job listing on LinkedIn, you should expect to get some applicants for the position. Every time someone applies for that job, you receive an e-mail from LinkedIn notifying you of the application. In addition, LinkedIn records the application in the Applicants tab of the Job Status window, next to the Overview tab. (Refer to Figure 11-7.)

When you're ready to review the applicants for your job, follow these steps:

1. **Hover your mouse over the Account & Settings button (on the top navigation bar on the right) and then select Manage (next to Job Posting) from the drop-down list that appears.**

   You should be taken to the Active Jobs screen, as shown in Figure 11-10.

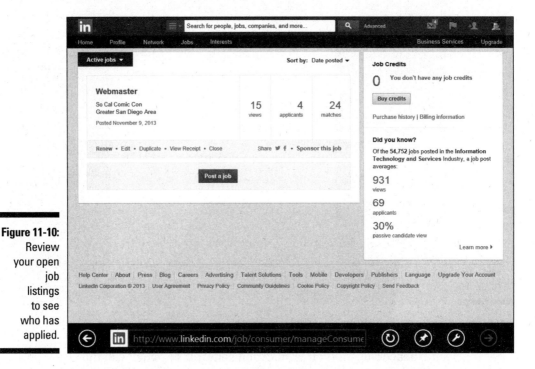

Figure 11-10:
Review your open job listings to see who has applied.

2. **Click the job title of the job listing you want to review, then click the Applicants tab (next to the Overview tab you're already on).**

   This brings up the Applicants page for the job listing, as shown in Figure 11-11. You should also see any recent applicants listed on the Overview screen for the job listing.

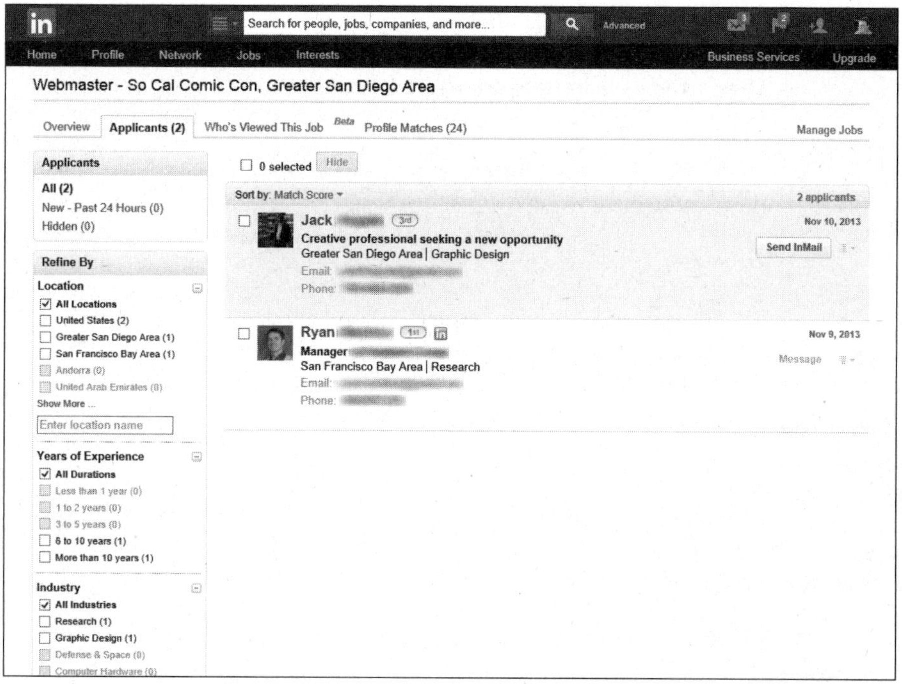

Figure 11-11:
Go through each applicant's information.

3. **Hover your mouse over an applicant's line item (on the right hand side below the date of the application) to access the links for viewing the applicant's resume. You can also click the applicant's name to see his LinkedIn profile; click the link associated with whatever you'd like to review.**

   Click the Send InMail or the Message button to contact the applicant, as shown in Figure 11-12.

4. **Click the Profile Matches tab to see additional potential applicants for this job.**

   In this example, LinkedIn analyzes the job listing and then looks through LinkedIn member profiles to see what is a match for the position based on the job description and skills requirements. When I click the Profile Matches tab, I am taken to a results page, as shown in Figure 11-13. LinkedIn displays the name, headline, photo, and location of each potential applicant and a score that indicates how closely they match, based on a 10-point scale. This helps you determine whether the person in the search result has the right skills as indicated by his profile.

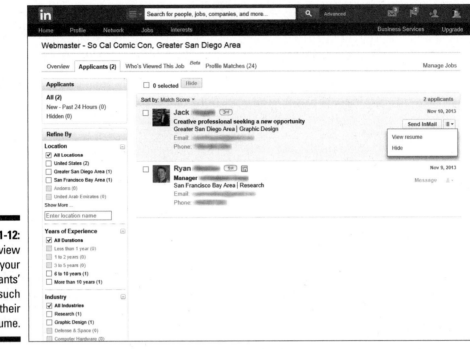

Figure 11-12:
Review all your applicants' data, such as their resume.

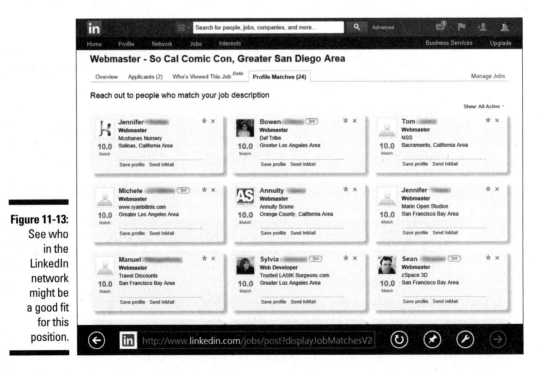

Figure 11-13:
See who in the LinkedIn network might be a good fit for this position.

At this point, you could go through the search results and look for applicants you'd want to approach to see if they'd be interested in the position. There are links in each search result box to save their profile or send them an InMail message. (As of this writing, each job posting gives you five free InMail credits to contact people.) If someone is a second- or third-degree network member, that degree is shown next to their name. Scroll to the bottom of the page and click the Show More link at the bottom to see more search results.

5. **Click the name of an applicant and contact her to see if she'd be interested in the job.**

   When you click any name in the search results, you bring up the person's profile. For example, if I click Bowen C, I see his profile as shown in Figure 11-14. If you think an applicant is worth pursuing for your job opening, you can use InMail or an introduction to send him a message (I cover both in Chapter 5) and inquire about his interest in the job.

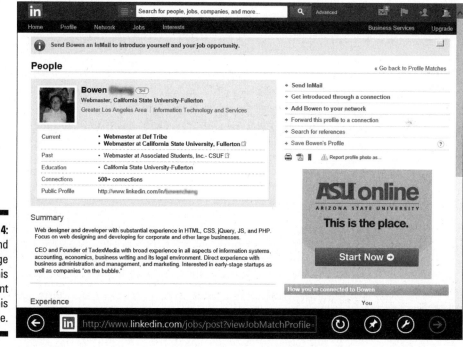

Figure 11-14: Send a message to this applicant through his profile.

Make sure the person is looking for a new job opportunity and is open to receiving incoming messages. You can do this by scrolling to the bottom of the profile and checking the Contact Settings.

Performing Reference Checks and Screening Candidates with LinkedIn

When you use LinkedIn to post a job request, the screening part of your hiring process clearly benefits. Rather than asking for references from the applicant and ordering a background check from a services company, you can use LinkedIn to verify a lot of the information in your applicant's resume and application at any stage of the process, without paying a dime!

Here are some reference search strategies to keep in mind:

- **Start by checking for the applicant's LinkedIn profile.** If the applicant has a common name, use additional information from her resume or application (such as past jobs, location, or education) to narrow your search. When you find her profile, compare it with her resume or application. Is she consistent in how she presents her experience?

- **Read through the applicant's recommendations and follow up.** If your candidate has received recommendations, go through them, pay attention to the date the recommendation was written, and see whether any are applicable toward your open position. Pay particular attention to recommendations from former bosses or co-workers. If necessary, ask your candidate whether you can contact the recommender through InMail and use that person as a reference.

- **See whether you're connected to your candidate.** When you pull up your candidate's profile, you see whether she is a second- or third-degree network member, which would mean there are one or two people who connect you with the candidate. If so, contact that person (or ask for an introduction to reach the correct party) and ask for more information about the candidate. Chances are good that you will get a more honest assessment from someone you know rather than the recommendations provided by the candidate. Understand, however, that while the two people may be connected, they may not know each other that well, or their connection may be outside the professional expertise you're looking to learn about from this job candidate.

- **Evaluate the candidate's total picture.** If your candidate mentions any Web sites, blogs, or other Web presences in her LinkedIn profile, click the links and see how they're involved. Take a look at the listed interests and group affiliations and see whether they add to (or detract from) your picture of the job candidate.

Because most LinkedIn users have already defined each company where they worked and the years of employment, LinkedIn offers an interesting and helpful application called Reference Search. It works like this: Say you're evaluating a candidate who says he worked at Microsoft from 2000 to 2005. You'd like to find out whether you know anyone in your immediate or extended network who might have worked with your candidate. LinkedIn scans everyone's profile and looks for matches in the company name and years employed and shows you possible matches. You can then follow up and hopefully get a much more honest, unbiased opinion of the candidate than someone the candidate has pre-selected to deliver a glowing recommendation. Beware, though, in case you get the ex-employee with an axe to grind.

There is one catch: You must have a paid premium account in order to use Reference Search. (I discuss the benefits of paid accounts in Chapter 1.)

Performing a reference check using Reference Search is easy; just follow these steps:

1. **Click the Advanced link at the top of any LinkedIn page. When the search screen comes up, click the wheel/cog near the top right, below your profile icon, and click Reference Search from the drop-down list that appears. You can also go directly to the Reference Search page by typing in** www.linkedin.com/rs **from your browser. (You may be asked to log in to your LinkedIn account.)**

   When you get to the Reference Search screen, it should bring up the window shown in Figure 11-15.

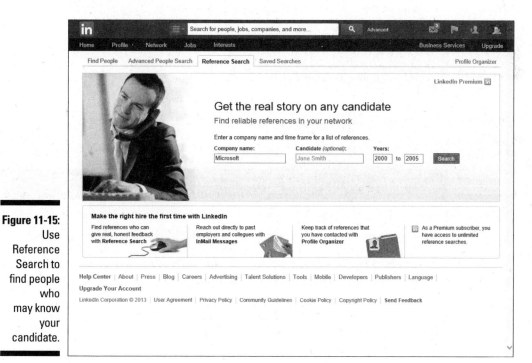

Figure 11-15:
Use Reference Search to find people who may know your candidate.

2. **Enter the company name and years of employment in the text boxes provided.**

   If the candidate is currently working at the company, enter the current year in the second year box. You can enter more than one company in the boxes provided; your results list contains anyone who matches at least one of the companies provided. If you like, you can also enter the candidate's name in the box provided.

3. **Click the Search button to start the reference search.**

   You see a results screen, as shown in Figure 11-16, that summarizes the number of first-degree connections as well as the number of their friends who match your reference search.

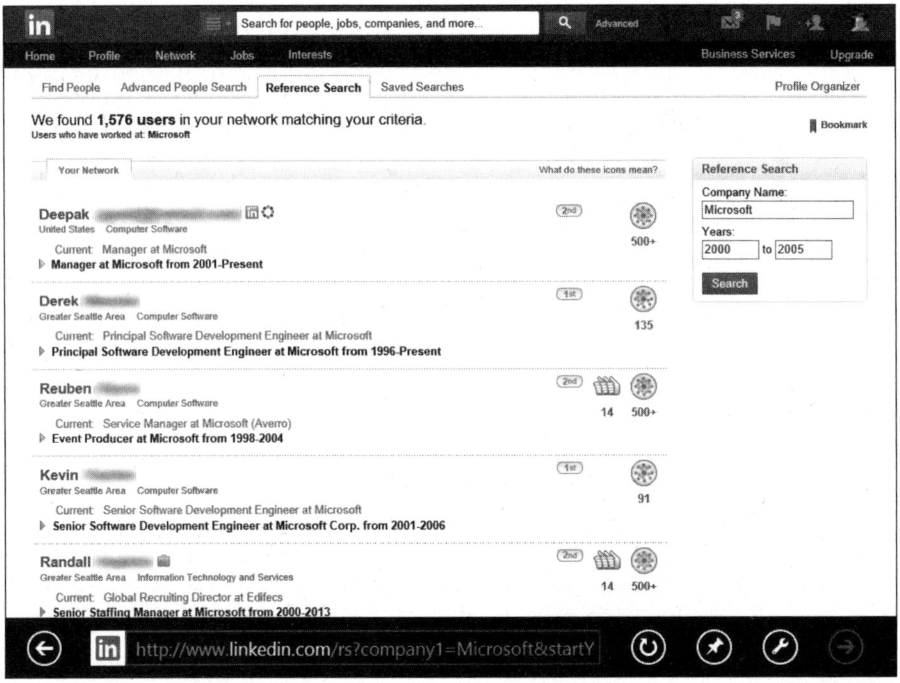

Figure 11-16:
See who
you know
might've
worked with
your
candidate.

4. **If you have a premium account — or decide to take the plunge to upgrade — you can evaluate each profile in your results list to see whether the applicant worked in the same division, and if so, contact the person in your results list for a reference.**

   Obviously, for a big company, such as Microsoft in my example, you may have to search multiple people to find the right division.

If you add a division name right after the company name (for example, you put Microsoft Excel instead of Microsoft), you severely limit your search to people who have defined their positions in that exact word order.

Using Strategies to Find Active or Passive Job Seekers

One of the powers of LinkedIn is its ability to find not just the active job seeker, but the passive job seeker or someone who doesn't even realize she wants a new job! You can tap an extensive network of professionals who have already identified their past experiences, skill sets, interests, educational backgrounds, and group affiliations. Also, through LinkedIn Answers, you can find out what they're thinking about or how knowledgeable they truly are.

The best piece of advice, in my opinion, for this type of search comes from Harvey Mackay and the book he wrote back in 1999, *Dig Your Well Before You're Thirsty*.

You should be building a healthy network and keeping your eye on potential candidates before you have a job opening to fill. The earlier you start, and the more consistent you are with the time you spend on a weekly or monthly basis expanding your network, the easier it is to identify and then recruit a potential candidate to fill your opening.

There are specific steps you should take to make your strategy a reality. Whether you start this process in advance or just need to fill a position as soon as possible, here are some tactics to consider:

- ✓ **Perform detailed advanced searches.** If you want the perfect candidate, search for that candidate. Put multiple keywords in the Advanced Search form, look for a big skill set, narrow your search to a specific industry, and maybe even limit your range to people who already live close to you. If you come up with zero results, remove the least necessary keyword and repeat the search, and keep doing that until you come up with some potential candidates.

- ✓ **Focus on your industry.** If you know that you're probably going to need software developers, start getting to know potential candidates on the LinkedIn site and stay in touch with them. Look for people to connect with, whether they share a group affiliation with you or respond to LinkedIn Answers, and actively network with these people. Even if they say no to a future job opportunity, chances are good that someone in their networks will be more responsive than the average connection. While Software Developer A may say no, that person probably has several software developers in his network who could respond favorably.

✔ **Start some conversations in the LinkedIn Groups section.** After you've found some LinkedIn Groups full of like-minded or interesting professionals, start exchanging information! Pose a question or start a group discussion that you would ask in an interview to potential candidates, and see who responds. Better yet, you'll see *how* the people respond, and you'll be able to decide from their answers who to focus on for a follow-up. You'll be able to see the public profiles of the people who provide answers and send messages to those people.

Chapter 12

Finding a Job

. . . .

. . . .

*O*ne of the most important ways that LinkedIn has benefitted people is how it helps improve their job search experience. Before LinkedIn, everyone remembers what was involved when you had a job search — making lots of phone calls and visits (and some e-mails) to people you knew, asking them whether they knew anybody who was hiring, asking whether they knew somebody at Company X who might talk to you, or asking something else related to your search. It was a tedious and inefficient process, and LinkedIn has improved it. Understand, however, that LinkedIn hasn't replaced the entire process. You still need to have some face-to-face meetings and make phone calls, but LinkedIn can help you find the right person before you pick up the phone. One of the most potent aspects of LinkedIn and a job search is the speed with which you can connect with people and find opportunities.

In this chapter, I discuss some of the ways that you can use LinkedIn to help find a job, whether you're an active job seeker (I need a job right now!) or a passive job seeker (I don't mind where I'm at, but if the right opportunity comes along, I'm listening). I start by talking about LinkedIn's job board and how you can search for openings. Then I move into more strategic options like improving your profile, devising specific strategies, searching your network for specific people, and incorporating functions like LinkedIn's JobsInsider tool when surfing the Internet.

Using LinkedIn to Search for a Job

LinkedIn offers lots of tools that can help you look for a job. The most direct way is to search for open positions on the LinkedIn job board, which I cover in the following section. There are other things to keep in mind when looking for a job, which I cover in the later sections, like improving your visibility and optimizing your profile. Part of the success of finding a job is to have an appealing LinkedIn identity so hiring managers can find you and want to contact you with an opening. According to *Forbes* magazine, 90 percent of employers are using social media sites to recruit employees, with LinkedIn being the most used of those sites. After all, the best search is when someone comes to you with an opportunity without you sweating the details.

Searching for an open position

The most obvious way to look for a job is to look through LinkedIn's advertised job openings. After all, someone is getting hired when a company runs a job listing, so why can't that candidate be you? When you search for a job on LinkedIn, you can see what skills seem attractive to companies these days, which you can keep in mind as you refine your job search and LinkedIn profile.

When you're ready to search for a job opening, just follow these steps:

1. **Click the Jobs link from the top navigation bar.**

   The Jobs home page appears, as shown in Figure 12-1.

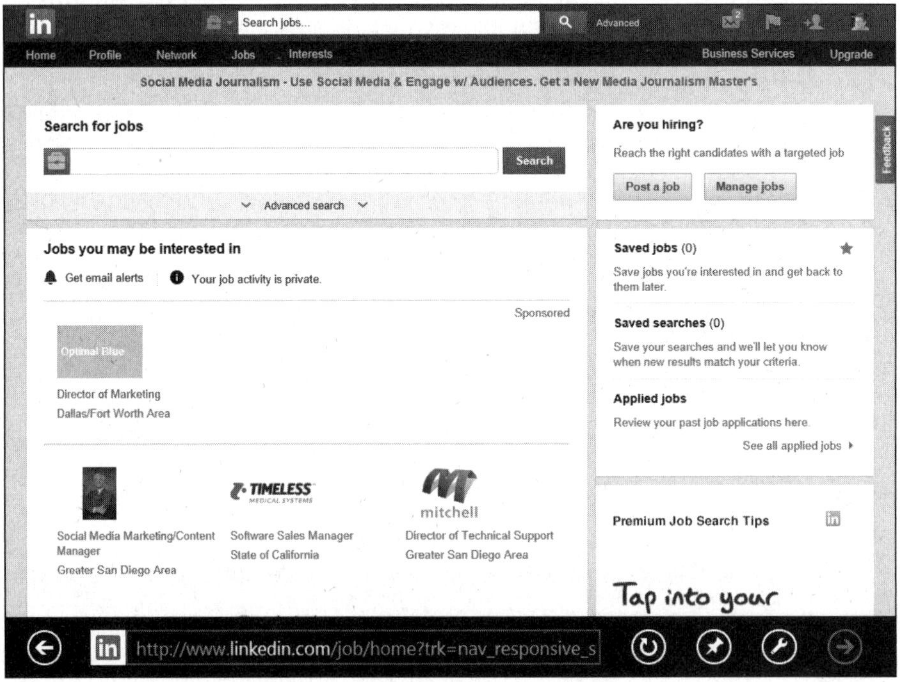

Figure 12-1: Look for a job on LinkedIn.

2. Enter keywords describing the job you want in the Search for Jobs text box.

To be more precise in your search, you can click the Advanced Search link below the Search for Jobs text box to bring up some Advanced Search additional criteria, such as Industry, Function, or Salary level. You can click the More Options link (next to the Search button) to see even more search options.

3. Click the Search button.

You're taken to a LinkedIn Jobs results screen like the one shown in Figure 12-2, where you see the basic components of the job listings, such as Company, Title, and Location.

To refine your job results, enter additional keywords or scroll down the left-hand side of the screen to use additional filters like the name of the company, how long the job posting has been online, and the location of the job.

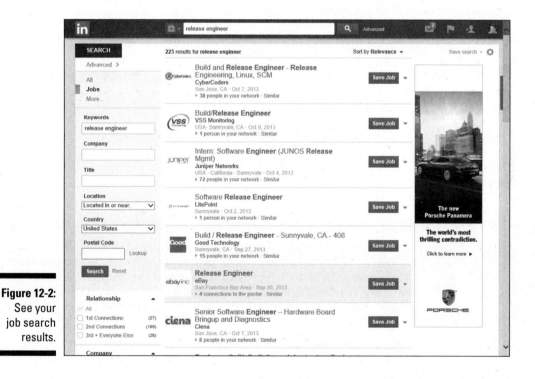

Figure 12-2: See your job search results.

4. Click an individual job title to see the details of that job posting.

You see the detailed write-up on the next screen, as shown in Figure 12-3, where you can find out more about the job and the job poster. If the person who posted the job is in your network and has opted to show her name, you will see who in your LinkedIn network can refer you to that person. In the example in Figure 12-3, you can see that four different first-degree connections, like Rachel M., can introduce me to the job poster, who is a second-degree network member.

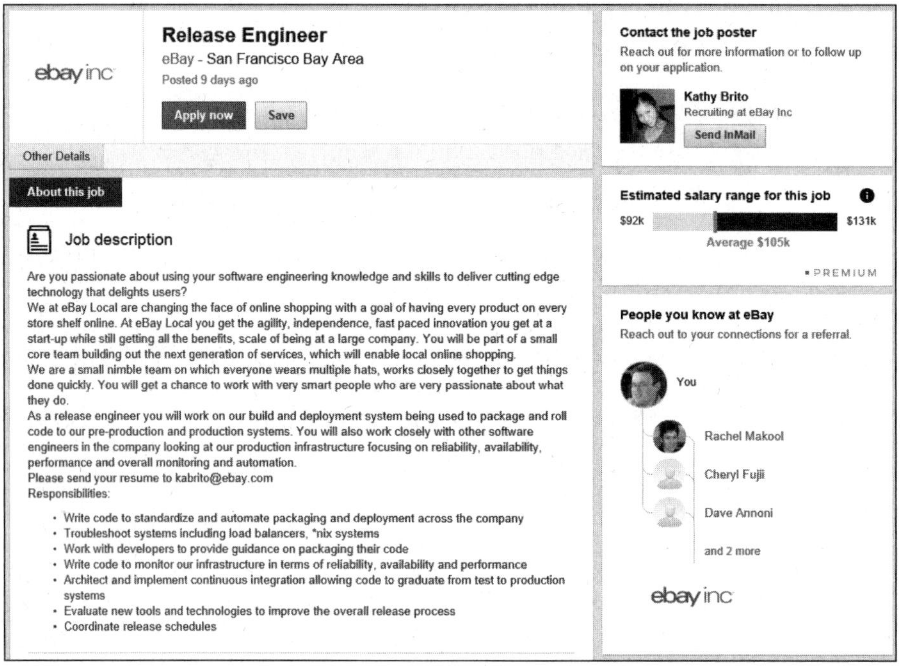

Release Engineer
eBay - San Francisco Bay Area
Posted 9 days ago

Apply now   Save

Other Details

About this job

Job description

Are you passionate about using your software engineering knowledge and skills to deliver cutting edge technology that delights users?
We at eBay Local are changing the face of online shopping with a goal of having every product on every store shelf online. At eBay Local you get the agility, independence, fast paced innovation you get at a start-up while still getting all the benefits, scale of being at a large company. You will be part of a small core team building out the next generation of services, which will enable local online shopping.
We are a small nimble team on which everyone wears multiple hats, works closely together to get things done quickly. You will get a chance to work with very smart people who are very passionate about what they do.
As a release engineer you will work on our build and deployment system being used to package and roll code to our pre-production and production systems. You will also work closely with other software engineers in the company looking at our production infrastructure focusing on reliability, availability, performance and overall monitoring and automation.
Please send your resume to kabrito@ebay.com
Responsibilities:

- Write code to standardize and automate packaging and deployment across the company
- Troubleshoot systems including load balancers, *nix systems
- Work with developers to provide guidance on packaging their code
- Write code to monitor our infrastructure in terms of reliability, availability and performance
- Architect and implement continuous integration allowing code to graduate from test to production systems
- Evaluate new tools and technologies to improve the overall release process
- Coordinate release schedules

Contact the job poster
Reach out for more information or to follow up on your application.

Kathy Brito
Recruiting at eBay Inc
Send InMail

Estimated salary range for this job
$92k $131k
Average $105k
• PREMIUM

People you know at eBay
Reach out to your connections for a referral.

You

Rachel Makool

Cheryl Fujii

Dave Annoni

and 2 more

ebay inc

Figure 12-3: Find out more about a specific job listing.

5. **When you see a job you want to apply for, click the Apply Now button.**

   LinkedIn may display a pop-up window, Apply with Your Profile, as shown in Figure 12-4, where your profile information is used instead of a resume. (In some cases, you're taken to the company's specific applicant tracking system — for example, any job from Google does this. In those cases, simply follow the instructions displayed to apply for that job.)

6. **Verify your contact information, then upload a cover letter (which you'll write from your word processing program) in the Resume/ Cover Letter section.**

   Include a brief summary of why you feel you are qualified for the job in your cover letter. If you like, you can update and reuse an older cover letter you've used to apply to a similar job: Simply open a word processing program (such as Microsoft Word), find the letter, copy the contents into your new letter, update it with the specific details of this job, and save it as a unique file, which you can upload to LinkedIn. (Be sure to check the letter using your program's spell checker before you upload it.)

The cover letter is a great chance for you to expand upon your experience and education to clarify to the employer why you are perfect for the job.

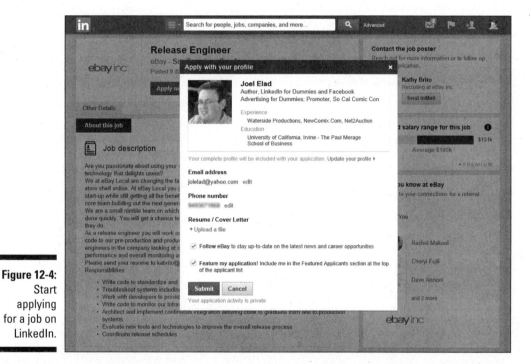

Figure 12-4: Start applying for a job on LinkedIn.

If the job poster is in your extended network, I recommend that you read her profile first, see what common interests you have, and incorporate that information into your cover letter. If you have the time, approach that person first with an introduction or InMail to get more information about the job posting before you apply. (I discuss introductions and InMail at length in Chapter 5.)

7. Click the Submit button.

Off your application goes!

Congratulations, you've applied for a job! Repeat Steps 2–7 to keep looking and applying for jobs.

Improving your visibility and attractiveness

When you're looking for a job, manually scanning job listings and sending resumes are only part of the process. You also have to prepare your job-seeking strategies. The most obvious examples of these are your resume (or CV) and your cover letter. When you include LinkedIn in your job search, you need to prepare your total LinkedIn profile and network in order to get the optimal job search experience.

Although no strategy can guarantee the job of your dreams, these strategies can improve your odds of getting the attention of the right contact person, an interview, or extra consideration for your job application that's in a stack of potential candidates.

Here are some strategies to keep in mind:

- **Connect with former managers, co-workers, and partners.** This might seem like an obvious strategy, but let me elaborate. Part of getting the job is communicating (to your future employer) your ability to do the job. Nobody knows your skills, potential, work attitude, and capability better than people who have worked with you and observed you in action.

  Therefore, make sure you have connected with your former managers, co-workers, and so on. When these people are part of your network, the introductions they can facilitate will carry extra weight because they can share their experience with the person you want to meet. You can encourage them to provide referrals for you to express to the entire community your capability and work ethic.

- **Look at your colleagues' LinkedIn profiles.** Using the search functions or your first-degree connections in your network, try to find people with goals and work experience similar to yours. When you see how they describe their work experience on their profiles, you might get some good ideas on how to augment your profile.

- **Get referrals from past bosses and co-workers.** After you add your past bosses and co-workers to your network, keep in contact with them, let them know your current job search goals, and ask for an appropriate referral or introduction. They can use their knowledge of your work history and their expanded networks to make more powerful introductions or requests than just a friend asking another friend, "Hey, can you hire my friend, Joel?"

  Don't be afraid to provide extra information to your past bosses or co-workers to help them make an effective referral. Before the Internet, when job seekers asked a past boss or co-worker to write a letter of recommendation, it was acceptable to include some bullet points of stories or points you hoped they would cover in their letters. The same is true in the LinkedIn world. Guide your contact to emphasize a work quality or anecdote that would be effective in the referral or introduction.

✔ **Collect your recommendations.** Nothing communicates a vote of confidence from your network quite like a recommendation. When anyone reads your LinkedIn profile, he can see exactly what other people have said about you. Because he knows that you can't alter a recommendation, he's more likely to trust the content and believe you're the right person for the job. (See Chapter 8 for more information on how to get more recommendations.)

Optimizing your LinkedIn profile

The core of your LinkedIn presence is your profile, which is included with every job application you make on LinkedIn. Odds are good that prospective employers are going to check your LinkedIn profile when evaluating you for a job, so you want to make sure your profile is optimized to make you as appealing as possible. Here are some things to keep in mind when bulking up your profile for a job search:

✔ **Complete all the sections in your profile with as much accurate information as possible.** It's easy to put up a skeleton of your employment history and never get around to fully completing your profile. Unlike a resume (where you could feel confined in terms of page length), you can be as expansive as you want with your LinkedIn profile. You never know what part of your profile will get you included in someone's search result, but the more information you provide, the better chance someone will find you. Most important, make sure your most recent positions are filled out, because many employers focus on those positions first.

✔ **Focus on accomplishments rather than duties.** I've seen a lot of people prepare their LinkedIn profiles in the same way they do their resumes, focusing solely on the duties they performed at each job. Although you want to give people an idea of what you did, hiring managers want to know the *results* of what you did, and the more concrete the example, the better. Saying you "organized procurement processes in your division" may demonstrate a skill, but saying that you "cut procurement costs by 16% in your first year" makes a bigger impact. Go back and talk to past co-workers or bosses, if necessary, to get whatever specifics they can provide on your performance.

✔ **Add all relevant job search keywords, skill sets, and buzzwords to your profile.** When prospective employers are searching for someone to hire, they may simply search for a core set of skills to see who can fill the position. Therefore, just stating your job titles is not enough. If your profile says "Software Developer," prospective hiring managers could assume that you're qualified, but the only way you'd be considered is if these managers ran a search on those keywords. Say that a hiring manager does a search for the programming languages C++, Java, Perl, and Python. If all those keywords are not somewhere in your profile, you won't show up in the list to be considered at all. If you're unsure about what keywords to use, consider asking people in your field or researching the profiles of people who have the job title you are seeking.

✔ **See how other people position themselves.** Imagine if you could get a book of thousands of resumes from current employees that you could then use as models to position yourself. Do a search for people with a job, education, or skill set similar to yours and see how they've worded their profiles or how they put their experiences in context. Use that insight to adapt your profile to make it clearer to others.

✔ **List all your job experiences on your profile, not just full-time positions.** Did you do any short-term or contract jobs? Were you an advisor to another company? Perhaps you're a board member for a local nonprofit group or religious organization. Your LinkedIn profile is designed to reflect all of your job experiences, which is *not* limited to a full-time job that provided a W-2 slip. Document any work experience that adds to your overall profile, whether you were paid for that job/experience or not.

Make sure that every experience you list on your profiles helps contribute to your overall career goals. After all, employers might not care that you were a pastry chef one summer — and will question why you thought it was so important that you listed it on your profile.

Implementing Job Search Strategies That Involve LinkedIn

When you're looking for a job, there are many potential ways you can include LinkedIn as part of your overall job search, beyond the direct task of searching jobs database listings and e-mailing a job request to your immediate network. In this section, I discuss various job search strategies you can implement that involve LinkedIn to some degree and can help add information, contacts, interviews, and hopefully some offers to your job search. Use one or use them all, but pick the methods you feel most comfortable with implementing.

A job search should be considered as a time commitment, even with the power of LinkedIn. Some of these strategies apply to working or unemployed people and might not instantly result in multiple offers.

Leveraging your connections

One of the biggest benefits of LinkedIn is being able to answer the question, "Who do my contacts know?" It's important to think of LinkedIn as not only the sum of your first-degree connections, but also as your extended network of second- and third-degree network members that your colleagues can help connect you with for information, referrals, and hopefully, a new career.

Therefore, keep these second- and third-degree network members in mind so you can best leverage your connections to achieve progress. Consider these points when you're working on your job search using LinkedIn:

- ✔ **Change the Sort option to Relationships instead of Relevance.** When searching for the right contacts (such as recruiters, headhunters, or company or job specialists), be sure to change the Sort option (on the top right of the screen) from Relevance to another option based on Relationships, or degrees of connections. This allows you to see which members of your extended network should be at the top of your list.

- ✔ **Ask for referrals whenever possible.** Exchange information first and then work your way up to request a referral.

- ✔ **Get your friends involved.** Let your immediate network know about your goals so they can recommend the right people for you to talk to — and hopefully, they'll generate the right introductions for you as well.

Finding people with the same or similar job

If you're looking for a specific job, one way to approach your job search is to ask this question: "Who out there could possibly know more about the job I'm interested in than those folks doing that job right now?" The answer to that question is "no one." This means one source of help should be people with the same (or very similar) job title or responsibilities. Although these people might not have hiring authority, they can help give you the right perspective, share the right insider tips about what the job truly entails, and let you know what skills or background the hiring manager considered when they were hired.

Because these people are already employed and not your direct competition, they're more likely to offer help and advice. They have practical knowledge of what it takes to do that job and what qualities will best help someone succeed in that position. When you're ready to implement this strategy, keep these points in mind:

- **Perform an advanced search for people with a similar job title as the one you're applying for.** Put the job title in either the keywords section or the title section.

- **Narrow and clarify your search by industry.** For example, Project Manager of Software Development is much different than Project Manager for the Construction industry. Pick multiple industries if they are similar enough.

- **When you find someone who has the job title you'd like to have, see whether she's interested in meeting for an informational interview (or if she's outside your geographic area, having a phone conversation).** Asking outright for a job lead will most likely not result in anything positive.

Taking advantage of your alma mater

Typically, people who share a school in common have an ongoing affinity, whether the school is an undergraduate or graduate college, or even a high school. You can rapidly increase the chance of someone considering your request if you and that person attended the same school. Therefore, take advantage of your alumni status and try to connect and work with people who went to one of the same schools as you. Here are some tips to help further this type of search by using LinkedIn:

- **Search for alumni association groups of any school you attended. Click Interests and then click Groups from the top navigation bar — and then go ahead and join those groups.** This gives you access to the member list of that group, so you can see other alumni, regardless of graduation year, and communicate with them.

- **Connect as a former classmate and ask for information first, referral second.** Your shared alumni status helps open the door, but don't expect a handout right away. Be ready to offer one of your contacts in exchange for the former classmate's help or consideration.

- **Check the connection list of any of your contacts who attended school with you.** This is a good safety check to look for any classmates on your contacts' lists who you might not have initially considered. (I discuss connection lists in Chapter 6.)

✔ **Try doing an Advanced People search with the school name as a keyword, and if necessary, try different variations of the school name.** For example, try the school name with and without acronyms. When I look for classmates from the University of California, Irvine, I search for *UCI* as well as *University California Irvine.* (I talk more about doing advanced searches in Chapter 4.)

✔ **If your school has changed or updated its name, do an Advanced People search for both the old and new names as keywords.** For example, because my department name at UCI has changed from the Graduate School of Management, or GSM, to the Paul Merage School of Business, I search for the old and new search terms because my classmates may have defined their educational listings differently.

Finding target company referrals

Sometimes your job search involves a specific company and not necessarily a job title. Suppose you know you want to work at one of the top computer database software companies. Now you can use LinkedIn to help you find the right people at those companies who can help you. Here are some points to consider:

✔ **Make a list of the ten companies you'd like to work for and do an individual Advanced People search for each company to find potential contacts at these companies.** Type the company name in the search box at the top right of the LinkedIn home page and then click the Search button. You should see a list of people on the Search results page that have the Company name in their titles who are in your extended network. For larger companies, you need to search for a specific department or industry area to find the right contact. Ask these people you've identified for referrals to someone in your target organization, like a hiring manager.

✔ **Follow the companies themselves.** LinkedIn allows you to "follow" companies through their Company page, so be sure to "Follow this company" after you're looking at the right Company page within LinkedIn Companies. When you know what companies you want to follow, simply hover your mouse over the Interests link in the top navigation bar, and click Companies. Then, type in the name of each company into the search box provided, click Search Companies, and when you find the company in the Search results list, click the Follow button next to the Company listing. Once you are following all your target companies, spend some time each week to review each Company page for news, information, job openings, and useful contacts.

✔ **If you can't find someone who currently works at your target company, look for people who used to work there and see what advice they can give you.** You do this through an Advanced People search, where you make sure the option under Company is set to Past. Many times, past employees still maintain contacts at their old company, and they can definitely attest to the work environment and corporate culture.

✔ **Get some information from the person you're replacing.** Find the person at the company whose job you're taking and ask her opinion of it, information about the hiring manager, company, and so on. (Understand, of course, that this person might not have left under the best of circumstances, so you may not always get a good or useful response.) If you can't find the person you're replacing, try looking for people with a past position like the one you're interviewing for. I got this tip from Garage. com founder Guy Kawasaki in his blog post entitled "How to Change the World: Ten Ways to use LinkedIn," which resides on `http://blog.guykawasaki.com`.

Chapter 13

Finding Companies on LinkedIn

● ●

In This Chapter

▶ Following companies using LinkedIn

▶ Creating a Company page

▶ Sharing company updates with the community

● ●

*T*wo of the main reasons why people search the LinkedIn network are to find a job and to find a new employee. In both cases, LinkedIn users are trying to learn more about the company, not just the job seeker or hiring manager. Millions of self-employed people who use LinkedIn to promote not only themselves, but also their services, are always looking for a way to expand their brand and advertise their own opportunities. LinkedIn organizes all these efforts under their Company pages.

LinkedIn maintains a directory of Company pages that allow people to learn about each company's products, services, and job opportunities. Each Company page has at least one administrator who can add his company to the directory, edit the information, connect his employees to the Company page, and provide company updates to the LinkedIn community. LinkedIn members can "follow" their favorite companies to get company and industry updates, and see how each member's network is connected to the employees of each company they follow.

In this chapter, I cover how you can search Company pages, follow different companies, and, if you are an employee or owner of your own company, create and update your own Company page.

Searching for Companies

When you need to learn more about your current industry or find a potential business partner for a big deal, your first step is to do some research. LinkedIn's Company pages allow users to explore companies of interest, whether it's a for-profit or non-profit company, and receive company updates and industry news, as well as research each company's products and services — and, of course, learn about job opportunities the company has to offer.

To search for a Company page, just follow these steps:

1. **Hover your mouse over the Interests link from the top navigation bar and select Companies from the drop-down list that appears.**

2. **On the Companies page, click the Search Companies link/tab (near the top of the screen).**

   The Companies Search home page appears, as shown in Figure 13-1.

   LinkedIn automatically shows companies based on the number of people in your network who are currently connected to each company.

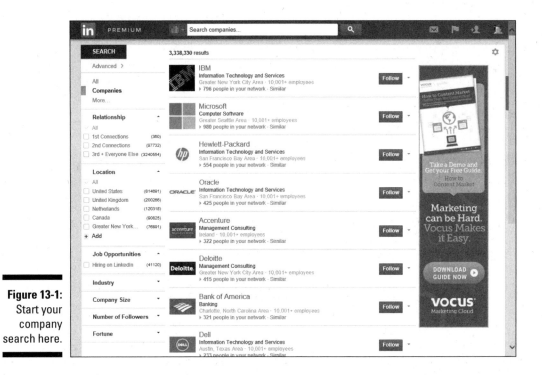

Figure 13-1: Start your company search here.

3. **In the text box along the top of the screen, enter the keywords for your company search. In the left pane, use the Relationship, Location, Industry, and other filters to refine your search.**

Let's say I'm looking for an Internet company in the United States where at least one person in my network is employed. Figure 13-2 shows the 29 companies that show up in my refined search, and this search used no keywords yet.

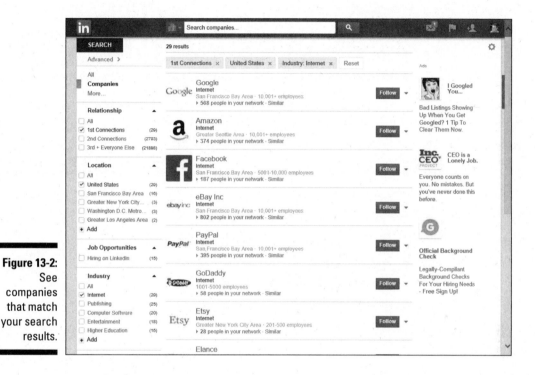

Figure 13-2:
See companies that match your search results.

If you plan on using any keywords in your search, enter those words first into a search before using the filters to narrow your search. Otherwise, when you enter keywords into the top navigation bar search box, you will automatically reset your search filters, like Relationship, Industry, or Location.

After you reach a page loaded with potential companies, use the following tricks to find the one that's just right for you:

✔ **Click the Follow button to keep track of that company.** When you click the Follow button next to any company listing, you add that company to your list of companies that you are following. This means you will see all the company updates in the Companies section of your LinkedIn page.

✔ **View the Company page and study your connections.** To see the Company page, either click the name of the company, or click the drop-down arrow next to the Follow button and then click the View link. You can study the information on that page before deciding whether to follow the company. You can also view how you're connected to people inside the company.

For example, I'm looking at Microsoft's Company page, as shown in Figure 13-3. On the right side of the page, under the How You're Connected header, I can see how many people in my immediate network, or first-degree connections, are associated with that company, and by extension, how many second-degree network members (that is, a colleague of a colleague, or a friend of a friend) I would have at that company. If I click the See All link in that section, I get a list of how I'm connected to people in that company, as shown in Figure 13-4. This page is a search results screen, so I can add more keywords or filters to get a defined list of how I relate to any given company.

Figure 13-3:
See how you're connected to a given company.

✔ **You can search based on location.** Let's say you're thinking of moving to a new city and are looking for potential companies to interview with in that city. Click the Location filter and either pick the Region that matches your destination, or click the +Add link and input your city. LinkedIn automatically pops up the region in their database associated with that city. (For example, if I type **Seattle**, LinkedIn eventually displays Greater Seattle Area.) When you see the correct region, click that listing to get a targeted search list of companies in that area.

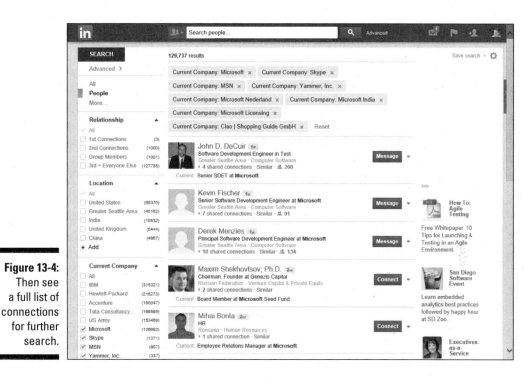

Figure 13-4:
Then see
a full list of
connections
for further
search.

Your search can include multiple locations, so you can select multiple regions, and the results list will include companies headquartered in at least one of those regions. Be aware that if you only want one specific region, you need to deselect your country filter, like United States, for example, and select only the region.

✔ **Decide who to follow by studying number of followers.** If you've got a lot of options for companies, you can use one of the newer filters, Followers, to refine your search based on the number of members who are currently following that company and show you the most-watched companies for your search criteria. Choosing the option 5001+, for example, shows only those companies that currently have more than 5,000 people following them.

Putting Your Company on LinkedIn

The flip side of understanding LinkedIn Company pages is to approach it on behalf of the company itself. Companies are always looking at ways to tell their story and engage interested members who want to follow their activities in a way that encourages word of mouth, highlights their products and services, and advertises career opportunities. LinkedIn Company pages allow companies to do all this as well as allow their customers to offer recommendations, which are spotlighted on the Company page.

As of this writing, there are more than 3 million Company pages on LinkedIn, and the number grows every day. The millions of LinkedIn users who follow these companies are current and potential customers, interested job applicants, business partners, and even curious industry watchers who want to hear the latest news, see the latest products and services, and reach out and interact with company leaders, managers, and employees. LinkedIn bills their Company pages as a "central hub" where millions of LinkedIn users can "stay in the loop" of company news and activities.

You can read more about the Company page benefits by going to `www.marketing.linkedin.com/company-pages/get-started/`.

Requirements for a Company page

When you decide to list your company on LinkedIn Company pages, understand that there are some requirements to protect the quality of this directory while making it accessible to companies of all sizes. Here are some things to keep in mind:

✔ **Your profile must show you're a current employee.** In your LinkedIn profile Experience section, you must have a position that defines you as a current company employee, manager, or owner. If you don't have a position defined, you will need to create that position in your profile before continuing with this process.

✔ **Have a company e-mail address defined in your account.** You are allowed to associate more than one e-mail address with your LinkedIn account, so make sure that one of your e-mail addresses for your profile is a company e-mail with the company domain name. This e-mail does not need to be your primary address for LinkedIn for you to have a Company page.

✔ **Your company's e-mail domain must be unique to your company.** One way LinkedIn controls the integrity of its Company page directory is to make sure that each e-mail domain can only be used once to create a Company page. Free e-mail providers like Yahoo! Mail, Gmail, and Hotmail are too generic to be associated with any one company (besides the e-mail provider itself), so an e-mail address from one of those providers is not sufficient.

If your company doesn't have its own e-mail domain, consider creating a LinkedIn Group for your company, instead of a Company page, so that your employees, customers, and business partners can stay in touch.

✔ **Your LinkedIn Profile Strength must be rated Intermediate or All Star.** LinkedIn uses a system called Profile Strength to rank its users' ability to create a robust profile, based on the number of sections a LinkedIn user has defined on her profile and network. LinkedIn wants its Company page administrators to have a strong understanding and ability to use LinkedIn so they can manage their page properly, so the Profile Strength rating must be Intermediate or All Star in order for them to create a Company page.

✔ **You must have several first-degree connections on LinkedIn.** Company page administrators on LinkedIn need to be part of the LinkedIn community in general, so LinkedIn requires that administrators have more than just one or two LinkedIn connections before they can create a Company page.

Adding a Company page to LinkedIn

After you've met the requirements for creating a Company page on LinkedIn, it's time to get started by adding the Company page to LinkedIn's system. To create your Company page, just follow these steps:

1. **Hover your mouse over the Interests link from the top navigation bar and then click the Companies link from the drop-down list that appears.**

2. **On the Companies page that appears, click the Add a Company link (on the right side of the screen).**

    You're taken to the first step in the process, the Add a Company page (see Figure 13-5).

3. **Enter the company name and company e-mail address in the fields provided, and then select the check box verifying you are the official representative of your company.**

    Make sure the e-mail address you are providing is your company e-mail address, with the unique e-mail domain for your company, and that your company e-mail address has been added and verified to your LinkedIn personal account first.

4. **Click the Continue button.**

    You're taken to the edit mode for your Company page (see Figure 13-6).

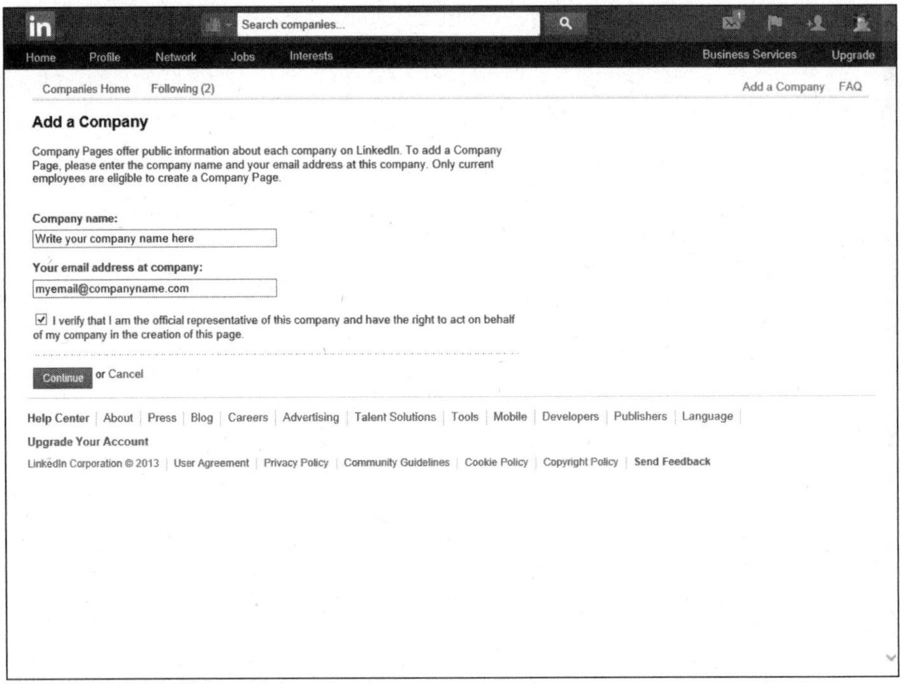

Figure 13-5:
Define your
Company
page on
LinkedIn.

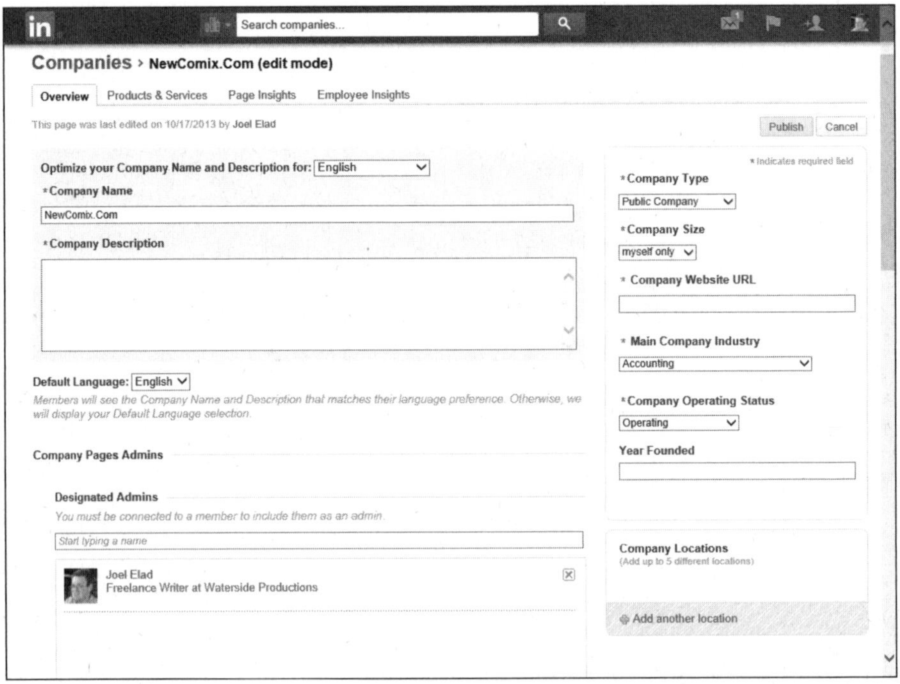

Figure 13-6:
Fill in the
details
for your
Company
page.

5. **Fill in the information in the fields provided: Company Name, Company Description, Company Type, and so on. Be sure to complete any field with a red asterisk, because those are required pieces of information for a Company page.**

6. **(Optional) Scroll down and provide a company image, a standard logo (100 by 60 pixels is recommended), or a square logo (50 by 50 pixels is recommended). List any company specialties and LinkedIn groups that are relevant to your company in the fields provided.**

7. **If you want to add another administrator for the Company page, enter his name into the field below the Designated Admins header.**

   The person you name as a page administrator must already be one of your first-degree connections on LinkedIn.

8. **Scroll back to the top of the page and click Publish.**

   You see a confirmation message that your Company page has been successfully updated, as shown in Figure 13-7. Now you can start to provide company updates, add products or services, or edit your page.

Figure 13-7:
Your
Company
page
has been
updated!

After your page is created, you should click the Follow button so your company has at least one follower. It's also a good check to see how company updates are showing up on a LinkedIn member's page (in this case, your page).

Now that you've created your Company page, think about incorporating your page management duties into your normal LinkedIn activity schedule. While it's important to properly set up your LinkedIn Company page, you'll want to spend some time on an ongoing basis to make sure you're properly communicating and responding with your followers and the community in large.

Here are some tips on how to proceed with administering your Company page:

- ✔ **Follow your competitors.** Not only will you gain insight into what your competitors are doing, you can see how they are using their LinkedIn Company page, which may give you ideas on how to position your Company page and what updates to share with your followers.

- ✔ **Add products or services.** Providing your basic company information is the first step. Next is defining the products or services that your company offers, so prospective customers can learn more about you and potentially try you out. Think about highlighting the right keywords and features that your customers want to see when defining your products or services on LinkedIn.

- ✔ **Ask your customers to recommend your company.** On LinkedIn, recommendations are not limited to those given to people. You can ask your current customers to write a recommendation for your company, which will appear on your Company page. Recommendations give any potential customers a great reason to consider your company.

- ✔ **Gain insight into how your company relates to your network.** When you click the Insights tab (located near the top of your Company page, below the Company name, next to the Overview and Products links), you can see some overall sets of information, like any former employees of the company that are in your own network, similar companies that were viewed by people visiting your page, your company employees with the most recommendations, and the skills that show up most often on your employees' LinkedIn profiles.

- ✔ **Keep an eye on the analytics.** LinkedIn provides a lot of information about how its members are viewing and interacting with Company pages. Click the Analytics tab (located near the top of your Company page, below the Company name, next to the Products and Insights links) to see how your followers are viewing and responding to your updates, as well as how many people you are reaching through your Company page — and how engaged they are with your Company page.

Part V
Using LinkedIn for Everyday Business

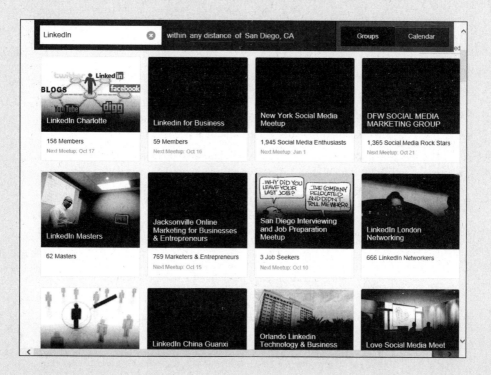

Find additional tips on using LinkedIn Groups at www.dummies.com/extras/linkedin.

In this part...

- ✔ Use LinkedIn Groups to meet like-minded people, expand your network, and grow your knowledge base.

- ✔ Get tips on how you can market your own business or start-up through LinkedIn.

- ✔ Understand how LinkedIn can help grow your business sales.

- ✔ Connect with venture capitalists and angel investors on LinkedIn and learn more about the company funding process.

- ✔ Discover some creative ways people have used LinkedIn to achieve their professional goals.

Chapter 14

Getting Connected with LinkedIn Groups

*W*hen it comes to the reasons why people get to know each other, there's more to a professional's life than colleagues and classmates. People have always been drawn to groups based on common interests, backgrounds, or goals, and this natural tendency to join together can be seen from sports teams to Boy/Girl Scouts, from social action organizations to nonprofit charity groups. Naturally, LinkedIn also offers a way for people to connect with each other as a group — LinkedIn Groups.

In this chapter, I discuss the benefits of value in LinkedIn Groups, from information and exposure to growing your network, and cover the overall idea and structure of LinkedIn Groups and what you can expect to find. I then talk about how to search for existing groups on LinkedIn, and I walk you through the steps necessary to join that group. Finally, if you see that there should be a group for something on LinkedIn but it doesn't already exist, I discuss how to start your own LinkedIn group and how to invite others to join it.

Reaping the Benefits of LinkedIn Groups

When people who are familiar with other social networking tools are first exposed to LinkedIn Groups, they see some similarities. The group interaction in LinkedIn Groups — members list, discussion threads, and so on — feels just like Yahoo! Groups or groups on most other social networking sites.

And yet, being a member of a LinkedIn group has extra benefits over other networking sites:

✔ **Connections:** Group members share a special sort of connection. Although you don't have access to their extended networks for introductions, you're considered directly connected to them, in that you can see their full profiles, and they can appear in your search results even if you aren't within three degrees of everyone in the group. Your search results can include fellow group members as well as your first-degree connections and second-degree network members.

✔ **Visibility:** By joining several groups — particularly large, open ones — you can increase your visibility in the LinkedIn network without having to add thousands of contacts.

✔ **Knowledge:** LinkedIn Groups share information and expertise among their members through the Discussions and Promotions pages of the group, which you can benefit from as a group member. Because there are thousands of groups for most industries and fields, LinkedIn Groups can be a valuable source of knowledge.

✔ **Recognition:** Employers like to see that you are connected with professional groups because it shows the desire to expand your knowledge base, stay current in your industry or field, and be open and eager to network with like-minded people.

✔ **Group logos:** The logos of the groups you're in are displayed on your profile. This is a sort of visual branding, reinforcing your association with those groups without a lot of words. For example, Figure 14-1 shows how the profile for a LinkedIn member who belongs to several groups might appear.

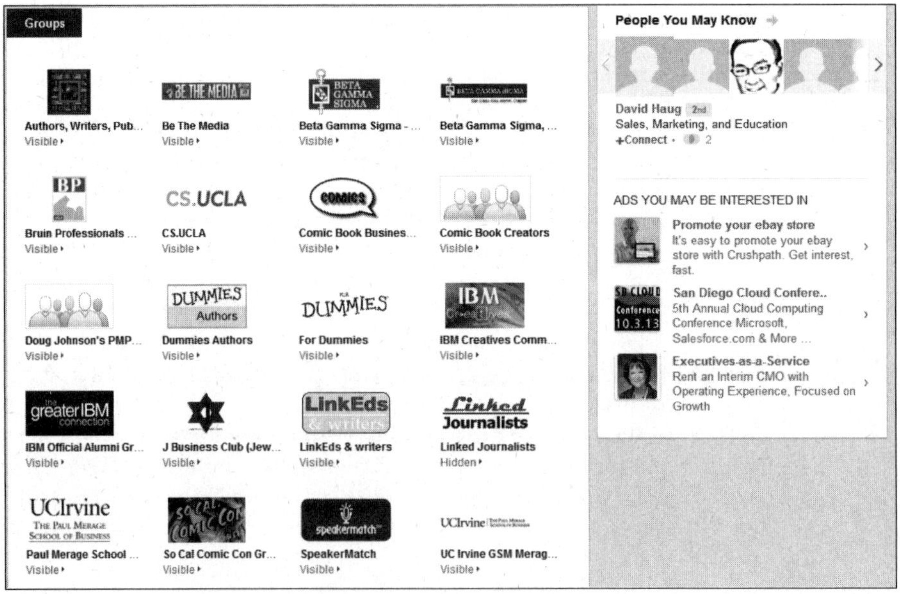

Figure 14-1: Group logos displayed on a profile.

Some LinkedIn Groups are extensions of existing organizations, and others are created on LinkedIn by an individual as a way to identify and network with people who share a common interest. In either case, they're useful tools for growing your network and leveraging your existing affiliations.

Understanding the Types of LinkedIn Groups

Because there are lots of reasons to create a group, LinkedIn has established the following six primary categories of groups:

- ✔ **Alumni:** These groups are alumni associations created by schools or teaching institutions as a means to keep in touch with past graduates. Graduates can also keep in touch with each other through an alumni group. As you develop your career, you can tap in to the alumni network of like-minded, qualified individuals. Loyalty to your alma mater makes you, and everyone else in the group, more likely to help a schoolmate than a complete stranger.

- ✔ **Corporate:** Because every company or organization has a unique culture, who better to understand that culture than current and past employees? Corporate groups allow employees from a single employer to stay in touch.

- ✔ **Conference:** For people planning to attend a particular conference, using a conference group to network with attendees before, during, and after the conference can be advantageous.

  Before the conference, you can relay important information, such as subject matter and agenda, and any events, lectures, seminars, parties, or other info that matters to the attendees. Perhaps there are last-minute changes or announcements that need to get disseminated quickly. During the event, you can quickly relay announcements, as well as news being generated at the conference and any on-site changes. After the conference, these groups allow attendees to stay in contact and help the conference organizers and presenters see how the subject matter and industries have changed or progressed.

  Also, if the conference becomes a yearly event, the conference group becomes a constant area of discussion and planning.

- ✔ **Networking:** A common interest is all that's needed to come together and meet similarly minded people. Networking groups are organized around concepts like women's networks, angel investors in new companies, or even Rotary Clubs. These LinkedIn groups allow you to stay involved in your interests and meet people with similar or complementary goals to your own.

✔ **Nonprofit:** After talking business all day, it's comforting to have a group where you can talk and plan any upcoming events that benefit your favorite nonprofit organization. These LinkedIn groups allow far-flung volunteers to organize, plan, and execute projects and events relating to their charity without being in the same room — which is especially convenient if everybody has a busy schedule. These groups also allow any nonprofit organizers to bring new members up to speed and answer their questions quickly so more people can become involved.

✔ **Professional:** Finally, who knows your career issues better than others in your industry or that share your job title? Professional groups allow you to network with people in the same line of work who are probably experiencing the same issues, problems, and potential solutions as you. Whether it's an organization of CFOs, workers in the wireless industry, or SAP Certified Consultants, these groups can be invaluable when it comes to furthering your career and giving you an avenue to evaluate job tips and industry news.

Joining a Group

When you look at the LinkedIn groups out there, one of the most important things to keep in mind is that you should join only those groups that are relevant to you. Although you might think it's fun to join another alumni association group besides your alma mater, it won't really help you in the long run.

As you use LinkedIn more and decide that you want to get involved by joining a LinkedIn group, you have a couple of options for getting started:

✔ Click the Group logo found on the profile of one of your first-degree connections to join the group yourself.

✔ Search the LinkedIn Groups Directory to find a group that interests you, then click the logo to join the group.

The first option may come about when you're browsing your first-degree connections list, and you see a group that you're interested in joining. After you click the logo, you simply click a Join This Group button on the next page that you see, and you've completed your part of the process. Keep in mind that some professional groups have special requirements and you may not be eligible to join due to your particular educational or professional experience.

If you plan to seek out a group to join, just follow these steps:

1. **From the top navigation bar, hover your mouse over the Interests link and then click the Groups link in the drop-down list that appears.**

   You're taken to your Groups page on LinkedIn, as shown in Figure 14-2.

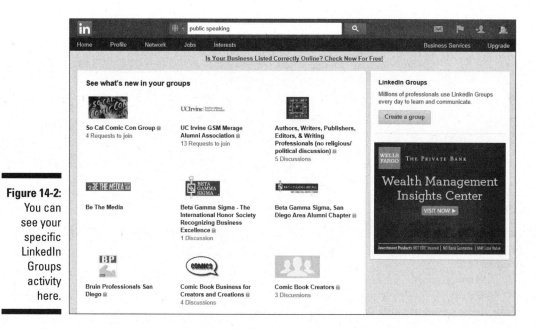

Figure 14-2:
You can
see your
specific
LinkedIn
Groups
activity
here.

2. **Enter keywords in the text box at the top of the page.**

   Use keywords to describe the group that interests you. If you're looking to join a group that promotes or encourages public speaking, for example, type **public speaking** into the text box.

3. **Click the Search button (it looks like a magnifying glass) to see a list of groups that match your keywords.**

   Go through the results list, as shown in Figure 14-3, and read the descriptions of each group on the list. If you need more information about the group, click the group name to see that group's summary page, which contains the group's contact e-mail, owner information, and member count. From this page, you can also contact the group owner and send him a message requesting a few details about the group.

4. **Click the Join button to join the LinkedIn group.**

   That's it! You see a confirmation message, as shown in Figure 14-4, and you're taken back to that group's home page. Depending on the requirements for membership, your request may be sent to the group manager for manual approval, instead of getting immediately approved, and if that occurs, you are returned to your Groups page from Step 1. As mentioned before, your request may not be approved depending on the criteria for that group.

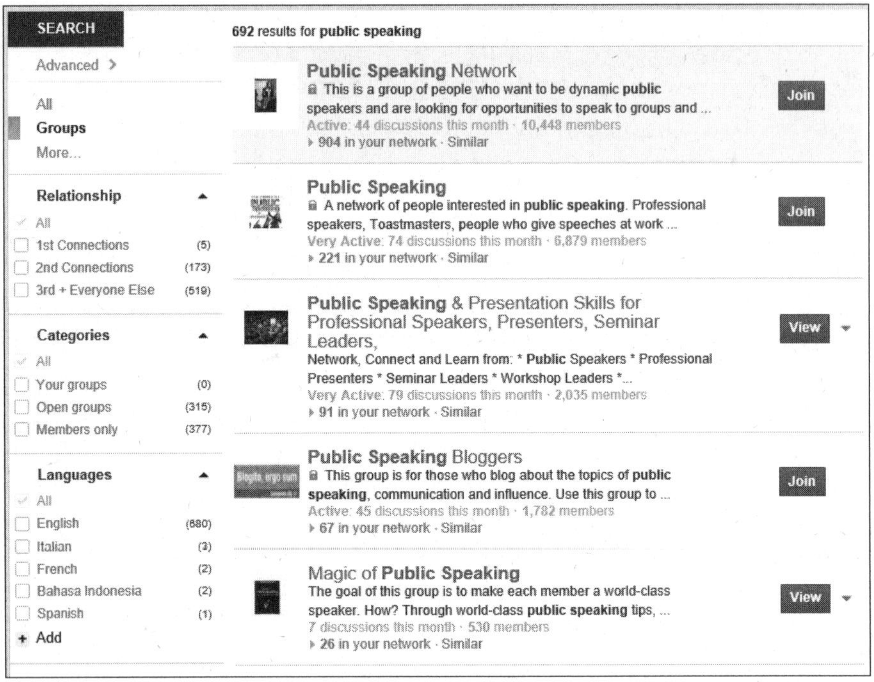

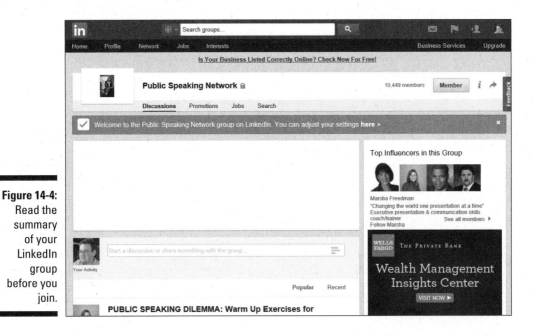

Figure 14-3:
Look
through a
list of poten-
tial groups
to join.

Figure 14-4:
Read the
summary
of your
LinkedIn
group
before you
join.

Searching a Group

After you join a group, you'll probably want to see who's in the group and how the group members are connected to you. After all, the point of these groups is to stay in touch with like-minded individuals and have them be part of your extended network.

To search a group, follow these steps:

1. **From the top navigation bar, hover your mouse over the Interests link and then click the Groups link in the drop-down list that appears.**

   Your Groups page appears.

2. **Look through the list of groups on this page, scroll down to the group's logo, and click that logo to bring up the Groups home page. On the page, click the link that contains the number of members in the group. (This link is to the left of the Member button.)**

   This brings up a search result of the members in the group, sorted by how many degrees they are away from you in your LinkedIn network, as shown in Figure 14-5.

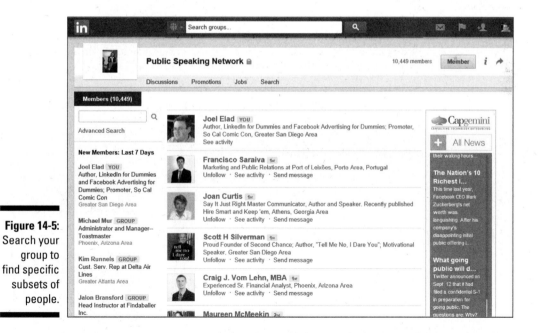

Figure 14-5: Search your group to find specific subsets of people.

Case study: Caltech gets connected

Caltech Alumni Association launched an official alumni group on LinkedIn in 2006. Of some 20,000 contactable alumni, it now has approximately 6,000 members in the LinkedIn group — about 30 percent. Andrew Shaindlin, Executive Director of the association, is one of the early adopters of using third-party social networking sites to help alumni stay connected.

With more than a year of experience running the group, Shaindlin noticed some cool things that his alumni members were doing with this new LinkedIn group, including the following:

✔ Graduates were making connections between their alumni network members and their non-alumni network members when they were networking.

✔ Alumni group members saw higher search engine placements for their member's names and more page views for Caltech in general.

✔ The Caltech Alumni Web site saw an increase of traffic from members clicking through from LinkedIn via the LinkedIn group Web site URL link.

✔ The Caltech Alumni Association has more graduates' e-mail addresses on file, attributed partially to their LinkedIn group.

✔ Most importantly, there are success stories about Caltech alumni finding jobs, employees, and investors through their LinkedIn group.

---

3. **(Optional) After you are on the search results screen, on the left-hand side of the screen, you can click the Advanced Search link and add other search criteria to get a more targeted results list.**

   This brings up an Advanced Search Results page, and you can see that the search is automatically limited to members of your group. Now you can scroll down the page and use more of the filters provided as search requirements, such as names, companies, user types, and locations.

4. **Click the Search button.**

   Your search is carried out according to the refined search criteria you entered.

Creating a Group

When you're ready to create your own group, just follow these steps:

1. **From the top navigation bar, hover your mouse over the Interests link and then click the Groups link in the drop-down list that appears.**

   You see your Groups page, with the main section See what's new in your groups and a Create a Group button along the right side of the screen.

2. **Click the Create a Group button.**

This step brings you to the Create a Group page, as shown in Figure 14-6. This is where you input all the information about your newly requested group.

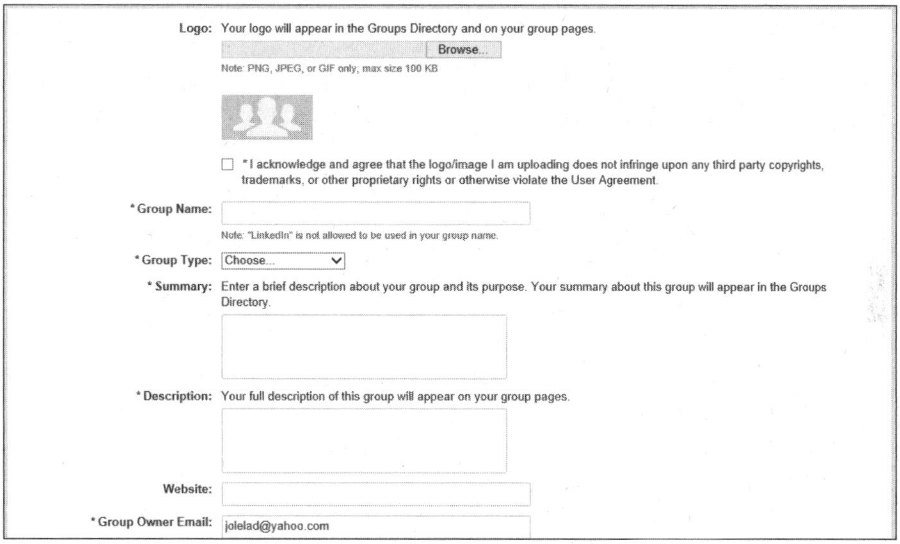

Figure 14-6:
Enter your
new group
information
here!

Logo: Your logo will appear in the Groups Directory and on your group pages.

Browse...

Note: PNG, JPEG, or GIF only; max size 100 KB

☐ *I acknowledge and agree that the logo/image I am uploading does not infringe upon any third party copyrights, trademarks, or other proprietary rights or otherwise violate the User Agreement.

* Group Name:

Note: "LinkedIn" is not allowed to be used in your group name.

* Group Type: Choose...

* Summary: Enter a brief description about your group and its purpose. Your summary about this group will appear in the Groups Directory.

* Description: Your full description of this group will appear on your group pages.

Website:

* Group Owner Email: jolelad@yahoo.com

3. **Upload the logo for your group.**

LinkedIn requires a logo. The file format must be PNG, JPEG, or GIF, and the memory size of the logo cannot exceed 100KB. Click the Browse button next to the logo box. In the Choose File dialog box that opens, locate the logo file on your computer so LinkedIn can upload it; then click Open.

"But where do I get a logo?" you might ask. Well, you can design your own logo at sites like www.logoyes.com or www.logoworks.com. If a logo already exists, like for an alumni association, ask one of the administrators for a high-resolution copy of the logo, or save a copy of the logo from the group's personal Web site — as long as you know you have the rights to use that image, of course.

Your logo can't exceed 100KB, so watch that file size as you create your logo.

4. **Provide your group information and settings, including group name, summary, description, type, Web site URL, manager e-mail, whether you want people to automatically have access to join or be pre-approved by you or another manager, and whether you want your group visible on your member's profile pages. (Refer to Figure 14-6.)**

You have only 300 characters in your group summary, so choose your words wisely.

If you're wondering what to write for your group description, search for similar groups using the search box at the top of the page and read through similar groups in your group type. Then, go back to the Create a Group page and enter your description. (If you check other group descriptions while writing your description, you'll lose whatever you typed.)

5. **If your group is located in one geographic region, select the appropriate check box.**

6. **Read through the Terms of Service and then select that check box.**

   At this point, your page should look something like Figure 14-7, where your logos and information are uploaded and ready for review.

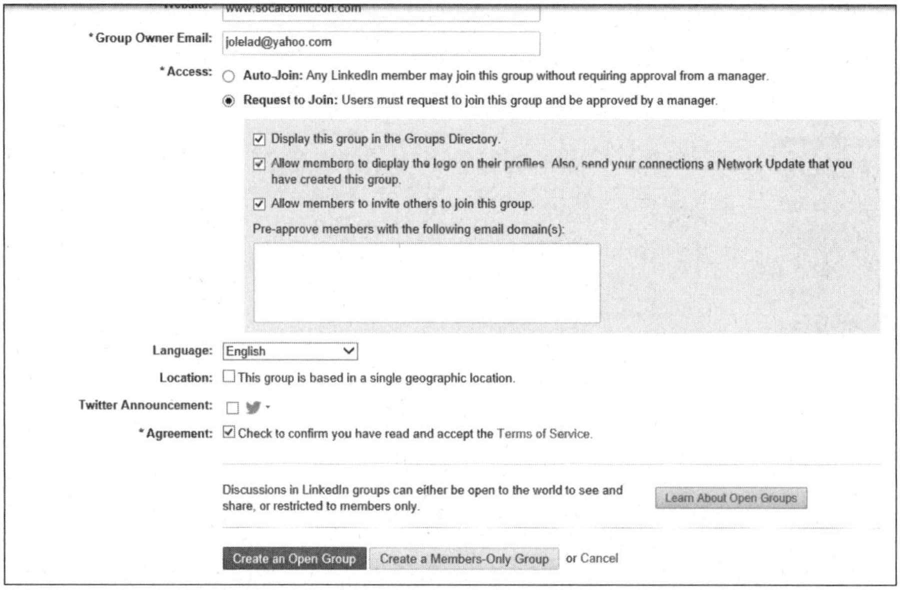

Figure 14-7:
Your group request is ready to be submitted!

Website:	www.socalcomiccon.com
*Group Owner Email:	jolelad@yahoo.com

*Access:
○ Auto-Join: Any LinkedIn member may join this group without requiring approval from a manager.
◉ Request to Join: Users must request to join this group and be approved by a manager.

☑ Display this group in the Groups Directory.
☑ Allow members to display the logo on their profiles. Also, send your connections a Network Update that you have created this group.
☑ Allow members to invite others to join this group.
Pre-approve members with the following email domain(s):

Language: English
Location: ☐ This group is based in a single geographic location.
Twitter Announcement: ☐ 🐦 ▾
*Agreement: ☑ Check to confirm you have read and accept the Terms of Service.

Discussions in LinkedIn groups can either be open to the world to see and share, or restricted to members only.   [Learn About Open Groups]

[Create an Open Group] [Create a Members-Only Group] or Cancel

7. **Click the Create a Group button to create your group on LinkedIn.**

   If you want your group discussions to be visible to everyone, click the Create an Open Group button. If you want your group discussions to be visible only to members, click the Create a Members-Only Group button. Either way, after you click that button, you're taken to the newly created home page for your new group, and your request is submitted.

   You should see your newly created group page, as shown in Figure 14-8. Your new group is ready for members!

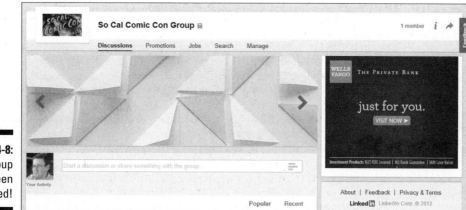

Figure 14-8:
Your group
has been
created!

Inviting Members

After you get your confirmation from LinkedIn that your new group has been created, your next step is to invite members to be a part of this group. This is actually a multi-part process:

1. **You have to define a list of pre-approved members of your group, which you upload to LinkedIn.**

   You should do this before you send out any invitations.

2. **You're allowed to e-mail your prospective members with an invitation to join your new group.**

   LinkedIn provides you with a Web page that you can use to generate your invitations.

3. **When someone clicks that link, LinkedIn checks to see whether that person is on your pre-approved list.**

   If so, she automatically becomes a member. If not, you (the group manager) see a member request in the Manage section of your group entry, which you have to manually approve so the person can officially join the group. The person's status shows up as Pending on her My Groups page until you approve her membership request.

Building your member list

The easiest way to build your list of members is to use a spreadsheet program like Microsoft Excel and create a Comma-Separated Values (CSV) file, which is simply a text file of members and their e-mail addresses. You should definitely have your member list in front of you before starting this process.

If many of the members are already connected to you in LinkedIn, you can simply export your connections to start building your member list. See Chapter 10 for more information on how to do this.

When you're ready to build your list of members, just follow these steps:

1. **Open a spreadsheet program, such as Microsoft Excel. Choose File⇨New from the top Excel menu to create a new blank document.**

2. **In the first row, create these entries for the three column headers:**

   • First Name

   • Last Name

   • E-mail Address

3. **Starting in the second row, fill in the members' names and e-mail addresses.**

   As you fill in your list, it should begin to look like Figure 14-9.

	File	Home	Insert	Page Layout	Formulas	Data	Review	View	

	A7	▾	*fx*		

	A	B	C	D	E
1	First Name	Last Name	E-mail address		
2	John	Doe	johndoe@mail.com		
3	Jane	Doe	janedoe@mail.com		
4	Loch	Ness	lochness@mail.com		
5	Big	Foot	bigfoot@mail.com		
6	Santa	Claus	santa@mail.com		
7					

Figure 14-9: Use Excel to build your group member list.

4. **Choose File⇨Save As.**

   The Save As window pops up, as shown in Figure 14-10.

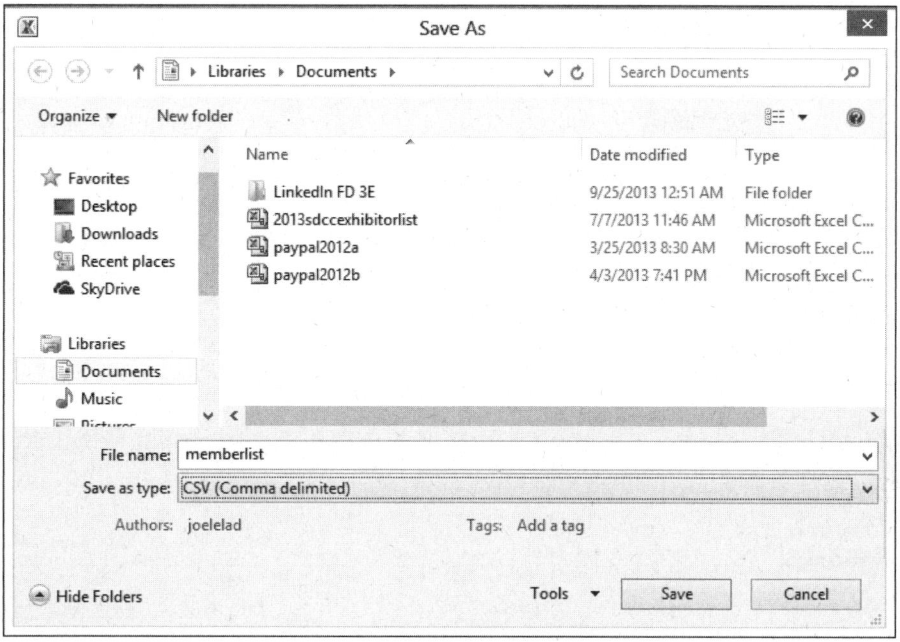

Figure 14-10:
Don't forget
to save your
file as CSV
(Comma-
Separated
Values).

5. **Make sure that the Save as Type option is set to CSV (Comma-Separated Values) and then click OK when prompted.**

6. **Go to your LinkedIn account and click the Interests link in the top navigation bar, then click the Groups link to bring up your My Groups page. Click the group logo to bring up your Group home page.**

7. **From your Group home page, click the Manage link to bring up the Manage Group page. Along the left-hand side of the Manage Group page, click the Pre-approve People option.**

   This brings up the Pre-approve People page for your group, as shown in Figure 14-11. At first, you're the only member of this new group.

8. **Click the Upload a File link below the Connections box in the middle of the screen.**

   This brings up the Upload a File page, as shown in Figure 14-12.

9. **Click the Browse button to find the CSV file on your computer.**

10. **After you specify the file you want, click the Upload File button to upload the file (containing your list of members) into your group.**

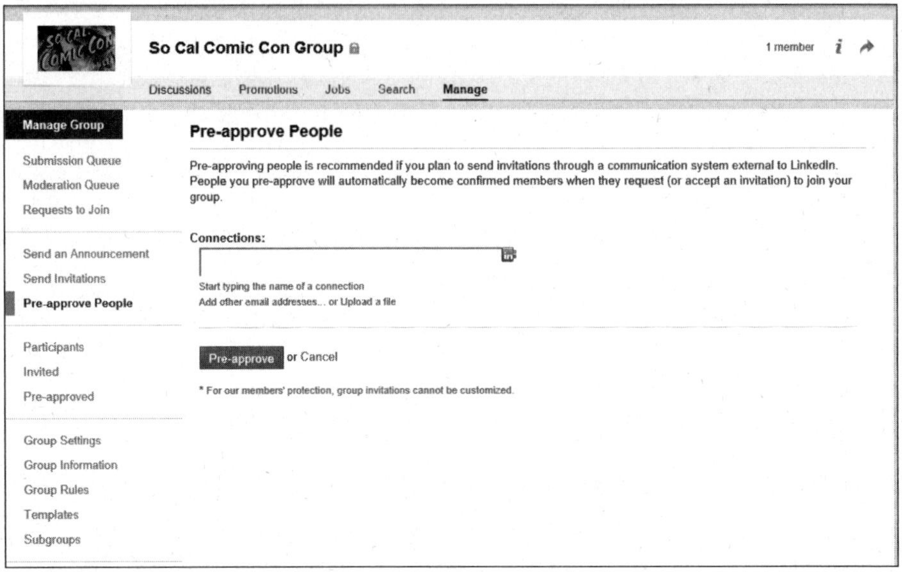

Figure 14-11:
The Pre-approve People page is one of many Manage Group tasks.

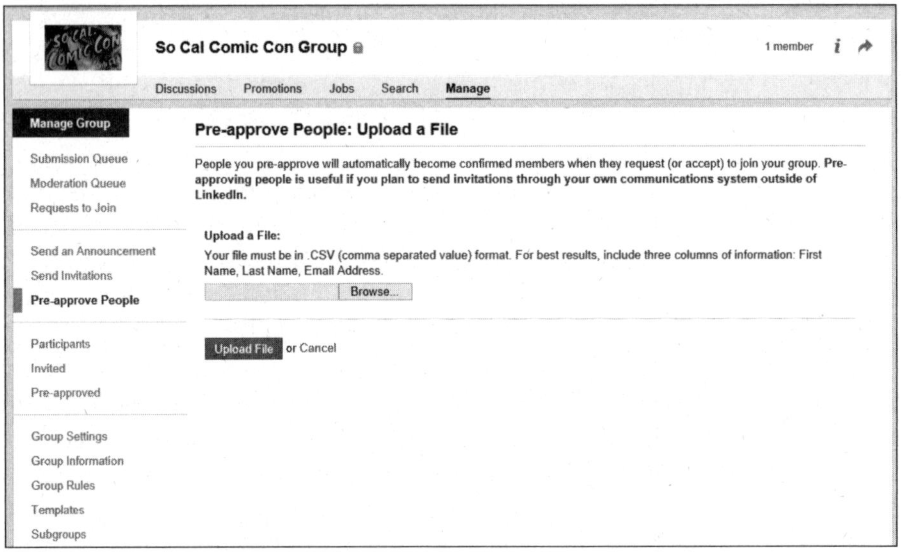

Figure 14-12:
Import your list of members here.

The next page attempts to determine whether the file was uploaded correctly. You should see your member list uploaded correctly, as shown in Figure 14-13. You have two options:

- **Finish Uploading:** If LinkedIn brought in the first few names correctly with the right text encoding — which pretty much assures everything went according to plan — click the Finish Uploading button.

- **Try Next Encoding:** If the names shown don't display correctly, click the Try Next Encoding link.

You're done! Your new members appear on the pre-approved list for this group.

You can always choose the Pre-approve People option and use the form to manually add names at any time.

If the e-mail address of a member's LinkedIn profile is different from the e-mail address you put in the pre-approved list, this member won't be automatically approved when he clicks the link. You have to manually approve him by clicking the Requests to Join link from the Groups page.

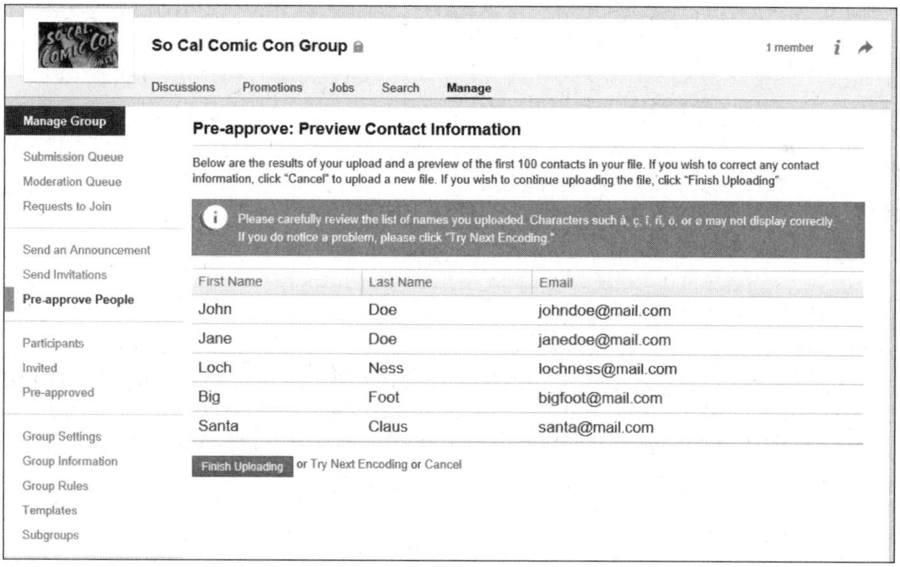

Figure 14-13:
Look through your list and add members to your group.

So Cal Comic Con Group   1 member

Discussions   Promotions   Jobs   Search   **Manage**

Manage Group

Submission Queue
Moderation Queue
Requests to Join

Send an Announcement
Send Invitations
Pre-approve People

Participants
Invited
Pre-approved

Group Settings
Group Information
Group Rules
Templates
Subgroups

Pre-approve: Preview Contact Information

Below are the results of your upload and a preview of the first 100 contacts in your file. If you wish to correct any contact information, click "Cancel" to upload a new file. If you wish to continue uploading the file, click "Finish Uploading"

Please carefully review the list of names you uploaded. Characters such à, ç, í, ñ, ó, or ø may not display correctly. If you do notice a problem, please click "Try Next Encoding."

First Name	Last Name	Email
John	Doe	johndoe@mail.com
Jane	Doe	janedoe@mail.com
Loch	Ness	lochness@mail.com
Big	Foot	bigfoot@mail.com
Santa	Claus	santa@mail.com

Finish Uploading   or Try Next Encoding or Cancel

Crafting your invitation e-mail

LinkedIn allows you to send group invitations from the Groups page because the folks at LinkedIn feel that invitations should come from the group owner — namely, you. Here are a few do's and don'ts to keep in mind as you craft your invitation:

✔ **Do relate the purpose and benefits of the group.** People are busy and need to understand why they should join this group. Explain the benefits of being connected to other people, the ability for professional development or advancement, and what you hope to accomplish with this group. Remember, you're sending this to LinkedIn members, so don't worry about explaining LinkedIn — just explain your group.

✔ **Don't go on forever.** One to two paragraphs is the maximum this invitation should be. Introduce yourself, introduce the group name, give people the benefits of joining, encourage them to join, include the link to the LinkedIn group page, and sign off. No one will read a long diatribe or laundry list of reasons to join. Use bullet points and short sentences whenever possible.

✔ **Don't put other offers in the e-mail.** Some people use this as an opportunity not only to encourage folks to join one group, but to push a second group invitation, or highlight a link to the group's non-LinkedIn Web site. The moment you start presenting multiple options for people, you lose their attention, and they won't sign up.

You can use any e-mail program to create an invitation to your group, or you can go to the Manage link of your group and click Send Invitations from the navigation options on the left-hand side of the screen. You simply type in the name of your first-degree connections (separated by commas), a Subject line, and a Welcome Message, which can look as simple as this:

Hello,

You are hereby invited to join the new So Cal Comic Con Group on LinkedIn. Joining this group will allow you to find and contact other people interested in the convention, so you can stay in touch, gain referrals, and view other attendees' LinkedIn profiles.

Hope to see you in the group!

–Joel Elad, Co-Promoter, So Cal Comic Con

After you send out the invitations, as members respond, they're moved from the pre-approved list to the current list of your group, and the small group logo appears on their profiles.

Approving members to your group

As more and more people find out about your new LinkedIn group, and as members start joining, you may find that some of the people who have clicked the link to join aren't on your pre-approved list. Perhaps they are people you didn't realize were on LinkedIn, or you didn't realize they were valid group members, or they clicked the wrong link and/or they don't belong in your group.

It can be helpful, from an administrative standpoint, to develop criteria or guidelines for people to join your group, so you can evaluate each request as it comes in. Consider talking to the governing members of your group to develop this in the early days of your group, so you don't have to worry about it later on when things get busy.

Regardless, you need to go into LinkedIn and either approve or reject people's membership requests so they can be members (or non-members) of your LinkedIn group. When you need to do that, just follow these steps:

1. **From the top navigation bar, hover your mouse over the Interests link and then click the Groups link in the drop-down list that appears.**

   By default, you should see your Groups page, although all your group options are just a click away.

2. **Scroll down (if necessary) until you see the name and logo of the group you are maintaining, as shown in Figure 14-14.**

Figure 14-14: You can manage your LinkedIn group membership.

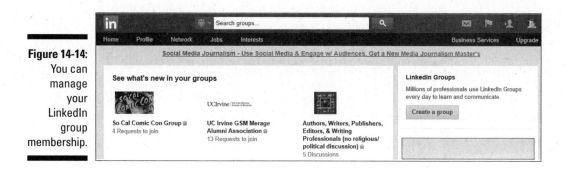

3. **Click the Requests to Join link below the name of your group to bring up the Requests to Join page.**

   This step brings up the list of people waiting to be approved for your group, as shown in Figure 14-15.

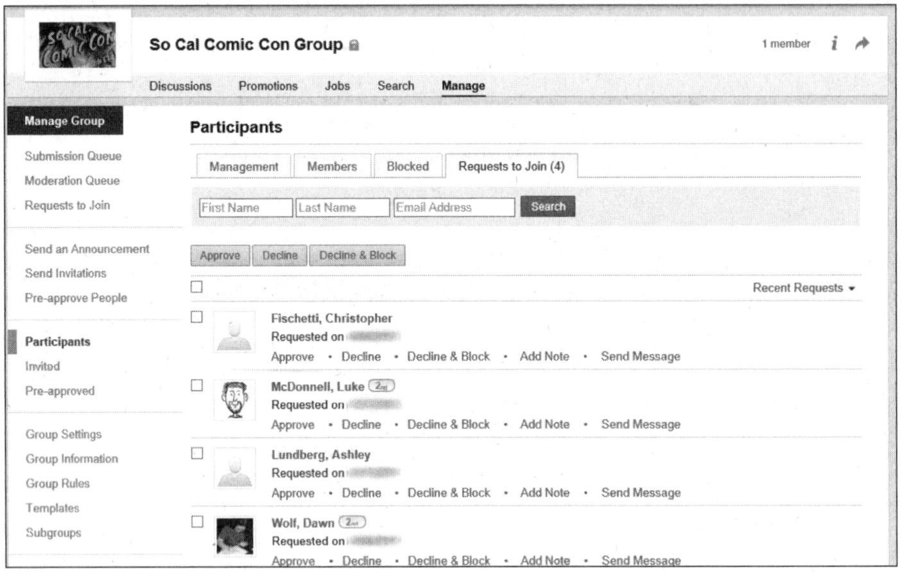

Figure 14-15: See who is waiting to be approved to your LinkedIn group.

4. **To accept people, select the check box next to each person you want to approve to join your LinkedIn group, then click the Approve button.**

   You can approve people individually or all at once if you want. You can always select the person's name on the list to read his LinkedIn profile and decide whether he belongs in the group or send him a message through his profile.

5. **To refuse membership, select the check box next to each person you want to decline membership to the group, then click the Decline button.**

   You can also click the Decline & Block button if you want to permanently block someone from trying to join the group.

Similar to the approval process, you can decline people one at a time or all at once. (The easiest way to select everyone is to select the empty check box at the top of the list; the one with no name associated with it.) In either case (approval or decline), the user's name disappears from the Request to Join page. Lastly, remember that you can remove someone from the group membership at any time after you initially approved him.

If you're going to decline someone, you may want to use the Send Message option first, before declining him, to let him know why you are declining his request. After you decline that person, you won't be able to send him a message without using the InMail system.

Chapter 15

Marketing Yourself and Your Business

*I*n this part of the book, you find out how to start applying everything the previous parts cover about how to use LinkedIn for specific situations and needs. After all, every great invention needs to fulfill some sort of purpose, and LinkedIn is no exception. Its value is not just in how it allows you to network and build your brand, but also in how you can use LinkedIn to handle other tasks more easily and effectively.

I start with the age-old discipline of marketing. In this chapter, I discuss how to generate sales and how LinkedIn can affect your entire sales cycle. LinkedIn can help you "spread the gospel" of your business mission by serving as a vehicle for positive and rich marketing messages about both you and your business, whether it's a start-up, personal service provider, or a Fortune 500 company. Part of the power of LinkedIn comes from involving others in your marketing initiatives, so I cover some ways for you to do that as well.

Marketing Yourself Through LinkedIn

When it comes to maximizing the benefit you receive from LinkedIn, you are your biggest advocate. Although your network of connections is instrumental in helping you grow, much of your marketing happens without your being involved. After you create your profile, that and any other LinkedIn activity of yours are read and judged by the community at large — on the other members' own time and for their own purposes. Therefore, you want to make sure you're creating a favorable impression of yourself by marketing the best traits, abilities, and features of you and your business. Because of the nature of LinkedIn, this marketing occurs continually — 24/7. So, you should look at LinkedIn as something to check and update on a continual basis, like a blog. It doesn't mean you have to spend hours each day on LinkedIn, but a little bit of time on a consistent basis can go a long way toward creating a favorable and marketable LinkedIn identity.

The following sections look at the different ways you interact with LinkedIn, and what you can do to create the most polished, effective LinkedIn identity possible to further your marketing message.

Optimizing your profile

In Chapter 3, I discuss building your professional profile on LinkedIn, which is the centerpiece of your LinkedIn identity and your personal brand. I refer to your profile throughout this book, but here, I focus on ways for you to update or enhance your profile with one specific goal in mind: marketing yourself better or more consistently. As always, not every tip or suggestion works for everyone, and you might have already put some of these into action, but it's always good to revisit your profile to make sure it's organized the way you intended.

To make sure your profile is delivering the best marketing message for you, consider these tips:

- ✔ **Use the Professional headline wisely.** Your Professional headline is what other LinkedIn users see below your name even when they're not looking at your full profile. I've seen some users stuff a lot of text into this field, so you should have enough space to communicate the most important things about yourself. If you have specific keyword phrases you want associated with your name, make them a part of your headline.

    A standard headline reads something like "Software Development Manager at XYZ Communications," but you can write entire sentences full of great keywords for your headline. My client Liz Goodgold's headline reads "Branding and Marketing Expert, Author, Coach, and Motivational Speaker." Think about how many people would want to connect with her!

- ✔ **Make sure you use keyword phrases that match popular keywords for you or your business.** The first step, as I just mentioned, is to put these phrases in your headline. The second step is to make sure these phrases are reflected in your Summary, Experiences, and Interests.

Be careful not to overuse your main keyword phrases. The search engines call this practice "stuffing," which is cramming as many instances of a phrase into your site as possible in hopes of achieving a higher ranking. If the search engines detect this, you will experience lower ranking results.

✔ **If you're available for freelance work, make sure to identify at least one of your current positions as freelance or self-employed.** Remember, people aren't mind readers, so you need to let people know that you're a freelance writer, Web site designer, dog walker, or whatever. If you look at Cynthia Beale's profile in Figure 15-1, you can see that she's listed her current position as self-employed.

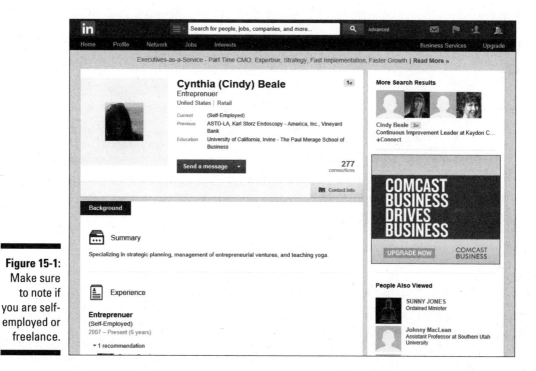

Figure 15-1: Make sure to note if you are self-employed or freelance.

✔ **Use the additional sections in your profile to include any relevant information that reinforces your marketing message.** For example, if you want to be seen as an expert in a given field, add the SlideShare application to upload presentations you've given, or update the Publications section of your profile to include the articles or books you've written, articles you've been quoted in, focus or advisory groups you belong to, and any speaking engagements or discussions you've participated in. LinkedIn has created sections like Projects, Patents, and Certifications for you to display specific accomplishments that are an important part of your professional identity.

✔ **Make sure your profile links to your Web sites, blogs, and any other part of your online identity.** Don't just accept the standard "My Company" text. Instead, select the Other option, and put your own words in the Web site title box, such as "Joel Elad's E-Commerce Education Web site." (See Chapter 3 for more information on linking from your profile to other Web sites.)

For an example of effectively linking your profile to other areas of your online presence, take a look at Scott Allen's profile, shown in Figure 15-2. His three Web site links replace the bland My Company, My Blog, and My Website with his own text — Momentum Factor, Linked Intelligence, and Social Media Is My Middle Name. Not only does this give more information to someone reading his profile, but search engines have a better idea of what those links represent.

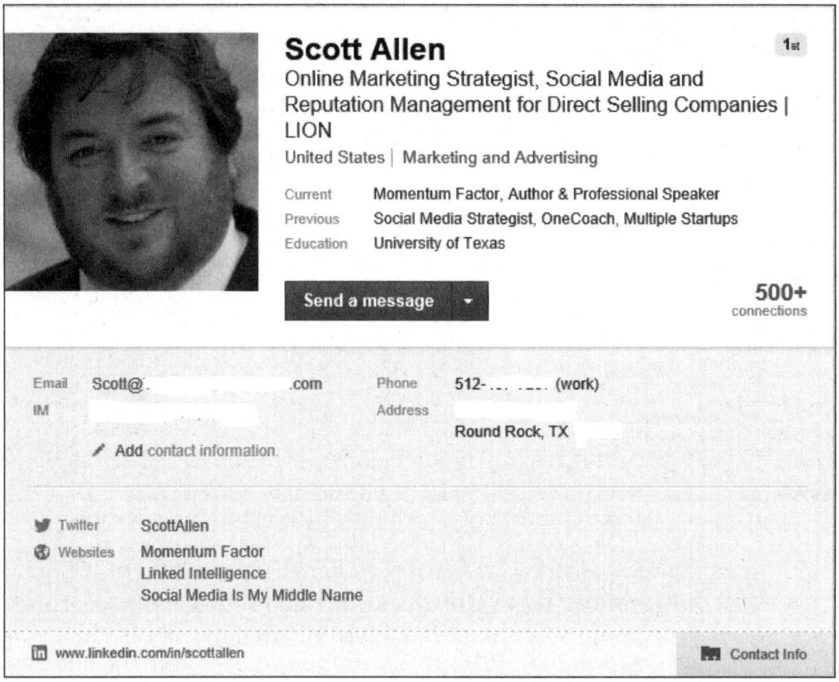

Figure 15-2:
Give your Web site links meaningful names.

Scott Allen   1st
Online Marketing Strategist, Social Media and
Reputation Management for Direct Selling Companies |
LION
United States | Marketing and Advertising

Current   Momentum Factor, Author & Professional Speaker
Previous   Social Media Strategist, OneCoach, Multiple Startups
Education   University of Texas

Send a message   **500+**
                                                   connections

Email   Scott@ .   .com   Phone   512- ... . (work)
IM   Address
                                                  Round Rock, TX
✎ Add contact information.

🐦 Twitter   ScottAllen
🌐 Websites   Momentum Factor
               Linked Intelligence
               Social Media Is My Middle Name

in www.linkedin.com/in/scottallen   Contact Info

Marketing yourself to your network

Optimizing your profile in the ways described in the previous section is one of the best ways to market yourself effectively using LinkedIn. Another is to be alert to how well you're communicating with your LinkedIn connections. Whether it's automatic (like when you update your profile and LinkedIn automatically notifies your network through a network update) or self-generated (when you use LinkedIn InMail or introductions to send a note to someone else, which I cover in Chapter 5), this communication becomes your ongoing message to the members of your network and keeps you in their minds and (you hope!) plans.

The most effective marketing occurs when people don't realize you're marketing to them. After all, the average American sees all kinds of marketing messages throughout their day. Your goal is to communicate often but not be overbearing about it so your message subtly sinks into people's minds. If you do that, people will think you're grrrr-*eat*! (Hmm, why am I suddenly hungry for cereal?)

So when you're contemplating how to effectively communicate with your network connections, keep these points in mind:

- ✔ **Update your profile when appropriate.** Updating your profile means that you're sending an update of your newest projects to your network so that your connections can consider involving you in their own current or future projects. You don't need to update your profile as often as you update a blog, but you certainly don't want to leave your profile untouched for months on end, either. Useful times to update your profile include

  - Getting a new job or promotion

  - Starting a new freelance or contract job

  - Launching a new company or venture

  - Adding a missing piece of your Experience section, such as adding a new position, updating the description of an existing job, or clarifying the role of a group or interest on your profile

  - Receiving an award or honor for your professional, nonprofit, or volunteer work

  - Being appointed to a board of directors or elected to a professional association board

  - Taking on new responsibilities or duties in any of your endeavors

✔ **Take advantage of the Network Update feature.** When you specify your current endeavors, several things happen. Your profile reflects what you enter here, your network connections see what you enter here when they read their network updates about you (see Chapter 9 for more on network updates), and you start to build your own microblog, in a sense, because people can follow your natural progression.

A similar example of a microblog is Twitter. As you update your Twitter profile with 140-character messages, other people can follow your activities and even subscribe to these updates. Tie your Twitter updates to your LinkedIn account, so if you "tweet" on Twitter, those updates are automatically reflected on your LinkedIn profile.

Some people use the Network Update feature to let people know that "Joel is getting ready for his next project" or "Joel is finishing up his first draft of *LinkedIn For Dummies.*" Other people use the messages to show progression of a certain task, like "Joel is currently conducting interviews for an Executive Assistant position he is trying to fill," then "Joel is narrowing down his choices for Executive Assistant to two finalists," and finally "Joel has made an offer to his top choice for Executive Assistant." See Chapter 9 for more on how to use this feature.

✔ **Search for, and join, any relevant LinkedIn Groups that can help you reach your target audience.** It's a good idea to participate in these groups, but whatever you do, don't immediately download a list of all group members and spam them with LinkedIn messages. When you join the group, you're indicating your interest in that group because your profile now carries that group logo. Membership in such groups gives you access to like-minded people you should be communicating with and adding to your network. Spend some time every week or every month checking out LinkedIn Groups and networking with group members to grow your network. See Chapter 14 for more about LinkedIn Groups.

✔ **Participate on a regular and consistent basis.** The easiest way to ensure a steady stream of contact with as many people as you can handle is to dedicate a small but fixed amount of time to regularly interact with the LinkedIn community. Some members spend 15 to 30 minutes per day, sending messages to their connections, reading through the Groups and Companies or Influencers page, or finding one to two new people to add to their network. Others spend an hour a week, or as long as it takes to create their set number of recommendations, invite their set number of new contacts, or reconnect with their set number of existing connections. You just need to establish a routine that works with your own schedule.

Marketing Your Business Through LinkedIn

LinkedIn can play a significant role in the effective marketing of your business. LinkedIn's value as a marketing tool gets a lot of buzz from most companies' finance departments, especially because they see LinkedIn as a free way of marketing the business. Although you don't have to pay anything in terms of money to take advantage of most of LinkedIn's functions, you do have to factor in the cost of the time you put in to manage your profile and use LinkedIn to the fullest.

Currently, LinkedIn offers your company promotion through its Company pages section. LinkedIn ties status updates, job titles, and other pertinent information from company employees' profiles directly into the Company page. From each page, you can see those people you know in the company, open career positions, recent updates from their employees, and other pertinent facts.

If you're a small business, you can create your own Company page. You need to have your company e-mail address in your LinkedIn profile and be established as a current employee/manager/owner of that company in your profile as well. Click the Interest link from the top navigation bar, and then click Companies from the drop-down list that appears to learn more.

Using online marketing tactics with LinkedIn

Marketing your business on LinkedIn involves working through your own network, employing both your current list of contacts as well as potential contacts in the greater LinkedIn community. Your efforts should also include making use of links from your online activities to your LinkedIn profile and promoting your business online from your LinkedIn identity. Here are some things to keep in mind as you develop your LinkedIn marketing strategy:

  ✔ **Encourage every employee to have a LinkedIn profile and to link to each other.** Extending your network in this way increases your exposure outside your company. And if anybody in your organization is nervous about preparing her profile, just tell her that LinkedIn can be an important asset in their professional or career development. You can mention that even Bill Gates has a LinkedIn profile. That should do the trick! (And then buy her a copy of this book to get her started.)

✔ **Make sure your business Web sites and blogs are linked to your LinkedIn profile.** By offering your Web site visitors a direct view to your LinkedIn profile, you're allowing them to verify you as an employee of the company because they can see your experience and recommendations from other people. They might also realize they share a bond with you and your business that they never would have discovered without LinkedIn.

✔ **Make sure your LinkedIn profile links back to your business Web site and blog.** You not only want your visitors and potential customers to be able to verify who you are, but you also want them to go back to your Web site and do some business with you! Make sure that you, and every employee of your company who's on LinkedIn, includes a link to your business's Web site and, if there is one, the company blog.

If you have a search engine expert working for you, that person may complain about something called a *two-way link,* which is a link from your LinkedIn profile to your Web site and a link from your Web site to your LinkedIn profile. This practice, known as *reciprocal linking,* hurts your search engine ranking. If so, have that person identify which of the two links is more important and implement only that link.

✔ **Make sure that your most popular keyword phrases are in your company or personal profile.** Use sites such as Wordtracker (www.wordtracker.com) or Good Keywords (www.goodkeywords.com) to find the hottest keyword phrases in your field. If your business is doing any online ad campaigns, make sure those keyword phrases are the same as the ones in your profile. Presenting a consistent image to potential customers makes you and your company look more professional.

✔ **Develop relationships with key business partners or media contacts.** When you search for someone on LinkedIn, you can be precise about who you want to reach. So, for example, if you know that your business needs to expand into the smartphone market, you can start targeting and reaching out to smartphone companies such as Apple, Samsung (maker of the Galaxy and Note), and HTC (maker of the One). If you want to increase your visibility, start reaching out to media members who cover your industry.

Promoting your services through a recommendation

Now, you may ask, "What if I *am* my business?" If you provide a professional service, such as consulting or freelance writing (to name just a few), be sure to take advantage of the fact that LinkedIn can classify you as a service provider. There are categories and subcategories of service providers that range from computer-related consultants to attorneys, accountants, and real estate agents. Although you can no longer search exclusively for a service provider, your recommendations for any service position still show up in your profile, which can be visible when people search LinkedIn, making it a potentially valuable addition to your business.

To request a recommendation from someone, just follow these steps:

1. **Click the word Profile in the top navigation bar, then click Edit Profile from the menu that appears. From your profile page, scroll down to the Recommendations section and click the Edit link (the pencil icon) to open up that section.**

   You see an expanded view of your recommendations, as shown in Figure 15-3, along with the Ask to Be Recommended link on the right side of the screen.

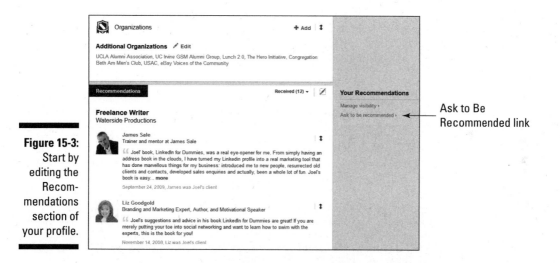

Figure 15-3: Start by editing the Recommendations section of your profile.

Ask to Be Recommended link

2. **Click the Ask to Be Recommended link to bring up the Ask for Recommendations page, shown in Figure 15-4.**

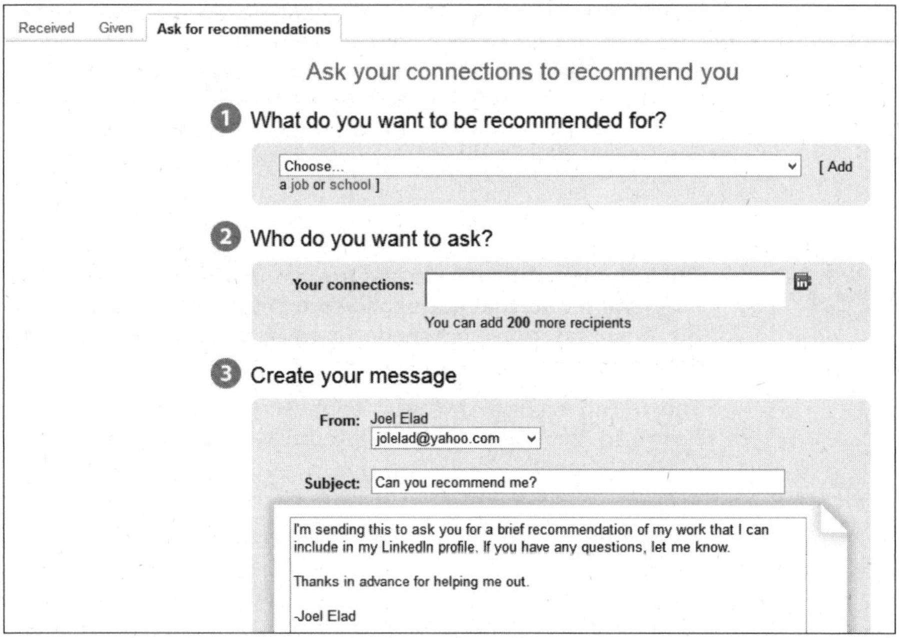

Figure 15-4:
Start your
service
provider
recom-
mendation
request.

3. **In the What Do You Want to Be Recommended For section, click the arrow for the drop-down list to find the position you want someone to recommend you for.**

   If you want your Services recommendation to be tied to a specific role, pick one of your positions that indicates that service, such as Freelance Writer or Web site Designer. If you don't see an appropriate position in your list, click the Add a Job or School link to add a new position to the Experience section of your profile. (For more information on how to update your profile, see Chapter 3.)

4. **In the Who Do You Want to Ask section, start typing the names of people to ask for a recommendation.**

   As you type those people's names, LinkedIn prompts you with the full name of that person. Click that prompt to have LinkedIn add that person to the list.

5. **Repeat Step 4 until you add all the people you wish to ask for a recommendation.**

6. **In the Create Your Message section, type a note to send to each person you selected, similar to the example shown in Figure 15-5.**

Although LinkedIn fills in this box with canned text (as shown in Figure 15-5), I recommend you personalize this text to make it sound as though it's coming from you. Most importantly, you should use this message to emphasize to the recommender what areas you are hoping they will comment on regarding your service. It's not about feeding them a speech to say about you, but pointing them to the areas you want mentioned in their recommendation.

TIP

Make sure the Subject line is appropriate, too, to help your chances of getting your intended requesters to actually open the e-mail and respond.

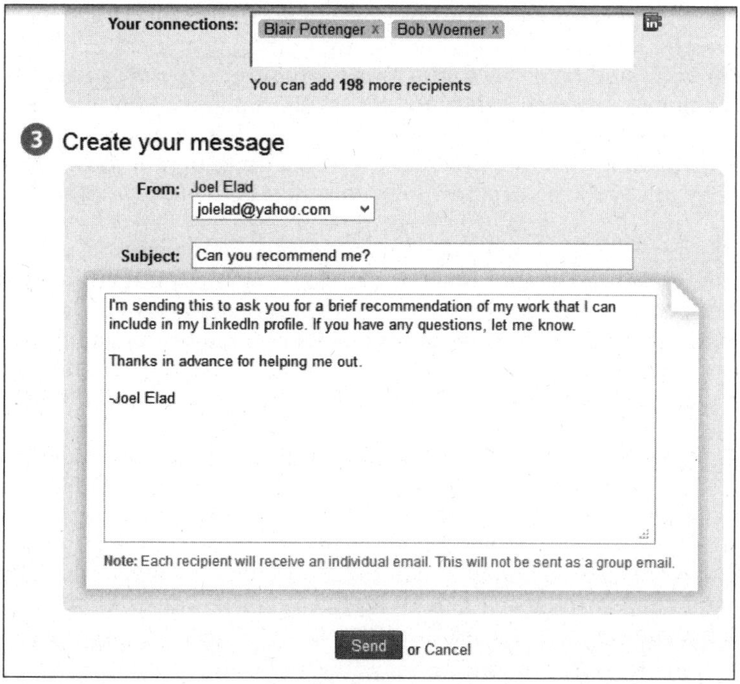

Figure 15-5:
Ask your network connections for a recommendation.

7. Click Send.

Your request is sent, and your selected connections receive a message from LinkedIn asking them to come to the site and complete a recommendation for you.

That's it! For information on how to complete a recommendation for someone who requests one from you, check out Chapter 8.

The best business etiquette involves a combination of online and offline methods, so don't be afraid to follow up with your recommenders through a phone call, e-mail, or face-to-face interaction after you send the request to make sure you can answer any questions they have and help them complete the process.

Finding Marketing Partners Through LinkedIn

When it comes to marketing on LinkedIn, your strategy typically involves more than just you and your business. Part of the success of marketing through LinkedIn is finding the right marketing partners to help you with your goals and take you to the next level. After all, you're connecting with like-minded professionals who have skills similar or complementary to yours, which helps both of you achieve your goals. In some cases, finding the right partner can make a big difference in the growth of your business, as I found out by interviewing Kristie Spilios, profiled in the following sidebar.

Odds are, you won't have all the answers when it comes to your strategic plan, marketing plan, or maybe even your business direction. Thankfully, when you're using LinkedIn, you're definitely not alone. LinkedIn allows you to search the collective knowledge of its community, enabling you to perform some market research on a variety of topics and get real-time responses without involving think tanks or putting out thousands of dollars in fees.

The key is to be honest, transparent, and (as odd as this might sound) grateful. After all, you are asking for people's advice and thoughts, so don't expect them to write a 30-page market analysis for you for free. Share your goals and intentions as a network update, get people discussing the idea and each other's comments, and be ready to listen. The best research results from the community's exchange of ideas, with a bunch of voices chiming in to validate or discount the theorem of the moment.

If you're really ambitious, you can set up a LinkedIn group that speaks to your target audience and your company's (or your) capabilities to gain more perspective and input. For example, if you're trying to reach accountants for financial services companies, to get the ball rolling you could start the Financial Services Accountants Group, spread the word to your target audience, and stay in touch with that audience via this group whenever you want to know more about your target audience.

No trouble starting TrebleMakers (with the help of a LinkedIn contact)

Several years ago, Kristie Spilios co-founded a company called TrebleMakers, which teaches music enrichment classes to young children. While she was building her marketing plan with her business partner, they realized that an important piece was the Web site and logo design they would be using. Given their limited preliminary budget, they were completely unable to find anyone who would address their needs. And then came salvation.

"When all hope seemed lost, I received a LinkedIn e-mail update that announced the connection of one of my contacts with an old, mutual friend from our high school days," relates Spilios. "This shared companion had just opened a consulting business and was enthusiastically eager to work with us despite our start-up woes."

Three months later, TrebleMakers received its "spectacular" Web site and "dazzling" logo (as shown in the following figure) for a reasonable fee that fell within their price range. The consultant even included some complementary business cards and letterhead stationery as appreciation for TrebleMakers' belief in him and his latest endeavor. TrebleMakers thrived and grew, and Spilios credits much of that success to having an informative Web site and prominent logo, saying that "We receive almost as many words of praise on our Web site and logo as we do on the music classes themselves!"

"Without LinkedIn and its awesome networking, my company would most likely still be searching for a cost-efficient marketing solution. But, instead of singing the blues, my

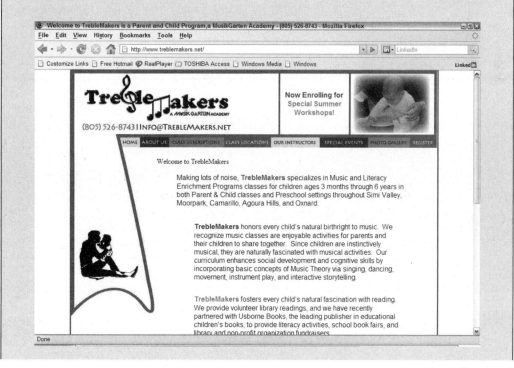

(continued)

(continued)

business partner and I both have happy harmony, all thanks to LinkedIn!"

Your first order of business is to use the LinkedIn Company page directory to start identifying potential partners. (See Chapter 13 on how to use the Companies directory.) You can look for service providers who may be two or three degrees away from you or you can target people you want to meet at specific companies by seeing who in your network can arrange an introduction. Here are some ideas to keep in mind during your search:

- **Pay attention to people's titles.** In the past, you might have searched for someone "who works at advertising sales for a major radio network." Today, with LinkedIn, you can look for an Advertising Sales Manager at Clear Channel Communications. Search for who you need to know, specifically, and LinkedIn shows you whether that person is connected to you by one, two, or three degrees.

- **Join the LinkedIn groups that would appeal to your business.** One of the quickest ways to signal your interest and find like-minded

businesspeople is to join a LinkedIn group that's relevant to your industry or niche. You can then search group members to find potential partners. Also, because your groups are listed on your profile, joining a group means that you have a lasting reference on your profile that lets people know you identify with this group. Also, members of the group who are experts are often willing to give you advice as you build your business, and they often have information on helpful resources for your business.

- **Read through your network updates and post accordingly.** You can learn about the reach of your network by seeing what your first-degree connections are sharing in terms of articles, updates, and information. Share relevant articles and see who comments or contacts you because of it, and always check the comments section of any articles that your connections post. See what articles or news LinkedIn Pulse recommends for you that are part of your update feed.

Chapter 16

Using LinkedIn to Increase Your Sales

*W*hen it comes to "making the sale," every edge you can gain over the competition is important. LinkedIn provides several ways to help you to get more competitive, close the sale, and even help deliver the winning solution. Throughout the entire sales cycle, a well-connected network and detailed profile can help you narrow the gap, identify with your potential lead, gain some trust, and make that sale. Even in the world of nonprofit organizations, LinkedIn can help you generate leads to potential donors, which are the lifeblood of any nonprofit.

In this chapter, I tell you about some of the ways LinkedIn can help you with sales. You find out how generating leads means more than just coming up with a pool of potential clients; you need to zero in on the decision maker — the person who's in the position to decide to buy your product or services. Then, after you identify your target, you can research your prospects using LinkedIn and, when you succeed in setting up a meeting with a prospect, you can use LinkedIn to prepare for that crucial meeting. Finally, this chapter covers how LinkedIn can help you deliver the winning solution after you have made the sale, and how you can report a positive experience with your customer, thereby leading to even more sales!

Mining for Clients

It's a big world out there. In terms of clients, you need to ask yourself who you're looking for. Is everyone a potential client, or do you have a specific demographic in mind? A specific skill set? Maybe you've written the greatest plug-in tool for accountants who work in the financial services industry, and you want to sell this tool directly to your likely users. With LinkedIn, you can conduct a search to find people who match your criteria. Then after you locate those people, it's up to you to approach them and close the sale, which I talk about in the "Closing the Deal" section, later in this chapter.

Before you start your search, ask yourself some questions that can help you with generating your leads:

✔ Are you looking for people with a specific title or in a particular industry?

✔ Are you looking for high-net-worth or well-connected donors for your nonprofit organization?

✔ Are you looking for decision makers within a company, or are you seeking a general audience? (That is, are you trying to sell into a company, or directly to people?)

✔ Besides your main target industry, can you approach related industries, and if so, what are they?

✔ Does the location of your potential contact matter? Does making the sale require an in-person visit (which means that the contact needs to live near you or you have to be willing to travel to this person)?

With your answers to these questions in mind, you're ready to start searching LinkedIn for your leads.

Generating leads with the Advanced People search

When you're ready to start looking for leads, I recommend jumping right in with the LinkedIn Advanced People search, which allows you to search the database consisting of tens of millions of LinkedIn members based on the criteria you've established for the leads you want to generate.

To start a search, first make sure that People is selected in the Search drop-down list in the top of the page and then click the Advanced link next to the Search text box. Say you need accountants who work in the Financial Services industry. To start such a search, you would fill in the Title and Industry fields of Advanced People search, as shown in Figure 16-1, and then click Search.

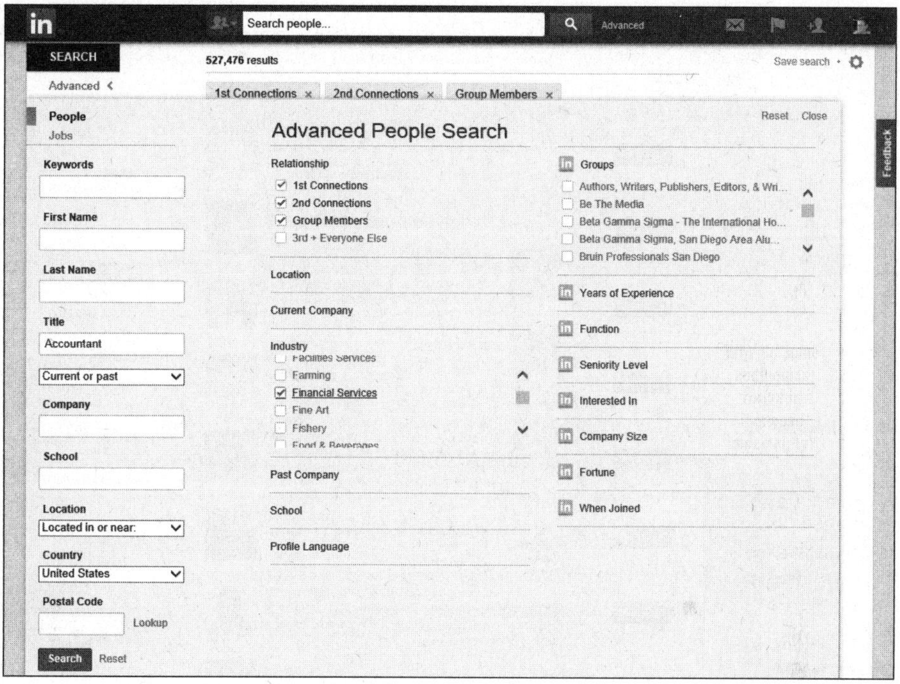

Figure 16-1:
Use the Advanced People search to find potential clients.

When you begin your search of the LinkedIn database, your own network can help you identify your *best leads* (people only two or three degrees away from you who you can reach through a first-degree connection introducing you) if you make sure that first-degree connections and second-degree network members are checked. When you see your search results with those options checked, you first see which results are closely connected with you via your connections. You can click each person's name to read his full LinkedIn profile, see how you're connected, and decide whether you have a potential lead. (This method gives you much more information than a simple Google search, which would provide only a LinkedIn member's public profile, instead of his full profile.)

After you identify your best leads, you can use LinkedIn to find out what connections you have in common: Simply click the Shared Connections link under the name for each search result. For example, say I click the 1 Shared

Connection link for Sarah S. from Figure 16-2. I see that my friend Heather O. is the shared connection between me and Sarah, as shown in Figure 16-3, and that helps me approach Sarah, because I can ask Heather for an introduction or for more information about Sarah.

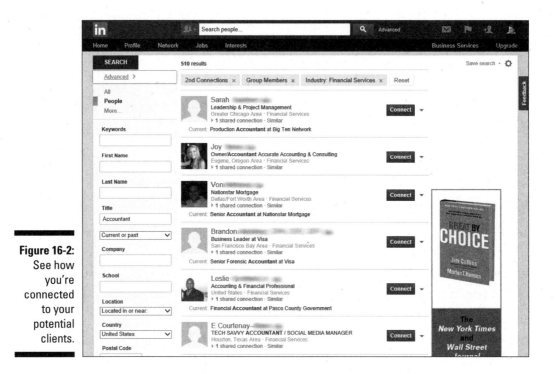

Figure 16-2: See how you're connected to your potential clients.

When doing general prospecting, surveying the market for that "perfect lead" or, at least, a lead in the right direction, keep these ideas in mind while filling in the appropriate Advanced Search fields for each strategy:

- ✔ **Generalize your search.** If you're looking for your ideal contacts independently of the company they work for, focus primarily on the Title and Industry fields to find your leads.

- ✔ **Narrow your search.** Use the Keywords field to narrow your results list when you need to reach people within a certain niche of an industry or job.

- ✔ **Target specific people.** Use either the Company or Keywords field, plus the Title field, to help you find specific employees in your target companies.

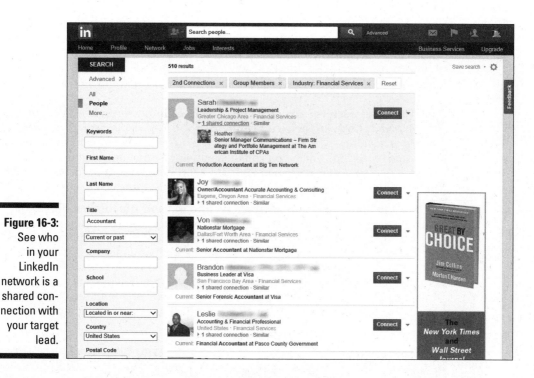

Figure 16-3:
See who in your LinkedIn network is a shared connection with your target lead.

✔ **Help your product or service sell itself.** Search for the customers of your customers to get those people excited about your product or service, so that they'll demand it from *your* customers! This strategy is also known as *pull marketing.* (See Chapter 15 for more information about how to use LinkedIn for marketing purposes.)

✔ **Reach out through service professionals.** Search for consultants who are hired by your potential customers by using the Title and Industry fields, or by choosing Consultants/Contractors from the Interested In drop-down list. Because LinkedIn might help you discover a shared connection or bond between you and these consultants, you can ask those consultants for help in reaching your potential customers.

Finding the decision maker

Although generating a list of potential leads is a great first step in marketing your product, being an effective salesperson often comes down to finding that "right person" with whom you can present an offer to buy something. This person is the *decision maker* (or the *final authority,* or even just *da boss*).

You can talk to as many administrative assistants and receptionists as you'd like, but without the exact name or contact info of the person who makes the purchasing decisions, your sales effort is stalled.

LinkedIn can help you reach that decision maker in the following ways:

- ✔ **When you perform an advanced search, include words like Account Manager, Director, or Vice President in the Keywords field.** If your results show someone who's in your extended network, now you have a specific name to mention when you call the company. I recommend you approach that person via LinkedIn and your mutual connections first, thereby making your first contact with her more of a "warm call" than a cold one.

- ✔ **Use the LinkedIn Company page to find out specific information about your target company.** If you're trying to reach someone within a company, see whether that person shows up as an employee on the Company page. To do so, click Interests on the top navigation bar and select Companies from the drop-down list that appears so you can search through LinkedIn's Company pages. Say, for example, that you need to reach someone within LinkedIn. When you bring up LinkedIn's Company page, as shown in Figure 16-4, you get some specific information right away.

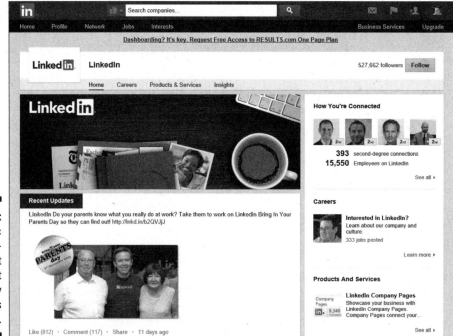

Figure 16-4: Get specific information about your target company through its profile.

You immediately see who in your network works for this company, so you know who to approach to pass along your request to the decision maker, or to tell you who that decision maker is. Be sure to click the other tabs for this page — Careers, Products & Services, and Insights — to views other useful information, such as former employees you may know, top skills and expertise at this company, similar companies or topics to this company, and most recommended people to connect with regarding this company (see Figure 16-5). You can then follow that company to see all its new updates and information as part of your LinkedIn News Feed, for example. At the top right of every company page is a Follow button, as shown in Figure 16-5. You can click the Follow button to stay in touch with that company's activities.

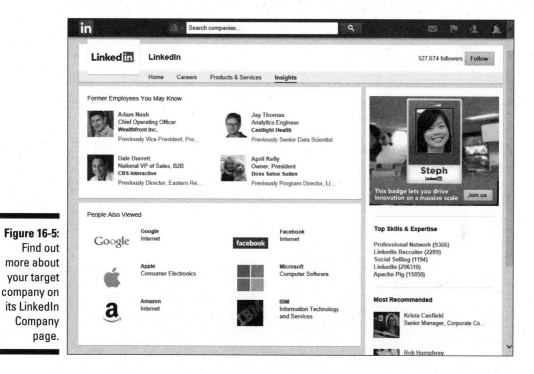

Figure 16-5: Find out more about your target company on its LinkedIn Company page.

✔ **Use your existing network to ask for an introduction, advice, or to point you in the right direction.** Using your network in this manner was basically the original intent of LinkedIn: You contact someone who works at your target company and ask that contact to introduce you to the decision maker. The decision maker is much more likely to be receptive to an introduction than a cold call. Your network connection might also recommend you to the decision maker, which carries some weight when you try to close the deal. In addition, you may have a select group of people in your own network that can provide advice on who to connect with, as well as advice or ideas on selling your product, service, or nonprofit organization.

✔ **Use InMail to contact people close to the decision maker.** You may find that, in some cases, the decision maker may not be on LinkedIn yet, or her profile is closed to introductions and InMail. If so, you can use LinkedIn to find the closest person to the decision maker and ask that person for help, for a connection, or for information to help you reach the next level.

✔ **Use InMail to contact the decision maker if she is on LinkedIn.** You may not have the time or opportunity to get introduced to your decision maker, and if you're using InMail to approach the decision maker, why not just go for the gusto and introduce yourself directly? This is a faster option than waiting or asking for an introduction, but there's the chance the decision maker will ignore your message. You have to decide what's best for your situation.

Closing the Deal

Establishing a connection to the right person (the one who makes the purchasing decisions) is half the battle in getting your product sold. However, you still have to convince the person and close the deal. In this section, I give you some pointers on how to put LinkedIn to work for you for the final phase of a sales effort: completing it successfully!

The key to getting the most out of LinkedIn for closing the deal is knowing that LinkedIn has more than just names — it has detailed profiles of its tens of millions of users, associations made through LinkedIn Groups, and corporate information through LinkedIn Company pages.

Researching prospects

After you identify your prospects, spend some time familiarizing yourself with them before you contact them. Gleaning some insight about a potential buyer can go a long way toward getting the person to respond, taking the time to listen to your pitch, and ultimately buying your product. Following are some tips concerning specific ways to research your prospective clients:

✔ **Read the prospect's *full* profile to discover all you can about his interests, likes, dislikes, and so on.** You can do far more than simply scan a person's profile looking for past jobs and view her education to see whether she shares an alma mater with you. A person's LinkedIn profile can be a gold mine of information about that person. For example, people may include links to their own Web sites, blogs, or company Web sites. Follow those links, especially to blogs or personal Web sites, and see what you can find out. In the prospect's profile, look over the Interests section and the Additional Information section. And don't forget the Contact Settings section — here's where you can find out under what circumstances this person wants to be contacted. Be sure to respect those wishes.

✔ **Read your prospect's recommendations for other people.** You can gain a lot of insight by seeing what qualities a person likes to praise in other people, especially if your prospect has left multiple recommendations. In this way, you also gain insight into the people he trusts, so check those people who received a recommendation to see whether you have a connection to any of *them*. If so, ask that person first for an introduction to your prospect.

✔ **See the activity your prospect has on LinkedIn.** If you pull up someone's profile, look for a section on his profile page below the summary box called Activity and scroll through that section to see updates and articles that person published, along with status updates, articles he liked, commented, or shared, and topics he follows, as shown in Figure 16-6. When you read these items, you might gain some insight into this person's preferences and "hot button issues" — what motivates or annoys him.

Preparing for the client meeting

Say that your initial conversations with your prospects have gone well and you have been granted a meeting with a potential client to make your pitch. Whereas you may have already used LinkedIn to gain more information about the specific person, you can now get details about the specific industry, the company, and the company's potential response to your business pitch. Here are some tips on gathering information about the company:

✔ **Try to get an informational interview with someone at the target company, preferably with someone you know.** Check your LinkedIn network to see whether you have a first-degree connection or second-degree network member at the company you're planning to pitch to. Ask that person to help you gather information about the company, and try to get some insights into company priorities and culture. Also see

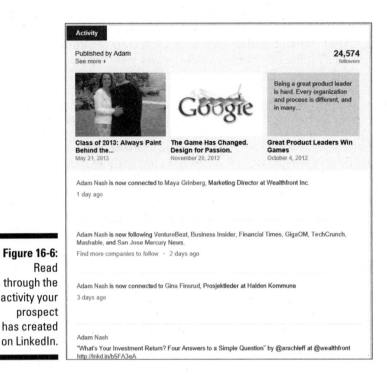

Figure 16-6:
Read
through the
activity your
prospect
has created
on LinkedIn.

what you can learn about the company's top motivation in purchasing decisions — what priorities or issues the company considers before buying something from a vendor. If you don't have a direct contact, look at the groups you're a member of for any potential contacts, or read up on LinkedIn members who might have mentioned the target company in some way.

✔ **Visit the LinkedIn Company page to review recent company activities.** As mentioned earlier in this chapter in the "Finding the decision maker" section, when you look at the Company page, you see sections such as New Hires, Recent Tweets, or Recent Blog Posts. Peruse these sections before your meeting with your potential buyer to find out who has been promoted or hired, the key statistics of that company, open job listings at the company, and even the most popular profiles of employees at that company. Doing so gives you more background information and there-fore more confidence; also, this type of knowledge helps you identify interests or commonalities to enhance your sense of connection with your buyer (and hers with you).

✔ **Use LinkedIn to get advice from the community at large or your network.** Search the channels within LinkedIn Pulse to see what is happening in your target field or company, or to find out how to approach companies in your industry. If you don't find anything directly related to what you're searching for, you can search for and join LinkedIn Groups that are related to your target field or company, and see what discussions or information are generated from other LinkedIn members.

All these efforts are meant only to prepare you and get you closer to your prospect or target company so that you can make your pitch. Obviously, to complete the sale, you still need to have a compelling product, pitch, and offer for this company. Have everything ready *before* you approach your prospect. Take the information you've learned; lay it out and organize it around the company, the person you're meeting, and the opportunity you're trying to gain; and prepare any potential questions (along with your answers to those questions) that may come up during the meeting.

Using LinkedIn to Help You Complete the Sale

At this stage you have, to borrow a famous phrase, "gotten to yes," meaning that you've contacted and met with your prospect and she has agreed to buy your product or service. Congratulations! You made the sale, and now it's time to deliver. Your membership in LinkedIn can continue to provide value by giving you some resources to help you deliver what you promised and ensure future sales success.

Getting help to deliver the solution

After you make the sale, go back to your company with the contract in hand and determine the resources and personnel necessary to deliver on your contract. In some cases, you may not have everything you need to deliver the order. As it can in earlier stages of the sales process, LinkedIn can assist you in this stage as well. Here are a few of those ways:

- ✔ **Find partners to create the winning team.** You've done the hard part: You got the contract. The customer trusts you to deliver on that contract, so it's your job to build the winning team. Your company may not employ full-time all the people you need, or you may have agreed to additional items to make the sale that require something where your business has to speed up development. In such a case, you can use your LinkedIn connections to find people who have the skill sets you need. (See Chapter 11 for tips on finding an employee.) You can also perform an Advanced People search for a consultant or part-time employee who has the skills you need to build your products or consult on your service offering.

✔ **Get some direction from the LinkedIn community.** You can create a question in LinkedIn Answers that polls your network and the greater LinkedIn community in the problem area you've been hired to solve. Get an idea of how other people would tackle this problem, and use the answers to identify potential partners or contacts you can use to deliver your solution. For example, polling the community about a part of your service offering (a part that isn't client-specific) may result in a LinkedIn member providing a new way of approaching the problem.

✔ **Hire the skills you need.** If you can't find a part-time person or tap into the skills you're seeking from someone in your LinkedIn network, it's time to post a job listing on LinkedIn Jobs. See Chapter 11 for the steps on how to post a job listing.

Reporting a positive sale

Reporting the completion of a sale is my favorite part of the business sales process. You made the sale, developed the solution, and delivered it to the customer. At this point, many people think, "Whew, I'm done. Nothing to do now but enjoy happy hour!" This is a common and natural response, but as a member of the LinkedIn world, your job isn't really done. You want to demonstrate your growth (and your company's growth) that resulted from handling this project to encourage future contracts to come your way. Here are some actions to consider after you complete the sale and deliver the solution:

✔ **Invite your customer to join your network.** You worked hard to earn this customer's trust and to meet (or exceed) his expectations by completing the sale. As a result, you should feel comfortable enough to send him an invitation to join your network. Doing so could keep you in contact with this customer for future opportunities. Studies have shown that it's six times cheaper to sell to an existing customer than to acquire a new customer.

✔ **Leave your customer a recommendation.** After you add a customer to your network, post a recommendation for him on the system if you feel it's deserved. Doing so gives your customer a sense of reward for being a positive contributor, but more important, it informs the community that you did a project for this person, which can help you in the future. Also, the customer may reciprocate by leaving you a recommendation, which strengthens your profile and makes you more appealing to future prospects.

✔ **Stay in touch with your customer.** You can keep track of your customer's activities by monitoring your network updates (if he is a part of your network). Routinely keep in touch about the solution you delivered, perhaps to open the conversation for selling additional products or services or maintenance contract work.

✔ **Update your profile with the skills you acquired or demonstrated through this sale.** To be ready for future prospects who search the LinkedIn database, it's important to have the right keywords and skill sets on your profile so that these prospects can identify you as someone who can provide a similar solution for them. If you're a consultant or freelance worker, you can add the project you just completed as experience on your profile as well. (See Chapter 3 for tips on how to update your profile.)

✔ **Tap the customer's network by asking him for referrals.** After you connect with your customer, keep an eye on his network. If you think you see a future prospect, consider asking your customer for an introduction or a recommendation. Usually, if you provided a quality solution, the customer may readily oblige your request, if they don't feel there is a conflict or a sense of uneasiness.

Chapter 17

Venture Capital and Angel Funding

● ●

In This Chapter

▶ Finding investors

▶ Getting the right advice

▶ Building your management team

▶ Using LinkedIn to get an investor

▶ Searching for investments

▶ Evaluating your potential investments

● ●

*W*hen you put lots of Internet-savvy, knowledgeable professionals who like to network on a big social networking site like LinkedIn, you're bound to have a community of people who are involved and interested in venture capital (VC), where specific firms provide millions (or tens of millions) of dollars in funding as well as support and board members for emerging companies that want to grow. Or you might run across professionals involved in *angel funding,* where wealthy investors invest up to a few million dollars of their own money in exchange for ownership percentages in emerging companies. You could say that LinkedIn has VC at its roots. LinkedIn founder Reid Hoffman is an angel investor who has invested in more than 60 companies besides LinkedIn, including Facebook, Digg, Flickr, Technorati, Tagged, and Ning.

LinkedIn has become an important tool for everyone involved in the VC or angel funding industry, from the casual observer to the hyper-extended dealmaker, for many reasons:

✔ LinkedIn can help entrepreneurs figure out how to connect with a VC firm.

✔ Entrepreneurs can use LinkedIn to build their management team before a proposal is made.

✔ Business owners can test their business ideas on fellow first-degree connections.

✔ VC firms can monitor LinkedIn Groups to get a perspective on up-and-coming trends.

✔ Experienced business veterans can become LinkedIn Influencers to give advice, encouragement, and a new perspective to first-timers.

In this chapter, I talk about how you can benefit from using LinkedIn when it comes to VC or angel funding, regardless of your role or position in the process. I cover different cases and stories on how entrepreneurs have benefited from LinkedIn, as well as how VC firms and angel networks have used LinkedIn to find, evaluate, or advance their deals.

Finding Potential Investors

So, you have a great idea for a company, you want to be the next big thing in your industry, and all you need is a blank check to make your dreams come true, right? Although LinkedIn can't guarantee that you'll find the right funding partner, get the money you need, and build your business with a great return on investment, it can help you improve your chances of success when dealing with the funding and growth of your business.

No matter what stage your business is in, whether you just thought of a new business idea or invention, you're building a prototype, you earned your first dollar of revenue, or you just hit $1 million in sales, LinkedIn can be an invaluable resource for reaching the next step and beyond. The following sections look at some of the ways LinkedIn can assist you in the quest for an investor.

Getting advice from LinkedIn Influencers

Although you may be an expert in your field, you could probably use some good advice from existing venture capitalists, angel investors, or successful entrepreneurs when it comes to obtaining financing. LinkedIn classifies important people in each industry as "Influencers," and LinkedIn allows you to follow a vast array of these knowledgeable folks who are experts in their fields and who gladly give general and specific information. And although Pulse, LinkedIn's news and insights aggregator, has a special channel for Entrepreneurship & Small Business, I focus on the channel of VC and angel funding here. If you're not ready for that big investment, definitely check out the Entrepreneurship & Small Business channel for information (see Figure 17-1).

When you're ready to follow LinkedIn Pulse's VC & Private Equity channel to get quality information from key Influencers and news sources on this topic, just follow these steps:

1. **Hover your mouse over the Interests link from the top navigation bar, then click the Pulse link from the drop-down list that appears.**

   You are taken to LinkedIn Pulse.

2. **Click the All Channels link under the Pulse header to bring up all the different channels you can follow. Scroll down the page to see the Entrepreneurship & Small Business channel, as shown in Figure 17-1.**

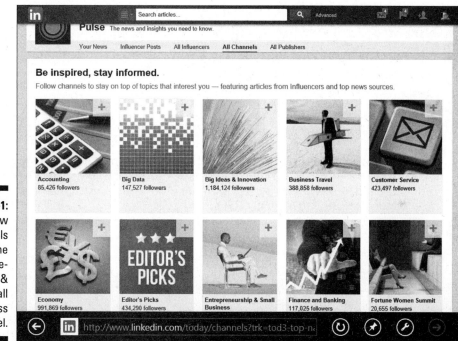

Figure 17-1:
Follow channels like the Entrepreneurship & Small Business channel.

3. **Scroll down to the bottom of the page and locate the VC & Private Equity box. Click the + sign in the top right corner of that graphic.**

   When you go to click the + sign, you see the Follow link appear on that box, as shown in Figure 17-2. After you click the + sign, you are marked as Following that channel. You can click the channel to see the collection of news stories and Influencer posts, as shown in Figure 17-3.

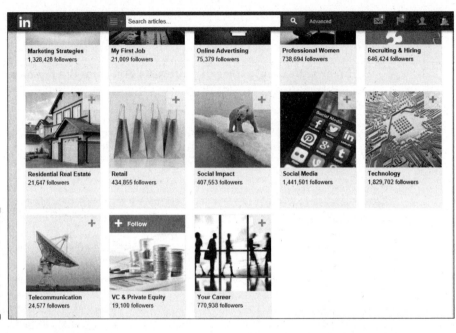

Figure 17-2:
Follow the Pulse channel for VC and private equity.

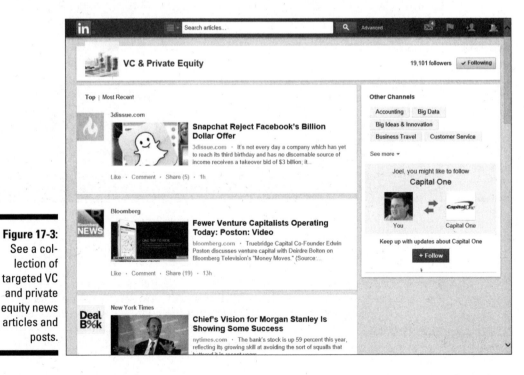

Figure 17-3:
See a collection of targeted VC and private equity news articles and posts.

Pulse channels like this one function similarly to Facebook in that members can Like, Comment, and Share the stories that are featured on the channel. You can see who in your LinkedIn network has Liked a particular story, learn more from your network and the larger community by reading the Comments, and expand your influence by Sharing relevant stories with the people in your immediate network who would benefit from reading them. You can sort between the Top and the Most Recent stories, and as you scroll down the page, LinkedIn continues to pull relevant stories that are tagged for this channel. As of this writing, news sources such as the Financial Times, The New York Times, Bloomberg, Forbes, USA Today, and CNBC provide rich content to this channel.

Building your dream team

When you're looking for funding of any amount, one of the top things any investor wants to see is your management team. No matter how great your idea is, it's the execution of that idea that determines your success. Investors see one way to mitigate the risk of their investment by rewarding strong management teams that have the skill to weather unexpected turns. If your management team is lacking in at least one key area, consider LinkedIn a source to find that missing person.

Here are some things to keep in mind when doing a search on LinkedIn for your next team member:

- ✔ **Experience is key.** Although desire, motivation, and interest are important, the way to improve your chances of getting funding is to have experienced personnel. When searching for potential candidates, you should study each person's profile to gauge her documented experience at past positions first; then see whether her interests match your company's interests.

- ✔ **Pick complements, not carbon copies.** It's tempting for an entrepreneur to seek out like-minded individuals with similar backgrounds to build a business. However, companies with the strongest growth have diverse management teams that can handle different situations because the teams' skills complement each other. Put your business needs ahead of your personal preference. Look for LinkedIn members whose profiles indicate strengths that aren't yet represented in your start-up.

- ✔ **Gauge the strength of the candidate's network.** Any time you look to add someone to your organization, you should ask what value that person can bring through his existing network. (After all, who you know can make the difference.) When you connect with someone, see who is a part of his network, if possible. See what groups and affiliations, Web sites, and Q & A are on the candidate's profile, because that indicates his overall reach into the greater network.

Putting it all together

Suppose you have your business plan, management team, market analysis, prototype or working model, and you've built up a customer set. You've done some research and are ready to start shopping around and looking for an investment. You've perfected your 30-second elevator pitch so you can quickly and accurately describe your business to anyone who's interested, and you can quote the facts and figures you need for any presentation. It's time to seek out a funding partner.

Although this is not the exhaustive list of what you can do, here are some tips that can help you find that partner using LinkedIn:

- **Do research on your leads.** Look up potential investors on LinkedIn and read their profiles. See what interests they have, what group affiliations they maintain, and what information they share or gather using LinkedIn Groups or Companies. Follow through on any Web sites, blogs, or profiles they link to from their profiles. See what you have in common or which benefit of your company might interest them the most.

- **Work your network and get them working.** Do advanced searches to see how your network can connect you with the right person. Maybe someone in your network knows a venture capitalist or an angel investor. Someone in one of your groups may have the right connection in one of her other groups. Let your network know what you're looking for and ask, respectfully, for help, advice, or a push in the right direction.

- **Get introduced or reach out yourself.** If a potential investor is a second- or third-degree network member, use LinkedIn introductions to ask your contacts to introduce you. If you have no direct connections, consider using InMail to make your own introduction. (Chapter 5 has more on introductions and InMail.)

- **Do your homework before any meeting.** Use LinkedIn to prepare for your meeting with a potential investor. Study her profile and check the LinkedIn Company pages for information about her company. If she's in your extended network, ask your connections (people who know her) for advice and information. See what companies she has invested in and research those companies as well.

Finding Potential Investments

Maybe someone in your VC firm needs to connect with someone in a particular industry, or perhaps your organization wants to invest in an emerging market or new technology. LinkedIn is a great place for you as a potential investor to look for your next investment.

Looking in your network

One of the benefits of a good investor is the network he brings with him to the investment. Although some venture capitalists recommend their own executive and/or board structure to their investments, other investors simply offer advice about any new hires or support personnel a new company may need in its growth phase. Sometimes, the right investor knows a new company's customer base well and can help the new company land a key account. This is all possible through a strong network, which makes LinkedIn one of the best ways an investor can grow and strengthen his network. Here are some ways that LinkedIn can help:

- ✔ **Monitor your network activity.** Your network is always working, and this point is clearly demonstrated in your network activity. Spend some time every day or week to look through your network activity to see which of your contacts has changed companies, started new projects, or participated in groups you may find relevant. (See Chapter 9 for more information on network activity.)

- ✔ **Monitor LinkedIn Groups and Influencers.** See what topics show up most often in your particular industry, and what comments other people are posting. Pay attention to channels like Entrepreneurship & Small Business, VC & Private Equity, and Technology.

- ✔ **Identify thought leaders.** As you watch your network, LinkedIn Influencers, and any relevant LinkedIn Groups, pay attention if certain names keep popping up. These people could be *thought leaders* in your intended industry — people respected as authorities in their given subject matter — and they are worth connecting to in order to stay ahead and scope out the best opportunities. Reach out to these parties through introductions or InMail (see Chapter 5) to see whether you can create a meaningful connection.

- ✔ **Strengthen your network.** Build good contacts in your field through regular networking and avenues like LinkedIn Groups. Identify people in your network who are a part of your desired industry and expand into their networks by getting to know their connections.

Doing your due diligence

As new proposals for investments come your way, or you meet an entrepreneur in one of your industries who could come to you later with an investment proposal, you have to evaluate these proposals and decide how to proceed. Here are some ways that LinkedIn can help you filter all this incoming information:

- ✔ **Evaluate your entrepreneurs.** When you're evaluating a proposal, do some research by seeing whether the requester has a LinkedIn profile. Compare notes between his business plan and his actual profile. Evaluate his entire management team.

- ✔ **Ask for endorsements.** If you're evaluating a proposal or contemplating adding someone to your network, see who in your network knows this person (or company). If you find a connection, ask your connection whether she would endorse or recommend this person.

- ✔ **Get a sense for your intended market.** See if any relevant LinkedIn Groups exist for your intended market on LinkedIn, and, if so, what discussions or activities are happening in those Groups. Search the LinkedIn Companies directory to see whether the requesting company has been profiled. If so, take a close look at the information.

Chapter 18

Miscellaneous Creative Uses of LinkedIn

• •

• •

*W*hen you think of a business networking site such as LinkedIn, the most obvious applications spring to mind pretty quickly: finding a job, finding an employee, meeting new people, building a new business, getting funding and partners for that new business, and so on. But LinkedIn has acquired even more uses than the obvious ones. The power of the Internet and tens of millions of LinkedIn members have encouraged people to use this large community to accomplish other goals, both close to home and around the world.

In this chapter, I give you a look at some of the "creative" uses that people have found for LinkedIn. Some people use LinkedIn in combination with other services, such as Google News Alerts. Other people use LinkedIn as a gathering place to find recruits to help mold a new venture. Yet others have been using LinkedIn to meet each other in person! I describe these endeavors as well as provide several case studies with some points to keep in mind if you feel like doing something similar.

Mashing LinkedIn with Other Services

One of the hotter trends on the Internet over the years has been the creation of mashups. No, I'm not talking potatoes here. A *mashup* is created when somebody takes data from more than one application and puts that data together into a single new and useful application. For example, say you combine real estate sales data from a database application with the Google Maps application, enabling a search result of the real estate data to be mapped onto a satellite image on Google. The satellite image represents a mashup because it's a new, distinct service that neither application provided on its own.

Something similar to the concept of mashups occurs with creative uses of LinkedIn. As LinkedIn continues to evolve and its members use more and more of LinkedIn's functionality, new uses for LinkedIn continue to emerge, especially as part of a user's Internet exploits. The following sections describe a smattering of these mashups.

LinkedIn and Google News Alerts

LinkedIn + Google News Alerts = Better-informed communication

I got this tip from Liz Ryan, a workplace expert, author, and speaker, as one of her top ten ways of using LinkedIn. It has to do with using both sites as a business tool when you're trying to reach out to an important potential business contact who you do not know. It works like this:

1. **Click the Advanced link next to the search box on the top of any LinkedIn page to bring up the Advanced People Search page.**

2. **Fill in the appropriate fields to search for the name of a person at a company who is relevant to your situation, and with whom you would like to connect.**

3. **Armed with the name that turned up in the results, set up a Google News Alert with the person's name and the company name so that Google notifies you when that person is quoted or in the news.**

When you go to Google's Alerts page (as shown in Figure 18-1), you simply enter the person's name and company name in the Search Query box, and then configure how you want Google to alert you by setting the Result Type, How Often, and How Many filters below the Search Query box. Finally, you set the e-mail address you want the alerts to be sent to with the Your Email drop-down list. Click the Create Alert button, and you're good to go!

When you receive a notice from Google News Alerts, you have a much better idea of what the person is working on as well as his impact at the company. This knowledge gives you an icebreaker you can use to strike up a conversation. Rather than send a random connection request, you can reference the person's speech at the last XYZ Summit or agree with his last blog post. You show initiative by doing the research, which can impress or flatter the contact and give you something to refer to when you talk about his accomplishments or innovations.

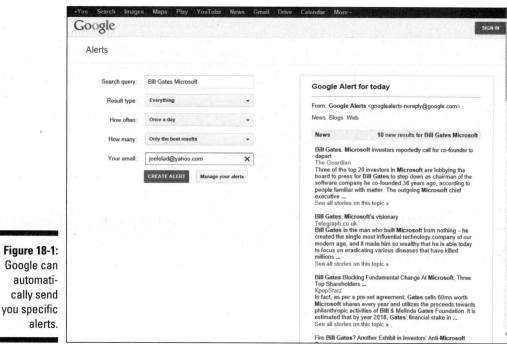

Figure 18-1:
Google can automatically send you specific alerts.

Don't overuse all this information you get when you contact the person, or, as Liz Ryan warns, he might think you're a business stalker.

LinkedIn Updates and RSS feeds

LinkedIn Updates + RSS feeds = Searchable information

Millions of people are updating, communicating, and broadcasting through their LinkedIn updates, and sometimes you may want one thread containing every update in your network instead of constantly having to check the site and remember people's updates all the time. Well, now you can subscribe to a live RSS feed and get automatic updates when someone posts an update or link.

What exactly is an RSS feed? Imagine if someone regularly sent you a file that contained only the newest updates to a Web page, instead of seeing every version of the Web page without knowing what was changed. An RSS feed is simply a file that contains only those changes that have been made to a file, like a Web page. Think of it as getting a stream of updates instead of hearing every version of the same story.

To benefit from this feature, just do the following:

1. **Log in to your LinkedIn account. Hover your mouse over the Account & Settings icon (your profile picture) from the top navigation bar, and then click Review (next to Privacy and Settings) from the drop-down list that appears.**

   Doing so takes you to the LinkedIn Account & Settings page.

2. **Pick the Account category from the bottom left side of the Settings box, below Groups/Companies/Applications, and click the Get LinkedIn Content as an RSS Feed link.**

   You are taken to the LinkedIn RSS Feeds page, as shown in Figure 18-2.

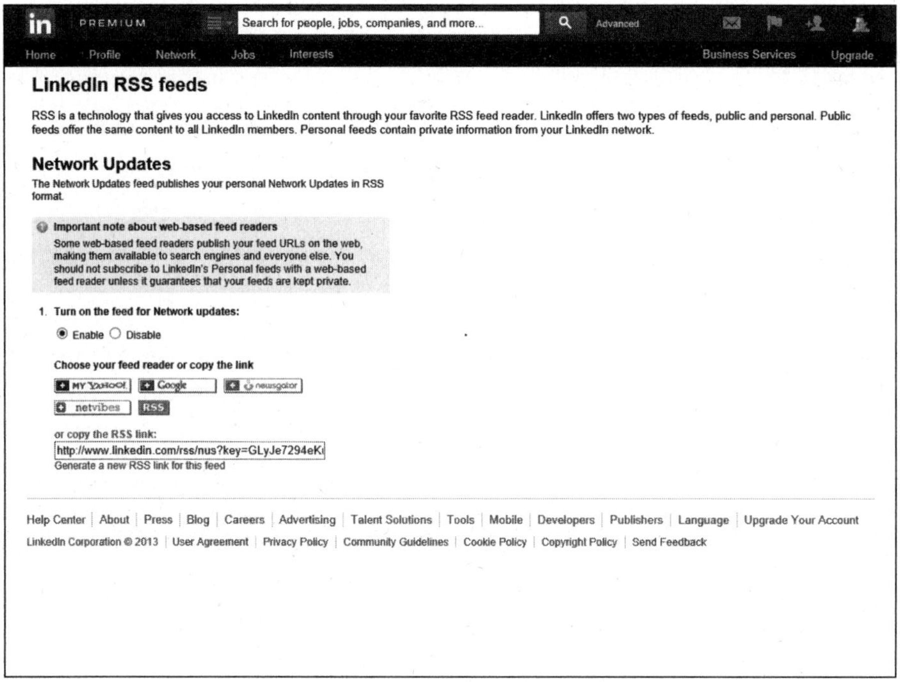

Figure 18-2:
Get your
LinkedIn
content
as an RSS
feed.

3. **Click the Enable radio button to turn on the RSS feed. This brings up a choice of RSS feed readers, as shown in Figure 18-2.**

   The *feed reader* is basically the software program that receives your RSS feed file and displays it to you so you can read it. You can either choose from the preprogrammed choices, like Google Reader or My Yahoo!, or cut and paste the link offered in the bottom of this window into your own RSS feed reader.

4. **Set up the news reader to handle the newly subscribed RSS feed(s) so that you can read all this information as it gets fed to you.**

   A popular RSS reader is Feedspot, which you can set up by going to www.feedspot.com and following the instructions there.

LinkedIn and the Xobni e-mail plug-in

LinkedIn + Xobni e-mail plug-in = More precise sender information

If you use Microsoft Outlook or Google's Gmail for your e-mail and you're constantly being deluged with e-mail from people you don't remember well, Xobni may be the tool for you. Xobni is a plug-in tool (available for Outlook or Gmail) that gives you a window of summary information for each sender of an e-mail you receive. Say that you got an e-mail from Adam Smith, but you can't remember exactly what Adam does, when and how often Adam e-mails you, and so on. With Xobni, the plug-in window shows you who Adam is and how you interact with him. Figure 18-3 shows an example of the kind of information Xobni can display.

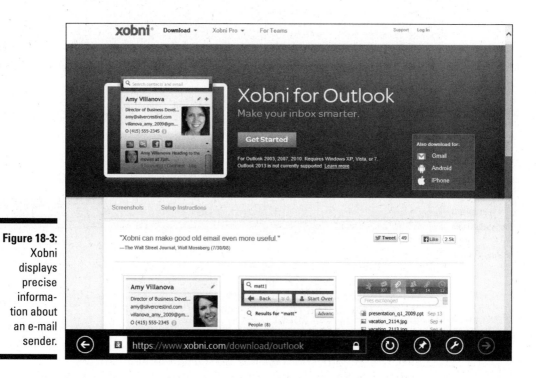

Figure 18-3: Xobni displays precise information about an e-mail sender.

Xobni has now integrated LinkedIn information into its plug-in window, so when someone's summary window is displayed, Xobni displays that person's employer, job title, and profile photo, and also offers a direct link to the person's complete profile on LinkedIn. To add this functionality to your Microsoft Outlook program, just follow these steps:

1. **Go to the Xobni site at** `www.xobni.com/download/outlook` **and download its newest plug-in application setup file.**

   The download should start up automatically when you go to the site's download page, shown in Figure 18-4.

Figure 18-4: Download the Xobni application.

2. **Run the downloaded file and follow the setup wizard that opens to install Xobni on your system.**

   The next time you run Microsoft Outlook, you should see the Xobni plug-in on the right side of your Outlook window.

If you use an e-mail program other than Outlook, there are tools that can help you as well. For example, if you use Google's Gmail service with Mozilla's Firefox browser, Google's Chrome browser, or the popular Safari browser

for Mac computers, you can download Smartr for Gmail by going to
`https://www.xobni.com/download/gmail` (as shown in Figure 18-5)
and repeating the same steps for downloading Xobni for Outlook.

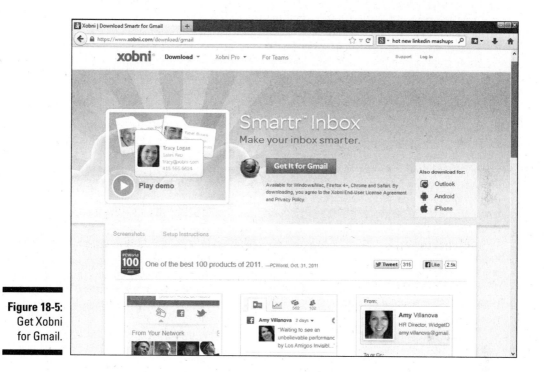

Figure 18-5:
Get Xobni
for Gmail.

Building Your Focus Group

In other chapters, I tell you about the potential for finding qualified partners
and customers using LinkedIn, and how LinkedIn can help you perform market
research and gauge reactions to a new product. Here, I want to take these
ideas one step further and discuss how LinkedIn can help you build a focus
group for your new or next project.

Here are some ideas to keep in mind if you want to build your own focus
group using LinkedIn:

- ✓ **Start by building your network.** Your best participants in this group
  are first-degree connections of yours (or of another employee of your
  company) because those people are most likely to join based on your
  recommendation and how well they fit your group's purpose. Try to
  network and invite potential candidates right away.

Who's ready to play DISC?

Cynthia (Cindy) Beale heard about LinkedIn the way most people do: She got an invitation from an old contact — a former high school classmate, in her case. After she joined, Beale at first used the site for typical purposes, but eventually she took her use of LinkedIn to the next level after co-founding her consultancy business, Stecin Leadership Solutions.

Beale and her co-founder, Steve Settimo, started Stecin as a consulting and training company focused on management and leadership training. The business partners spent two years developing an exclusive curriculum that can be customized for any size company. Then, they created a brand-new board game called DISCFunctional to demonstrate the power of understanding the DISC Quadrant behavior system (see the following figure for the layout). This game became a popular training tool, and Stecin's co-founders decided to use the power of their LinkedIn networks to help advance the game.

Beale explains, "Suddenly, we had a way to communicate information about our training and consulting business to a group of people that we already identified as knowing." They added

the game to their profiles and included a Web site link in each of their profiles so that potential customers could actually order the game. They updated their network with progress reports on how the game was doing, and then they created a special DISCFunctional group on LinkedIn for contacts who wanted to learn more.

This LinkedIn group became a focus group for Stecin Leadership Solutions, as they invited first-degree connections who expressed interest and potential customers who learned about the product elsewhere. Beale and Settimo were very careful about how they invited people to this focus group, doing research on each potential invitee, asking for introductions through their own personal LinkedIn networks whenever possible, and crafting a polished invitation.

Stecin has built a growing community that has been very influential in the game's development. Beale is happy to report that their first training contract came from a LinkedIn connection! She concludes by saying, "We are always looking for more ways to utilize LinkedIn to reach people who will benefit from our business offerings."

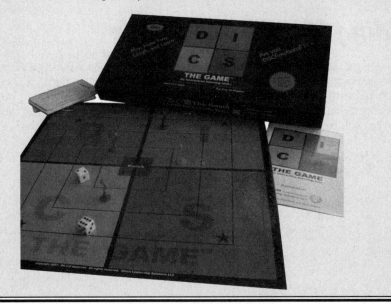

✔ **Build your accompanying Web site before building the group.** Your focus group participants will want to see something before deciding to join and participate, so make sure you've spent some time building an informational Web page, e-mail, FAQ, or other system that is available for viewing before you start to build your group.

✔ **Use your first-degree connections to expand your network.** After you've rustled up some involvement there, expand your group by asking for referrals or introductions to potential second- and third-degree network members or general LinkedIn members who might get some value and add some insight to your process.

✔ **Continually send out updates.** You should always be sending out some form of update, whether you do so by filling out the status update option, using LinkedIn Messages, or going through your own e-mail system. (See Chapter 9 for more information about these options.) Don't deluge people with messages — but also don't ask them to sign up and then be silent for weeks or months at a time. Keep your group members informed and ask for input when needed.

✔ **Ask for recommendations.** As group members get introduced to your product, ask them for a recommendation on your profile if they liked or approve of the product. Getting their feedback or recommendations helps build future involvement when your product is live and ready for the mass market.

Using Location-Based LinkedIn Ideas

It's easy to forget the importance of location when you have easy access to such a resource-rich community as LinkedIn. After all, you can communicate with your contacts through LinkedIn Messages, send recommendation requests or post questions, or grow your network without leaving your computer. When you're done using your computer, however, you need to interact in the real world, whether your interaction amounts to shoveling snow or catching a plane to a far-flung convention. When it comes to what I call "location-based" situations, meaning that the problem or situation is tied to a physical spot, you can discover solutions with the help of LinkedIn.

The best use of LinkedIn for location-based problems is this: Your network is typically spread out across the country and across the world. Therefore, not only can you tap someone's professional experience, you can also tap his knowledge or presence in a specific geographical area to help you solve a problem. Take a look at three different location-based situations.

Hello? Any opportunities out east?

Chuck Hester had a problem. He had to relocate his family from California to Raleigh, North Carolina, and he didn't have a job for himself when he would arrive. In fact, he didn't know anyone in Raleigh — but what he *did* have was a rich LinkedIn network. Hester quickly saw the value of LinkedIn and started contacting people and building relationships, driving his number of connections into the thousands.

Hester started networking with everyone he could who was located in Raleigh. He tapped his existing network to put him in touch with like-minded individuals who lived in the area and kept searching for contacts. One of the contacts he made was the chief executive of iContact, an e-mail marketing company. Hester turned this contact into a job interview, and he became the corporate communications manager for iContact. Even virtual persistence can pay off! Today, Hester continues to grow his LinkedIn network, and he even encourages his local contacts to network "Live," or use LinkedIn Live, to be specific — a feature that I cover later in this chapter.

Building your network before moving to a new city

These days, when you have to move to a new city, you can do a lot of planning for it on the Internet. You can research the neighborhoods, look into the school systems, and shop for homes online. You can take this one step further if you plan to move to a different country, and you need information on local customs, cultures, and practices. But what about the questions you can't seem to answer through a Web browser? What about the "local knowledge" of where to go and where to avoid? LinkedIn can help.

Every LinkedIn user has defined her location, so you can do a search and figure out which LinkedIn users live in your target area. If nobody in your network is from your target area, start networking and expand that network to include people who reside (or used to reside) in that area who can help.

Here are some specific actions you can take through LinkedIn to help you with the big move:

  ✔ **Use LinkedIn Groups to find your community.** Not every group on LinkedIn is directly related to software development or venture capital. You can look for specific groups of people who share a common skill through LinkedIn groups (see Chapter 14 for more information on how to do this), join the group and start a discussion topic with your question, and see what the community says in response. Take a look at Figure 18-6, which shows how a search for a specific city, such as New York City, yields thousands of possible groups. You can narrow your search by adding a specific profession or interest, then click Join to access the group.

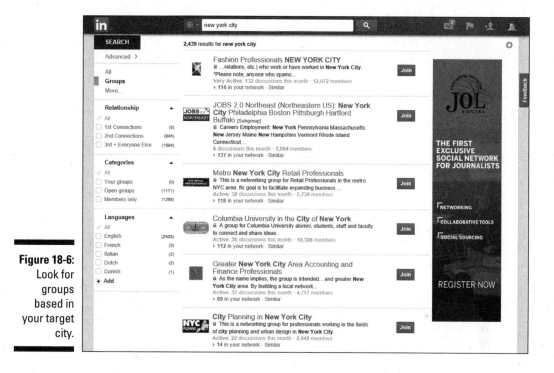

Figure 18-6:
Look for groups based in your target city.

✔ **Start as early as possible.** Building a region-specific network takes time as you recruit new members, ask your existing contacts for referrals, and search for specific people who match the location and either an industry or job title. As soon as you sense that a move is necessary, or maybe when you're mulling over whether to move, start building your network so that you can tap those people for location-specific information before you actually move.

✔ **Consider Chamber of Commerce groups.** Do an Internet search for Chamber of Commerce groups in your new area and see if they have a LinkedIn group or their own Web site. These groups often have excellent resources for people who are relocating and looking to learn more about the area, especially for local business needs.

✔ **Look for contacts who used to live in your new city.** You might try entering the location of your new city in the Keyword search field rather than the Location field. By doing so, you might find first-degree connections or second-degree network members who used to live in your target area but have since moved; they might reference their past locations in their profiles. Contact those people and see whether they can introduce you to any contacts they may still have in that target area, regardless of whether those contacts are on or off LinkedIn.

Arranging face-to-face meetings when traveling

LinkedIn can serve as a wonderful resource even when you're not moving to another city but simply traveling for business or personal reasons. Say that you know you have some extra time on your trip, or you want to make some local connections to reinforce your business trip. Why not tap your LinkedIn network and visit your contacts in person?

A growing practice of busy LinkedIn professionals who travel is to arrange face-to-face visits with other LinkedIn members during a business trip. This way, the traveler can meet with someone she is familiar with who could share similar interests and goals. Also, both people get a chance to expand their networks by creating a stronger connection. To bring about in-person meetings, most people either post something to LinkedIn groups or send a message to targeted members of their networks.

If you're interested in making your next trip more of a LinkedIn adventure, keep these tips in mind:

✔ **Provide enough notice to attract people's attention.** If you're putting up a post on Monday night that you're available for Tuesday lunch, you probably won't get many responses in time to set up anything meaningful.

✔ **Don't give too much notice, or your visit will be forgotten by the time you arrive.** Some notice is necessary to get on people's calendars, but too much notice will make people forget when your visit gets closer. More than two to four weeks in advance is probably too much notice.

✔ **Be specific about your availability.** It's great that you want to get together, but you probably have other plans when you're visiting. Therefore, when you contact other members, offer a few choices of when you can get together — and be specific. For example, you could say, "Hey, I'm going to be in San Jose for most of next week. Who's available either Monday night or Wednesday lunchtime to get together?"

✔ **Use your get-together to help prepare for business.** Your get-togethers with people in other cities don't have to be purely social. Say that you know you're traveling to that city for an interview. Perhaps you want to send a targeted message to a few contacts who used to work for your target company and ask to meet them in person before your interview so that they can help you prepare. Or maybe you want to practice your sales presentation on a knowledgeable person before you go into someone's office to do the real thing.

Networking with LinkedIn . . . in person!

Social networking is a great way to stay connected, grow your personal and professional contacts list, and learn about new opportunities. But after lots of e-mails, Instant Messages, and discussion boards, sometimes you just want

---

LinkedIn Live

If you use LinkedIn and you're in the Raleigh-Durham area of North Carolina, odds are you've heard of Chuck Hester. "I'm known as the Kevin Bacon of Raleigh," he smiles. "If I don't know a person, I probably know someone who does." He's the creator of LinkedIn Live Raleigh, an informal networking group formed in July 2007 and dedicated to having Hester's virtual connections meet each other in person so they can increase their own networking. By that time, Hester had built up more than 700 connections in the Raleigh area alone, so he sent out an invitation, and 50 people showed up to the event. The event was such a success that meetings were held every other month, and attendance grew exponentially, more than tripling in the first six months. In fact, Hester doesn't have to worry about the costs because he gets sponsors to donate the food, meeting space, and even door prizes! He expanded this group to the larger region in North Carolina by forming a LinkedIn group called Linking the Triangle.

Hester receives calls from more than a dozen other similar LinkedIn groups, each asking for advice on how to set up and maintain these live networking events. He's proud of the results from all this live networking, saying "At least 20–30 people have found new jobs from meeting someone at a LinkedIn Live." Of course, he used the opportunity to build brand recognition for his company, iContact, which he found by networking on LinkedIn. (See the "Hello? Any opportunities out east?" sidebar earlier in this chapter.) The LinkedIn Live Raleigh networking has also earned him mentions in the Fast Company blog, *The Wall Street Journal, Inc.* magazine, and *The New York Times.* You can find out more by reading Hester's blog at www.chuckhester.com.

the experience of meeting someone face to face. Many LinkedIn members feel this way and use the virtual power of LinkedIn to bring together people in the real world. Although online methods can expedite the process of finding the right people, they can't replace the power of face-to-face networking.

You can find all sorts of "chapters" of in-person networking groups inspired by people first meeting on LinkedIn and then connecting in-person with people from their network at a live event. Besides Linking the Triangle in North Carolina, I've discovered LinkedIn Live or LinkedIn Face-to-Face events in Miami, Dallas, and Denver — and there may well be more.

To find or organize a LinkedIn group from your network, keep these tips in mind:

✔ **Search your LinkedIn connections to see if they are involved with any local groups.** Do an Advanced People search to see which of your connections are located in the city you want to relocate to, for example, and scroll down their profile page to see which groups they belong to. You might find someone like Chuck Hester, who, besides starting Linking the Triangle near Raleigh, has helped others start LinkedIn groups in cities such as London and Miami. You can see these and other groups by going to the Groups section of his profile, as shown in Figure 18-7.

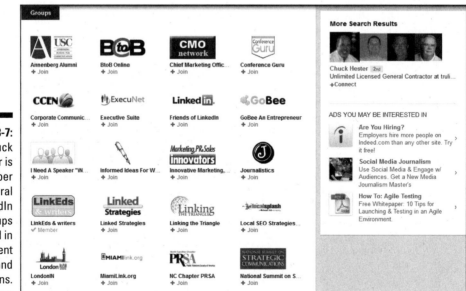

Figure 18-7:
Chuck Hester is a member of several LinkedIn groups located in different cities and regions.

✔ **Search LinkedIn Groups to see whether a group exists in your area.**
Click Groups and then do a search for terms like "LinkedIn Live" (don't
forget the quotes) to see what kinds of groups of LinkedIn members show
up. For example, when I searched for "LinkedIn Live," I saw LinkedIn
groups in places like Atlanta, Miami, and Charlotte, as shown in Figure 18-8.

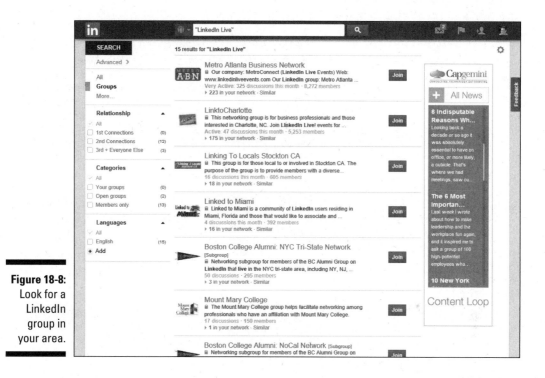

Figure 18-8:
Look for a
LinkedIn
group in
your area.

✔ **Use the Internet to look for social networking meetings.** You may have
to go outside LinkedIn to find an eager group of LinkedIn members. If
you do a search with a networking site like Meetup.com, you will find
a number of LinkedIn groups already established in cities around the
world, as shown in Figure 18-9.

✔ **If nothing exists, start your own live group.** Create something on
LinkedIn groups and build a core group for the first event. Send an
update or message to your network members who live in the area and
encourage them to pass along the message to their local friends who
are LinkedIn members.

Andrew Warner turned to LinkedIn to help find interest for a regular get-together of technology folks known as Lunch 2.0, for which companies involved in Web 2.0 technologies open their doors to hungry technology workers who then learn about their host company over lunch. He posted a question on LinkedIn to find a host company and got several responses, which led to some great meetings!

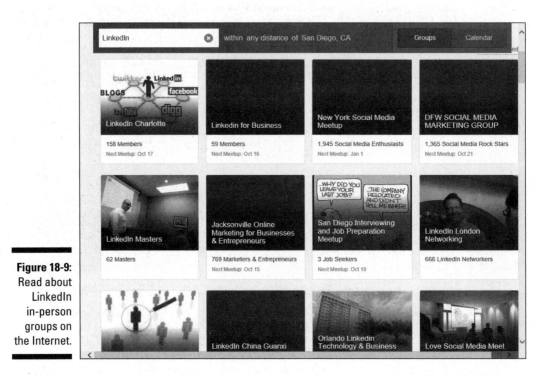

Figure 18-9: Read about LinkedIn in-person groups on the Internet.

Part VI
The Part of Tens

Enjoy an additional LinkedIn Part of Tens chapter at www.dummies.com/extras/linkedin.

In this part...

- ✔ Optimize your LinkedIn profile and communications for best results.

- ✔ Understand how to personalize your networking with LinkedIn.

- ✔ Find ten popular online resources to help you with your LinkedIn activity.

Chapter 19

Ten LinkedIn Do's and Don'ts

I cover a lot of ground in this book — so much that it might be hard to remember it all as you're going about your daily use of LinkedIn. So here are ten essential do's and don'ts to help you build relationships and get the most value out of LinkedIn.

Do Keep Your Profile Complete and Current

Even though LinkedIn has many features, your profile is still one of the most compelling reasons to use the Web site, which is why LinkedIn is one of the best searchable databases of businesspeople available. And if you want to be found by others, you need to make sure that your data is complete and current. Here are a few of ways to do that:

> ✔ **List all your former employers and schools.** Several features help users find and connect with former colleagues and classmates (see Chapter 6). Including your complete work and educational background in your profile can help you reconnect.
>
> If you've had a lengthy career, you don't necessarily need to include details about positions early in your career — just the companies and titles will suffice. A good guideline is to include details on just the past 7–10 years. Additionally, consider including only those positions relevant to your current work. I seriously doubt that my first job at a McDonald's is relevant to my current work as an author (except if I want to write the sequel to *Fast Food Nation*). I've also grouped a lot of my contract work under one experience heading with my own

consulting company name, because many of the consulting jobs were similar in nature. It's up to you how you want to present your experience to the LinkedIn community.

✔ **Update your profile (and headline) any time you achieve a new position, complete a major side project, or receive a special award or recognition.** Your direct connections will be notified (assuming they haven't turned off the feature) of the change. This is a subtle, unobtrusive way to notify your network of your career changes. And you never know when someone is going to be looking for what you have to offer. Make sure that if you have a new position, you update your e-mail address with your new corporate e-mail address so people can still reach and invite you. You can also provide status updates that go out to your network.

Don't Use Canned Invitations

There is never a good situation in which to use one of the default invitation text messages LinkedIn provides when you send someone an invitation to join your network on LinkedIn. Nothing says "You're not really worth a few extra seconds of my time" quite like the all-too-familiar "I'd like to add you to my professional network" message.

That doesn't mean every invitation has to be a lengthy personal epistle. Here are a few tips for keeping invitations efficient but personal:

✔ **Keep it short when you can.** With people you know well and have been in recent contact with, the canned messages are actually too long. The message can be as simple as this:

Great to see you last night, Jerry — let's connect.

✔ **Make sure you know whether the person is already a LinkedIn member.** Someone who's already a member doesn't need to be convinced of LinkedIn's benefits. Maybe it shouldn't be annoying to him that you're explaining something he already knows, but it's just an indication that you didn't really put any thought into making the connection.

✔ **If the contact isn't already a member, offer to help with the registration process.** You can try to explain the benefits of joining LinkedIn in an e-mail, but no matter what you do, it's going to come across as a sales pitch, or at least a bit evangelistic. The best way to persuade people is to offer to spend a few minutes on the phone explaining it and how you're using it. That also turns the invitation into an opportunity to strengthen your relationship with that person by offering your time to bring her something of value.

✔ **You can still personalize a batch of invitations.** You can give the invitation a personal touch even if you're sending it to multiple people. For example, you can send the same invitation to all the people you met or ran into at an event. Or you can send one invitation to everyone in your chamber of commerce. Just remember to write it as if it were going to one person, not the whole group.

For more on invitations, see Chapter 2.

Don't Expect Everyone to Network Like You Do

Setting rigid networking expectations can be a source of needless frustration and can actually prevent you from building relationships with some pretty great people. Here are some of the common issues that arise:

✔ **Different people have different standards for connecting.** Some people use LinkedIn to connect only with people they know very well. Some connect only with people with whom they share some common points of interest. Others connect with anybody. None of these approaches is wrong. If some people don't have the same standard for a connection that you do, don't take it personally, and don't judge them — they're doing what's right for them.

✔ **People might have perfectly good reasons not to allow other people to browse their LinkedIn connections list.** Don't hold anything against people who don't enable it. People may be concerned about client confidentiality, and thus be required to keep their connections private. Or they may be connected to a competitor and not want their bosses and co-workers to know about it. Or they may just be concerned about their time commitments and not want to handle a growing number of introduction requests if all their friends see their long list of connections. However, even if a person has disabled connections browsing, you can still get introductions to people that person knows. Frankly, if you're just browsing other people's networks, maybe you should think about a more focused approach.

✔ **Not everyone responds in a timely manner.** If your request doesn't get forwarded or you haven't gotten a reply to your InMail after a couple of weeks, don't take it personally. It doesn't mean that you're unimportant; it just means the people you're trying to contact are busy. If it's really urgent, pick up the phone, or consider sending another e-mail acknowledging that the other person is likely very busy but you were checking in one more time to see if he or she would be willing to set up a time to talk or converse online. Don't underestimate the power that a friendly and understanding note can have on the other party.

✔ **Some people are bad with names.** Just because you remember somebody's name doesn't mean that she remembers yours. Unless you're 100 percent certain that she will recognize your invitation, contact her via e-mail or phone or a LinkedIn introduction request before sending a connection request. Otherwise, don't be surprised when she declines your invitation or clicks the I Don't Know This Person link.

✔ **Relationships aren't always reciprocal.** For example, if you were someone's client, you might be able to provide a great recommendation for him. That doesn't mean he can do the same for you, so don't expect it.

✔ **Not everyone networks just to network.** Some people are extremely busy and not receptive to "I'd just like to meet you" requests. It's nothing personal, and it doesn't mean they're bad networkers. It just means that the demands on their time exceed the supply.

Do Your Homework

People provide you with all kinds of guidance, both direct and implicit, regarding what to contact them about and how. If you're the one initiating the communication, it's your responsibility to communicate on their terms. And showing that you took the time to do your homework about them demonstrates a certain level of commitment to the relationship right from the outset.

The most basic rule of good conversation is to listen. In the context of LinkedIn, that rule means simply this: Pay attention to what's on a person's profile. Any time you contact somebody, review her profile first as well as her contact settings. Respect what you see in her profile and contact settings.

For example, suppose you have a business deal or a job inquiry that you want to contact John Smith about, but his profile says he's not accepting such inquiries right now. Don't think that you know better than John does about whether he might be interested, and definitely don't try to pass off your deal or job inquiry as a mere "expertise request" or a "request to reconnect" and then tell him why you're really contacting him.

When you send an introduction request or an invitation to someone you don't know very well, don't put the burden on her to figure out what the common areas of interest or potential opportunities are. You took the time to read her profile and determine that it's a worthwhile connection. Save her the trouble of figuring out what you already know and put your common areas of interest in your introduction request or invitation.

Do Give LinkedIn Messages Equal Importance

Many people have a tendency to treat LinkedIn communications as less important or less time-sensitive than an official e-mail or phone call.

Nothing could be further from the truth. People get jobs, hire employees, gain clients, and make deals as a result of LinkedIn-based communications. They are every bit as much a part of your essential business correspondence as the rest of your e-mail. (If they're not, you're connecting with the wrong people!)

Here are some tips for managing your LinkedIn communications:

✔ **Don't turn off e-mail notifications.** Missing time-sensitive communications is one of the worst things you can do. If the volume of e-mail seems overwhelming, you can use e-mail rules to move LinkedIn requests into a separate folder, but as a general productivity practice, you want as few different Inboxes as possible.

To make sure you have e-mail notifications set up correctly, log in to your LinkedIn account and either visit the Communications section of the settings page, or go to www.linkedin.com/settings/email-frequency.

You see the Email Frequency screen, as shown in Figure 19-1. By clicking each category, such as Messages from Other Members (see Figure 19-2), you can set up what comes to you as an individual e-mail, a weekly digest e-mail, or no e-mail so you can decide what is most important.

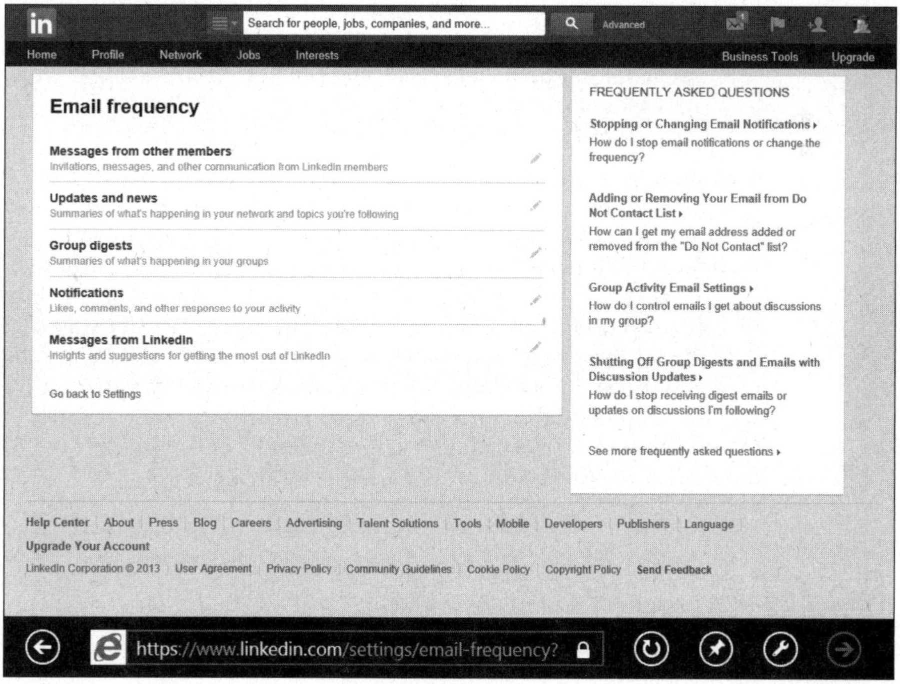

Figure 19-1:
Set your e-mail notification frequency so you don't miss an important message.

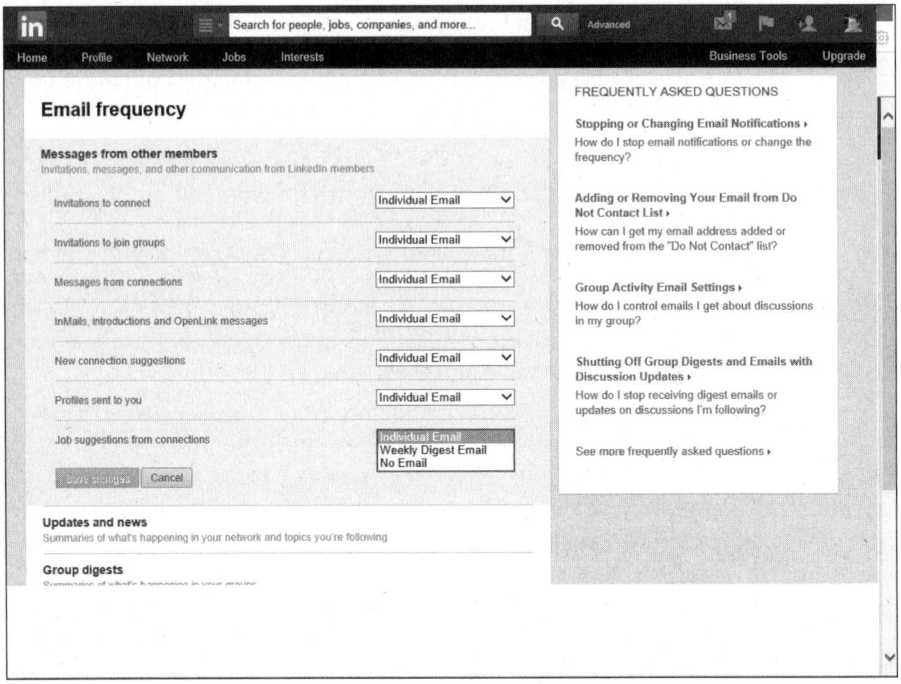

Figure 19-2:
Decide for
each cat-
egory how
often you
wish to be
contacted.

✓ **Check your LinkedIn Inbox every day.** Or at least every couple of days. You wouldn't go a week without checking your e-mail at work — don't treat LinkedIn messages any differently. (See Chapter 9 for more on how to manage your LinkedIn Inbox.)

✓ **Do it, delegate it, defer it, or delete it.** This technique from David Allen's book *Getting Things Done: The Art of Stress-Free Productivity* (Penguin, 2002) will help you keep your Inbox organized. As you're going through your Inbox, if you can handle a request in under two minutes, go ahead and do it. Or you can delegate it by sending on the introduction request or recommending one of your contacts as an expert to answer the person's question. If something in your Inbox takes a little more time, you can defer it by putting it into your work queue to handle later.

For additional tips on e-mail organization and productivity, check out David Allen's book *Getting Things Done,* and also take a look at 43 Folders' Inbox Zero collection at www.inboxzero.com.

Don't Spam

One person's networking is another person's spam. Better to err on the side of caution. There are plenty of ways to use LinkedIn productively without getting a bad rep as a spammer. Here are some basic rules of etiquette:

✔ **Don't post marketing messages or connection-seeking messages as Status Updates.** All these will get your message flagged and fairly quickly removed. Don't waste your effort. There's a fine line between market or product research that calls attention to your company and an advertisement.

✔ **Don't automatically subscribe your connections to your newsletter.** This is admittedly a gray area. Connecting with someone indicates a certain level of receptivity to receiving communication from him, and it's reasonable to assume that should include something more than just LinkedIn introduction requests. After all, he's supposed to be someone you know and trust, right? Well, that's not necessarily the same thing as signing up for a regular bulk newsletter.

I think it's better to be safe than sorry, so I don't recommend auto-subscribing folks to your newsletter. People can get ticked off if they suddenly start getting some newsletter they didn't subscribe to.

The best approach is simply to ask permission to subscribe your individual contacts to your newsletter. If you get their permission, even if they do complain later, you can politely point out that you asked first.

✔ **Don't send connection requests to people you don't know.** Unless they've given some kind of explicit indication that they're open to receiving invitations (for example, announcing it on a forum, stating it in their profiles, or being a member of an open networking group), you have to assume that most people don't want to receive LinkedIn connection invitations from strangers. LinkedIn has taken measures to curb such rampant inviting behavior, and it will get you suspended soon enough. Again, there's a simple solution: *Ask permission first.* Send an introduction request, or contact the person via e-mail or his Web site, and ask whether it would be okay for you to send him a connection invitation.

Do Be Proactive About Making New Connections

If you just set up a profile, connect with a few of your contacts, and then expect business to come your way, you're setting yourself up for disappointment. That's not to say that it can't happen, but being a little bit proactive goes a long way:

✔ **Search for people who can help you with your goals.** If you want to meet people in a particular city, industry, or target market, search for them specifically and make introduction requests. Some people are receptive to corresponding or talking just for networking purposes, but you'll get a better response if you have a specific need or opportunity as the basis of your contact.

✔ **Introduce people to each other.** LinkedIn's basic introduction paradigm is reactive. For example, an introduction is made when person A wants to connect with person C via person B. But an essential practice of a good networker is identifying possible connections between people in your network and introducing them to each other. You can do this by forwarding one person's profile to the other and Cc'ing the first person (see Chapter 5). You can send a LinkedIn message to both connections introducing them and telling them why you think they should get to know each other.

✔ **Get involved.** The Groups section is the main form of public group interaction on LinkedIn. You can come together with other people to talk about a shared interest, or as alumni of a school or university, or as former or current employees of a given company. After you join a LinkedIn Group, you have access to the other group members just as you do a first-degree connection or second-degree network member on LinkedIn, and group involvement is a great way to expand your network and further your education.

Do Cross-Promote

Your LinkedIn profile is just one Web page of your total Web presence. It should connect people to your other points of presence, and you probably want to direct people to your LinkedIn profile from other venues as well. Here are some good cross-promotion practices:

✔ **Customize your LinkedIn profile links.** As described in Chapter 3, you can create up to three links on your profile that you can use to lead people to your business site(s), personal site, blog, book, event, and so on.

✔ **Include a link to your LinkedIn profile in your signature.** You can use this both in your e-mail signature and also on discussion forums. If you don't have a centralized personal professional Web site, your LinkedIn profile is a good alternative. I cover how LinkedIn can help you create your e-mail signature in Chapter 10.

✔ **Link to your LinkedIn profile in your blog's About page.** Why rehash your entire bio? Put a couple of paragraphs that are relevant to the blog and then refer people to your LinkedIn profile for more details.

✔ **Install the LinkedIn app for your smartphone.** LinkedIn has added a lot of functionality to their mobile app, which is available for the iPhone or Android operating system. Using the mobile app will allow you to access LinkedIn when you're out and about, networking in person.

✔ **Put your LinkedIn URL on your business card.** More and more people are starting to do this.

Do Add Value to the Process

LinkedIn is based on the idea that existing relationships add value to the process of people meeting each other. If all you're doing is just passing the introduction "bucket" down the virtual bucket brigade, you're actually getting in the way of communication, not adding value.

To add value, you have to give those introduction requests some thought. Is it an appropriate fit for the recipient? Is the timing good?

Add your comments to the introduction request. Do you know the sender? Saying, "I worked with Michael Bellomo for several years as a co-author, and he was hard-working, trust-worthy, and ambitious" goes a lot further than saying, "Hey, Francine, here's this guy Michael to check out." For additional guidance on how to handle this tactfully, see Chapter 5.

Don't Confuse Quantity with Quality

Just because you're doing a lot of something doesn't mean you're doing something well. And when you think about it, is *more networking activity* what you really want? Or do you really want *more results with less activity?*

If you want to track your real progress using LinkedIn, don't measure it by meaningless metrics like number of connections, endorsements, or questions answered. Use metrics that you know directly tie to business results, such as

- ✔ Leads generated
- ✔ Joint venture/strategic partner prospects generated
- ✔ Qualified job candidates contacted
- ✔ Potential employers successfully contacted
- ✔ Interviews scheduled
- ✔ Speaking opportunities garnered
- ✔ Publicity opportunities created

Chapter 20

Ten LinkedIn Resources

A s you continue building your LinkedIn presence, you might want to take advantage of additional Web sites that keep you up to date on new features and possibilities on LinkedIn. These sites explore common and uncommon uses for the Web site and make you think about how to take advantage and enjoy the benefits of LinkedIn and social networking in general. I've rounded up a list of ten Internet resources that can provide extra information or functionality regarding your LinkedIn activities. Whether you use one or use them all, I'm sure you can find the resources that best match the way you like to learn and grow online.

The Official LinkedIn Blog

`blog.linkedin.com`

Mario Sundar, previously a LinkedIn "evangelist" who promoted the company on his own blog, was hired by LinkedIn to run its official company blog. Every week, Mario and various LinkedIn employees put up fun, informative, and timely blog posts about new functions or changes to the site as well as success stories, case studies, and practical information to make your LinkedIn experience that much more rewarding.

In addition, the blog posts live on forever, and you can search them to find out valuable information or post your own comments to give feedback!

You can also follow the official LinkedIn Twitter feed (@LinkedIn) and on Facebook at www.facebook.com/linkedin.

LinkedIn Labs

As LinkedIn employees think up new functions and possibilities to add to the LinkedIn Web site, there is the need to test those ideas, see whether the community finds them as valuable or relevant as first conceived, and understand how the user community would implement these new functions. LinkedIn Labs is the special site that hosts these new ideas.

LinkedIn employees post a small number of new projects or features and share them with the user base to find beta test users and gain feedback on these projects. Some projects may be promoted to become an official LinkedIn feature, while others disappear after a short time. Don't expect to find a lot of technical support for these new functions; they are here for you to play with and possibly gain your support. Keep an eye on this site to see the future of LinkedIn first-hand.

One great example of a LinkedIn Labs project is the Resume Builder (resume.linkedinlabs.com). This tool interfaces with your existing LinkedIn profile and allows you to select a template and instantly build Microsoft Word or PDF-ready resumes that you can print and/or distribute to potential employers. Why reinvent the wheel when your LinkedIn profile already has what your resume would contain? Be aware that the LinkedIn profile content and presentation may look different than your typical resume so you could do some reorganizing and editing.

LinkedIn Learning Webinars

help.linkedin.com/app/answers/detail/a_id/530

LinkedIn launched a set of webinars designed to help you use your LinkedIn account more effectively and to introduce you to LinkedIn's newest features and functionalities. These webinars and training videos are available from the LinkedIn Help Center. You can register for new webinars, which are typically held weekly.

MyLinkWiki

`http://linkedin.pbworks.com/MyLinkWiki`

A *wiki* is an Internet technology that allows multiple people to collaborate on gathering and presenting information. On a wiki site, anybody can create, add, or edit information, and those changes are then reviewed by other users, and ultimately approved or rejected. The best known example of this technology is Wikipedia, one of the fastest growing repositories of information on the Internet. This online encyclopedia has rapidly become a broad source of information because of the collaborative knowledge gathering it has fostered.

One great LinkedIn wiki is MyLinkWiki, where users comment on and update the width and breadth of LinkedIn's functionality and usefulness. As you become more familiar with LinkedIn, you can contribute to this growing community as well.

RSS Feeds with Feedspot

`www.feedspot.com`

The Web technology known as RSS (commonly referred to as Really Simple Syndication) works as follows: If you want to follow all the changes, additions, and updates of a Web site, blog, or profile page, the easiest way to do that is to read a list of just the changed or added information rather than combing the entire site over and over again. An RSS feed does precisely that by providing subscribers with this list of new information.

Many active LinkedIn users maintain an RSS feed for their profile so their friends and connections can get a list of the changes and updates. You can create an RSS feed of your network updates to keep track of your first-degree connections on LinkedIn. To get these updates, you need an RSS feed reader. I cover LinkedIn RSS feeds in more depth in Chapter 18.

Feedspot makes a great reader tool that you can use to handle all the RSS feeds you subscribe to, whether related to LinkedIn or not. You can install this free tool on practically any system. And a quick Google search for "RSS feed readers" can help you track down other feed readers to try.

Linked Intelligence Blog

`www.linkedintelligence.com`

When LinkedIn was growing in size and popularity during its earlier days, blogger Scott Allen put together the LinkedIntelligence site to cover LinkedIn and its many uses. Over the years, he built up a healthy amount of blog posts, links, and valuable information from himself and other bloggers regarding LinkedIn and how to use it.

One of his more ambitious projects, started in May 2007, is simply dubbed 100+ Smart Ways to Use LinkedIn. Allen had bloggers compete to provide valuable information and tips across all of LinkedIn's functions, and he created a table of contents of the best entries on his blog site. You can still find this handy resource at `www.linkedintelligence.com/smart-ways-to-use-linkedin`.

The large repository of links and information can be helpful to new, intermediate, or power users of the site. The blog posts are divided into dozens of helpful categories, from LinkedIn News to Training & Coaching.

Rock the World with LinkedIn — Podcast

`http://www2.webmasterradio.fm/rock-the-world-with-linkedin/`

The staggering popularity of the Apple iPod has given rise to a new way of broadcasting audio information to eager listeners — the podcast. Think of the podcast as a recorded audio broadcast that you can download to your iPod, smartphone, iPad, computer, MP3 player, or other device. You can subscribe to engaging and unique podcasts, regardless of where in the world they're recorded and played.

At Rock the World with LinkedIn, Mike O'Neil and Lori Ruff reveal their LinkedIn "secrets" and chat with all sorts of LinkedIn "rock stars" and experts and answer their listeners' most difficult LinkedIn questions. They've also got a wealth of archived shows that are available for download, so you can listen to success stories and all sorts of tips. You can subscribe to this show and hear great interviews, tips, and stories of how other people and companies connect online.

Digsby Social Networking/IM/E-Mail Tool

www.digsby.com

As you monitor your LinkedIn activity, you're most likely using other tools and networks as part of your overall experience, such as Facebook and Twitter. Rather than go to each site individually, you can use an *aggregator* — a special software tool you use to group all the information generated in all your social networks, and then present them in one tool.

One such application is Digsby, which promises to integrate your e-mail, Instant Messaging, and social networking accounts in one clean interface. After you download and set up Digsby, you can view a live newsfeed of all your friends and connections based on their events or activities on sites like LinkedIn, as well as manage chat sessions and see e-mail notifications. In the era of information overload, a tool like Digsby can help you make sense of all the messages and updates zooming to your computer screen.

Turn Business Cards into LinkedIn Contacts with CardMunch

www.cardmunch.com

If you're like many people who collect business cards at a networking event or conference, and you never get around to cataloging or responding to these new contacts, then CardMunch is for you . . . if you have an iPhone. CardMunch is a free iPhone app (owned by LinkedIn) that allows you to use the camera to take a picture of a business card, which CardMunch then converts into a contact for you, including that person's LinkedIn profile information and any connections he shares with you on LinkedIn.

Make sure you have iTunes installed on your computer *before* downloading CardMunch, because CardMunch relies on the iTunes program to work with your iPhone.

One Update for Multiple Sites with HootSuite

`https://www.hootsuite.com`

If you're active on LinkedIn and other social networking sites (Facebook, Twitter, Pinterest, and others), you probably hop from site to site to provide up-to-the-minute information about what you're doing and what you want others to know. Well, instead of site hopping, you can use one function to update your status across all your social networking pages and microblogs: HootSuite.

It works like this: You log on to the site and enter your message into the dashboard. You then select the sites you want to update with your new status message, and HootSuite does the rest, reaching out to your various pages to add your new status message. It's a great centralized way to keep all your various profiles as up to date as possible, and it's designed to update your LinkedIn status by answering the question, "What are you working on?" As of this writing, HootSuite offers a free plan that allows you to manage up to five social media accounts.

Index

• N •

• S •

About the Author

Joel Elad, MBA, is the head of Real Method Consulting, a company dedicated to educating people through training seminars, DVDs, books, and other media. He holds a master's degree in Business from UC Irvine, and has a bachelor's degree in Computer Science and Engineering from UCLA. He also operates several online businesses, including NewComix.Com, and is co-producing the So Cal Comic Con.

Joel has written seven books about various online topics, including *Facebook Advertising For Dummies, Starting an Online Business All-In-One Desk Reference For Dummies, Starting an iPhone Application Business For Dummies,* and *Wiley Pathways: E-business.* He has contributed to *Entrepreneur* magazine and Smartbiz.com, and has taught at institutions such as the University of California, Irvine, and the University of San Diego. He is an Educational Specialist trained by eBay and a former Internet instructor for the Learning Annex in New York City, Los Angeles, San Diego, and San Francisco.

Joel lives in San Diego, California. In his spare time, he hones his skills in creative writing, Texas Hold 'Em poker, and finance. He is an avid traveler who enjoys seeing the sights both near and far, whether it's the Las Vegas Strip or the ruins of Machu Picchu. He spends his weekends scouring eBay and local conventions for the best deals, catching the latest movies with friends or family, and enjoying a lazy Sunday.

Dedication

To my best friend Magda, who faces life and adversity as strongly as she values our friendship. You amaze and inspire me, and I hope you never give up on anything! Friends Forever — Joel

Author's Acknowledgments

First and foremost, I have to give the BIGGEST thanks to the great team at Wiley who made this book project possible. Thanks to Bob Woerner for pushing this project forward and having the confidence to put me in place. An absolute, huge, bear-hug thanks to Blair Pottenger and Lynn Northrup for putting up with my fast and furious submissions; they definitely kept me on track to make this book happen. And where would I be without my copy editor, who makes me sound so clear and grammatically correct!

Secondly, I want to acknowledge the absolutely terrific folks at LinkedIn for being open, eager, and absolute quality professionals to work with on this project. Doug Madey, Erin O'Harra, Adam Nash, Kay Luo, Mario Sundar, and Jay Thomas, thank you so much for your time, advice, stories, and access. You definitely made this book a better read because of your help.

I have to give a special thanks to Scott Allen, who was instrumental in getting this book project started, and I appreciate your help and support, as well as your infinite knowledge on the subject.

Thanks, as always, go out to my friends and new LinkedIn contacts who provided me with stories, examples, and endless amounts of encouragement. I especially want to thank Cynthia Beale, Michael Bellomo, Janine Bielski, Hal Burg, Eric Butow, Anthony Choi, Joan Curtis, Lynn Dralle, Greg Goldstein, Steve Hayes, Chuck Hester, Rob Keller, Kyle Looper, Carol Mendelsohn, David Nakayama, Blair Pottenger, Kristie Spilios, Jan Utstein, and Michael Wellman.

Lastly, thanks to my family for putting up with my late-late-night writing sessions and frequent seclusion to get this book ready for publication. Your support is always invaluable.

Publisher's Acknowledgments

We're proud of this book; please send us your comments at http://dummies.custhelp.com. For other comments, please contact our Customer Care Department within the U.S. at 877-762-2974, outside the U.S. at 317-572-3993, or fax 317-572-4002.

Some of the people who helped bring this book to market include the following:

Acquisitions and Editorial

Acquisitions Editor: Bob Woerner

Project Editor: Lynn Northrup

Copy Editor: Lynn Northrup

Technical Editor: Jane Finkle

Editorial Assistant: Annie Sullivan

Sr. Editorial Assistant: Cherie Case

Project Coordinator: Melissa Cossell

Cover Image: © iStockphoto.com/khalus

Apple & Mac

iPad For Dummies,
5th Edition
978-1-118-49823-1

iPhone 5 For Dummies,
6th Edition
978-1-118-35201-4

MacBook For Dummies,
4th Edition
978-1-118-20920-2

OS X Mountain Lion
For Dummies
978-1-118-39418-2

Blogging & Social Media

Facebook For Dummies,
4th Edition
978-1-118-09562-1

Mom Blogging
For Dummies
978-1-118-03843-7

Pinterest For Dummies
978-1-118-32800-2

WordPress For Dummies,
5th Edition
978-1-118-38318-6

Business

Commodities For Dummies,
2nd Edition
978-1-118-01687-9

Investing For Dummies,
6th Edition
978-0-470-90545-6

Personal Finance
For Dummies,
7th Edition
978-1-118-11785-9

QuickBooks 2013
For Dummies
978-1-118-35641-8

Small Business Marketing Kit
For Dummies,
3rd Edition
978-1-118-31183-7

Careers

Job Interviews
For Dummies,
4th Edition
978-1-118-11290-8

Job Searching with
Social Media
For Dummies
978-0-470-93072-4

Personal Branding
For Dummies
978-1-118-11792-7

Resumes For Dummies,
6th Edition
978-0-470-87361-8

Success as a Mediator
For Dummies
978-1-118-07862-4

Diet & Nutrition

Belly Fat Diet For Dummies
978-1-118-34585-6

Eating Clean For Dummies
978-1-118-00013-7

Nutrition For Dummies,
5th Edition
978-0-470-93231-5

Digital Photography

Digital Photography
For Dummies,
7th Edition
978-1-118-09203-3

Digital SLR Cameras &
Photography For Dummies,
4th Edition
978-1-118-14489-3

Photoshop Elements 11
For Dummies
978-1-118-40821-6

Gardening

Herb Gardening
For Dummies,
2nd Edition
978-0-470-61778-6

Vegetable Gardening
For Dummies,
2nd Edition
978-0-470-49870-5

Health

Anti-Inflammation Diet
For Dummies
978-1-118-02381-5

Diabetes For Dummies,
3rd Edition
978-0-470-27086-8

Living Paleo For Dummies
978-1-118-29405-5

Hobbies

Beekeeping
For Dummies
978-0-470-43065-1

eBay For Dummies,
7th Edition
978-1-118-09806-6

Raising Chickens
For Dummies
978-0-470-46544-8

Wine For Dummies,
5th Edition
978-1-118-28872-6

Writing Young Adult Fiction
For Dummies
978-0-470-94954-2

Language &
Foreign Language

500 Spanish Verbs
For Dummies
978-1-118-02382-2

English Grammar
For Dummies,
2nd Edition
978-0-470-54664-2

French All-in One
For Dummies
978-1-118-22815-9

German Essentials
For Dummies
978-1-118-18422-6

Italian For Dummies
2nd Edition
978-1-118-00465-4

Available in print and e-book formats.

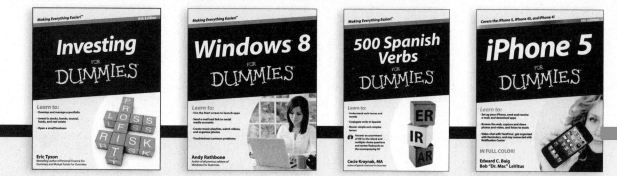

Available wherever books are sold. For more information or to order direct: U.S. customers visit www.Dummies.com or call 1-877-762-2974.
U.K. customers visit www.Wileyeurope.com or call (0) 1243 843291. Canadian customers visit www.Wiley.ca or call 1-800-567-4797.
Connect with us online at www.facebook.com/fordummies or @fordummies

Math & Science

Algebra I For Dummies,
2nd Edition
978-0-470-55964-2

Anatomy and Physiology
For Dummies,
2nd Edition
978-0-470-92326-9

Astronomy For Dummies,
3rd Edition
978-1-118-37697-3

Biology For Dummies,
2nd Edition
978-0-470-59875-7

Chemistry For Dummies,
2nd Edition
978-1-1180-0730-3

Pre-Algebra Essentials
For Dummies
978-0-470-61838-7

Microsoft Office

Excel 2013 For Dummies
978-1-118-51012-4

Office 2013 All-in-One
For Dummies
978-1-118-51636-2

PowerPoint 2013
For Dummies
978-1-118-50253-2

Word 2013 For Dummies
978-1-118-49123-2

Music

Blues Harmonica
For Dummies
978-1-118-25269-7

Guitar For Dummies,
3rd Edition
978-1-118-11554-1

iPod & iTunes
For Dummies,
10th Edition
978-1-118-50864-0

Programming

Android Application
Development For
Dummies, 2nd Edition
978-1-118-38710-8

iOS 6 Application
Development For Dummies
978-1-118-50880-0

Java For Dummies,
5th Edition
978-0-470-37173-2

Religion & Inspiration

The Bible For Dummies
978-0-7645-5296-0

Buddhism For Dummies,
2nd Edition
978-1-118-02379-2

Catholicism For Dummies,
2nd Edition
978-1-118-07778-8

Self-Help & Relationships

Bipolar Disorder
For Dummies,
2nd Edition
978-1-118-33882-7

Meditation For Dummies,
3rd Edition
978-1-118-29144-3

Seniors

Computers For Seniors
For Dummies,
3rd Edition
978-1-118-11553-4

iPad For Seniors
For Dummies,
5th Edition
978-1-118-49708-1

Social Security
For Dummies
978-1-118-20573-0

Smartphones & Tablets

Android Phones
For Dummies
978-1-118-16952-0

Kindle Fire HD
For Dummies
978-1-118-42223-6

NOOK HD For Dummies,
Portable Edition
978-1-118-39498-4

Surface For Dummies
978-1-118-49634-3

Test Prep

ACT For Dummies,
5th Edition
978-1-118-01259-8

ASVAB For Dummies,
3rd Edition
978-0-470-63760-9

GRE For Dummies,
7th Edition
978-0-470-88921-3

Officer Candidate Tests,
For Dummies
978-0-470-59876-4

Physician's Assistant Exam
For Dummies
978-1-118-11556-5

Series 7 Exam
For Dummies
978-0-470-09932-2

Windows 8

Windows 8 For Dummies
978-1-118-13461-0

Windows 8 For Dummies,
Book + DVD Bundle
978-1-118-27167-4

Windows 8 All-in-One
For Dummies
978-1-118-11920-4

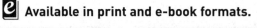 **Available in print and e-book formats.**

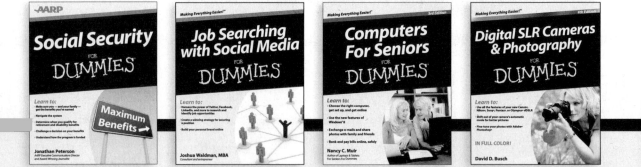

Available wherever books are sold. For more information or to order direct: U.S. customers visit www.Dummies.com or call 1-877-762-2974.
U.K. customers visit www.Wileyeurope.com or call (0) 1243 843291. Canadian customers visit www.Wiley.ca or call 1-800-567-4797.
Connect with us online at www.facebook.com/fordummies or @fordummies